Child

Kate, Age 7. Originally appeared in C. Milbrath, *Patterns of artistic development in children: Comparative studies of talent*, Cambridge University Press, 1998.

Children's
Understanding and Production of
Pictures, Drawings, and Art

Constance Milbrath
Hanns M. Trautner
(Editors)

Library of Congress Cataloging in Publication

is available via the Library of Congress Marc Database under the
LC Control Number 2007931770

Library and Archives Canada Cataloguing in Publication

Children's understanding and production of pictures, drawings, and
art : theoretical and empirical approaches / Constance Milbrath, Hanns
M. Trautner, eds.

Includes bibliographical references.
ISBN 978-0-88937-350-1

1. Children's drawings--Psychological aspects. 2. Children's
art--Psychological aspects. 3. Child artists--Psychology. 4. Drawing,
Psychology of. 5. Art--Psychology. I. Milbrath, Constance
II. Trautner, Hanns Martin, 1943-

BF723.D7C53 2007   155.4   C2007-904272-4

© 2008 by Hogrefe & Huber Publishers

PUBLISHING OFFICES
USA: Hogrefe & Huber Publishers, 875 Massachusetts Avenue, 7th Floor, Cambridge, MA 02139
            Phone (866) 823-4726, Fax (617) 354-6875; E-mail info@hhpub.com
EUROPE: Hogrefe & Huber Publishers, Rohnsweg 25, 37085 Göttingen, Germany
            Phone +49 551 49609-0, Fax +49 551 49609-88, E-mail hh@hhpub.com

SALES & DISTRIBUTION
USA: Hogrefe & Huber Publishers, Customer Services Department,
            30 Amberwood Parkway, Ashland, OH 44805
            Phone (800) 228-3749, Fax (419) 281-6883, E-mail custserv@hhpub.com
EUROPE: Hogrefe & Huber Publishers, Rohnsweg 25, 37085 Göttingen, Germany
            Phone +49 551 49609-0, Fax +49 551 49609-88, E-mail hh@hhpub.com

OTHER OFFICES
CANADA: Hogrefe & Huber Publishers, 1543 Bayview Avenue, Toronto, Ontario M4G 3B5
SWITZERLAND: Hogrefe & Huber Publishers, Länggass-Strasse 76, CH-3000 Bern 9

Hogrefe & Huber Publishers
Incorporated and registered in the State of Washington, USA, and in Göttingen, Lower Saxony, Germany

Printed and bound in the USA
ISBN 978-0-88937-350-1

In 2006 and 2007, researchers in psychology of the visual arts sustained a double blow. Two revered members of our community, John Willats and Rudolf Arnheim, passed away. Both of these men were avid and productive students of the arts, and although they did not share some of their theoretical positions, they did share a commitment to the rigorous pursuit of knowledge, impeccable scholarship, and methodical analysis. Above all, they shared a deep love of the visual arts and what the arts, at their best, could bring to humanity. Their erudition, humor, and synthetic flair will be sorely missed, but their rich and multiform contributions will continue to inform and generate discourse and research in our field for years to come.

> This book is dedicated to the memory of John and Rudy,
> whose legacies have provided much of the wisdom and inspiration
> for the contributions in this volume.

About the Editors

Constance Milbrath, PhD is a Senior Researcher at the Human Early Learning Partnership in the Department of Interdisciplinary Studies at the University of British Columbia, Canada. She is author of *Patterns of artistic development: Comparative studies of talent* (CUP, 1998) and a co-editor of *Biology and knowledge revisited: From neurogenesis to psychogenesis* (LEA, 2005). She has published widely in the fields of developmental and clinical psychology.

Hanns M. Trautner, PhD is Professor and Head of the Department of Developmental and Educational Psychology at the University of Wuppertal, Germany. He is author and editor of introductory and advanced textbooks on developmental psychology and co-editor of *The developmental social psychology of gender* (LEA, 2000). He has published widely on issues of gender development and cognitive foundations of child and adolescent development.

Contributors

Anna Silvia Bombi
Faculty of Psychology 2
University of Rome "La Sapienza"
Italy
annasilvia.bombi@uniroma1.it

Esther Burkitt
Centre for Childhood Development
   and Learning
The Open University
Milton Keynes
UK
e.burkitt@open.ac.uk

Tara C. Callaghan
Center for Research on Culture and
   Human Development
St. Francis Xavier University
Antigonish, NS
Canada
tcallagh@stfx.ca

Norman H. Freeman
Department of Experimental Psychology
University of Bristol
UK
n.freeman@bristol.ac.uk

Richard P. Jolley
Department of Psychology
Faculty of Health and Sciences
Staffordshire University
Stoke-on-Trent
UK
r.jolley@staffs.ac.uk

Anna M. Kindler
Departments of Art Education and
   Curriculum Studies
The University of British Columbia
Vancouver, BC
Canada
anna.kindler@ubc.ca

Christiane Lange-Küttner
Department of Psychology
London Metropolitan University
UK
c.langekuettner@londonmet.ac.uk

Lynn S. Liben
Department of Psychology
The Pennsylvania State University
University Park, PA
USA
liben@psu.edu

Constance Milbrath
Human Early Learning Partnership
The University of British Columbia
Vancouver, BC
Canada
constance.milbrath@ubc.ca

Sergio Morra
DISA – Department of Psychology
University of Genoa
Italy
morra@nous.unige.it

David A. Pariser
Faculty of Fine Arts
Concordia University
Montréal, QC
Canada
dparis@vax2.concordia.ca

Giuliana Pinto
Department of Psychology
University of Florence
Italy
pinto@psico.unifi.it

Philippe Rochat
Department of Psychology
Emory University
Atlanta, GA
USA
psypr@emory.edu

Sarah E. Rose
Department of Psychology
Faculty of Health and Sciences
Staffordshire University
Stoke on Trent
UK
s.e.rose@staffs.ac.uk

Hanns M. Trautner
Department of Psychology
University of Wuppertal
Germany
trautner@uni-wuppertal.de

Axel van den Berg
Department of Sociology
McGill University
Montreal, QC
Canada
axel.vandenberg@mcgill.ca

Table of Contents

Preface

The ideas and conception of this book grew out of symposia and poster workshops at several conferences and meetings in which many of the contributors of this volume were involved. Most of these symposia and poster workshops took place at meetings of the Jean Piaget Society (JPS).

The first personal contact of the two editors was at the 25th Annual Symposium of the JPS in Berkeley, CA, USA, 1995, where Constance Milbrath organized a symposium on *Hearing, Seeing, and Thinking in Music and the Visual Arts*, and where Christiane Lange-Küttner, Anna Silvia Bombi, Guiliana Pinto, and Hanns M. Trautner met in a poster session on drawings. A year later, Emiel Reith and Constance Milbrath organized a poster workshop at the Piaget Centennial Conference "The Growing Mind" in Geneva in 1996 (titled, *Contemporary Perspectives on the Nature and Development of Pictorial Representation in Children*), including eighteen posters that covered a wide range of issues. In the following years, varying groups of people doing research on the subject met again at conferences and exchanged ideas and research findings. Of particular note are the poster workshops, symposia, and individual papers at the 30th Annual Meeting of the JPS in Montréal, QC, Canada, in 2000 (poster workshop entitled *Children's Knowledge and Judgments About Drawings and Drawing Processes*, organized by the two editors), several presentations at the 36th Annual Meeting of the JPS in 2006, held in Baltimore, MD, USA, with the theme of *Art and Human Development*, and, recently, the symposium on *Artistic Representation and Aesthetics* (organized by the two editors) at the 37th Annual Meeting of the JPS in Amsterdam, The Netherlands, in 2007. The European contributors to this volume were also among the participants of two symposia at the 12th European Conference on Developmental Psychology in Tenerife, Spain, in 2005. Topics of the symposia were *Children's Perception and Depiction of Affective Information in Drawings* (organized by Hanns M. Trautner and Maria A. Tallandini), and *Productivity in Pictorial Space* (organized by Christiane Lange-Küttner and Anne Vinter).

In the course of the meetings of the past years, we noticed the rapidly growing interest of psychologists in children's theories about the way the self, others, and things in the world work and the numerous studies of children's metacognitive abilities in the areas of perception, language, and problem solving. However, at the same time, we saw little attention devoted to children's theory and knowledge of pictorial representation, drawing, and art, and how this knowledge evolves with age. In recent years, we are pleased to say, this trend has reversed and there are now a number of new and interesting empirical studies and theoretical advances that are starting to fill the gap in what is known about children's theories and metacognitive abilities in the domain of pictures, drawing, and art. Researchers have studied children's conception of what counts as a picture and of the role of the artist in picture production, how children adapt to specific drawing conditions and monitor their drawing processes, and children's appreciation of age differences in drawing performance, and their aesthetic preferences.

As these contributions are scattered across various journals and other sources (e.g., presentations at conferences), we felt the lack of a single book that surveys current theory and research in this domain. Building upon the fruitful exchanges with our colleagues at the several meetings, we developed the idea for this book as a means of bringing together researchers and theorists whose work contributes substantially to our knowledge of children's understanding and production of pictures, drawings, and art. This will be the first volume to focus explicitly on children's knowledge and interpretations of pictorial representations, including their understanding of the role of the artist as producer of pictures and of the viewer as beholder of pictures, in the context of their developing abilities to understand and produce pictorial representations. It addresses what children of different ages know about the nature of pictures as representations of the world, as intentional communications conveyed by artists, and as aesthetic objects, as well as what children of different ages understand about the different ways to depict objects and scenes.

The contributions of this volume should be of value for researchers of children's cognitive development, and particularly those working in the field of symbolic and representational development, and to researchers and educators in the field of art education who wish to understand young children's grasp of what pictures represent and their comprehension of the relationships between picture and artist and between picture and viewer.

We, as editors, were extremely pleased at the prompt response to our invitations to contribute to this volume. We wish to thank the authors for their collegial cooperation during the earlier process of writing, for their thoughtful responses to our many comments and suggestions, and for their effort to keep to the deadlines we set.

We have been helped by many people in preparing this book. We particularly wish to thank Johanna Baechli for her assistance in literature search and extracting research articles during an early stage of planning this volume. We are also grateful to Claudia Anders, Cornelia Rauschenbach and Manuel Teubert for their help in preparing the camera-ready copy of the manuscript and, in particular, for their adapting and processing the many complex figures in the volume. We also thank Robert Dimbleby and Christina Sarembe of Hogrefe & Huber Publishers for their encouragement and support and for taking over the responsibility for the production of the book.

Additional thanks of Constance Milbrath go to Gerald Cupchik, Jeanne Bamberger, Ross Fink, Gerald Lovelace, Carolyn Hildebrandt, David Pariser, and her husband Oscar Pelta, all of whom over the years have entertained many stimulating and formative discussions on aesthetics and the arts with her. Hanns M. Trautner would like to acknowledge also the eight years of productive collaboration with Heiko Hungerige and the ideas on metacognition and drawing generated from this collaboration, as well as the pleasant experience of our joint teaching and doing research on children's drawings with advanced students of our psychology department.

We hope that the approaches advanced in this volume will stimulate innovative research in the field of children's understanding and production of pictures, drawings, and art. Knowledge of how children think about pictures and drawings as representations and intentional communications about a *state of affairs*, and of art as aesthetic objects will deepen our understanding of the drawings they produce and provide valuable insights into children's comprehension of the many forms of graphic representation that are part of contemporary culture.

Constance Milbrath
Hanns M. Trautner

Part I

Introduction

Chapter 1

Children's Knowledge About Pictures, Drawing, and Art

Hanns M. Trautner
University of Wuppertal

Constance Milbrath
University of British Columbia

Introduction

When psychologists deal with pictures, drawings, and art (for ease of description, in the following: pictorial representation) they either use pictorial representations as an instrument for studying psychological processes and mental life or they are interested in pictorial representation as an activity in its own right (Reith, 1996). Pertaining to the first category (easily outnumbering the studies in the second category) is the use of pictorial representations to test cognitive abilities (e.g., intelligence, spatial cognition, perception, memory), to diagnose the personality of a person (e.g., traits, emotions, unconscious conflicts), as a means for planning or carrying out therapeutic interventions in clinical contexts, or to explain and illustrate tasks or verbal information. Piaget and Inhelder's classical book on the child's conception of space (Piaget & Inhelder, 1956) using children's drawings to verify their hypotheses about the development of spatial concepts is a typical example in developmental psychology.

The focus of our book is different. Our particular interest is directed at children's knowledge, ideas, and theories in the domain of pictorial representation. We are concerned with problems and research about the perception, production, and judgment of pictorial representation in itself and in the description and explanation of the developmental changes related to understanding and producing pictorial representations. Although we can build upon the extant developmental literature on the relation between cognition and drawing that has been published in the last decades (e.g., Freeman, 1980; Freeman & Cox, 1985; Lange-Küttner & Thomas, 1995; Van Sommers, 1984), we go beyond these traditional cognitive approaches by referring to more recent concepts under the umbrella of metacognition and theory of mind.

Cognition and drawing

Understanding pictures requires that one recognizes pictures as representations. Understanding the representational nature of pictures includes four components (Winner, 2006): to recognize "(1) the *similarity* between a picture and what it represents, (2) the *difference* between a picture and what it represents, (3) the *dual reality* of a picture as both a flat object and a representation of the three-dimensional world, and (4) the fact that pictures are made with *intentionality* and are to be *interpreted*." (p. 863). Understanding the representational nature of pictures also requires the ability to perceive the illusion of the third dimension in a two-dimensional picture, as well as to perceive aesthetic properties in pictures (Winner, 2006).

Drawing as symbol system

Cognitive approaches of pictorial representation are mainly focused on drawings as representations of the drawn object. The attention is on the relation between symbol and referent (symbol function). What children understand or misunderstand about the symbol-referent relation, about depiction as a symbolic or representational system, how this changes with age, and the situational factors that can influence this understanding are the main questions of this research.

It would be naïve to assume that children's drawings are a direct reflection of how they understand reality or of their mental representation of reality. On the contrary, most researchers today assume that the mental representation of an object drawn and the manner in which an object is drawn are rather independent of each other. According to Reith (1996) and Bremner (1996) there are several processes involved mediating between object (referent) and drawing, i.e., perception of the object, knowledge about the object, conceptual, visual (mental) images, experiential knowledge, representation of the drawing, knowledge of graphic symbolization systems, motor-skills, graphic planning, execution and monitoring of the drawing process and product.

The problems of the symbol-referent relation described above bear upon the relationships between seeing, knowing, and drawing. While Luquet (1927) stated that before reaching the stage of visual realism, children draw what they know, not what they see, Freeman (1980) argued that children draw what they know only if they don't know enough to draw in a different way. Others make the point that children draw according to their knowledge about how an object is depicted and by copying drawing schemata from other pictures, not necessarily according to their knowledge about the real world referent (Gombrich, 1977; Schuster, 1993). For them, "drawing is not a problem of seeing or knowing, it is a problem of drawing per se, that is, knowing the rules for translating knowledge and perceptual experience of real objects into forms on the page" (Thomas, 1995, p. 77). Goodnow (1977) terms this *creating graphic equivalents* of real objects. One reason for the loose relationship between what is seen and what is drawn, in particular by young children, is that children's spontaneous drawings are usually not drawn from life or by looking at the drawing object, but by relying on memory or by copying from other pictures (Milbrath, 1998; Thomas, 1995).

The preceding discussion of the symbol-referent relation and of the match between mental representation and drawing implies that the child's intention when drawing is to produce a more or less realistic representation of the referent; that is, to depict specific objects and spatial relations with a concern for accuracy and clarity. However, there might be other intentions behind children's drawings than a representational intention (Reith, 1996). The production of the drawing may aim to convey certain emotions or to induce specific effects in the observer (expressive intention). The child may want to tell a story or an episode with her drawing (narrative intention). Or the main purpose of the drawing may be to produce a composition of form and color that is pleasing or that serves a decorative function (aesthetic intention). Because cognitive approaches are mainly concerned with drawings as representations, the drawings are usually analyzed under the implicit assumption that the drawing follows a child's representational intention. As the drawing itself does not reveal the child's intention, to assume a representational intention is only justified when the child directly expresses a representational intention, or when the instruction for a drawing task warrants such an intention.

In dealing with the symbol-referent relation and the role of seeing and knowing in children's drawings, the distinction between figurative thought and operative thought, introduced by Piaget (1977), is of relevance. "Figurative thought relates to the mental reproduction of objects, events, and relationships experienced in the world, not to their transformation", and "includes perception, imitation, and the constructed visual image" (Milbrath, 1998, p. 11). Unlike figurative thought, "operative thought acts on objects, events, and relationships experienced in the world to modify or transform them", and "includes logical, mathematical, spatial, and causal reasoning" (Milbrath, 1998, p. 11). For Piaget, figurative thought was increasingly informed by operative thought in the course of a child's development. In his conclusions to the *Mechanisms of Perception*, Piaget states "that a direct analysis of operations shows that the irreducible elements they bring to figurative organizations supports [a] hypothesis …of an autonomous development of intelligence from action (sensory-motor activities) accompanied by a continuous enrichment of perceptual structures under the influence of the development of structures of action and of intelligence" (Piaget, 1969, pp. 310-11). The graphic equivalent even at its most realistic, therefore, is never simply a reproduction of the referent because it always includes the transformative actions the child performs a) in the remembered referent, b) to render 3-dimensional spatial relationships in a 2-dimensional space, and c) in the intentional and non-intentional transformations that serve the child's expressive, narrative, and/or aesthetic goals. Nevertheless, the degree to which children coordinate figurative and operative modes of thought may differ. For example, some children discover rules for graphic equivalents that produce more realistic visual equivalents because they appear more sensitive to the visual world (Milbrath, 1998; Munro, Lark-Horowitz, & Barnhart, 1942; Rosenblatt & Winner, 1988).

Conception, perception, and production in children's drawings

Milbrath (1998) describes three approaches that have had a major impact on research to the present time and that contribute to an understanding of children's drawings: (1) The first approach emphasizes conceptual development, regarding drawings as consistent with children's ability to reconstruct or internally represent objects and their spatial relationships. (2) The second approach emphasizes perception, focusing on the development of children's perceptual abilities and capacity to analyze objects and spatial relationships visually. (3) The third approach emphasizes the production of a drawing and views development in drawing as based on a child's ability to solve the multitude of problems inherent in graphic production. Similar to the time lag between comprehension and usage in language, the treatment of spatial information by the perceptual system is more advanced than its integration by the conceptual and production levels.

Two assumptions lay the foundations of the conceptual approach: that the stage of cognitive development determines a child's semiotic abilities (Piaget & Inhelder, 1956), and that the strategies that guide perceptual analysis are strongly influenced by cognitive development (Piaget, 1969). In the tradition of Piaget and Inhelder's book on the child's conception of space, drawings are mainly used to index conceptual knowledge (in particular, object knowledge and spatial cognition), and to show that object knowledge and object-centered views dominate the drawings of young children.

The perceptual approach attempts to explain children's drawings by emphasizing visual analysis and perception (Gibson, 1971, 1979; Marr, 1982; Willats, 1987). According to Gibson, perception is aimed at detecting aspects of the optic array that remain invariant under movement-induced transformations, which explains why young children's drawings are object-centered rather than viewer-centered. Using Marr's computational model of visual processing, Willats (1987) suggests a sequence in drawing development that starts with symbolic equivalents that stand for whole objects. Gradually the child differentiates the various lower levels processed by the visual system so that a shape that initially stood for the whole comes to stand for an object's surface and the lines that at first merely bounded the object come to stand for the object's edges.

The third approach emphasizes the difficulties young children have planning and executing a drawing, in particular the problem of translating three dimensions into two and to organize a coherent whole (Freeman, 1980; Van Sommers, 1984). Therefore, phenomena such as synthetic incapacity, intellectual realism, or mixed viewpoints are better explained as strategies for organizing a drawing than as failures in perceptual analysis or conceptual understanding of spatial relationships. Freeman concludes from his studies that young children have difficulty organizing a drawing because certain mental biases guide drawing production, e.g., canonical view of an object resulting from the child's inability to inhibit internal generic representations. This appears to be particularly true when children are asked to draw familiar objects in nontraditional orientations. A key point also is that production decisions made early in the drawing determine the direction a drawing takes.

Drawing as problem solving

In the eighties, several books were published that proposed a view of children's drawings as problem solving. Of special importance were the books *Strategies of Representation* by Freeman (1980), *Visual Order* by Freeman and Cox (1985), and *Drawing and Cognition* by Van Sommers (1984). According to Freeman (1980) the problem solving process consists of four sub-processes: planning, decision making, execution, and monitoring. If a child, for instance, is asked to make a drawing of "My friends and me", she has to solve at least the following problems: how many people to draw, in which situation, what figure first, what further sequence of fig-ures, where to place each figure, which spatial relations and perspective of figures and objects to draw, what size to make each figure and figure parts, which sequence and details of each figure to draw, in what order, and which sequence and direction of strokes.

When making a drawing, finding solutions for these problems has to take into ac-count the fundamental problem of transforming the three-dimensional reality onto a two-dimensional surface. This includes knowledge of denotation rules and graphic conventions, and how they relate to objects and scenes; that is, how children under-stand the relationship between the lines they draw and the objects they are drawing, as well as their knowledge of denotation rules associated with graphic representation (Willats, 1997, 2005).

To learn something about the way a child passes through the series of problem solving steps one has to analyze the drawing process. Analyzing only the end product of the drawing, may result in too quick an interpretation of certain details of the draw-ing, like the number, size, or the distance between figures in a drawing of "My friends and me". Observing the process during the making of a drawing, may reveal that a figure has been drawn small or far apart from another figure, because of previous deci-sions that, for instance, led to the consequence that there was little space left for the final figure.

Besides stressing the necessity of observing the actual drawing process, propo-nents of viewing drawing as problem solving argue for the use of experimental de-signs in drawing research. Systematic variation and control of task demands and drawing conditions, allows for disentangling children's conceptual and perceptual knowledge of drawn objects, their knowledge about denotation rules and graphic conventions, and their sensory-motor skills in transforming a three-dimensional reality onto the two-dimensional pictorial surface. Such experimental designs also offer the opportunity to test the flexibility of children's drawings when referents/models are varied, and to distinguish what children actually draw under specifiable conditions. For example, in varying the standard *Draw-a-Person* task by asking children to draw a human figure not only from imagination, but also by copying and by tracing a model drawing, Trautner (1995, 1996) observed significant differences in children's segmentation or contouring of body parts, as well as in the sequence in which the body parts were drawn.

Metacognition, theory of mind, and children's understanding and production of pictures, drawing and art

While traditional cognitive research puts pictures (drawings) at the centre of analysis, metacognitive approaches place minds rather than pictures at the centre of analysis. That means, one goes beyond studying the cognitive foundations of children's drawing performance and looks at children's explicit, objectified knowledge and theories of pictures, including their knowledge about artists as producers of pictures and about viewers as evaluators of pictures.

This perspective on drawing research guides the present book. It is a more recent focus and in comparison to other areas of cognitive development widely underrepresented. Developmental psychologists have dealt extensively with children's theories of mind, in particular the notion that young children reason about their world by building naïve theories about the way the self, others, and things in the world work. Accordingly, there is a lot of literature on children's theories in what are considered core domains of knowledge; in particular on children's understanding of others' minds and of mentalistic terms such as *know, belief,* or *desire* (Wellman, 1990), and on the notion that the young mind represents reality with naïve theories of biology, physics, and psychology (Karmiloff-Smith, 1992; Wellman & Gelman, 1998). There are also numerous studies of children's metacognitive abilities in the areas of perception, language, or problem solving (Gombert, 1992; Kuhn, 1999; Weinert & Kluwe, 1987).

Little attention, however, has been given to children's theories of pictures, drawing, and art, how these theories evolve with age, and children's metacognitive knowledge in this domain. According to Freeman (see Freeman, Chap. 3), the reason for this neglect is perhaps that art is not a unitary domain but rather arises from the confluence of domains "... a mentalistic competence communicative in nature, in which pictures are used prosthetically to extend the range of viewers' vision, in the sense of our visual understanding and our visual imagination" (p. 33). Another distinction, made by Gelman (2000), applies here, i.e., the distinction between core domains and noncore domains. While physics, biology and psychology, together with language and number may be classified as core domains in which to research children's theories of mind, making pictures, together with music, dance, play, and sculpture, may be regarded as noncore domains. In the case of the latter domains the product is left as an independent object external to the child while in the case of the former domains the outcome of the process is internal. Further, knowledge acquisition in core domains, according to Gelman (2000), builds upon a set of universal skeletal principles that help "to identify inputs that can be structurally mapped to its existing domain" (p. 855), whereas in noncore domains "the learner must acquire both the structure and the domain-relevant content pretty much from scratch." (pp. 855-856).

A model of metacognitive abilities applied to children's drawings

Two types of knowledge are usually distinguished when dealing with metacognition: factual or declarative knowledge (knowing *what*) in a particular content domain and procedural knowledge (knowing *how*) to organize cognitive activities to solve problems and take action. Flavell (1987) developed a general taxonomy of metacognitive variables that seems well suited to model the metacognitive abilities of relevance in the domain of children's drawings. He proposed to subdivide metacognitive knowledge into three categories: person variables, task variables, and strategy variables. While the person and task variables contain mainly declarative knowledge, strategy variables involve mainly procedural knowledge. However, Flavell (1987) points out that person, task, and strategy variables always interact, and that intuitions about their interaction also are acquired.

Person variables can be further subdivided into knowledge or beliefs about (a) intra-individual variation in one's own or someone else's aptitudes, (b) inter-individual comparisons between, rather than within, persons, and (c) universal aspects of human cognition or psychology, i.e., about the way the human mind works.

Task variables contain the knowledge about specific features and demands of a task that influence how it is conducted or performed and solved (e.g., the knowledge that it is easier to learn the essence of a story than to learn it verbatim).

Strategy variables concern the knowledge about the procedures that are adequate and promising in order to achieve task related goals or subgoals (e.g., knowing that you have to add up to get the sum of a list of numbers, or that you have to check the result of a procedure to feel confident that the goal has been achieved).

In addition to the variables of metacognitive knowledge described before, Flavell (1987) introduced the concept of metacognitive experience. This means conscious experiences that are cognitive and affective and often accompany ongoing cognitive activities, e.g., the sudden feeling that something is hard to perceive, comprehend, remember, or solve. Changes in the development of the child that might possibly contribute to the acquisition of metacognition are the developing sense of the self as an active cognitive agent and as the causal center of one's own cognitive activity, and an increase in planfulness, representing and interrelating past, present, and future actions and events (Flavell, 1987). One significant reason why young children seem to be so unintentional in their use of more effective strategies may be that they do not realize that they need them.

When applied to the metacognitive knowledge of relevance in the domain of children's drawings, the person, task, and strategy variables can be translated in the following way:

Person variables. Knowledge about one's own conceptual, perceptual, and sensory-motor skills, and those of others, in general, or to carry out a specific drawing task; knowledge about or evaluation of the age, talent, intention, individual style, or other individual characteristics of the artist behind the picture, and what it means to be a creative artist; and knowledge about people as cognizers of pictures, e.g., of viewers as evaluators of pictures.

Task variables. Knowledge about the referent object and the mental representation of the object; knowing that 3-dimensional objects can be depicted on a 2-dimensional surface; knowledge about the graphic equivalents for referent objects, the objects' possible depictions, and spatial relationships; and knowledge about criteria to evaluate the difficulty and the quality of a drawing.

Strategy variables. Knowledge about denotation rules and graphic conventions and how they relate to the depiction of an object; knowledge about possible drawing strategies for coping with different tasks, e.g., when drawing from memory, copying, or tracing; knowledge about drawing aids; knowledge about planning, executing, and monitoring drawing processes; knowing how to inhibit irrelevant or misleading information; and skills in instructing, advising, or monitoring others in drawing.

The contents of this book

This volume is one of the first to attempt a specific focus on children's metacognitive knowledge of pictures, drawing, and art, bringing together contributions from an international group of scholars, who either have been or are beginning to think seriously about how children develop a theory of pictures, drawing and art. The volume begins with three chapters that set the general foundations for metacognitive knowledge in the domain, as children take on the task of understanding how pictures as representations differ from their real world referents, become aware of and develop a theory about the mind of the artist that produces pictures, and acquire the domain-specific knowledge that yields strategies for increasingly effective and communicative representations. The three foundational chapters also attempt an answer as to why or how it is that young children begin to draw at all.

In the first chapter, Tara Callaghan addresses the foundations of symbolic development in infants and young children with the presentation of a model that proposes the perceptual, social, and cognitive skills that persons need to become symbol users. Critical to the emergence of symbolic competence in Callaghan's model, is the infant's drive to become a part of the socio-cultural environment that uses the culture's symbols, and the support that others in the culture provide as they bring the child into the symbolic world. Callaghan tenders three main phases in the transition from pre-symbolic infant to symbolic child. The first precursor phase is marked by the development of a set of core perceptual, social, and cognitive mechanisms that prepare the infant for the symbolic world. The following onset phase leads to the insight that pictures are a representation of their real world referents and is discernible as the beginning of symbolic functioning when young children deploy the core perceptual, social, and cognitive mechanisms to engage socially with others about pictures. In the final refinement phase, the representational intent and communicative function of pictures is more fully understood and it can be said that young children construct a theory of pictures.

The second chapter by Norman Freeman addresses some of the same issues as Callaghan but with a markedly different approach, attempting as Freeman does an integration of visual-computational approaches to pictorial competence with those that treat pictures as intentional manifestations of mind. Freeman focuses on what constitutes "the minimum ontology" that the pictorial domain must take into account and the minimum number of core domains that allow for its initiation. Basic to an ontology of pictorial competence is knowledge about artist, viewer, picture, and its referent or the *state of affairs* the picture purports to represent. Although these four basic ingredients are necessary, Freeman argues they are not sufficient to initiate knowledge in the area of pictorial competence. As sources, Freeman proposes a minimum of two core domains that are fundamental to children's intuitive theory construction; more specifically the crosstalk between the domain-specific representations of theory of mind and of naïve physics, as children's intuitive theories of optics (as one aspect of naïve physics) get extended to predictions about what is in the minds of others. Thus, while Callaghan sources the infants' social interactions with teaching infants about the referential function of pictures, Freeman proposes pictorial competence as an emergent property of the crosstalk between intuitive optics/physics and theory of mind. As such, the communicative function of pictures is one of the early discoveries a young child makes, and not grounds for the realization of the picture referent relationship. In a similar fashion, Freeman argues that pictures serve to extend the senses as a form of visual prostheses, making the case that "… while intention may be a clue to the shape that emerges on the page, likewise the shape that is seen on the page is a clue to what the artist had intended." (p. 46).

In the final chapter of this section, Sergio Morra focuses on the memory and executive control processes that form the foundations for children's drawing strategies and explains how these domain-general processes are coordinated with the domain-specific knowledge developed in drawing. Morra begins by describing the figurative and operative schemes that underlie the domain-specific knowledge necessary for drawing, noting that young children have a store of figurative (perceptual) schemes that represent how a topic should look and a corresponding repertoire of operative (motor) schemes to produce these drawing topics. Critical in the development of true graphic schemes from early scribbles to more advanced graphic solutions, is the coordination of these developing domain-specific figurative and operative schemes with domain-general processes, particularly with the capacity of working memory, defined as "…the information that we can hold in mind and work on," and with inhibitory and other control processes. Using examples from his own research and that of others, Morra demonstrates the role of combinatorial processes, invention, and flexibility in drawing development, and the constraints placed on these processes by a child's working memory capacity. Developmental changes are accounted for, not by stages in realism, but instead, by increases in working memory capacity and increased cognitive controls. Morra closes his chapter with an intriguing puzzle about a particular type of drawing, narrative drawing. The results from his preliminary research on these under researched types of drawings suggest that neither working memory nor control processes relate in any systematic way to the coordination of these drawings. This is counter to what one might predict given that sequencing the narrative itself would seem to present more of a challenge for the working memory of younger children than older children.

The next section on *understanding and developing pictorial competence*, addresses the representational rules children adopt when drawing, how they use color and adapt to specific drawing conditions, and suggests how some rules might differ cross-culturally. This section concludes with a chapter on the increasingly important artistic medium of photography and how children come to understand the representational qualities of photographs.

In the first of these chapters by Christiane Lange-Küttner, the relationship between children's graphic strategies and their emerging spatial concepts is examined. Historically, concepts of cosmological space have evolved from those that were geocentric with the earth at the center to those that construct an explicit spatial context of the universe. Lange-Küttner argues that the difficulties physics and astronomy have had in constructing a concept of universal space bear an interesting parallel to those encountered by children as they attempt to conceptualize the space on an empty sheet of paper. Using her own innovative research on developments in children's depiction of size and space, Lange-Küttner demonstrates convincingly that children begin with an object-centered concept of space and transition to an explicit spatial axes system in middle childhood. Integral but prior to this shift, children adopt new denotation rules that map scene primitives such as edges and contours into corresponding picture primitives such as lines. The disparity between depiction of object concepts and children's ambition to produce more visually realistic images propels these developmental changes. Lange-Küttner argues that although children have concepts for their drawings from the start, the changes which lead towards visual realism are also the result of a desire for specificity, immediacy, and flexible yet reliable visual communication.

Esther Burkitt, in her chapter, explores how children understand and use the emotionally expressive qualities of color in their drawings. As in the chapter by Lange-Küttner, the focus is on what children of different ages know about the depiction rules. Research on children's relationship to color as a form of artistic expression is relatively sparse as most studies are concerned with children's color preferences or the emotions children associate with different colors. Burkitt reviews studies carried out on children's use of color to express emotional experiences but notes that the diversity of experimental approaches makes it difficult to draw conclusions about whether children actually use colors to express a feeling toward a drawing topic or in relation to their more general color preferences. Burkitt reviews her own research demonstrating that both the emotional character of an assigned topic, and children's color preferences influence their color use. Not surprisingly, culture appears to play a role in children's choices for expressing emotion but this contribution is under researched. A variety of issues are reviewed as well that point to other difficulties with research in this area, such as the potential instability of an individual's color choice over time, lack of comparability across studies because color stimuli are not standardized, and the paucity of theory to interpret findings.

Guiliana Pinto and Anna Silvia Bombi take a decidedly cultural stance on children's representations of close interpersonal relationship in their chapter. They assert that despite the widespread use of drawings in clinical contexts, some caution is warranted as cultural norms vary as to how close interpersonal relationships are conceived and depicted in drawings. The authors briefly discuss the developmental importance of children's relationships with adults and peers and address the relevance of using drawings as a tool for gaining access to children's representation of relationships in psychological research and clinical practice. Theory and research on the pictorial strategies used by children of different ages and from different cultures, to draw human figures and to depict close social relationships (friendship, siblinghood, family) is reviewed with an emphasis on what can be gleaned about children's relationships from such drawings. Particular attention is paid to the studies these authors have conducted in order to develop and validate the PAIR method for collecting and analyzing children's drawings. This approach takes into account two main aspects of close relationships: cohesion and distancing, i.e., the creation of specific and stable links with the partner, and the maintaining of one's own identity and personal autonomy. The PAIR is proposed as a research tool for studying friendship and other close relationships particularly in younger children and across different cultural contexts.

The final chapter in this section by Lynn Liben, examines what children and young adults know about the representational conventions of photography. Photography has become an increasingly important artistic medium as previously difficult to access tools and techniques become widely available and easier to use. But it presents a particularly intriguing challenge for children as they attempt to interpret others' photographs and to produce their own. Significantly as viewers and creators of photographs, children and adults must overcome the widely held notion that photographs merely show the world as it is. Liben draws our attention to the fact that photographs are not simply automatic, two-dimensional records of an instance or moment of reality. Instead, they are the product of a myriad of intentional decisions as well as unintentional acts made by the photographer. Liben reviews the empirical work she and her colleagues have carried out to examine age-related differences in understanding of photographs and the way spatial qualities are linked to emotional expression of a given photographic referent. Liben concludes that children only gradually come to appreciate that qualities of photographs can differ from qualities of the referents they depict, and that the developing photographic eye is affected both by universal (e.g., spatial concepts) and specialized (e.g., photographic experience; parental guidance) factors.

The last section, *developing a theory of pictures and aesthetic preferences*, begins with presentation of two chapters that address children's early symbolic competence, first in relation to their developing understanding of the connection between artist, picture and referent and second in relation to their own drawing competence and their comprehension of pictures. The three final sectional chapters explore children's understanding of the aesthetic dimensions in pictures; what makes one picture better to the eyes of a viewer, when are the formal aspects, such as visual balance, appreciated by children, and how does culture and age influence the aesthetic evaluations children and adults make, are the questions addressed in the remaining chapters.

This first sectional chapter by Callaghan and Rochat is grounded in the model of symbolic development Callaghan presents in Chapter 2 of this volume. The authors present evidence from their own research that examines how children infer the referential function of pictures from engaging with others who are using pictorial symbols. As early as 12 months, infants emulate the actions others take on pictures, adopting a stance toward pictures that matches that of the adult (referential or manipulative). At this stage, Callaghan and Rochat propose that infants have an action-based understanding of picture symbols that they decipher from the actions of others; they are tuned in to others' actions on these special cultural artifacts. Later, preschoolers will imitate the intent to represent when that intent has been directly modeled by an adult. Still later, young children are able to read intent to represent from adult's indirect demonstrations, such as an adult's failed attempt. By the age of 5 years, children begin to construct a theory that others use pictures to represent the world, and that others' mental states will influence their pictorial representations. The findings from the studies the authors present address the origins of children's developing theory of the relation between artist and picture and suggest that the onset of intentional understanding is in infancy, but that fuller appreciation of the relationship is tied to the beginning of mentalistic reasoning found toward the end of the preschool period.

Although much research attention has been given separately to the development of children's drawings and to children's developing comprehension and appreciation of pictures, relatively few studies have examined the relationship between the two. Richard Jolley and Sarah Rose explore the interesting questions that an integrated approach to these two research streams suggests. It is widely accepted that at least in Western cultures children's drawings develop from basic scribbles to increasingly visually realistic drawings. Similarly, with respect to children's comprehension of pictures, there is evidence for an age-related shift from non-representational interpretations to an interest in visually realistic subject matter. By taking the commonality of visual realism and separating out cognitive from affective responses, Jolley and Rose attempt an explanation for the contradictory findings from studies that have compared children's own drawing skill level with their preferences for drawings that vary in degree of visual realism. Presenting their own research, the authors demonstrate that children's preferences are not tightly linked to their own developmental level of drawing skill, but they also show that younger and older children's choices do not reflect the same standards for realism or for affective preference. Children's understanding of developmental sequences for drawing as well as estimation of their own skill level appears to be more influenced by their drawing skill level than their preferences. In general, however, the authors' research points to the conclusion that production or drawing skill level lags behind a child's comprehension of pictures.

The chapter by Hanns Martin Trautner also addresses pictorial comprehension but with a focus on how children understand aesthetic rather than representational properties of pictures. Research on children's and adults' aesthetic sensitivity to artwork has shown that the comprehension and evaluation of aesthetic characteristics of the artwork of others changes significantly with age. Trautner begins his chapter by describing and evaluating extant models of aesthetic development and related research. He then reviews research findings on children's understanding of developmental sequences for drawing and of the expressive qualities of pictures. Besides observing a linear increase in judgmental accuracy and confirming the usual lag between comprehension and production, his own research points to the great importance of task demands as a major influence on achievement. The rest of the chapter addresses the debate from which age on children are sensitive to formal and stylistic properties of drawings and art, in particular, in the case of their being in conflict with subject matter. In this context, it is also explored what properties predispose one art work to be preferred over another. Again, findings vary considerably depending on kind of task and procedure. In a study investigating children's and adolescents' likes and dislikes of colored postcard reproductions by well-known artists or painted in the style of such artists, Trautner observed that the relative weights of subject matter, color and artistic style in subjects' reasoning about likes and dislikes varied considerably with the specific characteristics of the paintings. This intra-individual variation was larger than the observed age changes. Trautner closes his chapter arguing that future research on children's sensitivity to aesthetic properties, instead of putting the referent-picture link at the centre of analysis, should address also the artist-picture and the viewer-picture links.

In her chapter, Milbrath examines how the preference for and production of one particular aesthetic quality, visual balance, develops in children. Noting that current data from studies of infant perception support the Gestalt psychologists' supposition that the principles of perceptual grouping toward *prägnanz* and stability are operative in infancy, Milbrath proposes that at least hypothetically, very young children could demonstrate an appreciation for visually balanced works of art. On the other hand, children might use conceptual approaches, e.g., part-whole operations and compensation relations. In that case, compositionally balanced products would begin to appear only with operational forms of reasoning and develop sophistication as concepts support more abstract analysis. Milbrath explores these alternative developmental pathways through a series of studies she conducted with elementary, middle, and high school students that examine production, preferences, and understanding of aesthetic principles of visual composition in relation to age and talent. Surprisingly, Milbrath finds that production of sophisticated visually balanced compositions appear in advance of preferences for these types of compositions. Children's free productions evolved from symmetrical but static alignments in grammar school to the more difficult asymmetrical balancing strategies in older middle school and high school students. Across the same developmental period, however, preferences for true symmetry appear to increase until late adolescents. Most students regardless of age preferred visual balance. Older students showed a more sophisticated understanding of aesthetic principles of visual composition but with few exceptions, none of the students could discuss formal elements such as style in relation to an artist's communicative intentions. The author points to the absence of exposure and training in the arts in most school settings as a potential threat to the ability of students to engage meaningfully with art.

Pariser, Kindler, and van den Berg also address aesthetic preferences but from a cross-cultural perspective, giving emphasis to the results of a three-country study in which evaluations of a variety of drawing genres were made by experts and non-experts from each country. Their research was motivated by two considerations. One was the authors' interest in the potential cultural relativity of the original Gardner and Winner U-curved aesthetic development hypothesis. The second was to provide cross-cultural data relative to the Darras and Kindler model of graphic development, a model that privileges a much wider variety of graphic representations than is commonly considered under the rubric of drawing, including mastery of such diverse genres as visual realism, cartooning, map drawing and mixed renderings. The study included the full range of representational genres drawn by the different aged draftsmen/women from each of the three countries. Artist/experts and non-experts of varying ages from each of the countries then were asked to sort the drawings into three piles as to whether or not they were considered good drawings. Surprisingly, only the rankings from the artist/experts produced a U-shaped function, equating children's drawings with those of adult artists. The study points to a number of striking cultural contrasts in aesthetic judgments as well as to age biases in aesthetic preferences for genres. The authors suggest that cultural relativism extends to include differential preference for a variety of genres. Significant as well for pedagogy in the arts is that teacher and student may not share the same standards for graphic development. The authors discuss the implications their results have for teaching in the arts.

The concluding chapter in the last section takes stock of the diverse research and ideas presented in the volume and suggests further directions for fruitful research that addresses the questions raised by the contributions of the preceding chapters.

References

Bremner, J. G. (1996). Children's drawings and the evolution of art. In A. Lock & C. R. Peters (Eds.), *Handbook of human symbolic evolution* (pp. 501-519). Oxford: Clarendon Press.

Flavell, J. H. (1987). Speculations about the nature and development of metacognition. In F. E. Weinert & R. H. Kluwe (Eds.), *Metacognition, motivation, and understanding* (pp. 21-29). Hillsdale, NJ: Erlbaum.

Freeman, N. H. (1980). *Strategies of representation in young children: Analysis of spatial skills and drawing processes.* London: Academic Press.

Freeman, N. H. & Cox, M. V. (Eds.). (1985). *Visual order.* Cambridge: Cambridge University Press.

Gelman, R. (2000). Domain specificity and variability in cognitive development. *Child Development, 71,* 854-856.

Gibson, J. J. (1971). The information available in pictures. *Leonardo, 4,* 27-35.

Gibson, J. J. (1979). *The ecological approach to visual perception.* Boston: Houghton Mifflin.

Gombert, J. E. (1992). *Metalinguisitc development.* New York: Harvester Wheatsheaf.

Gombrich, E. H. (1977). *Art and illusion: A study in the psychology of pictorial representation* (5th ed.). London: Phaidon Press.

Goodnow, J. J. (1977). *Children drawing.* Cambridge, MA: Harvard University Press.

Karmiloff-Smith, A. (1992). *Beyond modularity: A developmental perspective on cognitive science.* Cambridge, MA: MIT Press.

Kuhn, D. (1999). Metacognitive development. In L. Balter & C. Tamis-LeMonda (Eds.), *Child psychology: A handbook of contemporary issues* (pp. 259–286). Philadelphia, PA: Psychology Press.

Lange-Küttner, C., & Thomas, G. V. (Eds.). (1995). *Drawing and looking.* New York: Harvester Wheatsheaf.

Luquet, G. H. (1927). *Le dessin enfantin.* Paris: Alcan.

Marr, D. (1982). *Vision: A computational investigation into the human representation and processing of visual information.* San Francisco: W.H. Freeman.

Milbrath, C. (1998). *Patterns of artistic development in children: Comparative studies of talent.* New York: Cambridge University Press.

Munroe, T., Lark-Horovitz, B., & Barnhart, E. N. (1942). Children's art abilities: Studies at the Cleveland Museum of Art. *Journal of Experimental Education, 11,* 97-155.

Piaget, J. (1969). *The mechanisms of perception.* New York: Basic Books.

Piaget, J. (1977). The role of action in the development of thinking. In W. F. Overton & J. MacCarthy Gallagher (Eds.), *Knowledge and development* (pp. 17-42). New York: Plenum Press.

Piaget, J., & Inhelder, B. (1956). *The child's conception of space.* London: Routledge and Kegan Paul.

Reith, E. (1996). *Some useful distinctions and concepts for understanding research on the development of pictorial representation in children.* Discussion presented at the Piaget Centennial Conference "The Growing Mind", Geneva, September 14-18.

Rosenblatt, E., & Winner, E. (1988). Is superior visual memory a component of superior drawing ability? In L. K. Obler & D. A. Fein (Eds.), *The exceptional brain: Neuropsychology of talent and special abilities* (pp. 341-363). New York: Guilford Press.

Schuster, M. (1993). *Die Psychologie der Kinderzeichnung.* [*The psychology of children's drawings*]. Berlin: Springer.

Thomas, G. V. (1995). The role of drawing strategies and skills. In C. Lange-Küttner & G. V. Thomas (Eds.), *Drawing and looking* (pp. 107-122). New York: Harvester Wheatsheaf.

Trautner, H. M. (1995). *The development from segmentation to contouring in children's human figure drawings.* Paper presented at the 25th Annual Symposium of the Jean Piaget Society, Berkeley (USA), June 1-3.

Trautner, H. M. (1996). *Drawing procedures in children's free drawing, copying, and tracing of the human figure.* Poster presented at the Piaget Centennial Conference "The Growing Mind", Geneva, September 14-18.

Van Sommers, P. (1984). *Drawing and cognition.* Cambridge, UK: Cambridge University Press.

Weinert, F. E., & Kluwe, R. H. (Eds.). (1987). *Metacognition, motivation, and understanding.* Hillsdale, NJ: Erlbaum.

Wellman, H. (1990). *Children's theories of mind.* Cambridge, MA: MIT Press/Bradford Books.

Wellman, H., & Gelman, S. A. (1998). Knowledge acquisition in functional domains. In D. Kuhn & R. S. Siegler (Eds.), W. Damon (Series Ed.), *Handbook of child psychology: Vol. 2. Cognition, perception, and language* (5th ed., pp. 523-573). New York: Wiley.

Willats, J. (1987). Marr and pictures: An information processing account of children's drawings. *Archives de Psychologie, 55*, 105-125.

Willats, J. (1997). *Art and representation: New principles in the analysis of pictures.* Princeton: Princeton University Press.

Willats, J. (2005). *Making sense of children's drawings.* Mahwah, NJ: Erlbaum.

Part II

General Foundations

Chapter 2

The Origins and Development of Pictorial Symbol Functioning

Tara C. Callaghan
St. Francis Xavier University

Introduction

The birth of a symbolic mind may be the most fundamental milestone in human development as it transforms all cognition once it is achieved. Symbols are the currency of communicative exchange, and communication is the glue that binds individuals to each other and to their cultures. Millennia of biological evolution and centuries of cultural evolution have prepared the human mind for symbolic functioning (Donald, 2001; Tomasello, 1999). Although human infants are not capable of symbolic functioning at birth, they come equipped with a variety of perceptual and cognitive abilities that will prepare them for that level of cognition. Once acquired, symbols will allow infants to explore and gain new types of knowledge about their world, a world where others are strongly motivated to bring young infants into the fold of their culture from the moment of birth. The challenge for developmental researchers is to determine the extent to which biological preparedness and cultural supports influence the onset and refinement of symbolic functioning in young human minds.

Symbols form a special class of cultural artifacts that are intentionally communicative in their function (Goodman, 1968; Wittgenstein, 1953). For any truly communicative exchange there has to be an intention to communicate on the part of the producer of the symbol, and an attempt to read those intentions on the part of the recipient of the message. For example, when a cloud floats by in the shape of a shark we do not think we are receiving messages from on high (usually), but if the pilot of a small plane maneuvers her flight path so that the exhaust leaves the trace of a shark, we may get out of the water fast. Understanding the intentions of others, and having an intention to influence others, is at the core of symbolic communication. This is not within the very young infant's sphere of abilities, but it is in the making. The task for researchers is to illuminate how it is that infants acquire this ability to read the intentions of others, especially the intentions others have toward them as they attempt to share meaning in communicative exchanges.

As young children leave infancy behind, they enter a world where communication with others is accomplished through a variety of symbolic systems. In my own research I have focused on pictorial symbols, with the premise that much of what is fundamental to the development of pictorial symbols applies to other symbol systems as well. In what follows, I outline a model of pictorial symbol processing. The central assumptions of the model are that there are core perceptual, cognitive, and social cognitive processes developing within the child that lay the foundation for symbolic development and that enlisting these processes in the service of symbolic functioning is accomplished within a highly supportive cultural context. When the foundations are in place, children can learn through others who are using symbols to share meaning with them. In general, they learn about the referential function of pictures in these communicative exchanges, and in particular, they learn about the unique meaning of given symbols.

Outline of the model

The model outlined here is a revision of an earlier account (Callaghan 2003, 2004; Rochat & Callaghan, 2005). There are three main phases of development proposed in the transition from pre-symbolic infant to symbolic child; the *precursor*, *onset*, and *refinement* phases (see Figure 2.1 for sample drawings, which indicate productive capacity of children at each of these levels). Above and beyond the description of symbolic understanding at each of the levels it is necessary to account for the processes that underlie this developmental trajectory. My colleague and I (Rochat & Callaghan, 2005) suggested that social supports from others and the basic drive to be a part of the social group were the main socio-cultural processes driving development through the three levels of symbolic understanding and functioning.

Phases of development

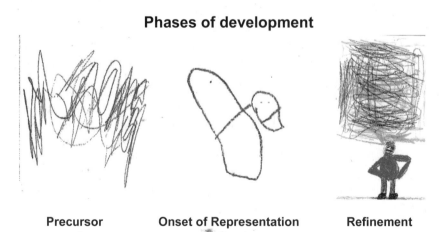

Precursor   Onset of Representation   Refinement

Figure 2.1 Sample drawings from children in Precursor, Onset, and Refinement phases of development.

Social supports for fledgling symbol users can be provided by the very act of directing symbolic communication toward infants, and this directed communication often occurs earlier than we expect the infant to comprehend the meaning of those messages. From birth, parents talk to their infants about such lofty topics as their goals and aspirations, their emotional states and their ideas about the world, albeit in the sweet song format that has come to be known as infant-directed speech (Werker, Pegg, & McLeod, 1998). Before their first birthdays, most Western babies are 'reading' picture books with their parents, who also point out the symbolic nuances of more complex pictorial symbols in infants' environments (Szechter & Liben, 2004). In their earliest social interactions with their infants parents often feign emotional states, typically mirroring the emotional states of the infants, which may help infants to develop the sense of self (Rochat, 2001) and may also expose them to pretense at an early age. Directing communicative acts such as these toward young infants provides a model of symbolism that can be copied. When the message is coordinated in such a way that the infant and adult jointly attend to the object of communication it eases the task for the infant who can more readily link the communicative act to the referent they are sharing with the adult. Joint attention, infant-directed communication, and models of symbolic acts are all examples of social scaffolding that adults provide to infants across most symbolic domains. Support for symbolic understanding may also accrue when more than one symbolic system is used redundantly in the symbolic act.

In the case of pictorial symbols, we propose that language is often used redundantly to highlight the meaning of the pictorial symbol (Ninio & Bruner, 1978; Szechter & Liben, 2005). This scaffolding of a novel symbolic system (pictures) with a familiar one (language) is another mechanism that facilitates the appreciation of the referential function of pictorial symbols (Callaghan, 2000a). Pictures piggyback on the previously developed understanding that language is used to convey meaning to others. Language itself may benefit from the use of gestures as a prop for intentional communication prior to first words, and the scaffolding benefits of gestures may diminish in importance as language is acquired (Tomasello, 2003; Tomasello, Carpenter, & Liszkowski, in press). For example, Iverson, Capirci, and Caselli (1994) report that children's use of gestures preceded that of conventional language, and that as children acquired conventional language the function of their gestures changed from being the primary mode of intentional communication to being more of a supplement to verbal language. Just as gestures facilitate verbal language, verbal language may play this scaffolding role for intentional communication at the onset of pictorial symbol functioning, only to recede in importance as proficiency in the pictorial symbol system is acquired. To summarize, the model proposes that social supports from others - in the form of rich joint attentional episodes, infant-directed pictorial symbolism, modeling of symbolic acts, and the redundant use of language - are critical to the process of discovering the representational function of pictures.

In addition to social scaffolding from others, the need to communicate and maintain social proximity with others arises early in life and provides a basic motivational backdrop for symbolic development in children. In earlier accounts of this theory, we labeled this need BAN, the basic affiliative need that infants and their caregivers have to ensure close, social interaction and sharing of experience through symbolic systems (Rochat & Callaghan, 2005). That children are drawn to symbolic interactions from birth is evident in three findings from the domain of language; the predisposition to categorize speech sounds from any language at birth in the same manner that adults who are native speakers of those languages categorize the sounds (Eimas, 1985; Werker, 1989), the preference at birth for human language over non-language sounds and for infant-directed speech (Werker et al., 1994), and the remarkable ability to hone in on meaningful characteristics of the speech stream very early in infancy (Jusczyk, 1997). As mentioned earlier, it is evident that the caregivers of those children are also tuned to enter into symbolic interactions with their infants. This is perhaps clearest in the case of language; adults direct rich language toward their infants from birth (infant-directed speech), adjusting their language in ways that make the speech stream easier to process (Werker et al., 1994), they coordinate their communications to the social responses of their infants (Bigelow, 1998), and they join into their infants' attentional focus providing rich linguistic information about the object of joint attention (Tomasello & Farrar, 1986). Thus, it appears as though infants and their caregivers alike are reciprocally pulled into communicative exchanges that may partly fulfill the BAN driving symbolic and non-symbolic social interactions.

These two mechanisms, one originating from outside the child (social supports) and the other from within the child (BAN), set the motivational context for symbolic development. However, to arrive at the game with a drive to join in and with a team that invites you to join in is not enough to understand how the game is played. You need to play the game with the others and learn through those interactions exactly what the game is all about. Learning to be symbolic is a dynamic process of social learning that occurs in the context of communicative acts with supportive other symbol users. The level of understanding that is achieved will depend on the extent to which other symbol users in the culture support that particular symbolic system, and on the foundations that infants bring to the context, foundations that can help set them up for understanding the symbolic acts of others. Research in our lab indicates that symbolic functioning develops first in the domain of language and later in the domains of pretense and pictorial symbols (Callaghan & Rankin, 2002). Preliminary findings from an ongoing cross-cultural study of symbolic development in our lab indicate that when adults in a culture do not interact using pictures or pretense with infants and young children, then comprehension and production of those symbols is delayed relative to cultures where adults engage in high levels of interaction using these symbol systems with infants.

In what follows I present empirical support for this theory of pictorial symbol functioning. The phases of symbolic functioning described below center around a turning point of representational insight, which in the case of pictures amounts to understanding that pictures are intentional representations of objects or events, real or imagined. As outlined, this insight develops with both the support of processes within the child (the perceptual and social cognitive foundations, a BAN), and the support of others who use pictorial symbols in social interactions with infants and young children.

Foundations for symbolic understanding

In the *precursor phase* of symbolic development, core mechanisms develop and provide a foundation for understanding the symbolic relation between pictures and their referents. These include the intertwined mechanisms of perception and analogical reasoning, and the interwoven mechanisms of intentionality and imitation. The child must have certain abilities related to these mechanisms in place in order to appreciate the communicative intent of others when they use symbols. These include, 1) an appreciation of the unique perceptual relation between pictures and their referents (i.e., pictures are similar to, but differ from, their referents), 2) an understanding that pictures form a special category of artifacts in that they all have this same/different relational link between symbol and referent that goes beyond a perceptual similarity (i.e., pictures point to, but do not replace, the referent), 3) an ability to reason by analogy that all pictures, even novel ones, have this same/different relation to their referents, 4) an ability to understand the communicative intentions of others when they interact using pictures, and 5) an ability to imitate the intentional actions, and eventually the intentional stance, that others take toward pictures.

The perception of similarity and difference relations between 2-D pictures and their 3-D referents were explored in habituation and visual preference studies decades ago. The results in this area suggest that very early in life infants have impressive perceptual abilities that enable them to perceive similarities and differences between pictures and their referents, and to use this knowledge to form categories. At birth infants perceive differences between pictures and their referents (DeLoache, Strauss, & Maynard, 1979; Dirks & Gibson, 1977; Rose, 1977; Slater, Rose, & Morison, 1984) and by 3 months they appreciate the similarity between the symbol and its referent (Rose, 1977). Infants also generalize across pictorial exemplars to form perceptual categories (Quinn & Eimas, 1996), suggesting that pictorial symbols may provide important information to infants as they categorize the objects in their world. Quinn's work provides evidence that infants can form even more complex categories based on spatial relations (Quinn, 1994). This suggests that during infancy the capacity to view pictures as a special kind of category, one that shares with other pictures the function of representation may be within reach. However, there have been no developmental studies that explore the formation of categories on the basis of representational relations.

Analogical reasoning may be required for such category building. Goswami (2001) argues that even very young infants engage in analogical reasoning that is perceptually based, and she proposes that they may build on these foundations to be able to reason about more complex relations during the preschool years. The ability to reason by analogy that novel pictorial symbols have a representational relation between the picture and its referent may be one such complex relation that comes within grasp during infancy and the early preschool years. Although many analogical reasoning studies employ pictorial symbols as stimuli, there are no studies that link the development of analogical reasoning ability to the onset of representational insight.

Understanding the communicative intentions of others, and then mirroring those intentions by using symbols as others do, are the remaining core foundations from early infancy that pave the way for symbolic development. Intentional understanding develops rapidly in infancy and stems from an early appreciation that other people have goals and tend to behave in a fashion that will help them to achieve these goals (Baldwin, Baird, Saylor, & Clark, 2001; Behne, Carpenter, Call, & Tomasello, 2005; Tomasello, Carpenter, Call, Behne & Moll, 2005; Woodward, 1999). Later, infants begin to understand that others will choose among alternative action plans the one that best suits their goal (Gergely, Bekkering, & Kiraly, 2002; Tomasello & Haberl, 2003). Still later, in social interactions with others whom they consider to be intentional agents, infants develop the capacity for shared intentionality, or collaboration, with others (Rakoczy, Striano, & Tomasello, 2005; Tomasello, 1999). In these collaborations, the infant shares goals and coordinates actions with the partner. It is in this context of shared intentionality that the infant begins to use the conventional symbols of their culture, such as language and pictures. Early in this process, infants will draw on their proficiency in imitating the specific actions that others take on objects in the world (Tomasello et al., 2005) and come to use words in ways that others use words toward them, and pictures in ways that others use pictures toward them (Callaghan, Rochat, MacGillivray, & MacLellan, 2004). *Acting-as-if* they are symbolic occurs before conceptual understanding of the referential function of all symbols, including pictures.

This apparently symbolic use of pictures by infants can often be deceiving to those attempting to measure their level of understanding. In our own studies we look for evidence of referential understanding in children's *actions*, particularly in their imitative actions in contexts where others have demonstrated referential use of pictorial symbols. These results, particularly those relevant to the development of intentional understanding of pictorial symbols, are discussed more fully later in this volume (see Callaghan & Rochat, Chap. 9). Very briefly, we find that infants are responsive to the communicative intentions of adults who use pictorial symbols in exchanges with them and will emulate referential actions following an adult's demonstration (Callaghan et al, 2004). On the basis of these findings, we proposed that an early stage in developing an understanding of the symbolic function of pictures is occurring between 6- to 12-months, wherein infants are acting toward pictures as others do, but without a conceptual understanding of the symbolic function. We call this *acting-without-knowledge* (Callaghan & Rochat, under review; Rochat & Callaghan, 2005), a variant of the concept introduced by Nelson and Shaw (2002) to capture children's use of language without knowledge of its referential function.

Achieving representational insight

Once infants have the perceptual and social cognitive foundations in place, they are poised for symbolic understanding. In the *onset phase*, children begin symbolic functioning by enlisting and coordinating the foundational mechanisms in social situations that involve the sharing of picture information with others and then come to the insight that pictures represent. As mentioned, we propose that three forces facilitate this insight; the readiness of the core mechanisms mentioned earlier, the pull from others who support development by using pictures to share meaning with the child, and the drive that the child has to become part of a symbolic community. The timing of the onset phase is also dependent on a number of contextual factors, including the familiarity of the particular symbols used in tests of symbolic functioning, degree of exposure to situations where others use pictorial symbols in interaction with the child, and the opportunity to support the pictorial symbols task with language.

Research has shown that children will comprehend the representational relation earlier when symbols common in their everyday environments are used to measure that understanding (Callaghan, Rochat, Lerikos, MacDougall, & Corbit, under review), and when they know the names for the objects depicted in those pictures (Callaghan, 2000a). We propose that children will also come to understand the referential function of pictures when they develop within a cultural context that supports the use of that particular symbolic medium. Callaghan (1999; 2000a) has argued that children have the perceptual motor capacity for drawing long before they have the conceptual understanding needed to intentionally produce a pictorial symbol. Only once children understand that pictures are used to represent, can they begin to produce their own symbols. Once they do have this ability, our studies with preschoolers suggest that they read the intentions in their own drawings by relying on form cues inherent in the pictures, both in tasks that require them to name what they meant to draw or to find the picture they just made (Callaghan & Rochat, under review). Thus, the child appears to focus on the picture-referent link when they first begin to produce pictorial symbols; making matches on the basis of perceptual similarity. Once children understand and produce rudimentary pictorial symbols they begin to refine this newfound skill.

Conceptualizing the symbolic function

In the *refinement phase*, children achieve a greater level of symbolic awareness, one that goes beyond the initial insight regarding the symbol-referent link that allows them to use pictures as symbols and to produce primitive representations. Now children understand representational intent in pictures produced by others and at the same time are sensitive to how others will receive their own symbolic messages. As they refine their understanding from a perceptual level to a conceptual level, children effectively construct a theory of pictures and keep others in mind as they use and produce pictorial symbols. Children's theory building in the sphere of pictorial symbols rests on the refinement of their earlier general understanding of the intentional actions of others. In this phase children understand others as intentional agents having beliefs, desires, emotions, and unique perspectives on the world. In the context of pictorial symbols, they understand that others will respond to pictures they have produced as meaningful symbols and will be misled when those symbols point to something other than their referents. When it is evident that the viewer does not understand their intended meaning, children will adjust their pictorial symbol so that it is more transparent (Callaghan, 1999). In the refinement phase, children are also able to comprehend and convey meaning beyond the simple forms used to symbolize concrete objects in their world. They can successfully judge such mentalistic concepts as emotion and thoughts in others' pictures (Callaghan, 1997; 2000b), and can portray those same concepts in their own drawings.

Toward the end of the preschool period, and coinciding with the onset of theory of mind reasoning, children begin to consider the intentions of the artist when processing pictorial symbols. Our own research indicates that children interpret the intentionality of pictures on the basis of the age, the emotional state, and the sentience of the artist (Callaghan & Rochat, 2003). Furthermore, preschool children are capable of reading the intention to represent from the symbolic actions of others. Callaghan and Anton (under review) report that some 3-year-olds and most 5-year-olds will imitate the intention to represent with pictorial symbols by drawing pictures to label the contents of boxes when an adult has demonstrated that action on a previous trial. By 7 years they will do so even when the intention is relatively obscure, as when an experimenter tries but fails to produce a drawing to label boxes. In contrast, the conceptual understanding that pictures are used by others to represent appears to be a relatively late-developing level of understanding. Callaghan et al. (under review) reported that it was not until 6 years that children successfully performed a pictorial version of a false belief task. In this task children watched an adult favor one set of toys that were placed in one of two identical boxes. When the experimenter left the room a second experimenter labeled the boxes with simple drawings and then the child and experimenter played a trick on the adult who had left the room by switching pictures on the boxes. Only children 6 years and older successfully predicted where the experimenter would look for his favorite toys when he returned. The ability to represent another person's representation of pictorial symbols is a sophisticated refinement of the symbolic function. Reaching this conceptual level of understanding of the referential function of pictures is a long way from the earliest stirrings of representational insight shown by infants (Callaghan et al., 2004), who held pictures and looked long and hard at them, or toddlers (Callaghan, 1999; 2000a; Callaghan & Rankin, 2002), who matched a toy to a picture of the toy in a choice task. The seeds of this understanding are present in infants and toddlers, but the flower has not yet bloomed.

Conclusions

The model presented here is a work in progress. The studies reviewed are relevant to a number of the proposed mechanisms that drive symbolic development in the domain of pictures and drawings, but there are still gaps in the research evidence. In particular, we know little about how the development of analogical reasoning skills during the toddler years may impact the conceptualization of pictures as symbols that are *similar to but different from* the objects and events they represent. This is an especially important question given that a great deal of this research uses pictures as tools to measure analogical reasoning (Goswami, 2001), and knowing what the child's concept of a picture consists of would be mutually beneficial to the interpretation of findings in both symbolic and analogical reasoning areas of research.

We have strong evidence now that imitation is a powerful mechanism for learning about what to do with pictures. From infancy through to early childhood children imitate actions that adults direct toward pictures. However, conclusions from these imitative actions need to be carefully drawn. When an infant mimics an action they have seen demonstrated successfully by an adult, we have no evidence of the symbolic knowledge underlying their imitative responses. We simply know they can imitate. The strongest test that children understand the intent behind pictorial symbol use is that they imitate intentional actions that were not successfully performed (Callaghan & Anton, under review), and they can predict how another person will act if their beliefs about a pictorial symbol are violated (Callaghan et al., under review).

We also have plenty of evidence that infants can match pictures to referents in a variety of tasks, both when the picture and referent are simultaneously presented and when they are not. However, like imitation studies, the actions of infants in matching tasks need to be carefully considered. Often infants can perform well on a pictorial symbol matching task because they have used language to do the match (Callaghan, 2000a). Language is a potential confound that is not acknowledged in most picture symbol tasks. It is also a likely candidate for an effective support system that is naturally used in pictorial symbol contexts by children who are fledgling symbol users. It is truly adaptive to scaffold a novel symbolic system with what you can from the one you have begun to test your wings on. And it is also adaptive to learn through others what to do with these novel symbols.

There is an intriguing anomaly in picture symbol research: Even though pictorial symbols share perceptual features with their referents, their function as symbols is not self evident to infants and young children. We suggest that children need considerable social support to become proficient symbol users in the visual domain, just as they do for any other complex symbol system. Research has shown that this support exists in typical mother-infant interactions within Western cultural contexts (Szechter & Liben, 2005) and can be used to facilitate picture symbol comprehension and production (Callaghan & Rankin, 2002). However, much more research is needed to address whether social supports are effective throughout all phases of developing an understanding of the symbolic function, and indeed whether they are necessary components of this process.

The research reported here adds the perspective of visual symbols to the growing literature, mostly coming from the domain of language, indicating that intentional understanding is a critical component in the development of a symbol system (Baldwin, 1991; Tomasello, 2001, 2003). It is highly likely that the ability to read communicative intentions is central to the acquisition of all symbol systems, systems that are fundamentally based on the need for sharing meaning among members of a cultural group. Understanding intentions behind simple actions begins as early as 12 months, and understanding of communicative intentions develops rapidly between 18 to 24 months. In our own research, we found that infants emulated a contemplative stance toward pictures beginning at 12 months, suggesting a degree of sensitivity to what others do with these artifacts, but still without full conceptual understanding of why they do it. There is a big divide between infants' contemplation of pictures at 12 months and either their use of pictures to guide search for objects at 36 months, or their production of pictures between 36 and 48 months. Future research on the origins of pictorial symbolism needs to focus on this age range (12 to 36 months) in order to determine why this gap between *acting-as-if* and *knowing that* a picture functions as a symbol exists.

If infants have successfully acquired the foundational mechanisms during infancy, and are gathering proficiency in other complex symbol systems (i.e., language) shortly following infancy, then what is holding them back with visual and other types of symbolic systems? The answer may lay in the relative value that cultures place on a particular symbol system. If a culture places only language cards in the symbolic basket, everyone talks by the time they walk, but there is little other symbolic activity. If cultures also engage their infants in stimulating interaction with other symbols, understanding and use of those symbols may also be facilitated. Studies that investigate the onset and refinement of symbolic functioning across cultures would contribute significantly to this long standing, but rarely researched question. In my own lab, we have begun to investigate the development of pictorial symbol understanding outside of the Western cultural context in traditional villages having very few pictorial symbols in infants' environments. Two themes are clear from our preliminary findings; infants who have never before held a photo in their hands will imitate a referential stance the adult has demonstrated, and very few school age children have begun to produce representational drawings. The foundations are within grasp, but without communicative acts that center on pictorial symbols those foundations alone will not produce a pictorial symbol user. Cultural supports appear to be necessary for entry into the symbolic world.

References

Baldwin, D. (1991). Infants' contributions to the achievement of joint reference. *Child Development, 62,* 875-890.

Baldwin, D. A., Baird, J. A., Saylor, M. M., & Clark, M. A. (2001). Infants parse dynamic action. *Child Development, 72,* 708-717.

Behne, T., Carpenter, M., Call, J., & Tomasello, M. (2005). Unwilling vs. unable? Infants' understanding of intentional action. *Developmental Psychology, 41,* 328-337.

Bigelow, A. E. (1998). Infants' sensitivity to familiar imperfect contingency in social interaction. *Infant Behavior and Development, 21,* 149-161.

Callaghan, T. C. (1997). Children's judgments of emotions portrayed in museum art. *British Journal of Developmental Psychology, 15,* 515-529.

Callaghan, T. C. (1999). Early understanding and production of graphic symbols. *Child Development, 70,* 1314-1324.

Callaghan, T. C. (2000a). Factors affecting graphic symbol understanding in the third year: Language, similarity and iconicity. *Cognitive Development, 15,* 206-236.

Callaghan, T. C. (2000b). Preschooler's judgments of emotion in museum art. *British Journal of Developmental Psychology, 18,* 465-474.

Callaghan, T. C. (2003). Nascita e primo sviluppo della rappresentazione grafica. [The birth and early development of graphic representation]. *Età Evolutiva, 76,* 51-63.

Callaghan, T. C. (2004). Developing an intention to communicate through drawing. *Enfance, 1,* 45-56.

Callaghan, T. C., & Anton, F. (under review). *Three- to seven-year-olds imitate referential intentions with pictures.*

Callaghan, T. C., & Rankin, M. (2002). Evidence of graphic symbol functioning and the question of domain specificity: A longitudinal training study. *Child Development, 73,* 359-376.

Callaghan, T. C., & Rochat, P. (2003). Traces of the artist: sensitivity to the role of the artist in children's pictorial reasoning. *British Journal of Developmental Psychology, 21,* 415-445.

Callaghan, T. C., & Rochat, P. (under review). *Intention to represent in the drawings of children aged 2 to 5 years.*

Callaghan, T. C., Rochat, P., MacGillivray, T., & MacLellan, C. (2004). The social construction of pictorial symbols in 6- to 18-month-old infants, *Child Development, 75,* 1733-1744.

Callaghan, T. C., Rochat, P., Lerikos, M., MacDougall, D., & Corbit, J. (under review). *Conceptual understanding of pictures and logos in 2.5- to 7-year-olds.*

DeLoache, J. S., Strauss, M. S., & Maynard, J. (1979). Picture perception in infancy. *Infant Behavior and Development, 2,* 77-89.

Dirks, J., & Gibson, E. (1977). Infants' perception of similarity between live people and their photographs. *Child Development, 48,* 124-130.

Donald, M. (2001). *A mind so rare: The evolution of human consciousness.* New York: WW Norton.

Eimas, P. D. (1985). The perception of speech in early infancy. *Scientific American, 252,* 66-72.

Gergeley, G., Bekkering, H., & Kiraly, I. (2002). Rational imitation in preverbal infants. *Nature, 415,* 755.

Goswami, U. (2001). Analogical reasoning in children. In D. Gentner, K. J. Hoyoak, & B. N. Kokinov (Eds.), *The analogical mind: Perspectives from cognitive science* (pp. 437-470). Cambridge; MA: The MIT Press.

Goodman, N. (1968). *Languages of art.* Indianapolis: Bobbs-Merrill.

Iverson, J. M., Capirci, O., & Caselli, M.C. (1994). From communication to language in two modalities. *Cognitive Development, 9,* 23-43.

Jusczyk, P. W. (1997). *The discovery of spoken language.* Cambridge, MA: MIT Press.

Nelson, K., & Shaw, L. K. (2002). Developing a socially shared symbolic system. In E. Amsel & J. P. Burns (Eds.), *Language, literacy, and cognitive development.* Mahwah, NJ: Erlbaum.

Ninio, A., & Bruner, J. (1978). The achievements and antecedents of labeling. *Journal of Child Language, 5,* 1-5.

Quinn, P. C. (1994). The categorization of above and below spatial relations by young infants. *Child Development, 65,* 58-69.

Quinn, P. C., & Eimas, P. D. (1996). Perceptual organization and categorization in young infants. In C. Rovee-Collier & L. P. Lipsitt (Eds.), *Advances in infancy research* (Vol. 10, pp.1-36). Norwood: Ablex.

Rakoczy, H., Striano, T., & Tomasello, M. (2005). How children turn objects into symbols: A cultural learning account. In L. Namy (Ed.), *The development of symbolic use and comprehension.* Mahwah, NJ: Erlbaum.

Rochat, P. (2001). *The infant's world.* Cambridge, MA: Harvard University Press.

Rochat, P., & Callaghan, T. C. (2005). What drives symbolic development? : The case of pictorial comprehension and production. In L. Namy (Ed.), *The development of symbolic use and comprehension*. Mahwah, NJ: Erlbaum.

Rose, S. A. (1977). Infant's transfer of response between two-dimensional and three-dimensional stimuli. *Child Development, 48*, 1086-1091.

Slater, A., Rose, D., & Morison, V. (1984). Newborn infants' perception of similarities and differences between two- and three-dimensional stimuli. *British Journal of Developmental Psychology, 2*, 287-294.

Szechter, L. E., & Liben, L. S. (2004). Parental guidance in preschooler's understanding of spatial-graphic representations. *Child Development, 75*, 869-885.

Tomasello, M. (1999). *The cultural origins of human cognition*. Cambridge, MA: Harvard University Press.

Tomasello, M. (2001). Perceiving intentions and learning words in the second year. In M. Bowerman & S. Levinson (Eds.), *Language acquisition and conceptual development*. New York: Cambridge University Press

Tomasello, M. (2003). *Constructing a language: A usage-based theory of language acquisition*. Cambridge, MA: Harvard University Press.

Tomasello, M., & Farrar, J. (1986). Joint attention and early language. *Child Development, 57*, 1454-1463.

Tomasello, M., Carpenter, M., & Liszkowski, U. (in press). A new look at infant pointing. *Developmental Science*.

Tomasello, M., Carpenter, M., Call, J., Behne, T., & Moll, H. (2005). Understanding and sharing intentions: The origins of cultural cognition. *Behavioral and Brain Sciences, 28*, 675-691.

Tomasello, M., & Haberl, K. (2003). Understanding attention: 12- and 18-month-olds know what is new for other persons. *Developmental Psychology, 39*, 906-912.

Werker, J. F. (1989). Becoming a native listener. *American Scientist, 77*, 54-69.

Werker, J. F., Pegg, J. E., & McLeod, P. J. (1994). A cross-language investigation of infant preference for infant-directed communication. *Infant Behavior and Development, 17*, 323-333.

Wittgenstein, L. (1953). *Philosophical investigations*. New York: MacMillan.

Woodward, A. (1999). Infants' ability to distinguish between purposeful and non-purposeful behaviors. *Infant Behavior and Development, 22*, 145-160.

Chapter 3

Pictorial Competence Generated from Crosstalk Between Core Domains

Norman H. Freeman
University of Bristol

It is bound to be the case that some researchers into cognitive development will put pictures at the centre of their analyses. After all, pictures are the tangible product of the labor of pictorially competent agents. The visual-computational approach puts pictures central to its account; and such an approach stops us misunderstanding what artists are up to, how pictures impel us to interpret them, and how children serve their apprenticeships in production (see Willats, 1997, 2005). Yet given that pictures are the objectives of artistic labor, one surely wants any such account to extend in principled fashion to give a place to artists' intentions to produce pictures. That immediately makes it comprehensible why there is an alternative approach to the picture-centric one.

It is bound to be the case that other researchers will put minds rather than pictures at the centre of their analyses. That is only reasonable because "The pictorial properties of pictures can have no causal effects upon the world except via agents who register those properties" (Schier, 1986, p. 81). Pictures by themselves do not do anything at all, they just inanimately hang around; it is agents who do things for people, and agents do things with pictures because the agents understand something of what pictures can prosthetic ally do for them. Picture-making is a tool to extend the senses and exercise the imagination. Agents interpret pictures and develop expectations of artists, and it is reasonable to put such facts near the centre of an analysis on the grounds that it is a "central fact about pictures ….. [That they are]….. an intentional manifestation of mind" (Wollheim, 1993, p. 134). We may add that that formulation clarifies another central fact about pictures, that the essentially communicative nature of pictorial competence is part of a lifelong mentalist-communicative endeavor (Freeman, 2000).

The idea behind this chapter is to incorporate the strengths of both approaches; for the approaches surely have to be complementary: without artists' minds there would be no pictures; and without pictures it would not be specifically pictorial competence that we were looking at. The formulation we arrive at is that pictorial competence is indeed a mentalist competence, communicative in nature, in which pictures are used prosthetically to extend the range of viewers' vision, in the sense of our visual understanding and our visual imagination. In the course of arriving at that formulation, we encounter a few possibilities and a few questions, such as the following.

Do we need a special explanation for why the young of our species so readily engage with the pictorial even as early as their third year of life?

Why might it not matter all that much whether we talk of the child as developing a theory of art or as developing a concept of the pictorial?

How far does a functional account of pictures get us towards an explanatory account?

I suggest that at least some of the confusion surrounding the question of where pictorial competence came from in the great sweep of phylogenetic change is perfectly comprehensible. Pictorial art was late in flowering in our species, yet it has evolutionary ancient roots in early-evolving core domains. Art itself does not constitute a unitary core domain, unlike intuitive physics or intuitive psychology (*theory of mind*); but it does arise from the confluence of the domains, the crosstalk that arises between them, as the title states. We leave it as an open question whether the crosstalk needed, and still needs, special cultural support to emerge and productively flourish in children.

One strategy when confronted by such large considerations and such broad questions, is, as adopted in what follows, to focus attention repeatedly on what are the fewest issues at base. Thus, the next section asks what is the minimum number of entities, the minimum ontology that pictorial competence encompasses. Later we ask what is the minimum number of core domains that feed into pictorial competence to get it effectively launched? In the final section, strands are brought together, focusing on new research possibilities, concerning how preschool children decide on how a picture should be interpreted by a viewer and whether the viewer should respect an artist's intention. Thus we arrive at the same key empirical issue as that of Callaghan (see Callaghan, Chap. 2)

Four ingredients of pictorial competence

One issue that is worth clarifying when starting to lay out the research is the issue of how far we should make value judgments on the pictures to be considered. At some stage it is essential to introduce a clear distinction between good displayable art and poorly done art; some such a distinction seems spontaneously to become salient in the conception of a picture in the minds of adolescents (Maridaki-Kassotaki & Freeman, 2003). Perhaps the distinction is related to a distinction between gifted and mundane artists? Yet conceptions of artistic giftedness change, and so do normative conceptions of ordinary talent due, in part to entanglement with the adult art world (see Korzenik, 1995); but I suggest that conceptions of giftedness change faster than conceptions of the mundane. Researchers and commentators who make prescriptive judgments on what counts as good children's art can pose problems for the development of experimental analyses of the ontogenesis of art. From a developmental perspective, a preschool child can take the role of artist just as firmly as anyone of any more advanced age (Gardner, 1980). We do agree that the identification of quality and talent is an essential second step in an analysis; but a second step needs a first step, a prior non-prescriptive analysis as a stepping-stone for launching an exercise in comparing and contrasting the superb with the mundane. Accordingly, let us enquire into what are the minimum considerations for an explanatory account of children's everyday, ordinary pictorial competence.

There are, of course, many things that go into an account of pictorial competence; but two things stand out as necessary, whatever one's prior predilections. The initial question to be borne in mind will therefore be how we might try and fit the two things together. They may safely be called *things* because they are two actual entities that go into the fundamental ontology of pictorial competence. One entity is the artist who produces the picture. The other entity is the general viewer who may inspect the picture; and who may or may not be the same viewer for whom the picture was produced in the first place. Indeed, some artists may produce pictures reserved solely for them to view; and some artists might even be too embarrassed to want their efforts put on display for other viewers. We do not for one moment deny that such considerations are important in the art world. But for the present purpose of evaluating the potential of explanatory accounts of the acquisition of pictorial competence, it is not very important who takes the role of artist and who takes the role of viewer or whether one person takes on both roles in turn; the two roles are always analytically separable.

In one obvious respect, the artist is the most important agent in the art world. Without the productive labor of an artist, we have no picture. An analysis of productive pictorial competence has to respect the hard work of picture-plane mastery because pictures are artifacts. Pictures are a particular sort of artifact: pictures serve us as communicative visual prostheses. Somewhat like things such as a telephone, a telescope or a periscope, pictures serve to extend our perceptual apprehensions into this particular world. Most entrancingly, pictorial prostheses can get us to extend our senses into non-arbitrary imaginative worlds. But the notion of an actively imaginative viewer brings with it another aspect of pictorial competence. Some viewers may or may not use their imaginations to understand the operation of the pictorial prosthesis at which they are looking, and they may or may not interpret the picture aright. Alternatively, some viewers may be so ready imaginatively to cooperate that they see pictorial representations where no representation really is being presented to be seen. That over-cooperative socialization is why one can trawl the electronic net and find John Travolta on toast (auctioned on e-bay early in 2006), as well as Jesus, his mother, Michael Jackson, and perhaps most pleasing, Aslan the eponymous lion, all making an appearance to co-operative viewers. Freeman (2006) analyzed such occurrences set in historical context; and Kemp (1998) briefly noted how some people's facial appearance really does seem to be suitable to being turned into icons. In 2006, Jesus appeared in an oil stain in a hardware shop. The finder asked a fellow employee if he too was of the same mind, and received the reassurance; "who else would come to give us a sign – Groucho Marx?" (The Times, 2006). Entirely reasonable.

In sum, an account of pictorial competence has to start by entering three terms into its analyses. The *picture* is a complex artifact with prosthetic functional potential. The *artist* is the productive agent who serves as the repository of knowledge and can model for us the expression of skill. The *viewer* is the receptive agent who may judge of the picture. What relationships do the three terms contract between them?

Those three terms are necessarily interdependent; just as they are for any communicative system whatsoever: an utterance, a speaker and a listener are analogously interdependent (see Heal, 1978). In that one fundamental respect, the pictorial medium is no different from any other communicative medium. A working concept of depiction should include the notion of "someone's attempt to communicate, preserve, or express" something (DeLoache, Pierroutsakos, & Troseth 1997, p. 3). In the verbal medium, "When noises have meaning they do not only have distinctive relations with human beings who use them or respond to them but also distinctive connections with some […] states of affairs" (Heal, 1978, p. 357). In the pictorial medium, *pictures* have distinctive relations with *producers* (artists, photographers), the *public* (viewers, curators), and *states of affairs* (what the pictures show). An overall concept of a picture consists, like any superordinate concept, of a "tight interconnection of concepts such that each one derives its meaning partly from the others" (Keil, 1989, p. 114). Parsons (1987) argued that children first learn to think about *pictures* in terms of what they represent as being *a state of affairs*, then in terms of how an *artist* expresses something and finally in terms of *viewers'* interpretative activity. Subsequent work showed that that strict ordering of phases of comprehension of the four terms needs some radical overhauling, but the ordering remains a productive starting point for any analysis (Freeman & Parsons, 2001). Irrespective of how well any particular analysis accounts for the evidence, all four terms and their relationships constrain the form of pictorial competence, as set out in Figure 3.1.

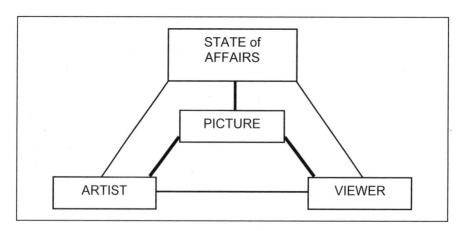

Figure 3.1 Entities and their relations that define pictorial function.

Something inside children impels them to develop sets of ideas about each domain of knowledge in which the children become immersed. Those four entities noted earlier are the prime constituents of the ontology of the domain; and are necessary but not sufficient to characterize what counts as knowledge in the domain (Freeman, 1996; 2004; 2006). So we now turn attention from ontological aspects to epistemological aspects of knowledge acquisition.

Pictorial expertise considered as mastery over a domain of knowledge

Any domain can be considered as composed of "A given set of principles, the rules of their application, and the entities to which they apply", according to the incisive formulation by Subrahmanyam, Gelman, and Lafosse (2002, p. 347). The authors go on to point out that sets of principles have functional significance in that they help learners to find inputs that engage mechanisms for problem-solving within that domain. For example, principles of number help someone find numerosity-relevant input. In such a way, for anyone gaining behavioral mastery over a domain, the domain becomes a domain of expertise. Thereby the expert is entitled to take on a title derived from the name of the domain: mastery over biology yields a biologist, mastery over chemistry yields a chemist, and mastery over their intersection yields a biochemist. In her fruitful model of cognitive development, Karmiloff-Smith (1992) organized her account of the acquisition of domain-specific expertise according to titles of expertise: "The child as a physicist; the child as a mathematician; the child as a psychologist" and so forth. What title does one get from attaining mastery over the pictorial domain? The answer surely depends on what one wants to include in the domain. Thus, the term *artist* certainly refers to picture-makers, but the term seems also to be extensible to someone who just does body-painting, or to a skilled make-up artist, and the term "artist" certainly gets extended to *performance artists*. It is hard to find a term that is restricted to those who master the use of making marks on a flat surface without thereby encompassing house-painters, room-decorators and even scribble-addicted "graffiti artists". Karmiloff-Smith (1992) ingeniously wrote of *the child as a notator*, in order to include mapping and other graphic symbol-generation, but the term *notator* understandably failed to catch on. Could it be that it is not clear what one gets from individual mastery over the pictorial domain? That marginal doubt is just sufficient to license raising the question of what did our whole species get from launching the propensity in the first place? Is there really anything hard and specialized to learn about pictures? At the time of writing there is no consensus on answers to these crucial questions. Yet progress towards consensus is being made. Let us start, as Karmiloff-Smith advocated, with the question of what there may be to learn in the domain of knowledge that makes it reasonable to talk about mastery and expertise in that domain.

There is indeed a great deal to learn about the pictorial domain, and a variety of skills in which to become expert. Each domain is bound to have its own peculiarities and its particularities, necessarily so because each distinguishable domain of expertise deals with a different set of inputs and outputs. At this point, there are two options concerning the main emphasis of an account.

One option is to regard some phase in the development of a set of ideas as constituting an intuitive theory of that domain. Children's conceptual change is a product of their interaction with states of affairs and with people who alter or maintain those states of affairs. Out of the interactions, children come to develop explicit theories; that is, children come to construct explanatory networks of beliefs along with rules of application to domains such as number, language, or physics (Karmiloff-Smith, 1992). A prime exemplar of that approach is theory of mind research. A theory is a set of interconnected concepts and beliefs which is the product of a certain type of learning, and it facilitates further learning. A theory can indeed become an intrinsic resource to empower children in their further development as the children work on the theory to increase its power in computations and its range of application. According to such a view, the appropriate way to characterize the development of pictorial competence is that children develop an *intuitive theory of art* (for discussion see Freeman, 1995; Freeman & Sanger, 1995).

The second option concerning the main emphasis of an account is not to talk so much about the child's *theory*. Instead, it is to regard some phase in the development of a set of ideas as constituting a sophisticated *concept* of the main entities in the domain. A prime exemplar of that approach is the tradition of research into the child's concept of number. A functional approach to concept-formation and concept enrichment assigns any concept a pair of functions, which are by no means straightforward to relate. Let us briefly note the two functions.

It is an important function of a concept of the pictorial that a child be able to categorize instances to which the concept should apply. The early steps in sorting out pictures from non-pictures are undertaken by young children (Thomas, Nye, Rowley, & Robinson, 2001). But there is more to having a concept than being able to identify things that fall under the extension of the concept. As Solomon, Medin, and Lynch (1999) put it, concepts do more than categorize. A concept is not just an input-filter for a domain; it is also something one uses to think about the things that the concept is of (see Fodor, 1998). Learning to be pictorially competent involves learning how to allocate attention to pictorial inputs, how to sort examples of different types of pictures appropriately, what to think about any example which falls under focal attention and then deciding on an appropriate output. It is straightforward to see all those processes going on when discussing with children advanced pictorial problems, such as whether a beautiful picture can be made of something ugly, or whether two viewers might reasonably agree to disagree about how a picture shows something, or what makes a picture worth hanging on the wall as an exhibition piece (Freeman 2000; Freeman & Parsons, 2001; Freeman & Sanger, 1993; 1995; Maridaki-Kassotaki & Freeman, 2003). It is not so straightforward to identify the principles that are needed to identify the early manifestations of developing orderly relations between all three aspects of having an effective concept: (a) accepting input and sorting it appropriately, (b) thinking about the input, and (c) deciding on a situation-appropriate output.

Consider a neat formulation by Flombaum, Santos, and Hauser (2002) who said that a domain "represents a finite computational problem space within which a given system operates. Thus, a domain-specific mechanism *becomes engaged* only when faced with particular types of problems, and operates by picking out certain relevant features, rejecting others, and using specialized learning mechanisms" (p. 107, italics added). *Allowing oneself to engage* with a domain is a vital part of allowing oneself to develop one's knowledge further. How is it that something about our species impels us into the pictorial domain at all? Some complex human activities can only be understood by supposing that we have a mental organ that sort of secretes something leading to the behavior (see Dennett's follow-up to his 1991 work). One might think of an *organ for language* or for visual perception, and so on. Yet the notion of some sort of *pictorial organ* is not an appealing idea to apply to the pictorial domain. Is there something intrinsic to the domain that pulls people into engaging with it? Or is there something extrinsic to the domain that pushes people into using the domain as a resource? Or, of course, there may be both pushing and pulling involved (as with most developments of a field of expertise). Whether one's own research is better conceptualized as a study of the child's theory of the pictorial or of the child's concept of the pictorial, one cannot avoid dealing with the question of why any such development at all is engaged in. We engage with art: What's in it for us?

What is the reason for engaging with the pictorial domain?

Gelman (2000) distinguished between two types of domain, *core-specific* and *non core-specific* domains, according to a suggested criterion that only the core domains are impelled from skeletal innate structures (see Carey, 2002; Carey & Spelke, 1996). Those innate structures perhaps operate by forcing the learner's attention to key inputs (such as numerosity in the number domain) which are relevant to knowledge acquisition within the domain (compare Geary & Bjorklund, 2000), as was earlier noted. It must be said that no amount of forcing attention to an input will guarantee that the learner makes anything at all of the input: hours spent taking a pet guinea-pig round the Louvre may or may not pay off in any respect at all.

Wellman and Gelman (1992) argued that there are three core domains within which children are innately prepared to construct theories: domains of physics (categorizing objects and the forces that operate on objects), of biology (objects that move by themselves and initiate activities) and of psychology (the significance of attention, intentions and mental representations of reasons for acting). A set of but three core domains is overly conservative as an estimate: it is necessary to take the list up to five by adding language and number. These five domains certainly seem to fit the bill to be Gelman's core domains which we human beings seem naturally to engage with.

Using such considerations as guide, how then do we categorize the other great human symbolic accomplishments? One option is to start with the broadest possible category *The Arts* whence to assign the pictorial a place. Alternatively, as we prefer here, it may be the case that there is no unitary domain *the arts* to be found anywhere in our mentalities. The arts may have emerged, piecemeal, impelled by other developments, perhaps in different mental subsystems. Let us briefly consider varieties of the arts.

There are many natural-seeming universal achievements: all of the performance arts for a start, music, dance, mime. Those are arts which are all presented to a public and are, as it were, ephemeral; in that once a performance is over, and the music dies away into silence leaving a memory of the doing. Rather like a grand gesture, in fact. And what are we to conclude about the non-performance arts, the making of pictures, sculptures, pots and baskets? Those arts and crafts are product-centered: the product is left as an independent object. No matter how polished and elegant the actions of doing may be, if the product itself doesn't turn out well, the enterprise has fallen short of its objective. Those are arts which are aimed at presenting a product usually without the actual crafting generally being on display so there is usually not even a memory of the doing. It may seem a bit odd of the *domain-specificity* researchers named above to omit our human propensities for object-making from being a core domain, a sort of demotion as it were from the key abilities that should be in the forefront of research. A core domain is something that certainly has a call on our attention for high valuation. Yet the high value-judgment may or may not accrue; for high valuation has to be earned. That is, a positive value-judgment has to come out of an analysis of the something in relation to other attainments. By the same token, to diagnose something as pertaining to a *non-core domain* should not degenerate into a value-judgment on the place of the something in the pecking-order of what makes us human. Underlying every valuation is some sort of functional conception, some conception of the activity in question as working well or as being effective in some respect or other. Functional accounts of the significance of outcomes are analytically distinct from phylogenetic accounts of evolutionary origins, and one can never use the one to supplant the other. The two *levels of analysis*, as they have been termed for half a century now, have initially to be kept separate and then tessellated somehow to generate any sort of satisfactory account (see Sherman, 1988, on how easy it can be inadvertently to generate an unsatisfactory account of any behavioral disposition). So exactly what qualifies a domain to be counted as *core*?

Core domains are those that were once biologically advantageous to the development of our species. Phylogenetic analysis claims no more than that we are as we are because something of adaptive significance happened to our ancestors to make us so (Dennett, 1995). Pinker (2002) endorsed the universality of art: "Art is in our nature [...] in the brain and in the genes" (Pinker, 2002, p. 404). Pinker immediately followed that formulation by noting that it does not follow that art is an evolutionary adaptation: he proposed that "art is a pleasure technology" serving the confluence of three other adaptations. That is, art-making may be a by-product, a realization of a need for status, the obtaining of aesthetic pleasure from direct experience of objects, and the ability to design artifacts to gain intended and willed ends. It may be so. Art might be something untidily emergent in the course of other developments in our species. That would be compatible with the appearance of paintings rather late in our historical record. By their very nature, we do not know directly about vanished performance arts. Pinker may have been right about arts serving status. But then so may most things be pressed into service in the social struggle. In fact, anything that can differentiate one human being from another, and anything that can be done better, can serve as a status symbol and motivate status striving. Functional accounts can be slippery things, prone to become formulated in terms which are too general. Of course, there may well be something about art-objects that renders them peculiarly suitable to be status symbols, their apparent non-functionality, for example, (art-objects being, on the whole, inedible and useless for digging with) or their capacity to soak up rich raw materials. That might be relevant to how the art domain becomes structured by powerful and aspiring adults. It will certainly not, on its own, explain the genesis of picture-making. Let us therefore take a fresh look at the functional question.

Pictures arise late in evolution, and late within the brief history of our species so far. Societies can get on perfectly well without making cave-paintings "whereas a society that banned the use of imagery could continue functioning, a society that banned the word would instantly grind to a halt" (Bryson, 1983, pp.16-17). To that extent, it is perfectly reasonable to maintain that pictures cannot have prime functional significance to our species, nor can one readily imagine selection pressure to develop pictorial competence and sensibility. Those considerations have led some researchers to leap to the conclusion that picture-making is a sort of cultural luxury, like developing a formal cuisine. Maybe so, but the fact that something is a luxury does not mean that is either arbitrary, or is just a matter of social convention. A gymnasium is a recent luxury, but it exercises, stimulates and develops individual action-powers. It is a sad comment on the human condition that we cannot get someone else to do our exercising for us while we get on with our drawing. Where a gymnasium stimulates something about the body (and mind, in the shape of action-planning), depiction stimulates something about the mind (and body, in the shape of the visual system). In sum, it is all too easy to over-estimate the fact of the late development of depiction in our history: it could be that depiction both exercises and challenges some innate propensity.

That takes us back to Pinker. In a neat offhand comment, he wrote: "I would guess that most [...] human 'cultural' practices (...narrative literature... ballet), no matter how much they seem like arbitrary outcomes of a Borgesian lottery, are clever technologies we have invented to exercise and stimulate mental modules that were originally designed for specific adaptive functions" (Pinker, 1994, pp. 426-427). There is no reason why *cultural* has to go in scare quotes; but it seems reasonable to propose that depiction exercises, stimulates, challenges and teases our computation of visual representations. It is inescapable that pictorial competence entails visual competence in some sense (with one proviso about blind drawing noted below); and therefore we have to consider visual characteristics in order to deduce what is peculiar to pictorial vision, as follows.

It is easy for us who have been over-exposed to pictures to forget that perceptual verbs are achievement words. The verb *to see (something)* is an achievement verb compared with *to look at (something)*, because one can look at something and yet fail to see it, or fail to see it for what it is. To look at does not exclude to overlook. It is likewise easy to forget how fundamentally even the simplest pictures challenge perception-action links. The first person who filled their mouth with pigmented dust and blew it over their hand pressed flat on a rock, then stepped back, could recognize the outline of their very own hand just out of reach, literally as steady as a rock, and saliently useless for reaching with. Depiction systematically perturbs the natural regularities that relate form to content, pattern-description to object-identification and surface-location. With the aid of no more than a finger dipped in paint as an instrument, pattern-descriptions can be lifted off object-identifications and the two played off against one another. Seeing the paint as surface markings jostles against having an object-recognition assigned: that is the famous dual reality of symbols. Milbrath (1998) wrote, when comparing her vision with that of artists, "where they saw edges, light, shade, and texture, I saw an orange, apple or bowl" (Milbrath, 1998, p. 3). Presumably, the latter object-identification as items of fruit has evolutionary priority, but the former appearance-parsing into aspects of appearance is no less real, for all that. It is the case that one needs both those facets of vision to characterize depiction as the "representation of things that have a visual appearance by using a medium to display a visual appearance" (Freeman & Parsons, 2001, p. 75).

We have evolved so that our visual systems are highly tuned to the business of picking up natural regularities that are of biological significance. If you see the surface of a tiger, it might be a reasonable bet that the rest of the tiger is close behind. There is often a correlation between how near the tiger is and how large it looms in the visual field. It is useful to recognize whether there is a leapable distance between you and it. Since most animals naturally tend to have front ends and back ends, it might affect your action-plan if you recognize which end of the tiger is which (an appearance of bilateral symmetry is a good guide to an animal's health: a lopsided or listing tiger might appeal to an escapee but not look so appealing to a tigress: there is natural viewer diversity). It is integral to our visual systems that they compute mental representations that turn natural regularities to our active purposes. Automatic mechanisms for processing some aspect of human figure appearance serve the purpose of recognizing others of our species (without secure conspecific recognition, sexual reproduction is almost a non-starter as an evolutionary trick). Maybe it is no accident that human figure drawing is just about universal as an entry point for young children as artists? Our visuo-motor systems are hives of representational activity ready to be exploited; and our species seems unable to keep its hands off any exploitable resource for very long. The implication is that the visual system has the status of something that has been harnessed as a resource when people make pictures. That way of looking at depiction evidently classifies the activity of depicting as a variety of tool-making, here, a tool to extend the senses and imagination. In such a case, crafting a tool and making a picture may have more in common than one might at first think. Certainly it makes depicting a very purposeful activity, and one that like all tool making is to be judged by what the tools can do and what we can do with the toolkit. Even counterfactual appearances can be put on display, an artist might prosthetically extend the concept of a periscope to show how things might look if light went round corners.

From that point of view, we can now more securely reaffirm that a most productive employment for visual resources is to use pictures to be "visual prostheses; they extend the informational system by gathering, storing, and transmitting visual information about their subjects in ways that depend upon and also augment our ability to identify things by their appearance" (Lopes, 1997, p. 144). The concept of pictorial prosthesis is truly generative if it be used sparingly (Harrison, 1997). Picturing certainly pertains to the visual system somehow. Maybe that seems banal. What else could a picture of someone look like if not something apprehended by the visual system? In fact, even the visual essence of pictures is by no means certainly the case. The flourishing of depiction by blind people is a hint that we may have to look deeper or more general than the visual system. Kennedy (1982, 1993) discussed a variety of pictorial metaphor that is now known to be spontaneously generated by blind people working with a pen that raised welts on the page, metaphors ranging from a picture of a businessman with a rabbit peering out of his head, to the sketchy lines that denote that something is speeding.

One always has to be careful in using a functional account. It may well be the case that, say, prosthetic tool making is the best category to use to encompass the mentality of mature artists who understand something of the visual world; but it does not follow that that takes us close to understanding how depiction arises in the first place. That is because a functional level of explanation has a different logic to an ontogenetic level of explanation (Tinbergen, 1963). Accordingly, it is to the ontogenetic level that we now turn.

Where children's minds come into the picture

When considering commonalities amongst the various domains of development, Karmiloff-Smith (1992) had noticed the extent to which the same developmental analysis as for core domains can be applied to "notation". That was a bold move because, as we noted earlier, unlike the evolutionarily-established core domains, the making of pictures is such a recent arrival in history that it does not even register on the clock face of evolution. *Notating* was conceived of as people's urge to "use cultural tools for leaving an intentional trace of their communicative and cognitive acts" (Karmiloff-Smith, 1992, p. 139). Cultural tool making leads the characterization in that formulation, but then the formulation departs from the visual characterizations in favor of the terms *intentional* and *communicative*. Why are those particular terms there? What is peculiar about incorporating the terms is that they seem to pertain to domains other than that of notation. Let us briefly consider them in order.

The term *communication* is usually so strongly associated with psycholinguistics that other researchers have had to resort to the term *nonlinguistic communication*, as though *linguistic* were the default value for communication. It is not: paralinguistic nonlinguistic communication arose long before our species was even a remote possibility. One could imagine boldly asserting the primacy of nonlinguistic communication, enrolling picture-making under that umbrella (Harrison, 1985). That is a perfectly productive position.

The term *intention* is best known from its appearance in theory of mind research. Long ago, Dunn (1991) recorded acute observations of 2-year-olds trying to tell whether something had been intended to happen or not. Something is impelling very young preschoolers to grapple with inferring people's *acts of intending*.

We shall now canvass the case for putting together the two main strands of the discussion so far. That is the case that pictorial competence is communicative in nature and springs from crosstalk between two core domains. The two domains will emerge as (a) domain-specific representations of theory of mind, and, unlikely though it may seem at first sight, (b) one strand of domain-specific naïve physics.

At the outset though, it would be imprudent to overlook something that appears to pose a rather difficult problem. The problem is that there is no *direct* evidence that nascent picture-making bears a biologically-specified relation to any communicative system, not even to a gestural system. It is still unclear what the emergence of scribbling signifies, especially given that 2-year-olds scribblers generally show at best only very transient interest in their own scribbles as objects of regard to be gazed at (Gardner, 1980; Thomas & Silk, 1989). That is, where the children may make vigorous efforts to have their gestures given their duly respectful attention, especially so for deictic pointing, the children seem to accord no such priority to their early scribbles. Maybe scribbles are produced solely for the hedonic pleasure of the activity? Against that view, Matthews (2004) argued that signs of symbolic action can clearly be seen in drawing in the second year of life. A multiple-component expansion of the genesis of intentional pictorial communication in preschoolers is to be found in the chapter by Callaghan in this volume. So perhaps we need not worry too much about the lack of direct evidence for scribbled communication. Maybe early scribbles do spring from hidden communicative roots; and maybe the lack of communicative intent attests to early scribbling being something akin to non-referential graphic babbling? All the same, we cannot confidently model the emergence of drawing as a specific pre-shaped medium of communication. All we are scientifically warranted in affirming is that drawing rapidly *becomes* a medium of communication whilst still in the scribbling mode (see Adi-Japha, E., Levin, I., & Solomon, S., 1998 for direct empirical evidence). That is to say, a communicative function to drawing may be one of the great *discoveries* made by young children before the age of three years. Is it that children have a powerful general urge to communicate and will press anything at all into service? Is there something special about depiction which means that the activity is impelled to gravitate towards communicative purposes? Consider the following case.

We noted earlier that Pinker did not derive depiction from a core domain but from confluence from other domains, what we termed cross-talk between them. And yet there remains the doubt mentioned earlier that we still need to explain how it is that the crosstalk eventuates in anything: how precisely does it come about that pictorial art can so readily provide a bottomless spring of products to serve extrinsic purposes, such as status-making? Consider a proposal by Lawson and Bertamini (2006) on the scope of a core domain. Research into the core domain of intuitive physics has concentrated on mechanical dynamics, such as predicting trajectories of falling objects, speeds of rotating wheels, or whether there is a tilt to the surface levels of liquids when containers move, and so forth. Yet as Lawson and Bertamini pointed out (2006), the scope of the intuitive physics domain encompasses much more than naïve statics and dynamics of entities and materials: the scope of the domain extends to *naïve optics*. Our representations of appearances, and thence our understanding of some of the determinants of appearances, have their base in the ways that light behaves and the ways our eyes responds to that. The understanding is highly relevant to pictorial presentation of appearances (basic optical theories and western art have long been interwoven in historical *optical themes*, Kemp, 1990). With the proviso noted above that a conception of the *visual* will have to be extended to the blind (perhaps somewhat after the manner in which "natural language" and "speech" have long been extended from vocal signals to the manual signing of deaf communities) it seems to be a reasonable proposition that pictorial competence has some of its foundational structure in a part of a core domain. So how does such a strand of core competence get extended into communication? Do we have to think up some special explanation?

It is interesting that the case made by earlier proponents of research into intuitive conceptions of optics is that no special explanation is at all needed (see Cottrell & Winer, 1994; Winer et al., 1996). That is because a prime function of intuitive optics is to understand the mentality of other viewers, or, as one might say, other users of those same optics. Thus, understanding how one's own line of sight can be occluded helps one to predict the knowledge state of someone else whose view gets blocked. In that way, intuitive optics from the core domain of physics seems to conduct crosstalk with the core theory of mind domain. That mentalistic domain encompasses belief-desire-intention reasoning. So it is now not such a puzzle that the term *intention* was contained in the formulation that we cited earlier: pictorial competence encompasses our capacity to "use cultural tools for leaving an intentional trace of their communicative and cognitive acts" (Karmiloff-Smith, 1992, p. 139).

Accordingly we suggest that the evidence on where children's minds come into the picture will be the same evidence as on where pictures come into children's minds. It is in the crosstalk between two domains that we should look for ontogenetic explanations.

Domain specific mechanisms are permeable; they are not sealed modules, witness the crosstalk between mechanisms of language and of theory of mind that can safely be inferred from the evidence and argument in Bloom (2000). It is to one strand of Bloom's work that we now turn to understand experimental evidence on the emergence of pictorial competence in preschool children. In particular, we look into evidence on the intimate connection between pictorial artifact, artist intention and the language of pictorial interpretation.

Evidence on cross-domain components of young children's grasp of depiction

It was noted earlier that pictures are prostheses, intentional artifacts for the extension of senses. The case to be considered is that something that applies to all artifacts, pictorial or otherwise, is that "children's naming is based on their intuitions about a creator's intent and how it relates to the design" (Diesendruck, Markson, & Bloom, 2003). There is a case to be made that while intention may be a clue to the shape that emerges on the page, likewise the shape that is seen on the page is a clue to what the artist had intended: "Children might call a picture that looks like a bird 'a bird' not merely because it looks like a bird, but because its appearance makes it likely that it was created with the intent to represent a bird. In general, appearance and shape in particular is seen as an excellent cue to intention" (Bloom and Markson, 1998, p. 203). Let us briefly note the evidence.

Bloom and Markson (1998) asked preschool children to draw different things that often come out very similar indeed under the preschool pen, such as two different people, or a lollipop and a balloon on a string. The authors claim that interviews established that if the intention had been to draw, say, a lollipop then in the eyes of the children the eventual product had to be called a lollipop, even though the picture could equally well be interpreted as a balloon. That firmness of purpose in young children is the first step in an intuitive theory of pictorial interpretation (for limitations on adult conceptions of pictorial intention see Baxendall, 1985; Beardsley, 1981). In the terms we used earlier, preschool children are acquiring a communicative theory of pictures in which an agent communicates something about a state of affairs to a viewer.

Now to re-examine the balloon/lollipop study. In order to give the widest scope to critical reflection that will generate testable predictions, let us imagine that we submit the experiment to someone who is immersed in the pictorial domain. That is, from an art-critical perspective, what issues would art critics say are involved here, issues more general than that of intention? In art-critical writings, one repeatedly recognizes a concern with terms like *authority* and its twin, *authenticity*. Who has the *authority* to put a caption (here, a name) to a picture? From that perspective, the Bloom-Markson design confounds (a) the child in the role of the artist actually producing the balloon/lollipop pictures, with (b) the child in the role of judge of the appropriateness of the caption *balloon* or *lollipop*. Accordingly, one would need to run a condition in which it was the experimenter who made the drawing. Will the child allow the experimenter-artist to change the interpretation of her own picture, seeing as how it was the experimenter-artist's prerogative to declare her intention in the first place? Or is it that once an intention has been stated, and a caption stipulated, the interpretation of the emergent picture is thenceforth set in tablets of stone?

We can try to find out whether the apparent faith of preschoolers in intention can be shaken, under what conditions; and if not at that early age, when? Fortunately for us, Browne and Woolley (2001) had already set out to answer that very question, for children aged 4 years and 7 years. The children were asked to choose names for drawings that they looked at; so that is rather the converse of Bloom and Markson's approach where the name was given first and the drawing came second. The drawings varied in the extent to which they looked like a possible referent, and the children were given information on what the artist had been trying to do. Intention was generally only a weak cue when pitted against *resemblance*. Indeed, to rely faithfully on stated intention here would run counter to the recognition that the apparent resemblance had triggered. So the children were judging sensibly. But when the drawings were so ambiguous that it was unclear what natural recognition was appropriate, intention came to the fore in judgment. Against that background, the important other finding was manifest in the older children: information on the artist's knowledge of the intended referent modulated the extent to which the children gave weight to the intention in determining the caption. That is, it is indeed feasible to think about enhancing or devaluing the value of being told the artist's intention when 7-year-olds are asked to name a drawing.

Enhancement was found by Jaswal (2004). For present purposes we focus on his use of the rather special case in which a drawing was made up of parts of two clearly recognizable referents, e.g. a bit of a cat and a bit more of a dog. Preschoolers turned to intention to decide on the balance of interpretation there. Further, Gelman and Ebeling (1998) showed preschool children rather vaguely done pictures and then counted the number of subsequent verbal label identifications (e.g., a *teddy*). When primed with the information that the pictures had been produced by accidentally knocking over a tin of paint, such labels occurred on nearly half the trials; but that level roughly doubled when told that the pictures had been done intentionally.

Devaluation of the value of knowing intention was attempted by Richert and Lillard (2002). The procedure on their third study was a rather special case that merits attention. The case was that there was a single drawing that looked like, say, a worm, and some trials involved telling the child that the artist (a space creature) intended to draw a stripy snake and did not know about worms, though her picture does look like a worm. To link back to the Bloom-Markson study, it is as though the child were shown someone drawing a lollipop and had the idea of a balloon put into their head along with a denial that the artist's mental state could allow them a balloon-producing intention. The outcome was that most 5-year-olds denied a role to the artist's mental state in assigning a caption to a drawing. Overall, the results were more complex than that, but the finding did come through that in this situation, where a strong recognition of a referent is triggered by the picture, children did not bother to consult the discounted alternative. It has to be said that logically, the children are wrong: no-one can be reasonably accused of drawing a worm even if all viewers see a strong resemblance to a worm in the picture if the artist has absolutely no idea that worms even exist. It would be interesting to push the design one step further, from the artist's ignorance to her false belief, by running a study in which the child sees for herself that the artist has the false belief that she is drawing a balloon when in reality she is looking at a lollipop as her model. In such a way one can hope to track an advancing contribution of theory of mind competence to the advancement of pictorial competence. And in relation to the model of pictorial competence that encompasses artist, picture, viewer and state of affairs, perhaps the simplest test would be to see children's processing of information about a *viewer* not knowing what a worm is. One could even extend the design to encompass two viewers with *contrasting knowledge* and see what the child makes of *viewer variability* in comparison with artist variability. It would also be straightforward to feed in information about artist skill: would young children give more credence to an artist's intention if they were told that the artist was a good, accomplished practitioner of her craft? Once one follows through the logic of the above studies on naming, all the familiar aspects emerge of charting the emergence of *pictorial reasoning* as laid out in Freeman and Parsons (2001).

Taking a perspective and drawing the threads together

At the start of the chapter, the point was made that there are two ways of approaching pictorial research. Both have a long intellectual history. One way is to put pictures at the heart of an analysis, as did Arnheim (1954). In the Introduction to the revised edition, Arnheim clarified the thinking behind the program he inaugurated: neither the role of the artist's relation with other people, nor the nature of the artist's striving, nor the psychology of the viewer "are the central focus of this book" (Arnheim, 1974, p. 4). The central place was accorded to the multiplicity of ways of pictorial perceiving. The contrasting concentration on what Arnheim relegated to the edges can easily be traced back to the first sentence on the first page of the first edition of Gombrich (1950). At that time, it was shocking for a book entitled *The story of Art* to begin: "There really is no such thing as art. There are only artists". The Gombrich tradition accorded central place to the human beings involved in the activities of the art world. The history of thinking about pictures has been bracketed by these two streams of thought. The discussion in this chapter has been framed so as to examine the extent to which current research fits into the divided intellectual tradition.

From the discussion so far, the conclusion is that we are seeing the roots of pictorial reasoning becoming visible through the confluence of two separate lines of work, one line on theory-of-mind and the other line on the psycholinguistics of naming. In the studies reviewed in the section above, the use of pictures has been largely a matter of convenience to experimentalists. That has certainly been advantageous for pictorial research. Even though pictures are appropriately in the centre of Figure 3.1, the suggestion is that in order to make progress in pictorial research, it is not essential to put pictures at the centre of one's research planning.

But it is useful to go one step further: it may actually be essential in the present phase of research actively to avoid putting pictures at the centre of an analysis. Indeed, that was the proposition in the second paragraph of this chapter. There it was noted that a line of commentary had concentrated on the pair of minds involved in the pictorial realm, the mind of the artist and the mind of the viewer. That trend towards a focus on minds, and their interconnections, characterized the philosophical work of Schier (1896) and of Wollheim (1993), with threads drawn together in Freeman (2000). It seems as though the heirs of Gombrich have inherited more research potential than have the heirs of Arnheim, at the present time. Perhaps the pendulum will swing back, but there is no reason to think that it needs to swing back soon.

In sum, the suggestion is that the present situation in developmental pictorial research can readily be characterized as a mentalistic phase, a phase in which the lessons of theory of mind research are being productively applied. That was exemplified in the section above that focused on the child's conception of the artist's pictorial intention. It is straightforward now to devise many experiments on that topic.

Yet it is important not to allow pictorial research to become merely a byproduct of mentalistic research. It was proposed above that our species' iconophilia arose from the crosstalk between core domains of theory of mind and one strand of naïve physics: optics. The special task of an artist is to operate on optic constraints so as to turn them into a visual prosthesis. It would be encouraging if pictorial research were to come to be capable of contributing something to the debate over domain specificity in human development. An exploration of crosstalk between domain specific mechanisms may be a way forward.

References

Adi-Japha, E., Levin, I., & Solomon, S. (1998). Emergence of representation in drawing: the relation between kinematic and referential aspects. *Cognitive Development, 13*, 23-49.

Arnheim, R. (1954). *Art and visual perception*. London: Faber.

Arnheim, R. (1974). *Art and visual perception: The psychology of the creative eye*. Berkeley, CA: University of California Press.

Baxendall, M. (1985*). Patterns of intention*. London: Yale University Press.

Beardsley, M. C. (1981). *Aesthetics: Problems in the philosophy of criticism*. Indianapolis, IN: Hackett.

Bloom, P. (2000). *How children learn the meanings of words*. Cambridge, MA: MIT Press.

Bloom, P., & Markson, L. (1998). Intention and analogy in children's naming of pictorial representations. *Psychological Science, 9*, 200-204.

Browne, C. A., & Woolley, J. D. (2001). Theory of mind in children's naming of drawings. *Journal of Cognition and Development, 2*, 389-412.

Bryson, N. (1983). *Vision and painting: the logic of the gaze*. London: MacMillan.

Callaghan, T. C. (2008). The origins and development of pictorial competence. In C. Milbrath & H. M. Trautner (Eds.), *Children's understanding and production of pictures, drawing, and art: Theoretical and empirical approaches* (pp. 21-32). Cambridge, MA: Hogrefe & Huber.

Carey, S. (2002). The origin of concepts: continuing the conversation. In N. L. Stein, P. J. Bauer, & M. Rabinowitz (Eds.), *Representation, memory, and development: Essays in honor of Jean Mandler* (p. 43-51). Mahwah, NJ: Lawrence Erlbaum.

Carey, S., & Spelke, E. (1996). Science and core knowledge. *Journal of Philosophy of Science, 63*, 515-533.

Cottrell, J. E., & Winer, G. A. (1994). Development in the understanding of perception: The decline of extramission perception beliefs. *Developmental Psychology, 30*, 218-228.

DeLoache, J. S., Pierroutsakos, S. L., & Troseth, G. L. (1997). The three R's of pictorial competence. In R. Vasta (Ed.), *Annals of child development,* (Vol. 12, pp. 1-48*)*. Bristol,: Jessica
Kingsley Publishers.

Dennett, D. C. (1991). *Consciousness explained.* London: Penguin Press.

Dennett, D.C. (1995). *Darwin's dangerous idea: Evolution and the meanings of life.* New York:
Simon & Schuster.

Diesendruck, G., Markson, L., & Bloom, P. (2003). Children's reliance on creator's intent in
extending names for artifacts. *Psychological Science, 14,* 164-168.

Dunn, J. (1991).Young children's understanding of other people; evidence from observations
within the family. In D. Frye & C. Moore (Eds.), *Children's theories of mind: Mental states
and social understanding* (p. 97-114). Hove, UK :Erlbaum.

Flombaum, J. I., Santos, L. R., & Hauser, M. D. (2002). Neuroecology and psychological modularity. *Trends in Cognitive Sciences, 6,* 106-108.

Fodor, J. (1998). When is a dog a DOG? *Nature, 396,* 325-327.

Freeman, N. H. (1995). The emergence of a framework theory of pictorial reasoning. In C.
Lange-Küttner & G. V. Thomas (Eds.), *Drawing and looking* (pp. 135-146). New York:
Harvester Wheatsheaf.

Freeman, N. H. (1996). Art learning in developmental perspective. *Journal of Art and Design
Education, 15,* 125-131.

Freeman, N. H. (2000). Communication and representation: Why mentalistic reasoning is a
lifelong endeavour. In P. Mitchell & K. Riggs (Eds.), *Children's reasoning and the mind*
(pp. 349-366). Hove, UK: Psychology Press.

Freeman, N. H. (2004). Aesthetic judgment and reasoning. In E. W. Eisner & Day, D. M. (Eds.),
Handbook of research and policy in art education (pp. 359-378). Mahwah, NJ: Lawrence
Erlbaum.

Freeman, N. H. (2006). Psychological analysis of deciding if something is presented in a picture. In R. Maniura & R. Shepherd (Eds.), *Presence: the inherence of the prototype within
images and other objects* (pp. 135-144). Aldershot: Ashgate.

Freeman, N. H., & Parsons, M. J. (2001). Children's intuitive understanding of pictures. In B.
Torff & R. J. Sternberg (Eds.), *Understanding and teaching the intuitive mind* (pp. 73-92).
Hove, UK: Erlbaum.

Freeman, N. H. & Sanger, D. (1993). Language and belief in critical thinking: Emerging explanations of pictures. *Exceptionality Education Canada, 3,* 43-58.

Freeman, N. H. & Sanger, D. (1995). The commonsense aesthetics of rural children. *Visual Arts
Research, 21,* 1-10.

Freeman, N. H. (1994). Associations and dissociations in theories of mind. In C. N. Lewis and
P. Mitchell (Eds.), *Children's early understanding of mind: Origins and development*
(pp.95-111). Hove, UK:Erlbaum.

Gardner, H. (1980). *Artful scribbles.* New York: Basic Books.

Geary, D. C., & Bjorklund, D. F. (2000). Evolutionary developmental psychology. *Child Development, 71,* 57-65.

Gelman, R. (2000). Domain specificity and variability in cognitive development. *Child Development, 71,* 854-856.

Gelman, S. A., & Ebeling, K. S. (1998). Shape and representational status in children' s early
naming. *Cognition, 66,* B35-B47.

Gombrich, E. H. (1950). *The story of art.* Oxford: Phaidon Press.

Harrison, A. (1985). Dimensions of meaning. In A. Harrison (Ed.), Philosophy and the visual
arts: seeing and abstracting (pp. 51-76). Dordrecht, FDR: Reidel.

Harrison, A. (1997). *Philosophy and the arts*. Bristol: Thoemmes Press.

Heal, J. (1978). On the phrase „theory of meaning". *Mind, 87*, 359-375.

Jaswal, V. K. (2004). Don`t believe everything you hear: Preschoolers' sensitivity to speaker intent in category induction. *Child Development, 75*, 1871-1885.

Karmiloff-Smith, A. (1992). *Beyond modularity: a developmental perspective on cognitive science*. London: MIT Press.

Kemp, M. (1998). *Icons of intellect. Nature, 395*, 551.

Kemp, M. (1990). *The science of art: optical themes in western art from Brunelleschi to Seurat*. New Haven, CT: Yale University Press.

Kennedy, J. M. (1982). Metaphor in pictures. *Perception, 11*, 589-605.

Kennedy, J. M. (1993). *Drawing and the blind: Pictures to touch*. New Haven, CT: Yale University Press.

Korzenik, D. (1995). The changing concept of artistic giftedness. In C. Golomb (Ed.), *The development of artistically gifted children: Selected case studies* (pp. 1-29). Hillsdale, NJ: Erlbaum.

Lawson, R., & Bertamini, M. (2006). Errors in judging information about reflections in mirrors. *Perception, 35,* 1265-1288.

Lopes, D. (1997). *Understanding pictures*. Oxford: Clarendon Press.

Maridaki-Kassotaki, K., & Freeman, N.H. (2003). Conceptions of pictures on display. *Empirical Studies of the Arts, 18.,* 151-158.

Matthews, J. (2004). The art of infancy. In E. W. Eisner & M. D. Day (Eds.), *Handbook of research and policy in art education* (pp. 253-298*)*. Mahwah, NJ: Erlbaum.

Milbrath, C. (1998). *Patterns of artistic development in children: comparative studies of talent*. Cambridge, England: Cambridge University Press.

Metro (2006). Potted news. *Metro*, Thursday May 11,16.

Parsons, M. J. (1987). *How we understand art*. Cambridge, England: Cambridge University Press.

Pinker, S. (1994). *The language instinct*. London: Penguin Books.

Pinker, S. (2002). *The blank slate: the modern denial of human nature*. London: Penguin Books.

Richert, R. A., & Lillard, A. S. (2002). Children's understanding of the knowledge prerequisites of drawing and pretending. *Developmental Psychology, 38,* 1004-1015.

Schier, F. (1986). *Deeper into pictures: an essay on pictorial representation*. Cambridge, England: Cambridge University Press.

Sherman, P. W. (1988). The levels of analysis. *Animal Behavior, 36*, 616-619.

Solomon, K. O., Medin, D. L., & Lynch, E. (1999). Concepts do more than categorize. *Trends in Cognitive Sciences, 3*, 99-105.

Subrahmanyam, K., Gelman, R., & Lafosse, A. (2002). Animates and other reparably moveable objects. In E. M. E. Forde & G. W. Humphreys (Eds.), *Category specificity in brain and mind* (pp. 341-374). Hove: Psychology Press.

The Times, (2006). *Bulletin for Wednesday* 1st March, p. 3.

Thomas, G. V., & Silk, A. M. J. (1989). *An introduction to the psychology of children`s drawings*. New York: Harvester Wheatsheaf.

Thomas, G. V., Nye, R., Rowley, M., & Robinson, E. J. (2001). What is a picture? Children's conceptions of pictures. *British Journal of Developmental Psychology, 19,* 475-491.

Tinbergen (1963). On aims and methods in ethology. *Zeitschrift fur Tierpsychologie, 20*, 410-433.

Wellman, H. M., & Gelman, S. (1992). Cognitive development: Foundational theories of core domains. *Annual Review of Psychology, 43,* 337-376.

Willats, J. (1997). *Art and representations: New principles in the analysis of pictures.* Princeton, NJ: Princeton University Press.

Willats, J. (2005). *Making sense of children's drawings.* Mahwah, NJ: Lawrence Erlbaum.

Winer, G. A., Cottrell, J. E., Karefilaki, K. D., & Chronister, M. (1996). Conditions affecting beliefs about visual perception among children and adults. *Journal of Experimental Child Psychology, 61,* 93-115.

Wollheim, R. (1993). *The mind and its depths.* Cambridge, MA: Harvard University Press.

Chapter 4

Memory Components and Control Processes in Children's Drawing

Sergio Morra
University of Genoa

Domain-specific and general components of cognition

There has long been a tension, in psychology and in the cognitive sciences, between the theoretical proposals that focus on general components or mechanisms of the cognitive system and those which focus on the role of domain-specific knowledge and abilities. This was reflected, for instance, in the debate on the nature of intelligence (e.g., Engle, Tuholski, Laughlin, & Conway, 1999; Eysenck, 1988). Another controversy regarding domain specificity concerns to what extent the mind is divided in modules (e.g., Karmiloff-Smith, 1992; Moscovitch & Umiltà, 1991).

Neo-Piagetian theories of cognitive development (e.g., see Case & Okamoto, 1996; Demetriou, 1988; Morra, Gobbo, Marini, & Sheese, in press) take into account – sometimes with different emphasis – both the domain-specific and the domain-general components of the child's information processing system. For instance, Pascual-Leone's theory of constructive operators (TCO; see Pascual-Leone & Goodman, 1979; Pascual-Leone & Johnson, 2005) includes two levels of constructs: schemes, a concept borrowed from Piaget, and metasubjective operators. Schemes have a specific content and are organized in networks according to their type and content; thus, a person's long-term memory can be conceived as a large, highly organized, individual repertoire of schemes. Metasubjective operators, instead, are general mechanisms for information processing that modulate the activation of schemes or the construction of new ones. The content of a person's consciousness depends essentially on the currently most activated schemes, whereas metasubjective operators as such are not consciously accessible.

If we assume that understanding performance in a specific domain (such as drawing) requires that we consider both domain-specific and general psychological mechanisms, which are the domain-specific and the general components that are relevant to children's drawings?

Let us consider first the domain-specific aspects. In keeping with the Piagetian and neo-Piagetian terminology, schemes can be divided in two types, figurative and operative. A figurative scheme is a mental representation of a state of affairs (e.g., an object, a particular arrangement of objects, or an object's feature). An operative scheme is a mental representation of a transformation, that is, the blueprint for an overt action or a mental act that transforms a state of affairs. Schemes are organized hierarchically; a scheme is a meaningful unit, and more complex schemes have simpler schemes as constituents. For instance, the hierarchical organization of the figurative scheme of an object often includes features, parts, and functional properties of the unitary represented item.

In agreement with Van Sommers (1984), one can define the graphic figurative schemes on which children base their drawings as long-term memory representations of the visual appearance of previous satisfactory solutions to pictorial problems. One can also state, following Willats (1995), that a graphic figurative scheme has a hierarchical structure, the parts of which denote the parts of the item to be drawn, according to rules of varying sophistication. I will discuss further the nature of such figurative schemes in the third section of this chapter. At this point, suffice it to say that the long term memory of a kindergartner or a primary school child typically includes a number of hierarchically organized figurative schemes that mentally represent how the drawing of a certain item should look like. How these representations are created, remembered, used, and eventually modified will be one of the leading themes of this paper.

Domain specific knowledge also includes operative schemes. First of all, one can mention motor schemes. These are very important in the early phases of learning to draw (i.e., scribbling). At subsequent ages the motor components of drawing are often automatized; fine motor control improves with age and this also affects drawing skill. Occasionally, however, attentional control of movement is required for high level performance, and in this case an account of what a child or an adolescent is doing must include consideration of the motor aspect of strokes or traits.

Another sort of operative schemes are those that represent spatial relations. These can be relations among the parts of an item (e.g., place the nose under the eyes) or relations between different items (e.g., place the wolf on the ground line between the trees, and place the sky above the trees). Some of these rules eventually become automatized; for instance, a child who has acquired a figurative scheme to draw a face does not any longer need any mental effort to place the nose under the eyes, and similarly also the use of a ground line and the use of the upper part of the drawing sheet for the sky become routine at some point. However, all that becomes routine at some point must have been discovered or learned with effort at an earlier point. Also complex rules (i.e., systems of operative schemes) can be acquired to organize the spatial layout of a drawing; this is the case of *drawing systems* (Willats, 1985) and *axial systems* (Case & Okamoto, 1996). Nevertheless, also in case an older child has acquired complex rules for space representation, a creative drawing often requires using some spatial operative schemes to plan the placement of certain items in relation to others. For a fuller account of the child's use of spatial operative schemes to organize a drawing, see also Morra (1995, in press; Morra, Moizo, & Scopesi, 1988).

Having thus assumed that a child's long-term memory can include a repertoire of more or less sophisticated figurative and operative schemes that constitute the domain-specific knowledge needed for drawing, let us return to the domain-general components of the developing information processing system. Which of them are involved in drawing, and how?

First, one should mention the role of working memory. The term working memory usually refers to the information that we can hold in mind and *work* on; thus, it does not refer merely to remembering information in the short term, but rather, to using it for any sort of processing. The nature of working memory is somewhat controversial; for some decades, the field has been dominated by a view that involved several separate *slave stores* (Baddeley, 1986). A theoretical view that is currently emerging as dominant suggests, instead, that we call *working memory* the subset of long-term memory units that are currently activated, and within this we can distinguish a more restricted subset of cognitive units that are currently in the focus of attention (e.g., Cowan, 2005). It is the focus of attention that is capacity-limited, although working memory development may include other aspects in addition to the growth of that limited capacity (Cowan, Saults, & Elliott, 2002). Also other authors (e.g., Case, 1995; Engle et al., 1999; Morra, 2000; Pascual-Leone, 2000) propose views of working memory and its development that emphasize the role of capacity-limited central attentional resources. In this chapter I will often use the concept of *M capacity* (Pascual-Leone & Johnson, 2005), which is similar to Cowan's concept of *focus of attention*. More precisely, Pascual-Leone defines *M capacity* as the number of schemes that an individual can simultaneously activate by means of endogenous attentional resources. Table 4.1 presents the growth of M capacity in the average child according to Pascual-Leone[1].

The role of working memory in various domains of higher cognition is widely recognized. I do not think that working memory capacity has a major role in predicting artistic giftedness.[2] However, I do believe that the development of working memory capacity has a major role in normal development of drawing ability, because children's limited working memory capacity constrains the degree of complexity and sophistica-tion of their solutions to pictorial problems. This is a main theme of this chapter.

Learning mechanisms are another type of general processes that affect drawing. They include both slow, cumulative learning that gradually enriches and refines the child's repertoire of schemes, and fast learning in which a new scheme suddenly emerges as a consequence of a personal insight or of direct teaching. The phenomena of organization of the visual field are another sort of general processes. The young child's

---

[1] To be fair, the terms *M capacity* and *working memory capacity* are not exactly synonymous. Pascual-Leone suggests that M capacity is a constituent of working memory, although a funda-mental one. However, these distinctions are beyond the scope of this chapter, where I shall use the term *working memory* in a general way, and the term *M capacity* when specifically referring to Pascual-Leone's theory. For a comprehensive discussion of working memory and neo-Piagetian theories see Morra et al. (in press).

[2] Even though I do not assume that working memory has a major role in artistic giftedness, there is some evidence that it has at least some role. For instance, individual differences in M capacity are a predictor of children's ability to invent pictorial metaphors for representing emotions (Morra, Caloni & d'Amico, 1994). For a comprehensive account of giftedness in drawing, see Milbrath (1998).

discovery of patterns in scribbles (Kellogg, 1969), and older children's use of compositional strategies driven by symmetry or dynamic balance (Golomb, 1992), are probably based on principles of perceptual organization (see also Milbrath, Chap.12). There are individual differences in sensitivity to the Gestalt of the visual field; a cognitive style called field dependence/independence (Witkin, Lewis, Hertzmann, Machover, Meissner, & Wapner, 1954) probably affects in various ways both drawing and aesthetic judgment.

Table 4.1 Development of M capacity according to the Theory of Constructive Operators

Age	M capacity for sensorimotor schemes	M capacity for symbolic (representational) schemes
1- 4 months	1	
4- 8 months	2	
8-12 months	3	
12-18 months	4	
18-24 months	5	
24-30 months	6	
30-36 months	7	
3- 5 years		$e+1$
5- 7 years		$e+2$
7- 9 years		$e+3$
9-11 years		$e+4$
11-13 years		$e+5$
13-15 years		$e+6$
15- years		$e+7$

Note. The ages indicated here are approximate and refer to the average child. The first symbolic activity emerges at about 12 months, and the first forms of executive control at about 2 years, but they emerge as a coordination of sensorimotor schemes (Pascual-Leone & Johnson, 1999). Only at about 3 years the child can activate a task executive (indicated by *e* in the table) *and* at least one figurative or operative scheme at a symbolic level of representation.

Also relevant to drawing are executive processes. Executive functions or control processes are often understood as the ones involved in selecting, planning, organizing and monitoring action or thought. They pursue experientially-based means-goal relationships, and thus they set in sequence, modulate, alter cognitive processes, or solve conflicts among them.

One relevant aspect is planning. The development of planning ability is itself constrained by working memory development. In drawing, one aspect of planning concerns the spatial location where a child intends to draw the various items that will be part of a scene (Morra, Moizo, & Scopesi, 1988). Another aspect of planning is time sequencing of actions. What one draws first and what next may be important, because the first items or parts that one draws place constraints and afford reference points for drawing the subsequent elements (Freeman, 1980). Young children (i.e., below five) are unlikely to do much planning before they start drawing, except for deciding the topic of the drawing; but after that age planning becomes more important. Even in young children, one can at least find monitoring and planning between the drawing of one and another part of an item – for instance, after having drawn eyes, they could decide that a mouth could be placed below the eyes and not in a random position on the page.

Inhibition of irrelevant or misleading information is another widely recognized executive function; it is among the predictors of academic giftedness, and it has been suggested that inhibitory control of cognition starts to develop early in childhood (e.g., Kirkham, Cruess, & Diamond, 2003). Not many drawing tasks seem to require inhibitory control; however, some of them do. Well-learned but inappropriate schemes could be activated, simple Gestalten may be tempting for the young artist, or misleading information can be salient in the context. All this calls for active inhibition of information that interferes with solving a pictorial problem. On the other hand, artistic creativity seems to involve an ability not to inhibit information that appears to be irrelevant, but rather, to incorporate it in ongoing performance. Pascual-Leone, Goodman, Ammon and Subleman (1978) speak of Interrupt/Disinterrupt control processes, referring to the ability to either inhibit or give up inhibition of information, thus alternating between a narrow and a wide focus of attention. Tests of fluency may operationalize the efficiency of those control processes.

As mentioned above, there are individual differences in sensitivity to the structure of the perceptual field. In artistic performance and judgment, sometimes a field-dependent cognitive style is advantageous, because the distribution and balance of the shapes is certainly one of the criteria by which we judge the quality of a picture. In other cases, however, a field-independent cognitive style seems advantageous, for instance in those situations where it is important to be analytic and attentive to the details. Field-independence is also useful in the situations where, as mentioned above, one should inhibit and disregard obvious solutions, such as a simple but inappropriate Gestalt. Pascual-Leone (1989) distinguishes between *rigid* and *mobile* field-independent persons; the latter, according to his account, can shift to a more field-dependent approach when appropriate; that is, they have efficient control processes to regulate their degree of sensitivity to the perceptual field according to the context and the task demands.

Metacognition fits well into this discourse. It is a particular type of domain-specific knowledge, that is, knowledge (awareness) of one's domain-specific knowledge, which derives from one's experience in drawing, from self-generated or environmental feedback about one's drawings, or from cultural standards explicitly or implicitly set on them. Even though it is a part of domain-specific knowledge, it clearly feeds back on control processes. Metacognition can assist a child in setting goals, selecting strategies, revising plans, discarding and inhibiting inappropriate ideas, monitoring the drawing activity and its outcome, allocating attentional resources.

Some aspects of the control processes are also related to personality differences. A creative personality with a preference for divergent thinking is also characterized by goals, strategies, and judgment processes that aim to produce unusual, original drawings and perhaps also to break the commonly accepted rules. An obsessive personality may manifest itself in control processes that have an impact on drawing style. Detailed consideration of personality differences, however, is beyond the scope of this chapter.

The emergence of drawing

So far, the argument has considered various aspects of cognition that affect children's drawings. Special emphasis has been placed on schemes that preserve and use domain-specific knowledge, on working memory as a resource that enables the child to use a limited (but growing with age) amount of available information, and on control processes that regulate the use of that information (and of working memory itself). But what is the origin of drawing? How can a young child take the giant step of using marks made on paper as a powerful means of representation?

In a Piagetian perspective, drawing can be regarded as a form of symbolization like delayed imitation, symbolic play, and language. However, even a superficial observer can note that children start to draw recognizable symbols much later than the onset of other forms of symbolic representation. Why?

A first reason is that symbolic play and delayed imitation do not require any particular symbolic language, because they use the same sort of actions or motor schemes that the child could also use in a non-symbolic context. Language uses words, but words are made of sounds that are produced naturally by specialized organs evolved with the human species, and the whole social context coaches the child to shape her spontaneous utterances as words of her native language. But evolution has not provided us with special organs for making marks. The ability to make marks on a surface with a drawing instrument is in itself a remarkable achievement for the child.

Actually, making even a totally uncontrolled scribble with a pencil (or another drawing instrument) on a sheet of paper requires the child to coordinate no less than five sensorimotor schemes, of which two are operative (motor) schemes and three figurative schemes (perceptual representations of aspects of reality that constrain scribbling). Namely, the figurative schemes involved are (a) the pencil, or whatever the child recognizes as a marking instrument, (b) the target surface, and (c) the point of the pencil, that must be in contact with the target surface; and the operative schemes are (d) grasping, and (e) moving the arm. Occasionally, young children make marks without using a drawing instrument (e.g., they move their hands in the sand, or they touch the mud or play with their own food) and to do so they need fewer schemes than to use a drawing instrument; but such actions only leave ephemeral traces. Using a pencil is a big achievement that even in the case of an uncontrolled scribble requires coordination of five sensorimotor schemes, which in turn demands the amount of M capacity that is typical of the age range from 18 to 24 months (see Table 1). That could be a reason why scribbling is observed seldom[3] in children younger than one year and a half, who are more likely to use a pencil as a drumming stick or a tasty delicacy. For the sake of comparison, consider that according to Pascual-Leone and Johnson (1999) the symbolic use of words requires coordination of only four sensorimotor schemes, and thus can take place approximately six months earlier, in the first half of the second year.

According to the foregoing account, mark making requires coordinating five sensorimotor schemes; however, that account is only assumed to be valid for un-controlled scribbling, that is, a motor activity that leaves marks by means of one of the spontaneous arm movements described by Matthews (1984), without any meaning attached and without any attempt to use visual feedback to regulate the movement. That would only be the least sophisticated form of scribbling. Early theories of drawing (e.g., Luquet, 1927) regarded scribbling as a purely motor ex-ercise, but more recent accounts emphasized quite different views. According to Kellogg (1969) children's interest is driven mainly by the visual aspect of their scribbles, and they progress through a series of visual patterns that are increasingly complex and better controlled. Others (Matthews, 1984; Quaglia & Saglione, 1976; Romano, Poddine, & Guindani, 1980) note children's use of scribbles as a form of representation through action, akin to symbolic play; the meaning would thus be conveyed by the action itself. For Adi-Japha, Levin, and Solomon (1998), some marks in a scribble may have a precursory referential meaning, although that meaning is not transparent for an observer (see also Yamagata, 2001). A possible expressive value of scribbles that have an emotional connotation has also been suggested (Quaglia & Saglione, 1976). Probably, there is some truth in all of these views. An emotional tone of the child who is scribbling does not add any informa-tion load on working memory; but either visual control or implied meaning of the scribbling do.

Let us consider first the case of visually controlled scribbling. A few months after their first scribblings, children start to use visual feedback and make experiments with the outcome of their movements, like younger children do in Piaget's *tertiary circular reactions*. They differentiate various sorts of scribbles, and produce what Kellogg (1969) calls placement patterns, that is, visually guided compositions of scribbles on the page. Visually controlled scribbling requires a fourth figurative

---

[3] The cases reported in the literature are not many and could have occurred in the context of in-teraction with adults who have a scaffolding role. This was the case of Yamagata (1997), while in other cases (Cox, 2005; Osterrieth, 1973; Quaglia & Saglione, 1976) where earlier ages are re-ported it is not stated whether only spontaneous scribbling was considered, or also scribbling in the context of interaction with a helpful adult. For instance, an adult could assist the child in grasping the pencil and orienting it with the point toward the paper, or model the marking be-haviour; such aids might enable effortless activation of one of the required schemes, thus reducing the working memory load.

sensorimotor scheme, in addition to the three figurative and two operative ones listed above; namely, the current pattern of scribbles visible on the paper, which feeds back on the arm movement and regulates it. According to the theoretical perspective taken in this chapter, six sensorimotor schemes can typically be coordinated by children aged 24 to 30 months; that could be a reason why controlled scribbling is not frequent in children younger than two years.

Once a child has acquired the ability to keep her scribbling activity under visual control, further developments are possible. For instance, the child could abstract shapes from the scribbles she has made, and intentionally produce such shapes in a new scribble. Kellogg (1969) calls *diagrams* the clear and simple forms – such as crosses, ovals, and roughly triangular or rectangular shapes – that children produce at this stage. According to Kellogg, these forms do not have a representational meaning, but the child is motivated to produce them by interest in the forms themselves and visual pleasure obtained from these good Gestalten. As Golomb (1992) puts it, "Drawing a single line that encloses an area and arrives back at the starting point demonstrates a remarkable visual-motor control. It speaks of an effort to subdue the impulse to make rotational whirls and thus to subordinate a preferred motor gesture to visual dictates." (p.15) I fully agree; here is an early case of inhibitory control that, as suggested in the previous section, is required by some drawing tasks.

Note that producing a pattern would require still one more figurative scheme than simple visually-controlled scribbling, namely, an expectation of the particular form to be produced; this would raise the working memory load to seven sensorimotor schemes (and, consequently, set the expected age for this achievement to 30 months). However, at this point, often the grip on the pencil has become more refined and to some extent automatized, and also the contact of the pencil point on the sheet may need lesser attention and monitoring. This frees up resources, also enabling the child to put together more complex structures of scribbles, comprising two or three diagrams (which Kellogg calls *aggregates*).

A quite different line of development is the one that involves meaning. If a purely motor scribbling activity requires coordinating five sensorimotor units, then, expanding attention to include an intended meaning of the arm movement (a symbolic meaning, like in symbolic play) would involve a sixth sensorimotor scheme, that is, the intended referent of the arm/pencil movement on the plane of symbolic play. Thus, the child would attribute meaning to the scribbling activity – not to the form of the scribble. This is sometimes called action representation (e.g., Matthews, 1984). However, action representation and meaning making are even more likely to take place when scribbling is visually controlled, which enables the movement to be more clearly defined. This entails that action representation by means of visually controlled scribbling involves seven sensorimotor units: (a) grasping or holding, (b) the pencil or marking instrument, (c) the target surface, (d) the pencil point on the surface, (e) the action, including the arm movement and possibly other movements, (f) the currently visible scribble, (g) the meaning attached to the action.

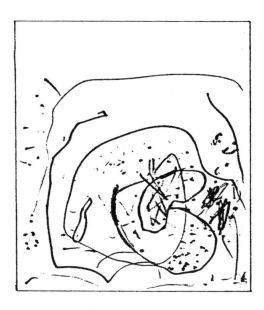

Figure 4.1 Action representation and meaningful scribbles: "This is all Jessica dancing with daddy." Source: Panchaud and Romano (1980).

Figure 4.1 provides an example of such action representation. The author, Jessica, is 2 years and 10 months old. Invited by her preschool teacher to draw a self-portrait, she draws a number of overlapping, closed or semi-closed shapes and then, with a series of rhythmic movements, adds many dots on the shapes or near to them, commenting: "This is all Jessica dancing with daddy." The closed shapes are, in Kellogg's terms, an aggregate of diagrams, with a meaning which is not self-generated but suggested by the teacher; spontaneously, the child adds to the required meaning the specification of *dancing with daddy*, and represents it with a rhythmic movement akin to symbolic play, which produces many dots on the paper. The currently visible scribbles drive the placement of such marks, but it is the action that conveys the meaning.

To summarize: a working memory capacity of five sensorimotor schemes is required for uncontrolled scribbling, six for visually controlled scribbling, probably seven for *diagrams* and combinations of diagrams, and six or seven for action representation (by means, respectively, of uncontrolled or controlled scribbling). This theoretical model was derived from a literature review and occasional observation; direct research on the relationship between scribbling ability and measures of working memory capacity appropriate for such young children (Alp, 1994) is now in progress.

If the model is correct, an important conclusion follows: the working memory capacity available to children below three years of age enables them to put together making marks and pursuit of visual form (as they do when they produce diagrams), or to put together making marks and symbolic meaning (as in action representation). However, putting together at the same time making marks, visual form, and symbolic meaning would be too much.

As both Freeman (1980) and Golomb (1992) remark in different terms, there is no abrupt transition between a pre-representational and a representational stage of drawing. Children who spontaneously scribble can, nevertheless, demonstrate representational competence. For instance, in drawing completion tasks, they can add parts to a stimulus drawing (Freeman, 1980; Golomb, 1981; Yamagata, 2001). Or, they can follow an adult's directions and draw *under dictation*, one at a time, the various parts of a figure. So, representation in drawing is not beyond their mentality – but they are still not able to put together a representational drawing by themselves.

Adi-Japha et al. (1998) report that children between two and three years occasionally attribute a representational meaning to parts of the scribbles they have made (especially in the second half of the third year). They are more likely to attribute representational meaning to angular curves than to smooth curves or straight lines, and only do so for scribbles that they have just made; they do not attribute meaning to scribbles drawn by peers, by themselves in the past, or by the experimenter. Adi-Japha et al. suggest that this attribution of meaning could be a precursor of pre-planned representational drawing, also because the part of scribble pointed at sometimes bears some shape resemblance with its stated referent. However, children hardly ever declared in advance what they were going to draw, and rarely did they attribute any representational meaning when asked about the entire scribble. The authors suggest that – although interpretation of angular lines in their own, just-finished scribbles is a genuine phenomenon – it is likely to take place a posteriori, and not be indicative of a pre-planned referential meaning of the scribble.

Luquet (1927) reported, and labeled as *failed realism*, evidence of children who had representational intentions, but could not translate them successfully into marks on the paper. Conversely, numerous studies (Adi-Japha et al., 1998; Cox, 2005; Freeman, 1980; Golomb, 1981, 1992; Matthews, 1984; Quaglia & Saglione, 1976; Romano et al., 1980; Yamagata, 1997, 2001) provide evidence of various precursors of pictorial representation in scribblers. Thus, there is no abrupt leap from non-representational scribbling to representational, schematic drawing; instead, there is a long period characterized by glimpses of representation that fleetingly appear among the scribbles, but do not precipitate as recognizable representational schemes.

Figure 4.2 illustrates well the characteristics of this transitional period. The author, Clara, is 2 years and 11 months old. She has a keen interest in children's books and can offer to the visitor extensive explanations about the pictures in hers – a clear evidence of her awareness of the representational value of pictures. On one occasion, she scribbles on some sheets of paper, but (even prompted with questions) denies any representational meaning to her scribbles, except one rectangular shape called *a window*. Thereafter, she picks up another sheet and, undisturbed by the fact that it already bears lots of *scribbles* (notes written by her father, a mathematician) she starts to produce Figure 4.2.

Figure 4.2 Another example of precursors of representational drawing: "A plane, flying in the sky".

First she draws the horizontal line in the lower part of the page, saying: "I make this line to keep it to the ground", then she draws the oval shape and the rectangular shape that makes contact with it at a corner, and says: "It flies ... it's flying with this ." At this point she draws the numerous vertical lines that start from the first horizontal line, and says: "All these lines to hold it still, because it's flying!" Upon questioning on what she was drawing, she answers "A plane ... It's flying in the sky" and then, indicating the lines that a few seconds earlier served the function of holding it still, she spontaneously declares: "They are all people." At that point, she makes several other marks, most of which dense and dark, and whispers "Something is still missing ... the background." Then, she turns the page over and makes numerous dots on the back of the sheet (of course, not visible in Figure 4.2) saying "A little dove"; perhaps, the repeated marking gestures symbolize the beat of the dove's wings. She adds quickly a few more marks on the rear of the sheet and then moves to the kitchen, apparently pleased of her completed performance. A few minutes later, upon questioning, she confirms that the people were traveling in the plane, but gives no account of the dark marks at the bottom and in the higher part of the page.

This episode presents several hallmarks of the transitional period. The child is not aiming at producing a coherent and recognizable picture on a page, because she simply ignores the signs already present on the paper, and completes her job on the rear of the page, so that not all of her product is visible simultaneously. Nevertheless, she is aware of the structure of a picture to the point that she states explicitly that a background ought not to be missing. Part of the meaning seems to be conveyed through action (the dots for the dove, and perhaps the vertical lines that "hold it still"). There is a shift of meaning in these lines, which first "hold it still" and then become "all people". But there is broad consistency in the overall theme of the drawing, and the initial declaration "I make this line to keep it to the ground" states in advance Clara's intention to draw a (so far unspecified) *it* that may take off the ground. Most of the marks on the page do not have a referential value, the vertical lines become *people* only on second thought, and the dark clusters of short, straight lines remain unnamed even after questioning. However, the central figure of the plane (in Kellogg's terms, two diagrams combined into a shape) is a closed figure of which Clara states that it's flying and, on questioning, labels it "a plane".

Even though it is not yet a schematic drawing of a plane, it is constituted by an oval and a rectangular form; indeed, planes do have a long and round fuselage and wide, flat wings, and perhaps not by chance while making the rectangular form Clara states "it's flying with this". Lowenfeld and Brittain (1975) would probably label the plane as pre-schematic and the rest of the drawing as a controlled scribble. Although I am not fully satisfied with the term *pre-schematic* (perhaps *early schematic* would fit better), one can regard it as a reasonable description inasmuch it conveys the idea of a separate shape with an intended meaning, articulated into components at least in a simple way, not necessarily recognizable by an observer, but where one can identify (perhaps with the assistance of the author's labeling) at least some initial use of denotation rules (in the sense of Willats, 1985).

As argued above, an average child aged between 30 and 36 months with an M capacity of 7 sensorimotor schemes should be able to do spontaneously advanced forms of scribbling, such as producing diagrams and diagram aggregates, or making visually controlled scribbles endowed with an intended meaning akin to symbolic play. In addition, children of this age can manifest early forms of representational competence, upon solicitation by adults in contexts that are less demanding than organizing a drawing by themselves. Following Pascual-Leone's model of capacity growth, about the age of three an average child could activate a task executive and a representational (symbolic) scheme. For instance, a child who wants to draw a house might activate a task executive carrying the goal and the plan of drawing a house, and a graphic figurative scheme that carries information on what the drawing of a house should look like.[4] The problem, however, is that to do so it is not sufficient to have enough working

---

[4] The task executive must include five constituents: a goal (the intended meaning, e.g., drawing a house), the use of marks standing for that meaning, a drawing instrument, a surface on which the drawing can be made, and a system of hand movements to produce marks with a drawing instrument. I assume that at this point the earlier motor schemes for grasping a pencil and moving the arm are unified in a single, well coordinated system of hand movements, refined through over a year of scribbling experience. All these components of the task executive are necessary; for instance, a child who wants to draw a house and has paper but no drawing instrument might go and fetch a pen. Also the graphic scheme can be decomposed into lower-order units, standing for the front, the door, the windows, the roof, etc.

memory capacity; it is also necessary to have in long-term memory a graphic figurative scheme for the house. Children may have the intention of drawing an item, such as a plane, a house, or a dog, and yet lack an appropriate scheme for that item. In this case, they could direct their efforts toward inventing a way for representing it; in other terms, they could try to create a pictorial representation by putting together the sensorimotor elements that they have already acquired.

How could that process work? A child could, for instance, hold in mind the various constituents of the task executive for drawing a house (see footnote 4), and tentatively think of a rectangular or another closed form (an already acquired diagram) standing for the house, and draw that. Using visual feedback from that form, the child could either be satisfied of having drawn a house, or perhaps consider that a house also has windows, and try to draw them. Other closed forms (such as smaller squares, or circles) standing for windows could be drawn in other parts of the page; in case the child also considers the topological relation between the windows and the house, the windows could even be placed inside the first, large closed form. Having drawn one or more windows, the child could either be satisfied of the outcome or consider, for instance, that a house also needs a pointed roof, and perhaps even take into account that the roof should be on top of the building; and so on. Such a process involves a lot of active experimentation by the child. For instance, on some occasion the child could be satisfied of having drawn a house as a single closed shape without any further details. On another occasion, that child may consider that the house has many rooms, try to represent both the house and the rooms, and get a messy, hardly recognizable outcome. Still another time, the child may draw windows as separate from the building. Extended practice, visual feedback, social feedback and cultural standards help the child to construct and refine a graphic figurative scheme for what a drawing of a house should look like.

Thus, through a combination of processes such as observation of traces obtained during action representation and visual patterns of scribbles, fortuitous discovery of resemblances between the shapes of scribbles and objects, unfulfilled early representational intentions, active experimentation to invent representational forms, and occasional teaching by adults and older siblings (on the effectiveness of social scaffolding, see Callaghan & Rankin, 2002), the child acquires a repertoire of graphic schemes. In the age range approximately from 2½ to 5 years one can observe a long and gradual progression, from predominance of scribbling with few elements of pictorial representation (as in Figure 4.2), to predominance of schematic representation with only occasional scribbling or action representation.

This long transitional period can hardly be divided into stages. Of course, processing resources – both M capacity and efficiency of inhibition – continue to grow during this age range, and at the age of about three the ability to activate a task executive plus a representational scheme enables the child to use more regularly the few available graphic schemes and to make attempts at creating new ones. However, the main progress during this phase is a series of *local revolutions* due to acquiring or restructuring pieces of domain-specific knowledge; one at a time, particular graphic figurative schemes are incorporated into the child's long term memory to represent, say, a person, a house, a tree.[5] Any of these figurative schemes carries information on a visual pattern, its intended meaning, and a set of motor actions that (possibly with variations, and not necessarily in a fixed temporal order) can produce the marks that compose that visual pattern.

During this transitional period, a child also acquires the first operative schemes for space representation. They are likely to be very simple ones, such as those for representing a form inside another (e.g., the eyes in the face, the windows in the house), or for representing relations among the parts of the same object. For instance, a child may realize that the mouth is better drawn below the eyes, and the roof on top of the house; these placements are not granted, even though they are facilitated by stimulus-response compatibility. From such experiences, a child could abstract constructively a rule (a spatial operative scheme) to place the marks that indicate X above the marks that indicate Y whenever in the real thing part X is above part Y. Once such a rule has been learned, it can function as a scheme and be used to solve new pictorial problems.

A last issue can be raised to conclude this section: Is it really necessary that children go through a scribbling stage, and the visual and motor experience with different scribble patterns, for representational drawing to emerge? Golomb (1992) argues that this is not the case, citing as evidence the fact that both blind children, and children from remote cultures without drawing instruments, quickly find out how to make representational drawings without passing through a phase of scribbling. This remark is certainly correct; indeed people can start drawing even at an old age, and discover rapidly how to do it. Hessel (1988) reports the remarkable case of Parr, an Inuit hunter who did his first drawings at the age of 68 and eventually became a renowned artist. His first drawings of persons, whales, and seals resemble in many ways those of young children, but are certainly representational. Having conceded that people can skip the *scribbling stage* and start out with representational drawings, it also seems appropriate to note that all the cases presented by Golomb (1992), not to mention Parr, are at least 5 years old. At that age children can coordinate two representational schemes in working memory; it should not be too difficult for them to combine mentally partial symbols, such as circles or lines that can stand for heads or limbs, and discover ways to put together a symbolic representation of a person. The blind children cited by Golomb (1992) are at least 9 years old, so they should be able to coordinate four symbols at a time; and even though they cannot have experience of visual symbols, there is evidence (e.g., Cornoldi & Vecchi, 2000) that blind people have an intact working memory that can manipulate efficiently spatial information, of course not coded visually but, for instance, kin-

---

[5] One could possibly identify a main turning point, during the transitional period from 2½ to 5 years, at about the age of 4 years, when a child has consolidated a repertoire of graphic schemes sufficient for schematic drawing to prevail over scribbling. However, the prevalence of either style of drawing seems hard to assess in an objective way. It also seems likely that the timing of such turning point is prone to large individual differences. At any event, I am not suggesting that working memory capacity or control processes affect that turning point. Rather, it may depend on long-term memory acquisition of graphic figurative schemes.

esthetically. In a similar vein, D'Angiulli and Maggi (2003) conclude that blind children's drawing is based not on pictorial conventions, but on spontaneous generativity that uses perceptual principles (derived not from vision but from touch). However, the drawings studied by D'Angiulli and Maggi were made by 12-year-old children.

Thus, I would like to qualify Golomb's remarks by adding that children can discover pictorial representation without going through the scribbling stage if they already have enough working memory capacity to manipulate a sufficient amount of symbolic information. Atypical development, due to sensorial impairment or cultural deprivation, may take atypical ways to reach the same endpoint. However, in our culture, children without sensorial or motor impairment do typically scribble, and through that experience they acquire a repertoire of hand movements, ocular-manual coordination skills, visual shapes, potential meanings of the visual shapes, and intended meanings of the motor actions. Such sensorimotor schemes are actually used by typically developing children as building blocks of their first representational drawings. However, they assemble graphic figurative schemes only when maturation of their working memory enables them to put together visual pattern, motor action and symbolic meaning at the same time. Until that point, children can put together only some of the necessary components, and thus develop the various precursory forms of representation discussed throughout this section.

Graphic schemes

Having thus accounted for the formation of children's graphic figurative schemes, we can briefly turn to their content. The schematic and stereotyped nature of children's drawings has often been noted (e.g., Lowenfeld & Brittain, 1975; Stacey & Ross, 1975), but what do children include in their figurative schemes for drawing people, houses, trees, or cows? Early researchers (e.g., Luquet, 1927) held that children draw what they know about those items, rather than what they see, and that their drawings reflect their *internal models* of the objects themselves. That view, however, is now superseded; as Picard and Vinter (1999) put it, to argue that symbolism in drawings directly reflects the underlying representations of the objects is quite absurd, given the disparity between the content of children's drawings and their knowledge of various topics. We can also note that for children it would be difficult to convey all their knowledge about a topic into a single drawing, because all of that knowledge should be translated into appropriate graphic symbols or marks, and all of those symbols and marks should be bound together in an organized way – not an easy task, indeed. Drawing schemes must be simpler than knowledge of the world. But what are they?

Van Sommers (1984) reports a longitudinal study of children drawing repeatedly the same objects, which documents various aspects of *conservatism* in drawing. His participants tend to maintain the overall visual appearance of a drawing over repeated performance, although they may change the presence, the position or the shape of some details. They also often change the temporal order of drawing various parts of an item, or the order and direction of the strokes, even though they can have favorite start points; thus, the scheme that children store in their long-term memory is not a motor program. Van Sommers regards drawing as a problem solving activity, and concludes that what a child remembers and replicates is the visual appearance of a previous satisfactory solution to a pictorial problem. For instance, when a child has found a satisfactory way to represent a pram, the visual aspect of that solution is retained as a visual figurative scheme and reproduced on need. If a child eventually encounters a new problem in representing a pram, then the adequacy of that scheme may be called into question, and thus the scheme could be modified, or in the extreme, a new, alternative scheme can be created.

Those figurative graphic schemes usually have a hierarchical organization, that we can understand better through the concept of denotation systems, that is, how objects and their features are mapped to elementary units of shape that can be regarded as the picture primitives (Willats, 1985, 1995). For instance the scheme of a cat could include simple shapes, such as circles and triangles, respectively used to denote the cat's eyes and ears; other features of the cat, such as whiskers, may be denoted not by shapes but lines. A child's use of more global units in denotation (e.g., using regions rather than edges) places a limitation on the degree of sophistication and flexibility of that child's drawing schemes.

The core of a graphic scheme is a mental representation of the visual aspect of a pattern of shapes that can stand for a certain item. The scheme comprises as its components a meaning, a visual pattern that is organized hierarchically with simpler shapes as sub-components, and a set of motor actions that can produce the sub-components of that visual pattern. The graphic scheme is not a motor program (Van Sommers, 1984); however, the mental image that is the scheme core needs to be accompanied by information on how the marks can be produced.

A recent study by Ross (2005) clearly suggests that both visual and motor experience are involved in forming a graphic figurative scheme. In the context of research on self-awareness and recognition of one's own drawings, she tested in different conditions children aged between 3 and 7. All children were required to draw an item (e.g., a mug or a crocodile), and after that a group was required to trace that drawing with a pencil, another group traced with a pencil a peer's drawing of the same item, still another group traced a peer's drawing with a non-marking instrument, and a fourth group did not trace anything, but looked at a peer who was drawing the same item. On a later session, they were asked to recognize both their own drawing and any other drawing that they had already seen. The interesting point here is that children could recognize the drawings that they traced with a pencil as well as their own drawings. The children who traced with a non-marking instrument or simply watched another child drawing, instead, were less likely to recognize those drawings. Note that the children who traced a peer's drawing made all the motor actions necessary to produce that drawing and obtained a full visual feedback of the outcome of these actions, whereas the children who traced with a non-marking instrument only had the motor experience (but no visual feedback from it), and the children who looked at a peer drawing had the full visual experience of the drawing being produced, but performed no motor action. This strongly suggests that both motor and visual experience are necessary for the child to construct a new graphic scheme, that can be used for subsequent drawing recognition. Once a scheme is formed, we can regard (after Van Sommers, 1984) the visual component as its core, and consider the motor program subcomponents at the service of the visual pattern to be produced.

A child's repertoire of graphic schemes is constantly enriched not only by acquisition of schemes to represent new items, but also by acquisition of new, more sophisticated schemes to represent items for which the child already had a scheme. For some time, a child can shift between the new and the older scheme (a phenomenon that Luquet, 1927, called *duplicité de types*) or use simpler and impoverished schemes when detail is not needed (e.g., draw many simple stick figures to represent a crowd).

One important aspect of children's scheme restructuring is the ability to construct outline figures; for instance, instead of drawing a human figure comprising a circle or oval for the head and another one for the trunk, to which other elongated shapes for the arms and legs are connected, a child may start to draw a continuous outline for the whole human figure. This ability starts to emerge at about age six (Barrett & Eames, 1996; Fenson, 1985; Lange-Küttner, Kerzmann, & Heckhausen, 2002; Trautner, 1995). It is related to using as picture primitives not regions that stand for surfaces or volumes, but lines that stand for edges or contours of the object (Willats, 1985; see also Reith, 1988), and its development throughout childhood is probably affected by several factors (Lange-Küttner et al., 2002). For the purpose of this chapter, suffice it to note that to construct a new graphic scheme characterized by a continuous outline a child must keep in working memory at least two representations – that is, both the overall, already available (segmented) graphic scheme for the item of interest and the shape of its part currently being drawn. Furthermore, the child must inhibit drawing the lines that do not belong to the outline of the figure.

Some graphic schemes can be created by differentiation from older schemes. For instance, there is evidence that schemes for animals are differentiated from the scheme of the human figure. This is the case of young children's schemes for four-legged animals (Silk & Thomas, 1986; see also Golomb, 1992). In a recent study (Morra, 2005), we asked kindergartners and primary school children to draw a kangaroo, with the assumption that its habitual upright position could induce children to use the human figure scheme as a base from which they differentiate the kangaroo drawing. In some cases, children's use of the human figure scheme is remarkable; Figure 4.3 presents the drawings of a kangaroo and a person made by two children, respectively aged 5 years, 6 months (above) and 8 years, 7 months (below).[6] However, not in all cases the person and kangaroo pictures were so similar; this issue will be discussed further in the next section.

---

[6] I am grateful to Floriana Ingravalle, who collected these drawings in the context of her thesis project.

Figure 4.3 Kangaroo (left) and human figure (right) drawn by a five-year old (above) and an eight-year old (below). The influence of the human figure scheme on the kangaroo drawing is rather extreme in these two cases; see also Morra (2005) for more typical examples.

The point of scheme modification and differentiation takes us to the so-called drawing flexibility. Karmiloff-Smith (1990) suggested that pre-schoolers' drawing procedures enable them to depict successfully many items, such as *a man*, but they cannot access their own drawing procedures and re-describe them at a higher level of awareness. Therefore, they would be bound to inflexible procedures that produce stereotyped drawings. However, subsequent research (Barlow, Jolley, White, & Galbraith, 2003; Berti & Freeman, 1997; Picard & Vinter, 1999; Spensley & Taylor, 1999; Zhi, Thomas, & Robinson, 1997), pointed out that Karmiloff-Smith's (1990) view may be too extreme, because young children seem to have access to their drawing procedures, and show some flexibility in drawing. These studies replicated the increase with age of drawing flexibility, but also found that pre-schoolers succeeded in Karmiloff-Smith's tasks better than reported in the original study, and documented various forms of pre-schoolers' awareness of goals, representations, and drawing procedures – as also Karmiloff-Smith (1999) has recognized. The results also showed that almost all children varied the motor sequence from one drawing to another (a finding consistent with Van Sommers, 1984; see also Trautner, 1996), and they were also able to make modifications to their productions in the middle of executing a drawing – which implies that "there was no evidence to support Karmiloff-Smith's hypothesis that young children are executing a simple procedure when they are drawing a man" (Spensley &

Taylor, 1999, p.310). Therefore, we need to explain the development of drawing flexibility, documented by Goodnow (1978), Karmiloff-Smith (1990), and other studies without basing our account on the concept of procedural representation. A neo-Piagetian account of drawing flexibility development is discussed in the next section.

How children's limited processing capacity affects drawing

So far, I have suggested how the growth of working memory capacity or M capacity, interacting with the child's repertoire of specific schemes and skills, permits the development of scribbling, the emergence of drawing and the construction of more sophisticated graphic schemes. Also inhibitory and other control processes, as mentioned above at various points, have a role in the development of drawing.

Previous research has provided empirical evidence for the role of working memory, particularly in the development of spatial structures (e.g., Case & Okamoto, 1996; Dennis, 1992; Morra, 2002; Morra et al., 1988; for a review, see Morra, in press). For instance, the growth of working memory enables the child to use increasingly complex systems of spatial axes (Case & Okamoto, 1996) and to plan the drawing of increasingly complex scenes (Morra et al., 1988).

For the sake of brevity, here I will illustrate in some detail only the issue of drawing flexibility, or children's ability to alter their own graphic schemes. As mentioned above, it is widely recognized that drawing flexibility increases with age, and now there is also broad agreement that representational redescription of rigid procedural knowledge is not an adequate explanation. No doubt, drawing flexibility also involves some degree of inhibition of habitual graphic schemes. However, the nature of the processes that enable a child to modify a habitual graphic scheme is still under debate.

Morra (2005) studied children's ability to modify their habitual scheme of the human figure to convey a certain meaning, and proposed that three factors are involved. Based on the distinction between *local* and *global* changes (Spensley & Taylor, 1999), that is, modifications of a specific part made on the spot, without being planned in advance, and more complex changes that need advance planning, Morra (2005) considered what information has to be held in working memory for either type of change. An example of local change would be drawing the upper half of a human figure, and only then deciding to draw the legs spaced farther apart than usual to convey the meaning that the person is running. This involves co-ordinating one figurative scheme (the mental image of a specific body part in a running person) and one operative scheme (for modifying the stereotyped drawing; e.g., to increase the angle between the graphic scheme components that stand for the legs). An example of global change would be drawing an inclined body axis; in this case, the child could not start by drawing a head in the usual way and then decide to tilt the body axis, because this decision would involve also drawing the head in a different position. Advance planning is necessary when altering some part of a drawing which also affects the way in which other parts must be drawn, i.e., the relationship between a totality and its part(s) must be taken into account. To plan a change of this sort, more schemes would need to be co-ordinated, i.e., a graphic figurative scheme for the human figure, one or more figurative schemes that represent the visual aspect of a person's global feature(s) that will be modified in the drawing, and (as in the previous case) an operative scheme that mentally transforms the intended feature(s) in the human figure graphic scheme. Therefore, to plan complex changes in advance, a child must activate several schemes simultaneously, and even for easier, *local* changes, two schemes are involved. An insufficient M capacity would prevent children from planning *global* changes or even from being able to perform *local* changes. On the other hand, a child with a larger M capacity might even hold in working memory one planned change while planning another, and thus be able to co-ordinate smoothly more than one modification in *global* features or relationships between parts. Thus, M capacity is expected to be a first factor involved in drawing flexibility.

A second factor is perceptual input, i.e., availability of an external model. When children draw from memory they need to activate all the relevant schemes using endogenous attentional resources. When a 3-d or a picture model is available, however, the perceptual input can activate some relevant figurative schemes that represent features, for instance, of the aspect of a running person. Therefore, activation of these schemes by perceptual input would reduce the information processing load (i.e., spare M capacity), and thus facilitate the drawing tasks.

As a third factor, Morra (2005) suggested that children's ability to modify their drawings can be improved when they are made aware of task demands. Such awareness could be obtained by explicit instructions (e.g., Barrett, Beaumontt, & Jennett, 1985), by manipulation of contextual conditions (e.g., Davis, 1983), or because of children's acquisition of a more advanced *theory* of pictorial representation (Berti & Freeman, 1997). In any of these ways, children's executive control processes would be enhanced. The executive functions involved in this case are those that represent an individual's current goals, and monitor resource allocation and ongoing performance.

To test these assumptions, Morra (2005) carried out a series of experiments. The first two involved representation of a person in movement, by means of tasks already studied by Goodnow (1978), such as drawing a person who is picking up a ball, walking, or running. The participants were in the age range between five and nine. Some children had a photo available as a model and others did not have it. The order of the tasks was manipulated so that some children would first make a drawing in a control condition (drawing a person who is standing still) and others would perform the control condition last – it was argued that having just drawn in the control condition could alert participants to the contrast between the two drawing tasks, and thus facilitate their monitoring that the drawing of a person in movement looks different from that of a person standing still. Furthermore, children's M capacity was measured with specific tests.

The results of both experiments strongly supported the theoretical predictions. Children's ability to alter their drawing schemes increased with age, but the effect of age was eliminated or largely reduced when M capacity was entered as a cova[ ]other sources of developmental differences can exist, the developme[ ]major cause of development in the ability to modify the human figur[ ]addition, M capacity proved to have a role also in accounting for individual differences, flexibility scores in all drawing tasks showed a positive correlation with M capacity that resisted partialling out age. However, it seems interesting to note that the relative importance of M capacity was different in accounting for developmental and individual differences. Whereas M capacity accounted for a large proportion of developmental variance in the ability to modify drawing schemes, it only accounted for a smaller proportion of individual difference variance. This is probably due to the existence of other important sources of individual differences besides M capacity, such as differences in reliance on visual imagery and figurative processes (Milbrath, 1998), in cognitive style (Morra, 1995, 2002), in metacognition, goal awareness and monitoring (e.g., Freeman, 1995; Berti & Freeman, 1997), and possibly, educational factors. At any event, it was clear that M capacity is a major factor in the development of drawing flexibility, and also a significant source of individual differences.

The experiments also showed that the presence of a photo that can be used as a model has a significant impact on children's performance. This was also theoretically predicted, because perceptual input from a model was expected to produce automatic activation of relevant schemes, which in turn facilitates drawing performance. This source of variance in drawing flexibility proved to be quite independent by other ones and not dependent of developmental processes

Finally, also the contrast induced by task order had a significant effect. This was probably due to specific executive control processes; an implicit request to make a different picture from the previously drawn stereotyped figure can lead the child to be alert, while drawing, to possible differences between a person in movement and a static person. In these experiments, the order of conditions affected as predicted the drawings of a person picking up a ball and a walking person, but not that of a running person (perhaps because the contrast between a running person and the static stereotype is very salient in itself). Task order did not interact with other factors and its effect remained unchanged when M capacity was a covariate, thus supporting the view that it involves still a different psychological resource.

A third experiment by Morra (2005) studied whether M capacity is relevant not only to drawing flexibility (modifying a graphic scheme) but also to scheme differentiation (using a graphic scheme to create a new and different one). In this experiment, already mentioned in the previous section, children listened to a short passage on kangaroos and were shown four pictures of them, before being asked to draw one. Once again, it was found that ability to draw a kangaroo as different from a human increases with age, and entering M capacity as a covariate removed over ¾ of the age effect, which dropped below statistical significance. In addition, the correlation between M capacity and the drawing score remained highly significant after partialling out age. Thus, the pattern of effects of M capacity on developmental and individual differences that was found for drawing flexibility was fully replicated for differentiation of a new scheme.

Another study (Morra et al., 1994) on metaphorical representation of emotions in drawing (e.g., drawing a happy tree or a scared ship) yielded results that are fully consistent with these views. It turned out that M capacity was a good predictor of the degree of complexity of the solutions that children could figure out to alter their scheme of a ship or a tree, in order to represent emotions metaphorically. In contrast, literal representation of emotions (i.e., drawing a person in an emotional state) was not correlated with M capacity, probably because many graphic devices for drawing people's emotions are culturally available, and therefore, drawing a person in an emotional state does not involve problem-solving that taxes working memory, but rather, it requires use of some well-learned cultural stereotype. Another result of that study was that children's ability to modify their drawings to represent different emotions was also correlated with verbal fluency, which, according to Pascual-Leone et al. (1978), can be considered as an indicator of Interrupt/Disinterrupt control processes.

Also children's ability to represent an object partly occluded by another one is related to M capacity (e.g., Morra, 2002). Morra, Angi, and Tomat (1996) suggested that children could make a visually realistic drawing of a partially occluded object by means of either of two different strategies, which respectively require coordination of two or three schemes. The results of those studies clearly supported this prediction. In addition, Morra (2002) discussed how the cognitive style of field dependence/independence affects children's partial occlusion drawings.

The mystery of narrative drawing

The foregoing sections of this chapter have discussed the role of domain specific knowledge (especially graphic schemes) and more general processing resources (emphasizing working memory capacity and the consequences of its growth). It has been noted occasionally that working memory capacity does not always have a role. For instance, metaphorical depiction of emotions in trees and ships correlates with M capacity but depiction of emotions in humans does not; and in tasks that involve drawing flexibility the automatic activation of relevant knowledge from a perceptual input is independent of the effortful activation of relevant knowledge by means of M capacity. The role of control processes and cognitive styles (that involve individuals' systematic preferences and biases in control processes) has also been noted. Still other factors are likely to affect children's drawing; for instance, goals (and awareness of them), social demands and conventions, beliefs and naive theories on drawing, and meta-cognition. The role of such factors is examined in detail in other chapters of this book.

One phenomenon for which we still have little explanation, and which is unlikely to depend on M capacity, is the organization of narrative drawings. By *narrative* I mean a drawing that represents a story or a sequence of events that unfold in time. Luquet (1927) discussed narrative drawing extensively, but since then only few authors have reconsidered it. This is a bit surprising, because children often draw scenes or characters from stories, movies, and other fictional narratives, or real life episodes. In addition, many of the pictures to which children are exposed illustrate narratives. Yet, we still know little on how children draw to represent a narrative.

One device that children sometimes use is repetition of the same item, drawn in various positions or conditions that represent different moments of an episode or a story. For instance, Luquet (1927) presents a child's drawing of the launching of a ship, in which the ship is depicted four times, at different points from the start to the end of her descent to the sea. Another feature that one can find in some narrative drawings is temporal syncretism, that is, depiction within the same scenery of events that occur at different times, and thus could not be seen together – although they do belong to the same story.

Even though temporal syncretism and item repetition are typically children's devices, also adult artists sometimes use them. For instance, in the Kariye museum of Istanbul one can observe a Byzantine mosaic that represents two distinct episodes (Joseph's dream and the journey to Bethlehem) depicted in a single scene and well integrated in a single landscape. Those episodes are connected in the story, because the first causes the second; nevertheless, they are distinct episodes. Moreover, in that mosaic one can observe a double representation of Mary, that is, Mary in Joseph's dream and Mary traveling to Bethlehem. However, temporal syncretism and item repetition are unusual in adult art – or at least, they have long been unusual, until some artistic trends of the 20th century (in particular, cubism and futurism) introduced devices that deliberately break visual realism, the single point of view of an observer and frozen time.

Luquet (1927) described four strategies or *types* by which children draw a narrative. The first is item repetition (in Luquet's terms, *successive type with repetition*); different moments of a story are represented in one drawing, and one or more items are depicted two or more times in the conditions or positions in which they are at different points of the narrative. The second is called by Luquet *successive type without repetition*; there is temporal syncretism as in the previous case, because episodes or elements that occur at different moments are represented in a single scene, but no item is depicted more than once. The third is akin to a comic strip (called *Épinal type* by Luquet at a time when comic strips were not yet popular in France); a sequence of distinct events are represented on paper, in such a way that the observer can recognize each separate scene as a different moment of the narrative. The fourth was called *symbolic type* by Luquet, and represents a single event or moment of the narrative.

Luquet (1927) related these types of narrative drawing to his theory of realism. The symbolic type, portraying a single moment of the narrative without any juxtaposition of elements that could not be visible together, was regarded as visually realistic (and therefore, the most mature type). The successive type with repetition was regarded as intellectually realistic (and the least mature), because it juxtaposes in the same picture information on various moments of the story, and shows the same item repeatedly, in different positions or conditions. Each of the other two types (successive without repetition and Épinal) would combine both intellectually and visually realistic features.

Duncum (1993) extended Luquet's classification, proposing ten types instead of four. Some of Duncum's additions are related to scribbling and action representation, in some other cases the narrative component is expressed not in the drawing itself but in language or thinking that accompanies it, and some of Duncum's types are further specifications of Luquet's types. Although Duncum (1993) broadens our perspective, Luquet's simpler classification can still be useful to describe children's different ways to represent narratives in drawing.

Luquet (1927) suggested that his four types are used by children at different ages; in his account, the Épinal type would not appear before age eight, and the symbolic type would be rare in children younger than eleven. Osterrieth (1973) expresses the opinion that the symbolic type appears earlier than that. However, all the studies by Luquet (1927), Osterrieth (1973), Duncum (1993) are based on drawings collected in uncontrolled conditions, and often only the verbal descriptions by the children who made them make clear what narratives they represent. We have considered that some degree of experimental control is necessary to clarify the age trends of narrative drawing and the factors that affect children's use of a strategy or another.[7] The method that we have used in a series of four studies consists in reading a story to each participant and, after checking for comprehension, requiring the child to make a drawing of that story. This enabled us to keep under control the narrative content to which the drawing refers.

A story that we have used often (adapted from Italo Calvino's collection of Italian fables) is entitled *The moon*. Its initial setting describes a village that always had dark nights. A boy and a girl from that village discover in a nearby village a shining ball hung at a tree. As a peasant informs them that it is called moon and illuminates that village every night, the children decide to steal it; they pull it off the tree and take it to their village with a horse-towed cart. The inhabitants of the village that suffered from the theft ask a wizard for help. The wizard goes to retrieve the moon and then flies to the sky and puts it up there, declaring his communist moral: now all villages will enjoy the moon and have some light, and nobody will be able to steal it anymore. This story seemed suitable for our study, not only as a fascinating narrative, but also because it involves different episodes which occur at different places, only some characters or objects are present in each episode, and from one episode to another the characters move in space both horizontally (from one village to the other) and vertically (up to the sky). Another story that we used (an adaptation of Gianni Rodari's *A taxi to the stars*) also involves different episodes that take place in different places on the earth and other planets, but contrary to the previous story it is centered on the interaction between two main characters (a taxi driver and an extraterrestrial) and its various episodes are not linked by a clear plot with strong causal connections. The third story we have used, *The cat with wings*, is an animal story with a cyclically recursive structure in which the main character, a flying cat living in a circus, meets other animals one after another and asks each of them essentially the same existential questions, until at the end he improves his way of life. Also this story, like the other two, involves both horizontal and vertical journeys of some characters, but its cyclic narrative structure is notably different from each of the others.

---

[7] I am very grateful to Annalisa Sedda, a preschool teacher and my former student at the University of Padova, who directed my attention to this problem and carried out the first of our studies on this topic. I am also grateful to Elisabetta Borsatti, Eleonora Cannioto, Sara Centofanti, and Chiara Pugno for carrying out the subsequent studies.

In some experiments we also had a control condition with a non-narrative drawing of the same elements. For instance, if the story to be read was *The moon*, in a first session we read to participants a list including two villages, a boy, a girl, a tree, the moon, a peasant, a horse-towed cart, and a wizard. The list was read repeatedly until the child could remember it all, and at that point she was required to make a drawing that included all those items; in a second session, the child was read the story and required to make a drawing of that story. Thus, a narrative and a non-narrative drawing of the same items could be compared.

With this overall design of the studies, we focused on two aspects, the child's overall strategy (Luquet's *types*) and the order in which the various items were drawn. Luquet's system of four categories proved reliable enough for analyzing the drawings; we retained Luquet's labels *successive with repetition* and *successive without repetition* but called *Épinal* and *symbolic* respectively *comics sequence* and *single moment*, in order to use terms that are clearer to contemporary readers.

In study 1 we tested 69 children from kindergarten to grade 2, using *The moon* as the narrative materials. More than half of the drawings were successive with repetition, but there were also 15 successive without repetition, 3 comics sequences and 13 single moments. The strategies varied with age; in kindergarten, 90% of the drawings were successive with repetition, while all the children who drew comics sequences were second-graders. However, contrary to Luquet's claims, a sizable number of children drew a single moment of the story, including one third of the first-graders and even a kindergartner.

In study 2 we tested 91 children from kindergarten to grade 5, using *A taxi to the stars*. We found that 12 drawings were successive with repetition, 22 successive without repetition, 19 comics sequences, and 38 single moments. This time there was no significant relation between age and drawing strategy. In particular, among kindergartners and first-graders those in advance with respect to the developmental schedule proposed by Luquet were almost two thirds.

Considering that children's strategies could vary according to some features of the story, we designed a third, larger study, in which 245 children from kindergarten to grade 5 were randomly divided into three groups and presented one of the three narratives. Furthermore, children were administered Raven's matrixes and a working memory test, the Counting Span.

Indeed, different stories yielded different strategy distributions. Single moment drawings were by far the most frequent for each story, but they were about two thirds for *The moon* and *Taxi to the stars*, while they were little more than 40% for *The cat with wings*. Comics sequences were almost one fourth for *The cat with wings* (the story with the most salient division in episodes), one ninth for *Taxi to the stars*, and only 7% for *The moon* (a story in which every episode is functional to the overall plot). Also successive with repetition drawings were more than one fourth for *The cat with wings*, but about one eighth for the other stories. These findings support the idea that the story structure (with a salient sequence of distinct episodes versus a highly coherent overall plot) affects children's use of drawing strategies that emphasize the different moments of the narrative.

Also age affected children's strategies; the main difference was the scarce use of comics sequences (less than 4%) in kindergartners and first-graders, while they were almost one fifth in the older age groups. Strategies were also related, albeit weakly, to scores in Raven's matrixes; the scores in the Counting Span were unrelated to drawing strategies.

Therefore, these studies provide some support for Luquet's claim that a comics sequence is a more advanced solution than a drawing of a *successive* type. In our studies, only few children younger than 7 drew comics sequences. Instead, Luquet's view that the *symbolic* type is still more advanced (being connected to visual realism), and rarely appears before age 10 or 11, clearly has to be discarded in view of our results. Among kindergartners and first-graders, drawings of a single moment were a minority (but not negligible) in study 1, and they were about half of the sample in studies 2 and 3, as well as in study 4 described below.

Figure 4.4 shows the age trends that emerge for each story from the pooled results of studies 1-4, with a total of 517 participants. In general, the single moment drawing is the most popular solution. Comics sequences are rare in kindergartners and first-graders, and steadily increase with age. The successive type with repetition, instead, declines with age. These trends are very clear for both *The moon* and *Taxi to the stars*, and somewhat less clear for *The cat with wings* – which is, however, the narrative for which we collected fewest drawings, and thus could yield age trends that are less reliable than the two other stories.

In the studies described so far we have found that drawing strategies are related to the structure of the narrative that is represented in drawing, but they seem to be unrelated to working memory capacity, only weakly related to intelligence, and also show a large variation in each age group. At this point of our search for an account of the various strategies, we have considered whether a control process based on story retrieval is involved. In particular, the successive type with repetition and the comics sequence may involve greater reliance on retrieving from long-term memory the various episodes of the story in their temporal order.

To test this hypothesis, we have computed for each participant the Spearman correlation between the order in which the main elements are drawn by the child and the order in which they are mentioned the first time in the story, and we took this as an index of how closely participants follow their own memory of the narrative as a guide for drawing. Most of these correlations were positive, with a median of .37 in study 1, .60 in study 2, and .50 in study 3, suggesting that children actually use to some extent their memory of the story to produce a drawing of it. However, there was no indication that different strategies are actually related to a differential use of retrieval of the story line. In study 1 the correlations calculated for individual children were not significantly different among groups that used different strategies; in study 2 there was a significant difference, due to the fact that children who drew a single moment of the story showed higher correlations (i.e., followed in drawing the order of the story) than those who made a successive drawing without repetitions; and in study 3 the correlations were unrelated to drawing strategies in the whole sample, but separating the subsamples that received different stories we found that children who drew a comics sequence showed the highest correlations with the narrative if they had received *The cat with wings*, but the lowest correlations if they had received *The moon*. In short, there was no evidence that strategy choice depends on retrieval-based control processes.

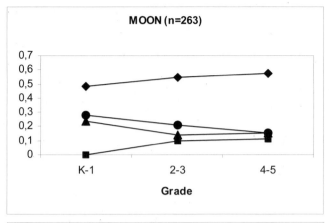

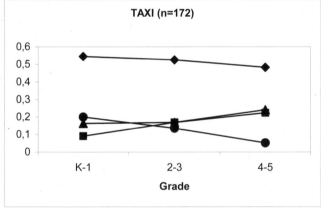

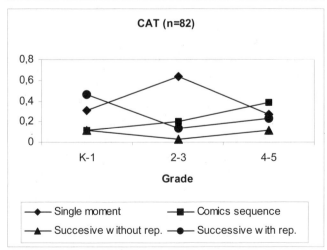

Figure 4.4 Proportion of narrative drawing types by story and grade.

At this point, we considered whether strategies can be related to children's communicative goals. We reasoned that certain forms of intellectual realism (as manifested in the successive type with repetition and the comics sequences) could reflect children's intention to represent the narrative content of the story, while adherence to aesthetic and stylistic conventions could induce children to draw a coherent scene, such as a single moment or a successive type without repetition. Previous research suggests that goals can be manipulated by means of instructions (e.g., Barrett et al., 1985) and creation of a communicative context (e.g., Light & Simmons, 1983). Thus, we designed an experiment in which different instructions could induce in children different goals and thus, by this way, different drawing strategies.

In study 4 we tested 112 children from kindergarten to grade 2, using only one story, *The moon*. Participants were randomly divided in two conditions; in one condition the experimenter required to "make a drawing of this story for your teacher, who does not know this story because she has never heard about it, so please make a drawing of this story in a way that your teacher can understand what goes on", in the other condition the request was to "make a beautiful drawing of this story, let's make a really beautiful drawing for your teacher, so we can show her how beautiful your drawing is". Children understood these instructions and could paraphrase them well, but they were not affected by them at all. More than half of the drawings were single moments, once again showing that even young children can produce the type of narrative drawing that Luquet called *symbolic*; only one was a comics sequence. The effect of age was significant, because the *successive* type, either with or without repetition, occurred more frequently in younger children. The instructions, however, had no significant effect.

Four studies on narrative drawing yielded results that clarify the age trends of narrative drawing and redress some of Luquet's claims about them; in addition, they strongly suggest that strategies for narrative drawing are affected by the structure of the narrative that is represented. Furthermore, they indicate that using stories as stimuli is a useful methodological tool for a better controlled study of narrative drawing. However, so far, our attempts to relate narrative drawing to information processing and control processes (in particular, to working memory capacity, retrieval from long-term memory, or representational goals) were unsuccessful. Perhaps some of these hypotheses need not be discarded altogether. For instance, our manipulation of children's processing goals might not have been strong enough, or could only be effective at older ages, and in this case future improved studies may find significant results. Concerning working memory, it seems reasonable to put forward the hypothesis that an M capacity at least two units (that typically develops at about the age of five) is required to produce a comics sequence. This is because a child should consider not only an overall scheme of the whole story, but also perform on it an operation of temporal unfolding, which enables isolating a particular event or episode at a time. In order to test this hypothesis, we should extend our research also to younger children.

Even though, according to the foregoing argument, it is still possible that representational goals or working memory have some influence on narrative drawing, they are likely to account only for minor portions of variance of children's representational strategies.

Thus, children's strategies for narrative drawing are a phenomenon that was not explained by Luquet's theory of realism, but is not yet explained either by current cognitive theories. This phenomenon remains an intriguing challenge for future research.

Conclusion

In this chapter, I have argued that drawing involves both domain-specific knowledge and general components of cognition. Domain-specific knowledge includes figurative graphic schemes and operative schemes for the representation of spatial relations, transformations that can be applied to graphic schemes and other specific rules that a child may learn to use. General components include working memory, executive functions, and metacognition. I have suggested that early development of working memory is involved in the development of scribbling and the transition to representational drawing. There is also evidence from several experimental paradigms that M capacity affects various aspects of drawing development, including the abilities to plan the composition of a complex scene, to modify one's well-practiced graphic schemes (drawing flexibility), to represent the three dimensions of space, as well as some more specific skills like representing partial occlusion or inventing metaphorical ways to represent emotion. Also control processes are involved in drawing ability from its early stages, as suggested by Golomb (1992) regarding the role of inhibitory control in the emergence of visually controlled scribbling. In older children, as argued at various points in this chapter, drawing involves executive functions such as planning and sequencing, inhibiting and releasing inhibition, and aspects of metacognition, such as awareness of goals and task demands, ability to select strategies and revise one's plans, and monitoring the ongoing activity. Also individual-difference dimensions, such as field dependence-independence and divergent thinking, are relevant to drawing.

Cognitive developmental research on drawing has made large progress since the first, pioneering studies in the Seventies (e.g., Freeman, 1972). Even though now we know a lot on the domain-specific and the general components of cognition that affect children's drawing, there are also important aspects about which we still know too little, such as the transition from scribbling to representational drawing and children's strategies for narrative drawing. Thus, we can expect that cognitive research on drawing development will continue to flourish in the next decades.

References

Adi-Japha, E., Levin, I., & Solomon, S. (1998). Emergence of representation in drawing: The relation between kinematic and referential aspects. *Cognitive Development, 13,* 25-51.

Alp, I. E. (1994). Measuring the size of working memory in very young children. *International Journal of Behavioral Development, 17,* 125-141.

Baddeley, A. D. (1986). *Working memory.* Oxford: Oxford University Press.

Barlow, C. M., Jolley, R. P., White, D. G., & Galbraith, D. (2003). Rigidity in children's drawings and its relation with representational change. *Journal of Experimental Child Psychology, 86,* 124-152.

Barrett, M. D., Beaumont, A. V., & Jennett, M. S. (1985). Some children sometimes do what they have been told to do: Task demands and verbal instructions in children's drawing. In N. H. Freeman & M. V. Cox (Eds.), *Visual Order* (pp.176-187). Cambridge: Cambridge University Press.

Barrett, M., & Eames, K. (1996). Sequential developments in children's human figure drawing. *British Journal of Developmental Psychology, 14,* 219-236.

Berti, A. E., & Freeman, N. H. (1997). Representational change in resources for pictorial innovation: A three-component analysis. *Cognitive Development, 12,* 501-522.

Callaghan, T. C., & Rankin, M. P. (2002). Emergence of graphic symbol functioning and the question of domain specificity: A longitudinal training study. *Child Development, 73,* 359-376.

Case, R. (1995). Capacity-based explanations of working memory growth: A brief history and reevaluation. In F. E. Weinert & W. Schneider (Eds.), *Memory performance and competencies: Issues in growth and development* (pp. 23-44). Mahwah, NJ: Erlbaum.

Case, R., & Okamoto, Y. (1996). The role of central conceptual structures in the development of children's thought. *Monographs of the Society for Research in Child Development, 61,* 1-265.

Cornoldi, C., & Vecchi, T. (2000). Mental imagery in blind people: The role of passive and active visuo-spatial processes. In A. H. Morton (Ed.), *Touch, representation, and blindness* (pp. 29-58). Oxford: Oxford University Press.

Cox, M. (2005). *The pictorial world of the child.* Cambridge: Cambridge University Press.

Cowan, N. (2005). *Working memory capacity.* Hove: Psychology Press.

Cowan, N., Saults, J. S., & Elliott, E. M. (2002). The search for what is fundamental in the development of working memory. In R. V. Kail & H. W. Reese (Eds.), *Advances in child development and behavior* (Vol. 29, pp. 1-49). San Diego: Academic Press.

D'Angiulli, A., & Maggi, S. (2003). Development of drawing abilities in a distinct population: Depiction of perceptual principles by three children with congenital total blindness. *International Journal of Behavioral Development, 27,* 193-200.

Davis, A. (1983). Contextual sensitivity in young children's drawings. *Journal of Experimental Child Psychology, 35,* 478-486.

Demetriou, A. (Ed.) (1988). *The neo-Piagetian theories of cognitive development: Towards an integration.* Amsterdam: North Holland.

Dennis, S. (1992). Stage and structure in the development of children's spatial representations. In R. Case (Ed.), *The mind's staircase* (pp. 229-245). Hillsdale, NJ: Erlbaum.

Duncum, P. (1993). Ten types of narrative drawing among children's spontaneous picture-making. *Visual Arts Research, 19,* 20-29.

Engle, R. W., Tuholski, S. W., Laughlin, J. E., & Conway, A. R. A. (1999). Working memory, short-term memory and general fluid intelligence: A latent variable approach. *Journal of Experimental Psychology: General, 128,* 309-331.

Eysenck, H. J. (1988). The concept of "intelligence": Useful or useless? *Intelligence, 12,* 1-16.

Fenson, L. (1985). The transition from construction to sketching in children's drawings. In N. H. Freeman & M. V. Cox (Eds.), *Visual Order* (pp. 374-384). Cambridge: Cambridge University Press.

Freeman, N. H. (1972). Process and product in children's drawing. *Perception, 1,* 123-140.

Freeman, N. H. (1980). *Strategies of representation in young children.* London: Academic Press.

Freeman, N. H. (1995). The emergence of a framework theory of pictorial reasoning. In C. Lange-Küttner & G. V. Thomas (Eds.), *Drawing and Looking: Theoretical Approaches to Pictorial Representation in Children* (pp. 135-134). London: Harvester.

Golomb, C. (1981). Representation and reality: The origins and determinants of young children's drawings. *Review of Research in Visual Arts Education, 14,* 36-48.

Golomb, C. (1992). *The child's creation of a pictorial world.* Berkeley, CA: University of California Press.

Goodnow, J. (1978). Visible thinking: Cognitive aspects of change in drawings. *Child Development, 49,* 637-641.

Hessel, I. (1988). The drawings of Parr: A closer look. *Inuit Art Quarterly, 3,* 14-20.

Karmiloff-Smith, A. (1990). Constraints on representational change: Evidence from children's drawing. *Cognition, 34,* 57-83.

Karmiloff-Smith, A. (1992). *Beyond modularity: A developmental perspective on cognitive science.* Cambridge, MA: MIT Press.

Karmiloff-Smith, A. (1999). Taking development seriously. *Human Development, 42,* 325-327.

Kellogg, R. (1969). *Analyzing children's art.* Palo Alto: National Press Books.

Kirkham, N. K., Cruess, L., & Diamond, A. (2003). Helping children apply their knowledge to their behavior on a dimension-switching task. *Developmental Science, 6,* 449-476.

Lange-Küttner, C., Kerzmann, A., & Heckhausen J. (2002). The emergence of visually realistic contour in the drawing of the human figure. *British Journal of Developmental Psychology, 20,* 439-463.

Light, P., & Simmons, B. (1983). The effects of a communication task upon the representation of depth relationships in young children's drawings. *Journal of Experimental Child Psychology, 35,* 81-92.

Lowenfeld, V., & Brittain, W. L. (1975). *Creative and Mental Growth.* New York: Macmillan.

Luquet, G. (1927). *Le dessin enfantin.* Paris: Alcan.

Matthews, J. (1984). Children drawing: Are young children really scribbling? *Early Child Development and Care, 18,* 1-39.

Milbrath, C. (1998). *Patterns of artistic development in children.* New York: Cambridge University Press.

Milbrath, C. (2008). Developmental preferences and strategies for visual balance in aesthetic compositions. In C. Milbrath, & H. M. Trautner (Eds.), *Children's understanding and production of pictures, drawing, and art* (pp. 261-291). Cambridge, MA: Hogrefe & Huber.

Morra, S. (1995). A neo-Piagetian approach to children's drawings. In C. Lange-Küttner & G. V. Thomas (Eds.), *Drawing and Looking: Theoretical Approaches to Pictorial Representation in Children* (pp. 93-106). London: Harvester.

Morra, S. (2000). A new model of verbal short-term memory. *Journal of Experimental Child Psychology, 75,* 191-227.

Morra, S. (2002). On the relationship between partial occlusion drawing, M capacity, and field independence. *British Journal of Developmental Psychology, 20,* 421-438.

Morra, S. (2005). Cognitive aspects of change in drawings: A neo-Piagetian theoretical account. *British Journal of Developmental Psychology, 23,* 317-341.

Morra, S. (in press). Spatial structures in children's drawing: How do they develop? In C. Lange-Küttner & A. Vinter (Eds.), *The development of drawing and non-verbal intelligence.* Cambridge, England: Cambridge University Press.

Morra, S., Angi, A., & Tomat, L. (1996). Planning, encoding, and overcoming conflict in partial occlusion drawing: A neo-Piagetian model and an experimental analysis. *Journal of Experimental Child Psychology, 61,* 276-301.

Morra, S., Caloni, B., & d'Amico, M. R. (1994). Working memory and the intentional depiction of emotions. *Archives de Psychologie, 62,* 71-87.

Morra, S., Gobbo, C., Marini, Z., & Sheese, R. (in press). *Cognitive development: Neo-Piagetian perspectives.* Hillsdale, NJ: Erlbaum.

Morra, S., Moizo, C., Scopesi, A. (1988). Working memory (or the M operator) and the planning of children's drawings. *Journal of Experimental Child Psychology, 46,* 41-73.

Moscovitch, M., & Umiltà, C. (1991). Modularity and neuropsychology: Implications for the organization of attention and memory in normal and brain-damaged people. In M. Schwartz (Ed.), *Modular processes in dementia.* Cambridge, MA: MIT Press.

Osterrieth, P. A. (1973). L'étude du dessin enfantin. In H. Gratiot-Alphandery & R. Zazzo (Eds.), *Traité de psychologie de l'enfant,* (Vol. 6). Paris: P.U.F.

Panchaud, I., & Romano, G. (1980). Autoritratti. In L. Franceschini, F. Guindani, N. Norcia, I. Panchaud, M. Poddine, G. Romano & E. Scotellaro (Eds.), *Tutto il tempo che va via: Mostra dello scarabocchio, catalogo* (pp. 47-57). Roma: MCE laboratorio di lettura e scrittura.

Pascual-Leone, J. (1989). An organismic process model of Witkin's field dependence- independence. In T. Globerson & T. Zelniker (Eds.), *Cognitive style and cognitive development* (pp. 36-70). Norwood, NJ: Ablex.

Pascual-Leone, J. (2000). Reflections on working memory: Are the two models complementary? *Journal of Experimental Child Psychology, 77,* 138-154.

Pascual-Leone, J., & Goodman, D. (1979). Intelligence and experience: A neo-Piagetian approach. *Instructional Science, 8,* 301-367.

Pascual-Leone, J., Goodman, D., Ammon, P., & Subelman, I. (1978). Piagetian theory and neo-Piagetian analysis as psychological guides in education. In J. Gallagher & J. A. Easley (Eds.), *Knowledge and development* (pp. 243-289). New York: Plenum Press.

Pascual-Leone, J., & Johnson, J. (1999). A dialectical constructivist view of representation: Role of mental attention, executives, and symbols. In I. E. Sigel (Ed.), *Development of mental representation: Theories and applications* (pp. 169-200). Mahwah, NJ: Erlbaum.

Pascual-Leone, J., & Johnson, J. (2005). A dialectical constructivist view of developmental intelligence. In O. Wilhelm, & R. Engle (Eds.), *Handbook of understanding and measuring intelligence* (pp. 177-201). Thousand Oaks, CA: Sage.

Picard, D., & Vinter, A. (1999). Representational flexibility in children's drawings: Effects of age and verbal instructions. *British Journal of Developmental Psychology, 17,* 605-622.

Quaglia, R., & Saglione, G. (1976). *Il disegno infantile: nuove linee interpretative.* Firenze: Giunti e Barbera.

Reith, E. (1988). The development of use of contour lines in children's drawings of figurative and non-figurative three-dimensional models. *Archives de Psycholgie, 56,* 83-103.

Romano, G., Poddine, M., & Guindani, F. (1980). Il processo della significazione. In: L. Franceschini, F. Guindani, N. Norcia, I. Panchaud, M. Poddine, G. Romano & E. Scotellaro (Eds.), *Tutto il tempo che va via: Mostra dello scarabocchio, catalogo* (pp. 21-37). Roma: MCE laboratorio di lettura e scrittura.

Ross, J. (2005, August 24-28). *I made my mark: An investigation of the mechanisms by which children recognize their own drawing products.* Paper presented at the 12th European Conference on Developmental Psychology, Tenerife.

Silk, A. M., & Thomas, G. V. (1986). Development and differentiation in children's figure drawings. *British Journal of Psychology, 77,* 399-410.

Spensley, F., & Taylor, J. (1999) The development of cognitive flexibility: Evidence from children's drawings. *Human Development, 42,* 300-324.

Stacey, J. T., & Ross, B. M. (1975). Scheme and schema in children's memory of their own drawings. *Developmental Psychology, 11,* 37-41.

Trautner, H. M. (1995, June 1-3). *The development from segmentation to contouring in children's human figure drawings.* Paper presented at the 25th Annual symposium of the Jean Piaget Society, Berkeley.

Trautner, H. M. (1996, August 16-21). *Drawing sequences in children's free drawing, copying and tracing of the human figure.* Poster presented at the 26th International Conference of Psychology, Montreal.

Van Sommers, P. (1984). *Drawing and cognition.* New York: Cambridge University Press.

Willats, J. (1985). Drawing systems revisited: The role of denotation systems in children's figure drawing. In N. H. Freeman & M. V. Cox (Eds.), *Visual Order* (pp. 78-100). Cambridge: Cambridge University Press.

Willats, J. (1995). An information-processing approach to drawing development. In C. Lange-Küttner & G. V. Thomas (Eds.), *Drawing and Looking: Theoretical Approaches to Pictorial Representation in Children* (pp. 27-43). London: Harvester.

Witkin, H. A., Lewis, H. B., Hertzmann, M., Machover, K., Meissner, P. B., & Wapner, S. (1954). *Personality through perception.* New York: Harper.

Yamagata, K. (1997). Representational activity during mother-child interaction: The scribbling stage of drawing. *British Journal of Developmental Psychology, 15,* 355-366.

Yamagata, K. (2001). Emergence of representational activity during the early drawing stage: Process analysis. *Japanese Psychological Research, 43,* 130-140.

Zhi, Z., Thomas, G. V., & Robinson, E. J. (1997). Constraints on representational change: Drawing a man with two heads. *British Journal of Developmental Psychology, 15,* 275-290.

Part III

Understanding and Developing Pictorial Competence

Chapter 5

Size and Contour as Crucial Parameters in Children Drawing Images

Christiane Lange-Küttner
London Metropolitan University

The commonly adopted approach in drawing research is that young children would draw what they know and show an attitude of *intellectual realism*, while older children draw what they see and thus have changed their attitude to one of *visual realism* (Luquet, 1927). This approach provided a testable hypothesis for research into drawing development for a long time. In the past this account was challenged to a large degree by devising experiments which tested whether these attitudes could be changed with experimenter instructions, to explore whether young children could be cued to draw what they see (e.g., Barrett, Beaumont, & Jennett, 1985; Barrett & Bridson, 1983). Awareness of projective spatial relations is poor in young children (Flavell, Green, Herrera, & Flavell, 1991), but begins to improve after age seven. However, in graphic constructions of older children and adults, only about ten per cent draw in viewpoint perspective (Hagen, 1985; Lange-Küttner, 1989, 1994). Viewpoint perspective involves drawing diagonals, which often has been found to be particularly difficult (Olson, 1970/1996; Perner, Kohlmann, & Wimmer, 1984). But the actual reasons why a diagonal line is more difficult than a vertical or horizontal one has remained unclear. The majority of children and adults can construct an orthogonal axes system which involves only 90°, or *right* angles (Hagen, 1985; Lange-Küttner, 2004, in press).

Projective space has two applications, one applies to individual pictorial objects, and one applies to the wider space, the latter will be called overall space, or space system, in the following text. The basic assumption in this chapter is that spatial objects are conceptually related to the type of space system which contains them, as would be predicted in Lewin's field theory (Lewin, 1951), where field forces have an impact on individual objects which happen to be in that field. The current chapter initially describes the problems both people and experts like astronomers are facing when they have to conceptualize an empty expanse which has no explicit spatial structure, and then reports how in pictorial space the increasing power of explicitly depicted space systems impacts on object parameters such as size and contour.

Conceptualizing empty space and apparent dissolving of the object

The problem of conceptualizing overall space when drawing images is very similar to the problem in astronomy and physics, as drawing involves a process where space itself has to be structured, albeit a very small one on a piece of paper, i.e., pictorial space rather than the universe. Astronomy research dates back to the philosophers Aristotle (384 – 322 BC) and Ptolemy (90 – 168 AD). They developed a *concentric* model of space, where it was correctly described that celestial objects have regular circular orbits. The early concentric model was a geocentric model of the empty space of the universe, i.e., with the earth at the centre, and the sun and all other celestial objects orbiting around it; see Figure 5.1 (1). This was the dominant theory for over a thousand years. The concentric model with the earth at the centre could also be seen as a psychologically egocentric approach (see also Piaget & Garcia, 1989). However, in the context of this chapter, it is more important that the space concept based on concentric object trajectories was a good, if small and imprecise model conceptualizing only a few objects. The notion of a powerful centre can also be found in conceptualizations of art (Arnheim, 1988) and in young children's search (Huttenlocher, Hedges, & Duncan, 1991). Kopernikus, and later Galilei began to modify this theory only insofar as they saw the sun at the centre (Evans, 1998), but not in terms of the geometric properties of the space system.

The empty space of the universe is especially difficult to conceive of, as it is different from empty expanses on the surface of the earth, which can be more easily delineated and segmented, as there are natural visual cues for spatial boundaries such as rivers, seas, mountains, plateaus or plains. Direct perception of the universe provides only perceptual impressions of visible celestial objects such as stars, planets, and comets in empty space, clustered in star systems which were later found to be embedded in entire galaxies. Similar to these early conceptions of space based on visible impressions, young children would also draw only the objects they can see, i.e., visible objects, and not objects and their parts which they cannot see. Please note that this is in stark contrast to the somewhat abbreviated understanding of how researchers into drawing development have understood Luquet (1927) in the past, i.e., that young children draw what they know. In fact, if young children draw objects, they do draw these with specific functional views they know, but (1) what is selected to be drawn must be directly visible, and (2) from a perspective of spatial projection systems, projection is still absent, and objects appear to float in an empty, unstructured pictorial space. So what Luquet really meant would be that young children draw what they know of objects they can see. Careful experimental research (Light & Humphreys, 1981; Light & MacIntosh, 1980), nevertheless, has revealed that children do not draw random spatial distributions, but can copy implicit spatial relations between aligned object models in an experimental setting, i.e., objects behind each other are depicted above each other on the sheet, and objects following each other are depicted to the left and right of each other on the sheet. This demonstrated that young children also show a clear mapping of top-bottom and left-right categorical spatial relations in their drawings.

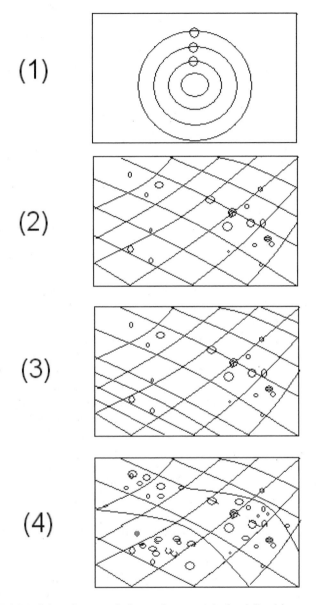

Figure 5.1 Models of power balance between (celestial) objects and space; (2)-(4) adapted from Clark (2007): (1) The celestial object-based *concentric* model, in the early version the earth is in the centre, in the later version the sun is in the centre, (2) the axes-based *cosmological constant* model with regular extensions (3) the *quintessence* model and *modified gravity* accounts with local fluctuations, and (4) the *inhomogeneous universe* model where local clusters of celestial objects distort the regular extension of space.

Also adults find it easy to attend to visible objects but are poor at coding spatial position per se, i.e., in the absence of an object occupying a particular place, or at coding empty regions of space (Humphreys, 1999). Explicit axes systems provide a projection system which makes it possible to measure the extension of space and to determine precisely the location of the objects within this space system. Thus, while we have assumed for many years that children draw a view of the world, this is only correct insofar as they draw objects of the world. It seems what really occurs when spatial context becomes explicit is that children develop models for the empty space on a sheet of paper, not unlike astronomers for the apparently empty universe.

The emerging explicitness of spatial axes structure is similar to the innovation of Einstein's (1920/1993) space concept, where larger weight was attributed to the actual reference frame than to the embedded celestial objects. While the computation of space-time and thus axes systems had become independent of the celestial bodies, Einstein assumed that in reality, multiple reference frames would interfere with each other due to the impenetrability of solid bodies. In his general theory of relativity, Einstein tried to reconcile the concentric gravitational fields of celestial objects with the linearly extending Gaussian axes systems. To achieve this, he conceptualized non-rigid reference bodies, which he called *reference-molluscs* (Einstein, 1920/1993, p. 99), and which could be modified in any way during movement. In this way, he theoretically abolished the independent existence of spatial co-ordinates versus objects, as space could be conceptualized as a truly homogeneous expanse insofar as every point on the mollusc would be treated as a space-point, and thus theoretically the object had become space. This *dissolving* of objects into space is still a problem in computerized picture processing (Willats, 1997). Sophisticated cognitive models have been developed either to describe how to identify an object shape in a space-based percept (Marr & Hildreth, 1980; Marr & Nishihara, 1978), or which rather assume an object-based mechanism (Driver, 2001), or object file (Pylyshyn, 2003; Treisman, 1993).

Einstein's theory provided some inspiration to the hypothesis of my research on size and contour in children's drawings, as it would be predicted that once children begin to draw explicit axes systems, objects and figures contained in these axes systems would become like *molluscs* and change their solid compositional quality of simple geometric circles with extensions to become modifiable in terms of dimensionality, contour and size.

When we note that children and adults find it difficult to construct diagonal projective axes systems in pictorial space, we must also notice however, that the kind of extension and shape of the empty space of the universe is still a matter of current controversy. Clark (2007) describes four approaches (see Figure 5.1). The first of these, the *cosmological constant* model, uses a regular force for extension as the basic parameter and thus produces what Einstein (1920/1993) as well as Piaget and Inhelder (1956) and many others have been thinking of as an Eucledian continuum. However, since then, in the more recent models the power balance between the gravitational fields of (celestial) objects versus the spatial axes systems is a central aspect and has been further elaborated.

It is particularly important for developmental psychologists to consider this debate, as in much recent research researchers are still busy with disconfirming Piaget and Inhelder's spatial model, which was the most advanced at the time, but in which the Eucledian vector space was the only interesting aspect and (celestial) objects did not matter much. *Figurative thinking* was presumed to be suppressed and subordinated as non-operational in development (Lange-Küttner & Reith, 1995; Piaget & Inhelder, 1971) in order to overcome the early, *concrete*, purely object-based conceptualizations.

The second model is the *quintessence* model, which assumes that space extends irregularly in different places and thus produces an irregularly spaced spatial axes structure. The third model is the *modified gravity* account where the gravity of celestial objects themselves exerts some power over how space is structured, also leading to local fluctuations, and the fourth model is that of an *inhomogeneous universe*, where this object-based power is multiplied insofar as clusters of celestial stars can distort the vector grid severely. Note that in every case there is an overall structure of space that determines the object and its pathway, but celestial objects have some power to distort the regularity of the spatial grid.

Another current model is the scale-relativity theory which assumes that regular fractal patterns of celestial objects could be observed within limited spatial scales of a universe (Célérier & Nottale, 2006). An assumption of a relativity of spatial scale was probably only possible once many more galaxies than our own were discovered. Also children draw many more figures with age, along with an increasing attentional span, which they size up against a larger spatial scale than when they focused on fewer objects (Lange-Küttner, 1997).

A profound difference between astronomical space and pictorial space, however, is that in the universe celestial objects are round and stay round, while in pictorial space, like in Einstein's theory of general relativity, indeed the shape of the objects (the mollusks) themselves begins to change when children begin to draw explicit axes systems. In the empty pictorial space of young children, objects are mainly composed of two types of picture primitives, i.e., round forms with extensions in various combinations to depict all kinds of objects, animate or inanimate (Kellogg, 1969, Willats, 1985, 1992). Thereafter, a split in the graphic repertoire occurs, i.e., firstly into forms consisting of closely monitored, perfect round circles which are drawn much slower for precision than the early round shapes (Lange-Küttner, 1998), as if to graphically construct pure geometric forms, and secondly into shapes with irregular contour for both whole and parts (Lange-Küttner, Kerzmann, & Heckhausen, 2002), as if to construct pure organic forms. In modern art, one can find various variations on this topic, from painters like Seurat, who would dissolve entire figures into dots, to Picasso, who would translate organic, soft matter figures into geometrical, hard matter creations, to Dali who would soften the geometric contours of hard objects such as clocks into bendy objects in his images.

Moreover, when older children begin to graphically construct explicit axes systems, object size can be regulated on a larger spatial scale than in implicit pictorial space (Lange-Küttner, 1997, 2004, 2007). Size also plays a role in the debate whether quantum, particle physics and classic, condensed matter physics are on the same scale, and where the transition from one to another would begin (Chown, 2007). In developmental psychology, it has been put forward that children can attend to the granularity of space, either fine-grained as in Euclidean vector extensions, or coarse-grained as in categorical spatial relations between objects (Newcombe & Huttenlocher, 2003). In drawing development, the transition seems to begin when children can draw entire figures in 3D pictorial space the size of a small fingernail (Lange-Küttner, 2004).

Drawing systems

When do explicit spatial axes systems emerge in drawings? Willats (1985; 1995; 1997; 2005) extended an approach used by art historians who differentiate between denotation (what is depicted) and connotation (what is this supposed to tell us) (e.g., Hauser, 1999). Willats used *mark systems* to categorize the actual physical marks on the picture surface in the first scribbled, idiosyncratic drawings of children (see also Campbell, Duncan, Harrison, & Mathewson, in press; Ross, in press), which do not yet denote a recognizable object. He held that *denotation systems* would map regions, lines and line junctions onto pictorial objects so that recognition would require less and less guesswork. *Projection systems* are still more elaborate, with an onset between nine and ten years of age (Willats, 1977). Willats classified projection systems into six categories (average age for the drawing system in brackets, in years and months), (1) no projection system, (2) orthogonal projection system (9;7), (3) vertical projection system (11;9), (4) oblique projection system (13;6), (5) naïve perspective (14;3) and (6) perspective (13;7) (see Figure 5.2).

Note that these drawing systems are not like stages; in particular the last three systems did not show an age trend. This reflects the difficulty to draw diagonals in projection systems. Angles in orthogonal systems are by definition always 90° and can be combined easily. However, the oblique angles created by diagonals can be of various degrees and thus there are many more degrees of freedom to make mistakes when constructing oblique angles, as lines can diverge into a multitude of different directions. Thus when drawing a house, the lines denoting a side which perceptually recedes into the depth of the background can be quite tricky, and many mismatches may result from the effort to coordinate several diagonal lines with each other.

Let us have a look at the overall spatial structure given to a blank sheet of paper. In a study with 9-year-olds, there were 12.7 % of a sample of $n = 63$ drawing diagonal axes to structure pictorial space (Lange-Küttner, 1989), but age-matched children with behavioral difficulties were drawing projection systems with diagonals significantly less often. Furthermore, in a longitudinal study from age 7 to 12, children from a rural population showed no drawing of viewpoint perspective at any measurement point, while in an urban sample of $n = 97$, 13.4 % were drawing in perspective (Lange-Küttner, 1994).

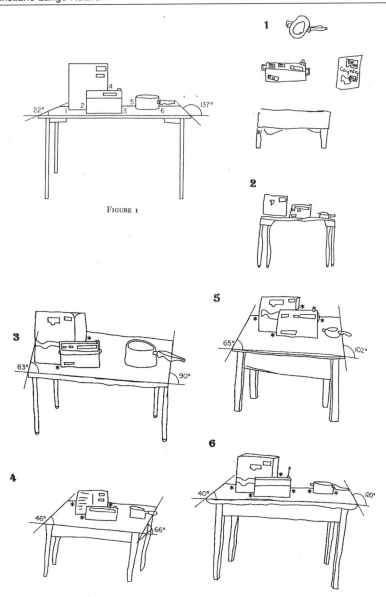

Figure 5.2 Drawing systems for object aggregates. Note the stars for the amount of overlap and the angle measurements at the table top for the assessment of the type of drawing system (Willats, 1977). Willats' classification system: 1 = No projection system, 2 = Orthographic projection system, 3 = Vertical oblique projection system, 4 = Oblique projection, 5 = Naïve perspective, 6 = Perspective. Reprinted with paid permission by the publisher Taylor & Francis Ltd.

When looking at the drawing of individual objects, the statistics look a bit better. In the study with the 9-year-olds, 21.1 % of a sample of $n = 66$ were drawing an oblique projection system when drawing a single object such as a table or cupboard, but again in children with behavioral difficulties this was rare (Lange-Küttner, 1989). Thus, it appears that constructing a third dimension in objects and in the space system on the page is related, with objects being depicted in 3D a bit more often than a 3D structure of overall space. Hence, in the longitudinal study, it was analyzed whether there was a contingency between indicators of depth such as intersection and overlap of objects, and the overall space system. A highly significant contingency was indeed found both at ages 9 and 12; children not structuring space with explicit axes systems were also very unlikely to draw intersection or overlap. Conversely, at age 9, more than 40 % of those who constructed orthogonal axes were also drawing overlap, while at age 12 more than 60 % of those who constructed orthogonal axes, and more than 70 % of those who constructed viewpoint perspective were also drawing overlap. Thus, it appears that indeed objects and space are expanded into the third dimension in pictorial space at the same *developmental* time, an assumption also made by astronomers when presuming that the universe and its celestial objects expanded in a *Big Bang*, although the exact mechanism is still unknown (Coles, 2006).

With the onset of explicit spatial axes, several types of axes systems emerge, horizontal axes systems which result in stripy pictures, orthogonal axes systems which allow the depiction of arbitrarily delineated areas, particularly in bird's eye view, and diagonal, viewpoint perspectives which allow the depiction of three-dimensional depth. In orthogonal or oblique mathematical space, objects are reduced to points in a co-ordinate axes system, uniform entities more defined by location than by shape (Lange-Küttner & Reith, 1995). But how do children conceptualize figures in projective pictorial space? Contour and size are two important parameters which need to be considered in order to understand the changing balance between objects and space in the development of drawing.

Drawing contours

Long-standing researchers of contour processing such as Kennedy (e.g., Kennedy, 1974; Kennedy, Nicholls, & Desrochers, 1995), Willats (1997) and Deregowski (e.g., Deregowski, in press; Deregowski & Dziurawiec, 1996) pointed repeatedly to the ambiguity of contours in children's drawing. Willats (1985, 1992) described that lines in young children's drawings denote either regions (when children draw round forms) or extensions (when they attach lines to these round forms) to build nearly any object they like. With the onset of visual realism, the parts which constitute the whole figure become represented in a much more specific and unique way than before. For example, Figure 5.3, left, shows human figures combined from circles and extensions, while Figure 5.3, right, shows irregularly contoured figures with shared common areas between parts (Lange-Küttner et al.,

2002, Study 2). Note that not only the silhouette has become more specifically human, but also the parts are identifiable as such. For instance, in the drawings of the 5-year-olds (Figure 5.3, left), *dots* denote eyes, nose and navel alike, *extensions* denote arms and legs alike, and *circles* denote head and trunk alike. Only the spatial position gives a clue as to the identity of the parts.

Figure 5.3 Left figures are typical combinations of circles with extensions drawn by 5-year-olds; right figures are typical irregularly contoured figures drawn by 11-year-olds, where some parts have dissolved into a common area within the silhouette (Lange-Küttner et al., 2002, Study 2).

Young children may occasionally use minimalist clues to the identity of parts, e.g., when asked to draw a person in a swimsuit, a girl would draw a flower emblem in the circle standing for the trunk, or a boy would draw additional shapes onto the arms to denote swimming aids (Lange-Küttner et al., 2002, Study 3, Fig. 7, p. 454), but without a verbal explanation, a viewer would not know what to make of it.

Willats had thus argued that young children would not draw true contours but *boundaries* of regions, as their shapes would be an *enclosure* drawing (see also Piaget & Inhelder, 1956), a kind of false positive for a contour. Willats referred to experiments from Moore (1986) and by himself (Willats, 1987) showing that children under six years of age often draw the multiple sides of a multi-colored cube into the one square they have been drawing. This was indeed strong evidence that children read more meaning into their depictions than a viewer could be aware of. But it could also be that it is not contour drawing as such that is absent, but that young children use simple forms as a minimalist approach to denote more complex forms they only do not yet know how to construct (Picard & Vinter, 2005). Reith (1988) showed that when drawing the model of a kangaroo with an irregular, organic contour, most young children would use circles and extensions, but a small proportion of children at all ages would draw the correct outline silhouette, but empty, i.e., without parts. This empty outline drawing strategy could also occur when children were asked to draw two squares above each other, then the upper one was moved half-a-length sideways, producing a figure which had many more angles than before, and more than each of the two squares, i.e., its constituent parts (Lange-Küttner & Reith, 1995). Thus, it is contour complexity which seems to make part-whole integration difficult.

Contour is also important when drawing overlapping figures, as overlap between two objects can only be depicted when one is drawn as a part-figure or half-a-figure. In the early days of drawing research, Freeman (1980) called this necessary omission of contour *hidden line elimination*, as if a line is being thought of, but needs to be erased, either in reality using an eraser on the drawing sheet, or even better in anticipation before the unnecessary line is actually drawn. Thus, some figure parts may need to be omitted, but young children frequently show not only an inability to omit half the object along a spatial axis (Lange-Küttner, 2000, in press; Picard & Vinter, 2006), but blacken out some parts (Karmiloff-Smith, 1990), and can show *deletion spreading* once they have started to eliminate parts (Berti & Freeman, 1997). Interestingly, although children indicated more segmentations on a photo of the human figure with a stick than adults, this was not correlated with the inability to draw half-a-figure (Lange-Küttner, 2000). Instead, drawing half-a-figure was significantly correlated with detection of missing small figure parts (object violation) in perceptual and composition tasks, as well as with copying the Navon figure, where 72.7 % of the 5-year-olds and 45.5 % of the 6-year-olds would copy only the overall shape (Lange-Küttner, 2000).

While young children seem to have a problem in integrating parts and whole (Lange-Küttner, 2000; Picard & Vinter, 2006; Vinter, Picard, & Fernandes, in press), this problem may become even more aggravated with objects that have a particularly complex outline. Picard and Vinter (2006) asked children to merge an animate object (a human figure) with an inanimate object (a house) into one new object. It appeared as if most children chose to draw the irregular-to-geometric contour transformation, rather than the alternative geometric-to-irregular contour transformation. This may have occurred because it takes years in middle childhood until the human figure is entirely transformed from an additive accumulation of circles and extensions into the smooth silhouette whose irregular contour integrates body parts completely (Lange-Küttner et al., 2002). A specific difficulty of complex organic figures such as a kangaroo, or a human figure, might be that in their 3D volume some parts protrude or recede out of a common area with the whole, while in an angular object such as a 3D house, sides are just simple add-ons, rather than peculiar out-growths.

Barrett and Eames (1996) convincingly explained the difficulty of drawing the smooth, irregular contours of parts of the human figure as open shapes, rather than as combinations of picture primitives, as an inability to stop the drawing movement in the middle of a line. Indeed, counter to the increasingly faster information processing capacity with age (e.g., Kail, 1991), and also counter to Piaget (Piaget, 1936/52) who would limit the significance of sensori-motor learning to infancy, some drawing movements need to be slowed down for precision and visually realistic contour. For example, using psycho-physiological measures, it could be demonstrated that children showed very fast speed when drawing overlapping circles but slowed down when drawing spread-out loops. They were drawing open forms significantly *slower* than closed forms, and round forms *slower* than angular forms (Lange-Küttner, 1998).

It is especially astounding and theoretically paradoxical for developmental psychologists that the newly emerging angular forms are indeed easier to draw than the earliest round forms, which children have used since the very beginning of their drawing activity. A circle denoting everything round has now acquired a new, narrowed down, literal meaning as a circle, which is a geometric entity. This firstly shows that not all is what it seems in drawing development, secondly, that a simple emergence theory does not suffice to account for task difficulty in the changes of graphic representation, and thirdly, that fine sensori-motor skills are an integral part of the new visual cognition gradually unfolding in view-specific graphic representations. Indeed, Toomela (2002) showed in a large survey study that the only additional parameter, beyond block building and mental rotation, that predicted drawing in middle childhood in comparison to young children were fine motor skills. Thus, it may be that the theoretical paradox between emergence theory and task difficulty could be reconciled here by assuming that the different modalities of intelligence such as visual perception and motor skills do not drop-out to achieve a pure and completely mentalistic approach to graphic problem solving, but become enhanced by reconfiguring themselves at crucial points in development.

Drawing size

As in physics, where smaller and smaller particles were discovered, also in drawing, drawing smaller parts becomes more important with development. In fact, young children love to *start large*. Freeman (1975, 1980) showed that very young children at the very beginning of their drawing activities frequently run into planning problems, e.g., when drawing a human figure, they draw the head first, and so large that there is no room to attach the trunk, so they just attach arms and legs to the head producing a tadpole. If a head-trunk is pre-drawn for them, arms and legs are attached in the normal way, and the child does not use the head as a trunk to produce a tadpole. This was a first impressive demonstration of the importance of size, and further studies showed that the problem also pertains in preschool children when drawing a dog larger than his owner (Silk & Thomas, 1988; Thomas, 1995). Thus, size appears to be a crucial variable for planning, both in terms of inclusion of more detail within a single figure (Silk & Thomas, 1986), and in terms of inclusion of more figures into overall space (Lange-Küttner, 1997).

Most likely, the number of figures children draw has to do with the development of memory capacity (Morra, 1995; Morra, Moizo, & Scopesi, 1988, see also Morra, Chap 4). Children find it more difficult to include more detail in an object when drawing from memory than from a model (Chen & Cook, 1984), but they also include more detail when the topic is interesting, e.g., in all groups between ages 5 to 9, drawing a television set attracted more attention to detail than drawing a house (Picard & Vinter, 2005).

However, there are also domain-specific problems which emerge when drawing more detailed figures and more figures on the page, i.e., the lack of available space. While a figure can usually be drawn larger in order to accommodate more detail (Silk & Thomas, 1986), a sheet of paper is a limited expanse which sets spatial constraints, so that the more figures there are, the more they would be in competition for pictorial space, and thus the smaller they would have to be drawn. Lange-Küttner (1997, 2004) compared spatial constraints on object size in relation to the number of objects and complexity of the spatial axes system. Would figure size regulation be object-driven or axes-driven? The prediction was that initially object-driven size modification should prevail, but that the more adept children would become at planning explicit spatial structure, the more they would be able to regulate size based on the respective space system.

To investigate the effect of a space concept which is based on competing objects, with a space concept which is based on axes systems, the number of figures was counted in a drawing task asking children from different areas in Iceland to draw themselves with their friends at play near home or school, in a longitudinal design at ages 7, 9 and 12 (Lange-Küttner, 1997). The spatial system that children had constructed was rated by experts, and figure size measured and averaged. Indeed children were drawing more figures with age. However, when children were 7 years old, figure size actually depended more on the type of community and environment in which the children lived, than on either of the two hypothesized factors. Children from agrarian communities, where spatial expanses are in the focus, were drawing figures smaller, while children from service and trade communities, where the customer is important, were drawing figures larger. This corresponded to earlier research on selective domain-specific cognitive development of children in Norway and Hungary, where social isolation in remote communities enhanced Piagetian-type logical spatial reasoning, while in more populated areas role play was better developed (Hollos, 1975; Hollos & Cowan, 1973). However, both domain-specific rules of object- and axes-driven size modification became more powerful predictors for size at ages 9 and 12. The Icelandic, Norwegian and Hungarian studies were all carried out some time ago (Edelstein, Keller, & Schröder, 1990), thus it was considered appropriate to replicate the study with a more recent cohort in Scotland

(Lange-Küttner, 2004). In this second study, the expected age sequence for the best predictors for figure size was found, that is, at age 7 the number of objects predicted size, while at age 9 and 12 it was the axes system, with no effects of community at any point in time. This was explained with an early onset of schooling at age 5 in the UK, in combination with a nation-wide curriculum for all school subjects, instead of local agendas of teachers.

In these studies there was a problem, however, which has been mentioned before, and that was the low occurrence of diagonal, viewpoint spatial systems. A way around this problem was to present children with ready-made pre-drawn spatial systems (see Figure 5.4) into which they could draw the figures. Children were given the ready-made space systems in a simulated developmental sequence (empty space, horizontal axis, orthogonal axes, diagonal axes), so that every single participant would be encountering the visually most complex diagonal axes system.

Another improvement in the experimental design was to control the topic by specifying a ball game instead of leaving all options open, and to prescribe the number of figures, in this case pairs of two figures versus peer groups of five figures (Lange-Küttner, 2004). Thus, in this third study, the spatial constraints caused by the number of objects vs. the space system were systematically varied for all children. It was found that at all ages children reduced the size of the figures more, the more complex the space system, and this became more pronounced with age.

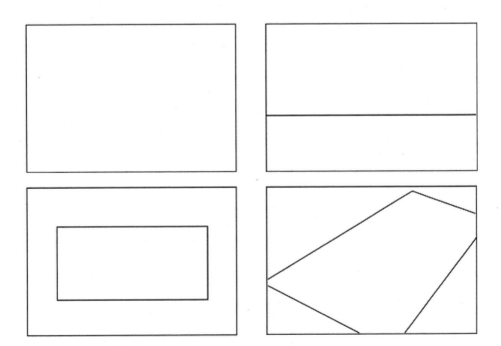

Figure 5.4 Ready-made pre-drawn spatial axes systems used in Lange-Küttner (2004, Study 2) simulating the developmental acquisition sequence.

Different factors, however, were responsible for size modification in each age group. Only at age seven, three factors combined to impact on figure size. On the first page with empty space, children could construct an explicit axes system themselves, and ambitious 7-year-old children under the highest spatial constraints, that is drawing five figures, plus spontaneously constructing their own explicit space system on this first empty page, showed the smallest figure size and did not reduce size any further during the drawing series. All other 7-year-olds were drawing initially relatively large figures and then gradually reducing their size. In the older age groups the own effort to construct an explicit spatial system on the empty page was not significantly related to figure size. In 9-year-olds, both object-driven (number-of-figures) and axes-driven (space system) experimental design factors were significant for size modification, while in the 11-year-olds only the type of ready-made space system was relevant. This was again in accordance with the prediction that object-driven size reduction would drop-out, while the power of explicit space systems to determine figure size would increase.

In a fourth study (Lange-Küttner, under revision) still more controls were introduced. In the first control condition, one group of children was asked to continuously repeat the drawing task on empty pages, the second group was given the ready-made space systems in the simulated developmental sequence like in the previous study, and the third group was given the space systems in a randomized order.

The assumptions were that (1) if young children have a robust space concept, it would survive the random sequence and size reduction would occur in the same way as in the simulated developmental sequence of space systems, and (2) unless a motor practice effect would support gradually smaller size drawing, repeated drawings in empty pictorial space would produce random fluctuations of size. It was found that the 7-year-olds were drawing a kind of habitual size, without a significant difference between the repeated condition and the two space system sequence conditions. However, within this habitual size range, 7-year-olds were reducing size along with increasing complexity of the space system when the space systems were logically pre-sorted for them, while for the 11-year-olds it had become irrelevant whether space systems were pre-sorted or in random order. Size modification was again much more pronounced in the 11-year-olds than in the 7-year-olds. The transition mechanism appeared to be the recognition of spatial constraints, as only in 9-year-olds did a significant difference between simply repeated drawings in empty space and the ready-made space systems emerge. This was similar to the construction of boundaries of areas for common space, which the majority of children also only show at nine years of age (Lange-Küttner, 2006). Thus, this study could identify awareness of spatial constraints as a major factor in the development of projective size.

The power balance of objects and space

From a visual perception and art perspective, Willats (1984) had argued for a long time that the biological design features of the human visual system would cause a mismatch between competence in perception and competence in production that would drive developmental change, as children would aim to match their drawings to the perceptual input. While this claim is not entirely unjustified, based on more recent models of the power balance between (celestial) objects and space systems, it was suggested here that the emergence and increasing power of explicit pictorial space systems that structure the empty page may actually also change the child's concept of the object and necessitate increased attention to their contour and size.

In conclusion, while in implicit space objects were competing and defining space, and shapes were holistic and sometimes had more meaning than apparent, the transition to explicit space systems required that objects can be segmented, re-composed, shrunk in size to insignificance or expanded to larger-than-life size. The new power balance between objects and space also makes objects more specific so that they become more detailed and immediately identifiable in their specificity. The current chapter pointed to the multi-factorial nature of this process that defies many simplistic developmental theories.

Although visual realism is nowadays technically realized as a mechanical and computational approach that could be delegated to machines such as photo, film and video cameras, scanners, and drawing software, the current chapter demonstrates that many conceptual issues in modern art have their roots in the difference between and transition from implicit space to an explicit spatial context. In particular, Einstein's theory of the *mollusk* appears to be nearly more applicable and valid for objects in simulated pictorial space, whose size and contour is controlled by the spatial system, than for celestial objects in the universe. We will need much more research on the interaction of objects and spatial systems in pictorial space to investigate the causative links between increase in cognitive resources, attentional span, fine motor skills and spatial concepts.

References

Arnheim, R. (1988). *The power of the center: A study of composition in the visual arts.* Berkeley, CA: University of California Press.

Barrett, M., & Eames, K. (1996). Sequential development in children's human figure drawing. *British Journal of Developmental Psychology, 14,* 219-236.

Barrett, M. D., Beaumont, A. V., & Jennett, M. S. (1985). Some children sometimes do what they have been told to do: task demands and verbal instructions in children's drawings. In N. H. Freeman & M. V. Cox (Eds.), *Visual order. The nature and development of pictorial representation* (pp. 176-187). Cambridge: Cambridge University Press.

Barrett, M. D., & Bridson, A. (1983). The effect of instructions upon children's drawings. *British Journal of Developmental Psychology, 1,* 175-178.

Berti, A. E., & Freeman, N. H. (1997). Representational change in resources for pictorial innovation: A three-component analysis. *Cognitive Development, 12,* 405-426.

Campbell, R. N., Duncan, P. A., Harrison, A. L., & Mathewson, L. C. (in press). Can four-year-old children recognize their own drawings? In C. Lange-Küttner & A. Vinter (Eds.), *Drawing and non-verbal intelligence.* Cambridge: Cambridge University Press.

Célérier, M. N., & Nottale, L. (2006). The Pauli equation in scale relativity. *Journal of Physics A: Mathematical and General, 39,* 12565-12585.

Chen, M. J., & Cook, M. (1984). Representational drawings of solid objects by young children. *Perception, 13,* 377-385.

Chown, M. (2007). Forever quantum. *New Scientist, 193,* 36-39.

Clark, S. (2007). Heart of darkness. *New Scientist, 193,* 28-33.

Coles, P. (2006). *From cosmos to chaos: The science of unpredictability.* Oxford: Oxford University Press.

Deregowski, J. B. (in press). On contours drawn and contours seen. In C. Lange-Küttner & A. Vinter (Eds.), *Drawing and non-verbal intelligence.* Cambridge: Cambridge University Press.

Deregowski, J. B., & Dziurawiec, S. (1996). The puissance of typical contours and children's drawings. *Australian Journal of Psychology, 48,* 98-103.

Driver, J. (2001). A selective review of selective attention research from the past century. *British Journal of Psychology, 92,* 53-78.

Edelstein, W., Keller, M., & Schröder, E. (1990). Child development and social structure: A study of individual differences. In R. M. Lerner (Ed.), *Life-span development and behavior* (pp. 152-187). Hillsdale, NJ: Erlbaum.

Einstein, A. (1920/1993). *Relativity. The special and the general theory.* Authorised translation by Robert W. Lawson. London: Routledge.

Evans, J. (1998). *The history and practice of ancient astronomy.* New York: Oxford University Press.

Flavell, J. H., Green, F., Herrera, C., & Flavell, E. R. (1991). Young children's knowledge about visual perception: Lines of sight must be straight. *British Journal of Developmental Psychology, 9,* 73-87.

Freeman, N. H. (1975). Do children draw men with arms coming out of the head? *Nature, 254,* 416-417.

Freeman, N. H. (1980). *Strategies of representation in young children.* London: Academic Press.

Hagen, M. A. (1985). There is no development in art. In N. H. Freeman & M. V. Cox (Eds.), *Visual order* (pp. 78-100). Cambridge: Cambridge University Press.

Hauser, A. (1999). *The social history of art.* London: Routledge.

Hollos, M. (1975). Logical operations and role-taking abilities in two cultures: Norway and Hungary. *Child Development, 46,* 638-649.

Hollos, M., & Cowan, P. A. (1973). Social isolation and cognitive development: Logical operations and role-taking abilities in three Norwegian social settings. *Child Development, 44,* 630-641.

Humphreys, G. W. (1999). Neural representation of objects in space. In G. W. Humphreys, J. Duncan & A. Treisman (Eds.), *Attention, space and action. Studies in cognitive neuroscience* (pp. 165-182). Oxford: Oxford University Press.

Huttenlocher, J., Hedges, L., & Duncan, S. (1991). Categories and particulars: Prototype effects in estimating spatial location. *Psychological Review, 98,* 352-376.

Kail, R. (1991). Processing time declines exponentially during childhood and adolescence. *Developmental Psychology, 27,* 259-266.

Karmiloff-Smith, A. (1990). Constraints on representational change: Evidence from children's drawings. *Cognition, 34,* 57-83.

Kellogg, R. (1969). *Analyzing children's art.* Palo Alto: Mayfield.

Kennedy, J. M. (1974). *A psychology of picture perception.* San Francisco: Jossey-Bass.

Kennedy, J. M., Nicholls, A. L., & Desrochers, M. (1995). From line to outline. In C. Lange-Küttner & G. V. Thomas (Eds.), *Drawing and looking* (pp.62-74). Hemel Hempstead: Harvester Wheatsheaf.

Lange-Küttner, C. (1989). *Raumbegriff und Objektbeziehungen beim Kind* [Space concept and object relations in the child]. Frankfurt/Main: Lang.

Lange-Küttner, C. (1994). *Gestalt und Konstruktion. Die Entwicklung der grafischen Kompetenz beim Kind* [*Gestalt and construction. The development of graphic competence in the child*]. Bern: Huber.

Lange-Küttner, C. (1997). Development of size modification of human figure drawings in spatial axes systems of varying complexity. *Journal of Experimental Child Psychology, 66,* 264-278.

Lange-Küttner, C. (1998). Pressure, velocity and time in speeded drawing of basic graphic pattern by young children. *Perceptual and Motor Skills, 86,* 1299-1310.

Lange-Küttner, C. (2000). The role of object violations in the development of visual analysis. *Perceptual and Motor Skills, 90,* 3-24.

Lange-Küttner, C. (2004). More evidence on size modification in spatial axes systems of varying complexity. *Journal of Experimental Child Psychology, 88,* 171-192.

Lange-Küttner, C. (2006). Drawing boundaries: From individual to common region. The development of spatial region attribution in children. *British Journal of Developmental Psychology, 24,* 419-427.

Lange-Küttner, C. (under revision). *Habitual size and projective size: The logic of spatial systems in children's drawings.*

Lange-Küttner, C. (in press). Figures in and out of context: Absent, simple, complex and halved spatial fields. In C. Lange-Küttner & A. Vinter (Eds.), *Drawing and the non-verbal mind: A life-span perspective.* Cambridge: Cambridge University Press.

Lange-Küttner, C., Kerzmann, A., & Heckhausen, J. (2002). The emergence of visually realistic contour in the drawing of the human figure. *British Journal of Developmental Psychology, 20,* 439-463.

Lange-Küttner, C., & Reith, E. (1995). The transformation of figurative thought: Implications of Piaget and Inhelder's developmental theory for children's drawings. In C. Lange-Küttner & G. V. Thomas (Eds.), *Drawing and looking* (pp. 75 - 92). New York: Harvester Wheatsheaf.

Lewin, K. (1951). *Field theory in social science.* New York: Harper Brothers.

Light, P., & Humphreys, J. (1981). Internal spatial relationships in young children's drawings. *Journal of Experimental Child Psychology, 31,* 521-530.

Light, P., & MacIntosh, E. (1980). Depth relationships in young children's drawings. *Journal of Experimental Child Psychology, 46,* 41-73.

Luquet, G. H. (1927). *Le dessin enfantin.* Paris: Alcan.

Marr, D., & Hildreth, E. (1980). *Theory of edge detection.* Proceedings of the Royal Society of London, B 207, 187-217.

Marr, D., & Nishihara, N. K. (1978). *Representation and recognition of the spatial organisation of three-dimensional shapes.* Proceedings of the Royal Society, 200, 269-294.

Moore, V. (1986). The use of a colouring task to elucidate children's drawing of a solid cube. *British Journal of Developmental Psychology, 4,* 335-340.

Morra, S. (1995). A neo-Piagetian approach to children's drawings. In C. Lange-Küttner & G. V. Thomas (Eds.), *Drawing and looking* (pp. 93-106). New York: Harvester Wheatsheaf.

Morra, S. (2008). Memory components and control processes in children's drawing. In H. M. Trautner & C. Milbrath (Eds.). *Children's understanding and production of pictures, drawings, and art: Theoretical and empirical approaches* (pp. 53-85). Cambridge, MA: Hogrefe & Huber

Morra, S., Moizo, C., & Scopesi, A. (1988). Working memory (or the M operator) and the planning of children's drawings. *Journal of Experimental Child Psychology, 46,* 41-73.

Newcombe, N. S., & Huttenlocher, J. (2003). *Making space. The development of spatial representation and reasoning.* Cambridge, MA: MIT Press.

Olson, D. R. (1970/1996). *Cognitive development. The child's acquisition of diagonality.* Mahwah, NJ: Erlbaum.

Perner, J., Kohlmann, R., & Wimmer, H. (1984). Young children's recognition and use of the vertical and horizontal in drawings. *Child Development, 55,* 1637-1645.

Piaget, J. (1936/52). *The origins of intelligence in children.* New York: International Universities Press.

Piaget J., & Garcia, R. (1989). *Psychogenesis and the history of science.* New York: Columbia University Press.

Piaget, J., & Inhelder, B. (1956). *The child's conception of space.* London: Routledge & Kegan Paul.

Piaget, J., & Inhelder, B. (1971). *Mental imagery in the child.* London: Routledge & Kegan Paul.

Picard, D., & Vinter, A. (2005). Development of graphic formulas for the depiction of familiar objects. *International Journal of Behavioral Development, 29,* 418-432.

Picard, D., & Vinter, A. (2006). Decomposing and connecting object representations in 5- to 9-year-old children's drawing behaviour. *British Journal of Developmental Psychology, 24,* 529-545.

Pylyshyn, Z. (2003). *Seeing and visualizing. It's not what you think.* Cambridge, MA: The MIT Press.

Reith, E. (1988). The development of use of contour lines in children's drawings of figurative and non-figurative three-dimensional models. *Archives de Psychologie, 56,* 83-103.

Ross, J. (in press). Drawing production, drawing re-experience and drawing re-cognition. In C. Lange-Küttner & A. Vinter (Eds.), *Drawing and non-verbal intelligence.* Cambridge: Cambridge University Press.

Silk, A. M. J., & Thomas, G. V. (1986). Development and differentiation in children's figure drawings. *British Journal of Psychology, 77,* 399-410.

Silk, A. M. J., & Thomas, G. V. (1988). The development of size scaling in children's figure drawings. *British Journal of Developmental Psychology, 6,* 285-299.

Thomas, G. V. (1995). The role of drawing strategies and skills. In C. Lange-Küttner & G. V. Thomas (Eds.), *Drawing and looking* (pp. 107-122). New York: Harvester Wheatsheaf.

Toomela, A. (2002). Drawing as a verbally mediated activity: A study of relationships between verbal, motor, and visuospatial skills and drawing in children. *International Journal of Behavioral Development, 26,* 234-247.

Treisman, A. (1993). The perception of features and objects. In A. L. W. Baddeley (Ed.), *Attention: Selection, awareness and control* (pp. 5-35). Oxford: Clarendon Press.

Vinter, A., Picard, D., & Fernandes, V. (in press). Graphic syntax and representational development. In C. Lange-Küttner & A. Vinter (Eds.), *Drawing and non-verbal intelligence.* Cambridge: Cambridge University Press.

Willats, J. (1977). How children learn to draw realistic pictures. *Quarterly Journal of Experimental Psychology, 29,* 367-382.

Willats, J. (1984). Getting the drawing to look right as well as to be right: the interaction between production and perception as a mechanism of development. In W. R. Crozier & A. J. Chapman (Eds.), *Cognitive processes in the perception of art* (pp. 111-125). Amsterdam: North-Holland.

Willats, J. (1985). Drawing systems revisited: the role of denotation systems in children's figure drawings. In N. H. Freeman & M. V. Cox (Eds.), *Visual Order* (pp. 78-100). Cambridge: Cambridge University Press.

Willats, J. (1987). Marr and pictures: an information-processing account of children's drawings. *Archives de Psychologie, 55,* 105-125.

Willats, J. (1992). The representation of extendedness in children's drawings of sticks and discs. *Child Development, 63,* 692-710.

Willats, J. (1995). An information-processing approach to drawing development. In C. Lange-Küttner & G. V. Thomas (Eds.), *Drawing and looking* (pp. 27-43). New York: Harvester Wheatsheaf.

Willats, J. (1997). *Art and representation. New principles in the analysis of pictures.* Princeton, NJ: Princeton University Press.

Willats, J. (2005). *Making sense of children's drawings.* Mahwah, NJ: Erlbaum.

Chapter 6

Children's Choice of Color to Depict Metaphorical and Affective Information

Esther Burkitt
Open University

Introduction

The view that colors are associated with emotional qualities has a long standing history in popular culture and various academic fields. In everyday language, moods are described in color terms, such as feeling blue, seeing red, green with envy, and colors are used by artists to evoke certain feelings in the viewer. Despite this understanding of the relation between color and emotion, children's use of color has been largely neglected relative to the great research interest in formal aspects of children's drawing and art. However, the use and significance of color has been the topic of various emerging research strands which can be broadly distinguished.

One research tradition has concentrated on children's knowledge of realistic coloring and the development of the communication of this knowledge in drawing (e.g., Golomb, 1992; Lowenfield & Brittain, 1970). A second line of research has focused on the kind of understanding children have about the relation between color and affective information, as indicating the mood of the artist and/or the emotional quality of the art work, or the feelings aroused in the viewer (Boyatzis & Varghese, 1993; McNiff, 1998). Researchers have also examined the color preferences of children and the ways in which these preferences may influence children's depiction of objects and scenes (Burkitt, Barrett, & Davis, 2003a; Burkitt & Newell, 2005; Zentner, 2001). In a related strand of research, interest has also been shown in the felt emotional quality that children associate with specific colors and in how children use single or multiple colors in relation to affect-eliciting topics (McNiff, 1998; Nelson, Allan, & Nelson, 1971). Lastly, researchers have given some attention to the fixation or flexibility of the relation between color and affective information across age, individuals, cultural groups and drawing conditions (Burkitt, Tala, & Low, 2007; Nelson, Allan, & Nelson, 1971). The relationships between children's color preferences, the felt quality children associate with colors and the way children use color to depict affect-eliciting topics is a neglected issue in the literature. More is known about children's liking for certain colors over time and their understanding of the felt qualities of particular colors than is known about how children actually use color to convey how they feel about the topics which they draw.

Children's drawings, and the use of specific colors, continue to be interpreted by parents and professionals for signs about the emotional state of children and for information about how the children feel about the topics they draw (Hammer, 1997; Hunsley, Lee, & Wood, 2003). It is therefore important to understand how children use color to convey emotion and to assess whether children's color use can be interpreted reliably for information about the emotional significance of the topics children draw. In this chapter I will address the progression of research in the area of children's color use in relation to affect eliciting topics. It will be shown that although claims as to the emotional content of children's drawing production have often been based on limited research, we are beginning to see that children's use of color is sometimes related to how they feel about the colors that they have been given to draw with, the felt quality children associate with particular colors, and the topics that they are drawing. Issues which continue to surround investigations in this area will also be presented, as will suggestions for possible future directions for research.

Children's color use in relation to affect-eliciting topics

A common view is that children's choice of color can be influenced by the feelings that they hold towards a drawn topic, and also by the way they feel about the colors they have been asked to use (e.g. Alschuler & Hattwick, 1943, 1947; Burkitt et al., 2003a; Brick, 1944; Hammer, 1997; Winston, Kenyon, Stewardson, & Lepine, 1995). However, although color use in children's drawings has been regarded as emotionally significant to the child, the majority of existing claims have tended to have been based on professional observation and often on the basis of drawings from a limited number of children (Hammer, 1997). In the following review of early and recent research it will be shown that some research studies have failed to include appropriate control groups, that some studies have used restricted age ranges, and that the majority of work has overlooked systematic independent validation of the artist's feelings towards the colors used and the topics drawn. It will be made evident that existing findings are also difficult to compare due to methodological differences such as the provision of different types and amounts of colors and requests for children to depict different topics and emotions across studies.

Relatively little experimental work investigating color use in relation to affect-eliciting topics has been conducted with children from mainstream populations, and such work within an experimental framework has had distinct limitations. For example, in examining children's use of color when painting, Alschuler and Hattwick (1943, 1947) made claims about aspects of children's personality traits on the basis of whether the children selected specific colors to paint a range of topics. For example, it was posited that children who used yellow were happier and possibly more neurotic than children who used other primary colors such as blue or red. However, the research suffered from neglecting to assess the children's feelings towards the colors they selected, leaving the resulting claims subject to question and alternative interpretation. It could for example have been argued that the children were responding on the basis of color preferences rather than on the basis of a particular affect related personality characteristic.

Early research designed to examine whether children's reaction to colors was based on a biological or a learned process has received the criticism that an appropriate age range was not included. For example, Lawler and Lawler (1965) found that even 3 and 4 year old children consistently associated yellow with happy pictures and brown with sad pictures and argued that the results showed support for Guilford's (1940) biological claim. However as Cox (2005) pointed out, these young children may have already had the opportunity to learn conventional color-affect associations as such associations are arguably relatively easy for young children to learn compared to other drawing skills. Whilst not convincingly explaining the children's behavior, such early research did establish a link between even very young children's emotional responses to color and the affective character of the pictures they were asked to draw.

The kind of topics and emotions to depict

A difficulty with concluding whether or not children reliably relate specific colors with specific emotions in drawing production is that existing research varies in the kinds of objects and experiences that children have been asked to portray and the kinds of emotion that they have been asked to represent. For example, research differs in terms of whether children have been asked to depict an experience of someone else or of themselves and whether the given experience is a positive or a negative one.

In a departure from the more projective orientation favored by earlier researchers, where color use was hypothesized to relate to personality traits and states, later work addressed the question of whether children would depict their own experiences due to the association of temporary mood states with particular colors. For example, Mumcuoglo (1991) conducted a study where kindergarten children were asked to draw their experiences of a negative emotion-eliciting experience, namely the experience of having head-lice. The finding that most children tended to depict head-lice in black led to the claim that children used black when depicting unpleasant experiences, and that their anxiety about the experience was translated into their drawings through such color use. However, no control group was included, children were not provided with a range of colored crayons from which to choose alternatives, and no account was taken during the interpretation of the findings of the point that head-lice appear black to the eye in real life and for this reason are often depicted in dark colors. Additionally, this work was based upon an assumption that the children held negative feelings towards head-lice, thereby assuming that the children's feelings were translated into their representations via the use of black.

Other researchers have asked children to draw affectively positive and negative described topics. In a sequence of studies Golomb (1992) asked children to depict positive or negative themes such as a happy, sad or angry child and initially found no association between the themes children were asked to portray and the colors they chose to depict them. She argued that this may have been due to the unengaging nature of the drawing topic and conducted a further study where children were asked to draw more salient topics based on their own personal experiences, such as a happy or a frightening dream.

Under these conditions, the 6 to 12 year olds were found to use brighter colors for happier dreams and darker colors for scarier dreams suggesting that when the drawing topics were made more salient, the color affect associations were translated into the drawings. As with earlier research, however, neither the children's feelings towards the dream scenes nor the colors provided were assessed by measures which were independent from the drawings themselves.

Researchers have also asked children to represent emotional themes of which they have not had direct experience with tasks designed to make the emotional qualities of color more salient to the children. For example, Winston et al. (1995) examined children's use of color to represent expressive themes in relation to events such as ageing and dying. Children were divided into groups, either using a restricted range of four non-representational colors which had been previously judged by children to have expressive qualities (for example, yellow being judged as a happy color), or using a larger range of colors which were judged by the researchers as representational of realistic colors for the topics. When color use was restricted, there were no age differences between 1st and 7th graders in their expressive use of color and ability to report that they had used a color for its expressive qualities. The authors argued that the provision of a restricted range of colors had focused children's attention towards the expressive properties of colors. Winston et al. also proposed that such use was deliberate on the part of even the youngest of the children. This research indicates that when children are encouraged to show differences between happy and sad scenes, they use combinations of colors differently to represent different emotional themes. It is not clear, however, from this study whether the children felt differently towards the events they were drawing or whether they were feeling the related emotion during drawing production. Yet, as with Golomb's (1992) research, this work highlights the importance of ensuring that the drawing topics which are interpreted for emotional relevance to the child are indeed salient to the children in the anticipated way.

It has also been found that when children are given a free drawing task, that is when they can select the subject of the picture, children between the ages of 4 and 9 years consistently use brighter colors for happier topics, pastel shades for calmer themes and a wider selection of colors to depict sadder themes (Callaghan & MacGregor, 1997). However, as Cox (2005) highlighted, and as has been outlined above in relation to Mumcuoglo's work, color and form are often confounded in that it is difficult to tell whether children are selecting colors that correspond to the realistic colors of the theme, or to the emotion in question. There is subsequently a need for future research to tease apart these competing explanations.

One such study was conducted by Zentner (2001) who asked children to select colors in relation to happy, sad or angry faces. This design was intended to control for drawing topic in that whilst the emotional character of the faces was already depicted in a literal way, the children were free to choose a color to color in the faces to convey the emotion in a more metaphorical way. He found that even the 3-year-olds chose brighter colors, especially yellow, to convey happy faces and darker colors to convey sad faces, while red was selected to show angry expressions. With the exception of the association between angry and red, these findings were replicated by Platten (2003), suggesting that when subject matter is controlled even children as young as 3 years of age can choose colors metaphorically to convey a specified emotion (see also Trautner, Chap. 11).

Hence, in the collection of recent research presented above it can be seen that the research differs greatly with respect to a variety of features. Children have been asked to portray their own experiences, the experiences of others, and they have been given the option to use colors in combination with other drawing strategies and in isolation to complete pre-drawn stimuli. In addition, no standardization of colors has been ensured across the research with different studies offering children different numbers of colors which possibly also vary in hue and tone. This diversity makes it difficult to compare the research claims and to assess whether children reliably associate certain colors with certain experiences and topics in their drawings or to assess whether the children were actually feeling the appropriate way towards the colors and topics in question at the time of drawing.

This last point is important to the interpretation of why children choose certain colors in relation to specific emotions as it could be argued that the above research has overlooked the important consideration that children may, at least in part, have chosen colors in relation to their color preferences rather than in relation to their feelings towards the topics in question. The majority of research in the field has not directly assessed the children's alleged feeling towards the topics in their pictures and has also largely overlooked the role that color preferences may play in drawing behavior. We turn then to an emergent line of research which has developed the methodologies of previous work in an attempt to understand the possible influence of color preferences on children's color use for emotionally characterized figures.

The influence of color preference on color use

The relationship between children's color preferences and color choice when depicting affect-eliciting topics has received some experimental study. Nelson et al. (1971) examined the influence of color preference and cultural group on Northwest Canadian children's color choice when drawing affect-eliciting topics. Children were permitted to use multiple colors with color preference defined as a preference for hue rather than tone. Color preference was measured by differences in crayon weight before and after the drawing session. The authors claimed that a hierarchy of color preference predicted cultural membership, yet they found no significant difference in crayon weight between the crayons used in drawings of daily events and the drawings of supposedly more affect-eliciting dream scenes. The lack of crayon weight difference was interpreted to show that there was no difference in preference for the colors that children chose to depict the different drawing types. Problematic for the claims of this research, however, is the point that the authors were not present at the administration of the test, and even though it is reported that all precautions were taken against the crayons chaffing and incurring weight loss during posting, it still may be possible that differences between the use of preferred colors were masked by such procedural difficulties. In addition, the influence of the affective characterisations on color use can only be assessed if, unlike the above work, independent ratings of the children's perception of the different significance of the topics and of the colors used are included.

A recent sequence of studies has attempted to systematically examine the impact that children's color preferences have on the choices children make to color pictures of emotionally characterized topics. Derived from a paradigm originally used by Thomas, Chaigne, and Fox (1989) to assess the impact of emotional descriptions on the size of children's human figure drawings, Burkitt, Barrett, and Davis (2003a) asked 330 children aged 4-11 years to complete two counterbalanced test sessions. In one session the children rated and ranked their favorite colors from a range of ten colors. In the other session they were asked to color in a baseline uncharacterized outline figure, followed by two further outline figures characterized as nice and nasty in counterbalanced order. The children rated their feelings towards each figure immediately after the completion of each drawing. To ensure that the children's color preferences and use of specific colors could be analyzed in relation to the emotional character of the drawing topic, color choice was restricted to one color per drawing for each outline figure. It was found that children across the age range used colors in relation to both their color preferences and the emotional characterisation of the human figures. More preferred colors were chosen for the more liked nice figures and least liked colors were chosen for the less liked nasty figures. In addition, children's choice of particular colors indicated overall that primary colors were predominantly selected for the baseline task, and a wider range of mainly primary and secondary colors were chosen for completion of the nice task. In all age groups, for all topics, black was the most discriminating response when completing negatively affectively characterized models in line with claims from earlier studies (e.g., Hammer, 1958, 1997; Machover, 1949; Mumcuoglo, 1991).

Whilst supporting the majority of past findings that darker colors tend to be more closely associated with negative topics and brighter colors for positive topics, this work also showed that color preferences directly influenced the specific colors children chose for their drawings. Indeed, when the emotion terms of happy and sad rather than nice and nasty were used to describe the drawing figures, Burkitt and Newell (2005) found a similar tendency. The 4- to 11-year-old children selected colors in relation to their color preferences in line with the emotional descriptions of, and their own feelings towards, the topics.

There is also some evidence that the specific colors children regard as happy or sad are educationally specific. For example, in contrast to the dark colors used in drawings of negative figures by the children in Burkitt et al.'s (2003a) study of children sampled from mainstream schools within the United Kingdom, children who had exclusively attended Steiner schools in the United Kingdom tended to select yellow as the predominant color to depict sad figures. Recent work has also shown that some colors are used differently between different cultures in relation to happiness and sadness, suggesting that some color-affect associations are acquired through cultural mechanisms from an early age (Burkitt, Tala, & Low, 2007).

The results from such recent research indicate that children do alter their color choice during color completion tasks in response to differential affective topic characterization, and also are consistent with the suggestion that children can use color symbolically from a young age (Golomb, 1992; Winston et al., 1995). Taken together, these findings high-light the value of ascertaining children's color preferences for the colors provided at the time of drawing when an interpretation of children's color use is made.

Thus, recent studies have indicated that children's changes in color choice are re-lated to their preferences for particular colors and the way that the children feel about the happy, sad, nice and nasty figures that they have been asked to portray. These re-sults, however, are in contrast with the earlier work of Nelson et al. (1971) who found no differences in color preferences for the colors used in children's drawings of a dream scene and a daily event. However methodological differences between their work and that of Burkitt et al. (2003a) may account for the conflicting findings. Firstly, different measures of color preference were used. Burkitt et al. used rating and ranking measures of preference whereas Nelson et al. inferred preference from the difference in crayon weight before and after the children had produced their drawings. Such a definition does not entail that the children necessary liked the particular colors they were using. Secondly, Burkitt et al. restricted children's color use to the choice of one color per drawing. The use of one color was intended to allow assessment purely of color use, not as it might relate to drawing ability or other drawing strategies (Nel-son et al., 1971; Winston et al., 1995), whereas Nelson et al. allowed children to use more than one color. Children in their study may well have been employing a different strategy influenced by using colors in certain organizations. Thirdly, a wider range of crayons was provided in the more recent research (Burkitt et al., 2003a, 2005; Burkitt & Newell, 2005; Burkitt et al., 2007), and it may be that children's preferred colors were not included in Nelson et al's study. Lastly, children's differential perceptions of, and feelings towards, a dream scene and a daily event was assumed by Nelson et al. with the assumption that the dream scene represented a topic with greater emotional significance than the topic of a daily event. Clearly there are core differences between the methodologies of the two approaches to the study of children's color use. It could be argued, therefore, that such results are not directly comparable, only that the series of studies by Burkitt and colleagues provided additional experimental support, and independent evidence for, the children's feelings towards the colors offered and topics in question. The work also gives further support for the idea that children will use spe-cific colors in relation to certain affective stimuli in certain drawing contexts. How-ever, whilst research in this area has advanced methodologically to systematically as-sess children's application of color-affect associations in drawings of affect-eliciting figures, certain issues persist which limit the research claims. An examination of some of these limitations and suggestions for future research will now be presented.

Changeability of color preferences and colors used

One limit on the generalizability of research investigating the impact of color preferences on color use regards the possibility that children's color preference ratings are unreliable over time and vary across different situations. For example, Gelineau (1981) conducted a study with adults looking at the reliability of their color preferences, administering a color preference sort task twice, at the beginning and end of a five week period. Color choices on the two sessions were computed using the Q technique (Stephenson, 1953), and the range of correlation coefficients were found to vary from 0.39 to 0.86. Gelineau (1981) concluded that while some people were consistent with their choices, others were not. Interestingly, there was a sex difference. Females gave more consistent color preference ratings than males. Additionally, people who stated that they were deliberately choosing a different order of colors on the second occasion unintentionally resulted in ranking preference in the same order, implying, according to Gelineau, a dependable process in some individuals which is perhaps unconscious.

Although the measures of color preference in recent research have correlated highly (Burkitt et al., 2003a, 2005), it is an open question as to whether children would produce a different profile of preference on different occasions and whether this pattern would vary between the genders. Indeed there is evidence that boys and girls have markedly different favorite colors in early and middle childhood (Boyatzis & Varghese, 1993; Burkitt et al., 2003a). In addition, research with clinical groups has shown that girls integrate more color in their responses to the Rorschach test (Ames, Metraux, & Walker, 1971) than boys, and use color at an earlier age than boys in their drawings of common objects (Milne & Greenway, 1999). Longitudinal research with attention to individual differences might show that the particular colors chosen in relation to affective stimuli would vary over time, between the genders and maybe within the same individuals.

Which colors to provide?

Another consideration for future research is a point raised by Zentner (2001) who argued that results across existing studies cannot be compared as the research varies in the types and amounts of colors provided and rarely the exact hues and tones of the colors involved are reported. Such a development is necessary in order to be confident about comparing the use of the same and different colors across studies. For example, a red in one study may not be the same red as that employed in another study. Thus some standardization of colors in future research would help to clarify children's use of color-affect associations in their drawings. It is also necessary for future research to ascertain whether children are choosing their favorite color in relation to hue and tone in general or whether the color is chosen as it is their relative favorite from the range provided in an experimental setting.

Flexibility and developmental change of color-affect associations

In line with claims from literature focusing on cognitive and motor factors involved in drawing production, it seems that even young children have a wide range of strategies to draw upon when portraying figures, and that there is flexibility within these graphic routines (Arazos & Davis, 1989; Barrett, Sutherland, & Lee, 1987; Burkitt, Barrett, & Davis, 2003a; Crook, 1984; Davis, 1983; Light & McEwan, 1987; Sitton & Light, 1992; Trautner, 1995, 1996). The results of recent research (Burkitt et al., 2003a; Burkitt et al., 2007; Golomb, 1992; Winston et al., 1995) lend weight to the claim that even very young children can use color-affect associations in a flexible way when portraying affectively characterized figures. However, it is not yet clear how and when this learning begins. Future research with measures to assess very young children's color-affect associations and color choices would be needed to clarify these points. Children could be tested using drawing tasks along with perceptual tasks (Cotterill, 1989; Jolley, 1995) to assess when children are responding from realistic or expressive color conventions in their drawings, and to assess at what age such behavior begins.

It has been claimed that both the quality and quantity of children's use of symbolic drawing activity in relation to apparently affect-eliciting topics increases with age (Gardner, 1978; Ives, 1984) and future research could be developed in order to assess how children's use of color and other drawing strategies interplay over time to convey emotional character in drawings of topics where children have feelings towards the topics involved.

Future research questions

Are children deliberately choosing color in line with preferences?

It remains an open question as to whether children's color choices in relation to color preference are the result of a deliberate strategy, namely whether the children (in line with Winston et al.'s, 1995, claims) planned to use colors to signify the emotional character of the drawn figures and how they felt about the figures. It may be the case that children's color preferences influenced their behavior in a less direct way in line with Parson's (1987) stage theory where favoritism is a key feature of the early stages of aesthetic development. It could be argued that favoritism guided the younger children's aesthetic preferences for color, but as children aged they were able to be guided by more formal aesthetic aspects of color use within a picture. One possibility is that children simply use their favorite colors but as they mature, color is used to express first the "real" color of the subject depicted and later the affective tone the artist wishes to convey.

Within therapeutic settings, children are frequently asked to discuss their drawings and their graphic intentions, yet well-controlled research in this area is only beginning to elicit knowledge about children's drawing intentions (Kindler, 2000; Rostan, 2000; Winston et al., 1995). There are clearly concerns for using verbal reports to assess intention with young children in that they are likely to underestimate children's understanding of their own behavior (Housen, 1983; Rosenstiel, Morison, Silverman, &

Gardner, 1978). However, if care is taken to validate children's self-reports with adult observations of the use of color in the same drawings, understanding of children's intent regarding expression and/or depiction of emotion through color choice could be further advanced.

Using color to communicate affect?

Children's color use often continues to be seen as a resource for children to communicate their feelings to an audience (cf. Hammer, 1997; Hunsley et al., 2003), yet this proposition has not been explicitly tested using systematic study. Children have been shown to change their graphic responses during communication tasks (Callaghan, 1999; Light & Simmons, 1983; Sitton & Light, 1992), and it would be of interest to assess whether a communicative context would increase the salience of the characterized topics, and lead children to alter their use of color to communicate emotional character. Freeman's (1995) proposition, that children become increasingly aware of intentional relationships between the artist, the drawings, and the audience, could be tested in relation to color use as it is conceivable that children would alter their use of color depending on who they understand will comprise the audience.

Where is the emotion?

A central difficulty in understanding how and why color-affect associations influence drawing behavior is the point that while various researchers have claimed that emotion is related to children's color use, these theories vary about where exactly the emotion resides in the process; namely that children's color use may be related to the way children feel about a color (Nelson et al., 1971; Winston et al.,1995), to the level of emotional adjustment and personality of the artist (e.g. Alschuler & Hattwick, 1943, 1947; Brick, 1944; Hammer, 1958, 1997), to the emotional qualities associated with the colors themselves (Miljkovitch de Heredia & Miljkovitch, 1998; Mumcuoglo, 1991; Winston et al., 1995), and to the topic which they are representing (Mumcuoglo, 1991). More recently, research has shown that children's color use is influenced by the provision of emotional characterisations of a topic, and to children's color preferences (Burkitt et al., 2003a, Burkitt & Newell, 2005; Burkitt et al., 2007). It is not clear, however, from this research whether or not the relationship between color choice and color preference is as causal as has previously been claimed (Nelson et al., 1971). If children are applying a common convention it remains an area for future research to uncover the source of this behavior and to clarify in what ways affect interacts with such conventions. Future research could also assess the extent to which color use is culturally relative, reinforced by educational and/or domestic values, and whether cultural differences in emotional expression may influence the tendency of color preference to be related to color use to convey emotional character.

Is emotion activated at the time of drawing?

Although there have been claims that children are motivated to use color by the way they feel about the color (Burkitt et al., 2003a; Burkitt et al., 2007; Burkitt & Newell, 2005; Nelson et al., 1971) and by the figures they are drawing (Burkitt et al., 2003a; Zentner, 2001), it still cannot be claimed on the basis of existing research that the children's emotions were activated at the actual time of drawing production. To say this would require independent measures of the children's actual feelings at the time of color choice, possibly through the use of observational data and/ or physiological measures taken at the time of testing. The use of such measures would increase the validity of claims attesting to the direct impact of emotion on drawing behavior.

Other future directions?

Previous research has shown that topic significance can be successfully manipulated by the provision of emotion terms. The findings have provided some reason to believe that, while the tendency to use color in relation to preference is relatively insensitive to the exact sets of emotion terms employed, the choice of particular colors seems to vary in relation to whether children draw happy and sad figures or nice and nasty figures (Burkitt et al., 2003a; Winston et al., 1995). Thus, there is reason to assess the generalizability of the present findings using the same paradigm in situations where other sets of contrasting emotion terms are used, for example angry versus calm.

The majority of research attesting to the role of affect in children's color choices has been established with children from mainstream populations. To enhance the theoretical and applied value of work in this area, future research could examine the development and use of color-affect associations of children with different developmental pathways, especially with those children whose drawings are used as part of assessment and therapeutic procedures where their drawings and color use continue to be interpreted for emotional salience. A range of drawing tasks could also be employed in order to advance to naturalistic relevance of the research, for example, where children are free to choose multiple colors, additional drawing strategies, and to nominate their own drawing topics.

Conclusions

Unlike earlier research in the field, recent work has not assumed that children's choice of color reflects aspects of the child's personality or emotional state but has instead attempted to understand the ways in which color choice is related both to the children's feelings towards the drawing topics in question and the children's feelings towards the colors they use. Overall it seems that while primary and secondary colors are more highly associated with neutral and nice and happy figures (Burkitt et al., 2003a; Burkitt & Newell, 2005; Golomb, 1992; Winston et al., 1995), brown and black are predominately associated with children's drawings of nasty and sad figures (e.g. Alschuler & Hattwick, 1943, 1947; Burkitt et al., 2003a; Burkitt & Newell, 2005; Miljkovitch de Heredia & Miljkovitch, 1998; Mumcuoglo, 1991), and children's preferences for specific colors also influence how they depict more or less liked topics (e.g., Burkitt et al., 2007; Nelson et al., 1971).

Systematic research examining children's feelings in relation to color use is at a very early stage, and a small collection of research has shown that effects of topic salience and characterization on color choice do occur (e.g. Burkitt et al, 2003a; Golomb, 1992; Winston et al., 1995). Support for the claim that young children use color symbolically in relation to affect-eliciting topics is growing (Golomb, 1992; Nelson et al., 1971; Winston et al., 1995), even when children are not restricted to the use of symbolic colors (Winston et al., 1995).

However, as argued above, future research is needed to further examine the reliability of children's color use over time across different drawing contexts and with different populations of children. Standardization of colors across the research is also required in order to make valid comparisons between research findings. It is also the role of future enquiry to develop a more comprehensive theory about the various mechanisms which influence children's color use than have previously been ventured in the literature. Overall, the existing findings suggest that a complex interplay between a range of factors (e.g., color preference, affect, educational background and cultural values) influences children's use of color in drawings of characterized figures and salient topics, and that we are only beginning to understand the basics of how children's color-affect associations are translated into children's drawing behavior. A theory which can account for children's color choices over a range of contexts would be valuable in order to enhance the accuracy with which children's colors choices are interpreted as signs of their feelings toward the topics which they draw.

References

Alschuler, R., & Hattwick, L. A. (1943). Easel painting as an index of personality in pre-school children. *Journal of Orthopsychiatry, 13*, 616-625.

Alschuler, R., & Hattwick, L. A. (1947). *Painting and personality. Volumes I and II.* Chicago: The University of Chicago Press.

Ames, L. B., Metraux, R., & Walker, R. (1971). *Child Rorschach responses: Developmental trends from 10 to 16 years.* New York: Brunner-Mazel.

Arazos, A., & Davis, A. (1989). *Young children's representation of gender in drawings.* Poster presented at the British Psychology Developmental Section Annual Conference, Guildford, Surrey, September.

Barrett, M. D., Sutherland, A., & Lee, F. (1987). *Visual realism in children's drawings: The effects of instructions.* Paper presented at the British Psychological Society Developmental Section Annual Conference, York, September.

Boyatzis, C.J., & Varghese, R. (1993). Children's emotional associations with colors, *The Journal of Genetic Psychology, 155*, 77-85.

Brick, M. (1944). The mental hygiene value of children's art work. *American Journal of Orthopsychiatry, 14*, 136-146.

Burkitt, E., Barrett, M., & Davis, A. (2003a). The effect of affective characterisations on the use of color within children's drawings. *Journal of Child Psychology and Psychiatry, 44*, 445-455.

Burkitt, E., Barrett, M., & Davis, A. (2003b). The effect of affective characterisations on the size of children's drawings. *British Journal of Developmental Psychology, 21*, 565- 584.

Burkitt, E., Barrett, M., & Davis, A. (2004). The effect of affective characterizations on the use of size and color in drawings produced by children in the absence of a model. *Educational Psychology, 24*, 315-343.

Burkitt, E., Barrett, M., & Davis, A. (2005). Drawings of emotionally characterised figures by children from different educational backgrounds. *International Journal of Art and Design Education, 24*, 71-83.

Burkitt, E., & Newell, T. (2005). Effects of human figure type on children's use of color to depict happiness and sadness. *International Journal of Art Therapy, 10*, 1-8.

Burkitt, E., Tala, K., & Low, J. (2007). Finnish and English children's color use to depict affectively characterized figures. *International Journal of Behavioral Development, 31*, 1-6.

Callaghan, T. C. (1999). Early understanding and production of graphic symbols. *Child Development, 70*, 1314-1324.

Callaghan, T. C. & MacGregor, L. (1997). *Children drawing emotion and experiencing emotion.* Unpublished manuscript, St Francis Xavier University, Nova Scotia.

Cox, M. (2005). *The pictorial world of the child.* Cambridge: Cambridge University Press.

Cotterill, A. R. (1989). *Children's production and judgements of drawings of emotionally significant topics.* Unpublished manuscript, University of Birmingham, School of Psychology, Birmingham.

Crook, C. (1984). Factors influencing the use of transparency in children's drawings. *British Journal of Developmental Psychology, 2*, 213-221.

Davis, A. M. (1983). Contextual sensitivity in young children's drawings. *Journal of Experimental Child Psychology, 35*, 478-486.

Freeman, N. H. (1995). The emergence of a framework theory of pictorial reasoning. In C. Lange-Küttner & G. V. Thomas (Eds.), *Drawing and looking: Theoretical approaches to pictorial representation in children* (pp. 135-146). New York: Harvester Wheatsheaf.

Gardner, H. (1978). *Developmental Psychology: An Introduction.* Boston: Little Brown.

Gelineau, E. P. (1981). A psychometric approach to the measurement of color preference. *Perceptual and Motor Skills, 53*, 163-174.

Golomb, C. (1992). *The Child's Creation of a Pictorial World.* Berkeley, CA: University of California Press.

Guilford, J. P (1940). There is a system in color preferences. *Journal of the Optical Society of America, 30*, 455-459.

Hammer, E. F. (1958). *The clinical application of projective drawings.* Springfield, IL: C. C. Thomas.

Hammer, E. F. (1997). *Advances in projective drawing interpretation.* Springfield, IL: C. C. Thomas.

Housen, A. (1983). *The eye of the beholder: Measuring aesthetic development.* Unpublished doctoral dissertation, Harvard University Graduate School of Education, Boston.

Hunsley, J., Lee, C. M., & Wood, J. M. (2003). Controversial and questionable assessment techniques. In S. O. Lilienfeld, S. J. Lynn & J. M. Lohr (Eds.), *Science and pseudoscience in clinical psychology* (pp. 39-76). New York: Guilford Press.

Ives, S. W. (1984). The development of expressivity in drawing. *British Journal of Educational Psychology, 54*, 152-159.

Jolley, R. P. (1995). *Children's production and perception of visual metaphors for mood and emotion in line drawings and in art.* Unpublished doctoral thesis. University of Birmingham, Birmingham.

Kindler, A. M. (2000). *Drawing development through the lenses of age and culture.* Poster presented at the 30th Annual Meeting of the Jean Piaget Society, Montreal, June 1-3.

Lawler, C., & Lawler, E. (1965). Color-mood associations in young children. *Journal of Genetic Psychology, 107,* 29-32.

Light, P. H., & McEwan, F. (1987). Drawings as messages: The effect of a communication game upon production of view-specific drawings. *British Journal of Developmental Psychology, 5,* 53-60.

Light, P. H., & Simmons, B. (1983). The effects of a communication task upon the representation of depth relationships in young children's drawings. *Journal of Experimental Child Psychology, 35,* 81-92.

Lowenfield, V., & Brittain, W. (1970). *Creative and mental growth,* 5th Edition. New York: MacMillan.

Machover, K. (1949). *Personality projection in the drawings of the human figure.* Springfield, IL: C. C. Thomas.

McNiff, S. (1998). *Art-based research.* London: Jessica Kingsley publishers.

Miljkovitch de Heredia, R. M., & Miljkovitch, I. (1998). Drawings of depressed in-patients: intentional and unintentional expression of emotion states. *Journal of Clinical Psychology, 54,* 1029-1042.

Milne, L. C., & Greenway, P. (1999). Color in children's drawings: The influence of age and gender. *The Arts in Psychotherapy, 26,* 261-263.

Mumcuoglo, K. Y. (1991). Head lice in drawings of kindergarten children. *Israel Journal of Psychiatry and Related Sciences, 28,* 25-32.

Nelson, T. M., Allan, D. K., & Nelson, J. (1971). Cultural differences in the use of color in NorthWest Canada. *International Journal of Psychology, 6,* 283-292.

Parsons, M. J. (1987). *How we understand art: A cognitive developmental account of aesthetic experience.* Cambridge, MA: Cambridge University Press.

Platten, M. (2003). *Can children use color expressively? Specific color associations with happiness, sadness and anger.* Unpublished undergraduate project, University of York.

Rosenstiel, A. K., Morrison, P., Silverman, J., & Gardner, H. (1978). Critical judgement: A developmental study. *Journal of Aesthetic Education, 12,* 95-107.

Rostan, S. M. (2000). *A study of the emergence of an artistic and creative identity.* Poster presented at the 30th Annual Meeting of the Jean Piaget Society, Montreal, June 1-3.

Sitton, R., & Light, P. (1992). Drawing to differentiate: flexibility in young children's human figure drawings. *British Journal of Developmental Psychology, 10,* 25-33.

Stephenson, W. (1953). *A study of behavior.* Chicago: University of Chicago Press.

Thomas, G. V., Chaigne, E., & Fox, T. J. (1989). Children's drawings of topics differing in significance: Effects on size of drawing. *British Journal of Developmental Psychology, 7,* 321-331.

Trautner, H. M. (1995). *The development from segmentation to contouring in children's human figure drawings.* Paper presented at the 25th Annual Symposium of the Jean Piaget Society, Berkeley, June 1-3.

Trautner, H. M. (1996). *Drawing procedures in children's free drawing, copying and tracing of the human figure.* Paper presented at the Piaget Centennial Conference, Geneva, September 14-18.

Winston, A.S., Kenyon, B., Stewardson, J., & Lepine, T. (1995). Children's sensitivity to expression of emotion in drawings. *Visual Arts Research, 21,* 1-14.

Zentner, M. (2001). Preferences for colors and color-emotion combinations in early childhood. *Developmental Science, 4,* 389-398.

Chapter 7

Children's Drawing of Friendship and Family Relationships in Different Cultures

Giuliana Pinto
University of Florence

Anna Silvia Bombi
University of Rome "La Sapienza"

Introduction

In this chapter we will address the use of drawing as a means to study children's representations of interpersonal relationships in different cultures. After a brief review of the developmental importance of relationships with adults and age mates, we will discuss the relevance of the children's representation of relationships for psychological research and practice. We will then clarify why drawing can be considered a valuable tool to investigate children's representation of relationships. We will compare the traditional projective tests with PAIR (Pictorial Assessment of Interpersonal Relationships), a new instrument we created, which makes a communicative use of drawing. In this section, we will underscore merits and limitations of the two approaches, we will describe the structure of PAIR and we will present some instances of the empirical data on which it is based.

In the final section we will address some questions about children's ability to produce pictorial representation of human figures in relation to cultural norms as a base for research on children's pictorial representation of their social life. We finally summarize the results of studies, conducted with PAIR by us or by other researchers in order to study children's relationships in different cultures, beginning with our early work on friendship, carried out in a comparative vein, and then moving towards more recent studies, centred on the cultures themselves.

The importance of interpersonal relationships

Children do not develop in isolation: "Far more than any other species, humans seem programmed to form relationships with others, to rely on their relationship partner for support and assistance in times of trouble and to derive a sense of well-being from the relationships they create and cultivate" (Schneider, 2000, p. 1).

Children obviously depend on parents for physical and emotional security (Ambert, 1997) and, as the attachment theorists have demonstrated, these early relationships extend their effects over time. Early relationships not only create the basis of the personal self worth: they are the cradle of emotional competence and social understanding. As children grow older, other relatives besides mother and father (especially grandparents, Brussoni & Boon, 1998) and adults outside the family (such as teachers, Pianta, 2006) begin to play an increasingly important role in children's lives. Experienced members of society support and guide the younger, less experienced individuals, as they acquire information and develop new skills in a kind of apprenticeship (Rogoff, 1990).

The relationships with other children, for a long time undervalued by psychological research, have proved to be equally essential as the adult-child relationships, if not more important than them, as the provocative approach of Harris (1995) suggests. To experience sustained interactions with peers is essential for children's psychological adjustment (Bukowski, 2003), and both siblinghood (Kramer & Bank, 2005) and friendship (Berndt, 2004) provide significant developmental opportunities for experiences of this sort in the playground and in other contexts. Based on the seminal work of Piaget (1932) on moral development, several scholars have in fact demonstrated that the confrontation of perspectives which are different from one's own, but not so radically as those of a child and an adult, is crucial for cognitive and social development (Doise & Mugny, 1981; Selman, 1980).

In short, positive relationships with adults and age mates help the growing child to build a sense of security and self-esteem, to understand and express emotions, to develop his/her cognitive abilities and to acquire social norms and values; the links between positive social experiences in childhood and subsequent resiliency are well documented in longitudinal studies in contexts as different as North America (Coie, Lenox, Lochman, & Hyman, 1995), Europe (Stattin & Magnusson, 1989) and China (Chen, Rubin, & Li, 1995). On the other hand, the lack of such experiences deprives the child of basic opportunities and negative relationships can seriously harm children's development. In fact, violence in the family can be a school of aggression (Feldman & Weinberg, 1994; Patterson, 1995) and even when the adults' behavior does not reach the extremes of maltreatment, the poor quality of early relationships has been found to be crucial to later emotional and cognitive development (Baumrind, 1991; Sroufe 1995). On the other hand, peers can teach the child deviant values (Agnew, 1991) or can destroy his/her well-being, inflicting painful experiences of exclusion or victimization (Olweus, 1993). The negative effects of poor early relational experiences can be just as long-lasting as the positive effects of good relational experiences (Schneider, Richard, Younger, & Freeman, 2000; Waters, Merrick, Trebouse, Crowell, & Albersheim, 2000).

Why and how to assess the representation of interpersonal relationships

Given the importance of interpersonal relationships, the way in which children represent them has attracted scholars and practitioners alike; for these latter, to get information from children about their relationships with parents, teachers and peers is an important component of psychological assessment, certainly easier than direct observation and often more reliable than adults' reports. Researchers, on the other hand, consider the representation an intrinsic component of relationships themselves.

Relationships can be defined as psychological entities that require at least two participants and a series of interactions over an extended period of time (Hinde, 1979). Nevertheless, one cannot identify a relationship on the basis of observed interactions only; some relationships survive even if the partners cannot have any kind of interaction, and vice versa, social exchanges, even if frequent, do not grant that a relationship is formed. This amounts to saying that a relationship exists not only for its behavioral components, but also for some kind of partners' awareness and feeling. Moreover, in a relationship, actual interactions are affected by previous ones and may affect the following ones (Berscheid & Reiss, 1998); the continuity between interactions that take place in different circumstances is guaranteed by the way in which the partners perceive and remember them. In fact, the influence of previous interactions on following ones depends not only on what really happened, but also on the representations the partners have of their respective behavior, as well as of the underlying intentions. On this basis, Hinde argues that, "some of the most important characteristics of interpersonal relationships lie in the affective and cognitive components" (Hinde, 1997, p. 40). The emphasis on the cognitive/affective aspects of relationships led psychologists to consider not only what goes on between two individuals but also what goes on within each individual. In short, to fully understand interpersonal phenomena, it is important to know how relationships are represented.

This theoretical assumption has provided the rationale for numerous studies on representations of relationships, especially on adults (Duck & Gilmore, 1986), but also on children; these latter have been mostly conducted in revised versions of Piagetian theory, such as in the work of Damon (1977) or Selman (1980). By and large, this developmental literature shows a progression that reflects the course of cognitive development (O'Mahoney, 1989). Children seem to pass from a limited and somewhat self-centred social perspective to a broader appreciation of personal and societal factors (Kennedy & Itkonen, 2006; Lang, Reschke, & Neyer, 2006). In the early and middle childhood, when this progression is still midway, children interviewed about their social life give the impression of experiencing only "fleeting alliances precipitated principally by the momentary pleasure of sharing enjoyable activities" (Schneider, 2000, p. 130). Unfortunately, this portrait bears little resemblance to the children's social behavior, which is often very competent (as it has been widely documented by observational studies, such as those conducted by Dunn, 1993).

In our opinion, this paradox depends on the prevalent use of verbal tools such as interviews, questionnaires or written reports in which children are required to describe and/or conceptualize the relationships in which they are involved (Crutcher, 1994). Verbal reports can be of great value in providing information about the nature and quality of the children's relationships, but the developmental accuracy of these reports has often been questioned (Furman, 1996); in particular, the data about the children's social lives are inseparable from the linguistic competence on which they can count in order to talk about themselves and their partners. It is well known that as children grow older, their mastering of language increases (as a function of intellectual development and larger experience) allowing for the expression of increasingly elaborate concepts: and, in fact, the development of social competence from pre school through high school years parallels the developing language skills (Gallagher, 1993). The risk here is to interpret changes in children's language as changes in their social knowledge. In other words, the poor models of interpersonal relationships expressed by younger children could be (at least in part) a function of their linguistic limitations.

Theoretical perspectives on the drawings of relationships

The above considerations led us to reconsider drawing as an alternative means of expression, to complement, if not substitute, verbal tools in the assessment of children's representation of relationships. Drawing requires different representational abilities from verbal language, and reduces the risk of an overlap between conceptual and expressive limitations. Drawing is a form of iconic representation that reflects the distinctive features of the represented experience (Bruner, 1964), a "graphic speech" that conceptualizes an internal representation (Vygotsky, 1978). Children's representations of their relationships can be considered instances of "spontaneous concepts" as described by Vygotsky (1934), i.e., concepts that develop from the child's personal experiences, not from adults' verbal instruction such as scientific concepts. Spontaneous concepts might in fact be best expressed at the implicit level of children's pictorial expression, before an explicit (linguistic) mastery of them would be acquired. For these reasons, drawing can be "user friendly" for young children, who are indeed highly motivated towards graphic activity, one of their favorite and regular activities.

Other non marginal advantages of drawing lie in the nature of analogue representation, which includes, literally "in a glance", many features of a situation, which would require a flow of words to be described. A single, general instruction ("draw yourself and your best friend, to let me know what friendship means for you") can lead the child to elaborate quite complete information about the required theme, without the need for prompts typical of interviewing.

The use of children's drawings of salient relationships, in particular family (Corman, 1967), has a long tradition in psychology. This tradition is based on the psycho-dynamic approach of Freudian derivation, and posits that the child, thanks to the defensive mechanism of projection, unconsciously borrows – while drawing – symbolic forms which will be then "readable" by an external viewer; more recently a similar use of drawing has been made by attachment theorists (Fury, Carlson, & Sroufe, 1997).

This symbolic approach to children's drawings, even though widely used in clinical practice (within whose boundaries it maintains some value), has not received solid empirical support (see Thomas & Silk, 1990, for a review); in particular the symbolic interpretation of the drawing almost inevitably leads to subjective judgments. We tried to avoid the criticisms levelled against the projective approach, proposing to use drawing as a communicative instrument, a perspective that has been adopted by a limited number of scholars. Examples of such an approach in the field of children's direct social experience include Tallandini's investigation (1991) on the representation of school and Weber and Mitchell's research (1995) on the conceptualization of teacher, as well as the more recent work by Trautner and Campos-Ramirez (2004) on the representation of an ideal woman and an ideal man. Large scale social phenomena were also investigated through drawings, as in the studies of peace and war conducted by Povrzanovic (1997), and by Walker, Myers-Bowman, and Myers-Wall (2003). More abstract concepts of social relevance were also studied by means of drawing: children's knowledge of science (Peterson, 1997); children's perception of health and safety (Wetton & McWhirter, 1998); children's knowledge about literacy (Kendrick & McKay, 2004).

In a communicative perspective, it is not necessary to postulate the existence of defensive, unconscious mechanisms; moreover, drawings can be *read* without having recourse to always debatable interpretations of symbolic features. We only posited that children have ideas about their social world, and that some of these ideas are more easily visualized than verbally described. We assumed that when a child is asked to draw a picture of himself with another person he has to engage in a "search for meaning and likeness" (Golomb, 1981) or "search for equivalents" (Goodnow, 1977) which adequately demonstrates what he/she knows about interpersonal relationships. The subject does not necessarily have to be explicitly aware of his/her understanding of interactions, social rules, and so on, nor of his/her own efforts to realize the appropriate graphic representation of such understanding; it is sufficient to assume the existence of a tacit understanding (Grieve, 1990) about the theme which has to be drawn and the rules of graphic representation.

Rejecting a symbolic approach in favor of a communicative perspective entails some consequences. Validity of the data no longer depend on the ability of the psychologist to interpret the drawing produced by the child, because the drawing content has to be considered objectively, renouncing the use of the emotional reaction of the viewer as a source of knowledge (see Freeman, 1991, for an alternative model of the relations between viewer, artist, picture and reality; see also Freeman, Chap. 3). For this reason, informative drawings can be obtained without those cautions that are necessary to ensure validity to projective tools, namely a significant relationship between the psychologist and the child, within an appropriate clinical setting. A very short and simple training is sufficient to become able to collect drawings with a communicative purpose, and valid data can be easily gathered from large samples, making our method particularly useful in research contexts.

What of a social relationship can we see in a drawing?

When a child is required to draw two or more related persons he/she will necessarily arrange the characters in the page (near or far from each other, side by side or facing each other, etc.); details of the environment could be used to create a sense of proximity (e.g., by including two figures in a common area) or of distance (separating two figures by means of a pictorial element). Face, body and clothing of the characters will be more or less similar and, to the extent to which they are not identical, their differences will be open to convey a diversity of value (e.g., one figure bigger or more complete than the other). Characters could also be represented while doing something and their facial expressions and gestures could show some kind of emotion. Are these features sufficient to say something about human relationships?

Several models of interpersonal relationships, only partially overlapping, can be found both in the psycho-social and developmental literature. One of the more complete list of the features characterizing close relationships is that proposed by Clark and Drewry (1985), which includes the following seven dimensions: *Proximity, Intimacy, Shared Activity, Similarity in Attitudes, Similarity in Values, Conflict* and *Conflict Resolution*. Comparing these dimensions with the features of drawing described above, one could easily see that *Proximity* and *Intimacy* can be measured by the spatial arrangement of the figures; *Shared Activity* can be directly seen if the characters are represented while doing something; *Similarity in Attitudes and Values* can be metaphorical expressed by the similarity of bodies, faces and clothing. *Conflict* can be shown by the characters' actions, as well as by their emotional expression. In short, several features of close relationships can be illustrated in a drawing.

More difficult would be for a child to depict *Conflict Resolution*, at least if the drawing does not include speech balloons for the characters; and, in general, to reintroduce language in one way or another seems the only way (not exactly iconic!) to capture the temporal dimension of relationships, which is inevitably "frozen" in a single moment when a specific scene is chosen to represent the ongoing relationship. However, we can also find in a drawing something more than the dimensions proposed by Clark and Drewry (1985).

One relevant aspect is the distance between the characters, which is not simply the opposite of *Proximity*, neither pictorially, nor conceptually. In a drawing, two persons can be put near to each other to indicate *Proximity / Intimacy,* and at the same time they can be distanced by an interposed object; conversely, two persons can be drawn at the opposite ends of a page, but they can convey a remarkable sense of connection by looking to each other. In terms of how interpersonal relationships are conceived, it is almost self-evident that to be related to someone, while requiring to set up specific and stable links with the partner, does not entail the complete loss of one's own personal autonomy; on the contrary, a harmonious relationship requires a balance of connection and individuation (White, Speisman, Costos, & Smith, 1987). These twofold aspects of human relationships have not been treated exhaustively in the developmental literature. Only recently, as a results of the keen interest shown by developmental researchers in theories about the close relationships in adults, has the need been felt to consider the processes of individuation as an integral part of the building of social relationships, not only between child and adult, but also between child and child (Youniss & Smollar, 1989).

A second aspect not mentioned by Clark and Drewry (1985) is the differential value of the partners; but again, we have here something more than the lack of *Similarity.* Psychological affinity cannot be so extreme as to destroy the individuals' identities, and when two persons differ in one way or another, a space is created for a hierarchy. In a drawing, characters can be distinguished from each other by neutral features (i.e., characteristics that do not carry any sense of value, such as a yellow or a blue shirt, curly or straight hair, etc.) or by features that clearly convey a sense of value (such as a dominant position in the portrayed scene or a larger size). Here we use the term *value* as a generic indication of a qualitative difference, which can be metaphorically connected to the idea of personal worth, importance or power. These are very important organizers in social life shaping the nature itself of our relationships (Fiske, 1992): e.g., a child recognizes parents or teachers as endowed with more power than him / herself, but wants to be equal to a friend in this respect. Moreover, we use social comparison to assess our own worth, and we tend to judge both our partners and ourselves in such a way that we reach a positive outcome of one sort or another (*Self Evaluation Maintenance Model,* Beach & Tesser, 1995). For instance, if I am better than my friend in something, I can be proud of myself, but if it is my friend who is the best, I can be proud to be associated with him/her (Tesser, Campbell, & Smith, 1984). The importance of comparisons for personality development is fully acknowledged by the traditional pictorial tests, which take into consideration of the figures' value, both in comparative terms, as in the drawing of the family (Corman, 1967), and in absolute terms, as in the drawing of a person (Machover, 1949). It is important to note, however, that our procedure for the assessment of a figure's value does not re-introduce those symbolic interpretations we were just trying to avoid. In fact, we have considered as pictorial indices of value only quantitative differences between the figures and two indices of almost universal iconographic meaning, namely the figures' dimension and respective positions (for more detail, see Bombi & Pinto, 1993; 1998).

There is one more feature of our approach to be mentioned, namely the explicit inclusion of the self in the representation, which is not typical of the verbal studies: on the contrary, often children have been interviewed about "relationships in general".

However, as Rochat (2001, p. 129) points out "inter-subjectivity entails a basic differ-entiation between the self and others, as well as a capacity to compare and project one's own private experience onto another (the 'like me' stance)". This is why, apart from the cases in which the reference to the self would be unethical[1], we have typi-cally asked children to draw themselves with one or more partners. Besides the rele-vance of this procedure for a more in-depth understanding of children's relationships, the inclusion of the self in the drawing is procedurally useful, as we will explain later (see the section about Data collecting).

In short, indices of *Cohesion* and *Distancing*, *Similarity*, *Value*, *Emotions* and *Con-flict* have been included in an instrument, called PAIR (*Pictorial Assessment of Inter-personal Relationships*), which has been described , in progressively more refined ver-sions, in Italian (Bombi & Pinto, 1993; 2000) Spanish (Bombi & Pinto, 1998), and in English (Bombi, Pinto, & Cannoni, 2007). In the following section, we describe the PAIR.

Scales comprised in PAIR, their structure and function

Cohesion

Cohesion informs on the degree of the interdependence between the partners. It comprises six subscales, each providing a dichotomous score (0 = absence; 1 = presence)
1. *Looking at*: Is one figure in condition of looking at the other?
2. *Moving towards*: Does the posture of one figure tend to reduce the space between one-self and the other?
3. *Coordinated activity*: Is the activity of one figure coordinated to the presence and/or the activity of the other figure?
4. *Proximity*: Are the two figures near one another?
5. *Common area*: Are the two figures located in a common area, distinct from the re-maining space?
6. *Union*: Are the two figures united by a graphic element?

Subscales 1, 2 and 3 refer to the direction of partners' action; subscales 4, 5 and 6 refer to space organization.

Distancing

Distancing informs on the degree of autonomy of the partners. It comprises six subscales, each providing a dichotomous score (0 = absence; 1 = presence)
1. *Looking away*: Does one figure actively avoid looking at the other?
2. *Moving away*: Does the posture of one figure tend to increase the space between one-self and the other?

---

[1] For instance, when we have compared the representation of good and bad parents (see p. 141 in this chapter), we have not required children to portray their own family.

3. *Independent actions*: One figure acts by itself?
4. *Remoteness*: Are the two figures far apart?
5. *Individual area*: Is one figure set in an area of its own, distinct from the remaining space?
6. *Separation*: Are the two figures separated by a graphic element?

Subscales 1, 2 and 3 refer to the direction of partners' action; subscales 4, 5 and 6 refer to space organization.

Similarity

Similarity informs on the psychological affinity between the partners. It comprises five subscales, each giving a score ranging from 0 (no similarity) to 2 (maximal similarity).

1. *Height*: Are the two figures the same height?
2. *Position*: Are the two figures in the same position?
3. *Body*: Are the two figures the same as regards the form of the face and body?
4. *Attributes*: Do the figures display the same attributes?
5. *Color*: Are the two figures the same as regards the colors of body and attributes?

Subscales 1 and 3 refer to stable figures aspects; subscales 2, 4 and 5 refer to changeable figures aspects.

Value

Value informs on the comparative value of the two figures. It comprises five subscales, each giving a score ranging from 0 (parity) to 2 (maximal disparity):

1. *Space occupied*: Do the figure occupy the same amount of space?
2. *Dominant position*: Are the two figures on a par as regards their location on the page?
3. *Body detail*: Do the two figures have an equal number of parts?
4. *Number of attributes*: Do the two figures display the same number of attributes?
5. *Number of colors*: Do the two figures display the same number of colors?

Subscales 1, 2 and 3 refer to personal importance, subscales 4 and 5 refer to the figures embellishment.

Emotions

Emotions informs on the mood displayed by the two figures. It comprises three nominal categories, mutually exclusive:

1. *Well-being*: Does the figure show a positive emotion (joy, love etc.)?
2. *Hostility*: Does the figure show an aggressive emotion (anger, contempt etc.)?
3. *Malaise*: Does the figure show a negative emotion (sorrow, fear, pain etc.)?

The emotions show by the two figures can be combined to assess the Emotional climate of the relationship.

Conflict

Conflict informs on the disruption of the relationship. It comprises three ordinal categories:
1. *Opposition*: Does a figure dissent verbally or act in opposition to the other?
2. *Aggression*: A figure aggresses the other verbally of physically?
3. *Closure*: Does a figure refuse to interact with the other?

Capitalizing on the growing literature on children's drawings conducted in the framework of the *Human Information Processing* approach, and especially on the seminal works by Freeman (1980) and those summarized in Freeman and Cox (1985), we took into account not only the final product but also the process which results in the drawing. We found evidence in previous studies for the children's ability to draw intentionally the pictorial elements scored in each scale; where necessary, we conducted new studies and experiments, some published as independent papers, other summarized in books. Overall, these studies examined various possible constraints that could limit children's freedom of expression in their pictorial representation of relationships. For instance, we described how children vary the canonical human figure to show interacting characters (Pinto & Bombi, 1996); we verified that, from 6 years of age, children can control the shape and color of two human figures to maximize or minimize their similarity; we showed that neither the dimension of the figures nor the density of environmental elements has any impact on how the figures are drawn as near or apart from each other (Bombi & Pinto, 1993). Some validation studies have demonstrated that PAIR has a good psychometric structure and gives convergent information with open ended interviews (Bombi & Pinto, 1993; Bombi et al., 2007). Its application has repeatedly proved that PAIR is able to discriminate between different relationships (such as friendship and siblinghood) and catches individual differences (such as the diverse perspectives of boys and girls on friendship). Comparing siblings with non-identical and identical twins Lecce and Pinto (2004) have also provided very compelling evidence that children are not hindered by strict adherence to a realistic constraint when they try to depict a relationship. In fact, the similarity that identical twins introduce when asked to draw themselves to illustrate "what does it mean to have a sibling who is not perfect," matches the level of similarity found in the other dyads (siblings and non-identical twins); moreover, in all the dyads, identical twins included, similarity decreases when children are asked to represent themselves and their sibling in a moment in which they are in conflict or expressing negative feelings towards each other (see Figure 7.1).

Characteristics of PAIR

The validation and refinement of PAIR took a long time (see Bombi et al., 2007); here we will only report the main characteristics of this instrument, especially focusing on those which distinguish it from its more well-known predecessors. These characteristics, in extreme synthesis, can be classified in two groups: the manner of collecting the drawings, and the method of coding them.

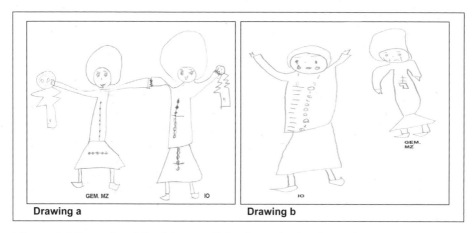

Drawing a   Drawing b

Figure 7.1 Example of flexible use of *Similarity* in drawings of a monozygotic twin (girl, 8 years old); drawing a: Twins in harmony, drawing b: Twins in conflict (Lecce & Pinto, 2004).

Data collection

The way in which children draw is highly contextual; they may scribble when they are annoyed, invent very creative forms when they are drawing for themselves, and adhere to canonical, "safer" representations when they know that their work will be submitted to a judgment of merit. For this reason the method we suggest for collecting drawings departs radically from projective tests. In those instruments the task is purposefully ambiguous, leaving space for the unconscious drives to unfold. Instead the researcher following our method will ask as clearly as possible (while avoiding suggestion) what the child has to represent: "Make me a picture of yourself with ... (a friend, a sibling, one or both parents, etc.), in order to let me know what it means for a child like you ... (to have a friend, a sibling, a mother and/or father, etc.)". The request to represent oneself as one of the portrayed characters is a powerful antidote to the use of stereotypical figures or to copying, even inadvertently from classmates when the task is not administered individually.

Even though it is possible to limit the task to a single drawing, as we did in our earlier studies, we found more and more evidence that it is highly useful to ask each child to produce *two drawings*, representing two comparable relationships (e.g., child-father vs. child-mother), or two aspects of the same relationship (e.g., friends in harmony vs. friends in conflict). Proposing the task in this contrastive form has two main advantages: for the child, it makes the task even clearer, helping him/her to focus on the relevant characteristics to be included in the drawing; for the experimenter it reduces the unnecessary variability (that could arise if children did not understand the task clearly) and at the same time it makes available more information about the graphic abilities and stylistic idiosyncrasies of the individual child. This is very important if one doesn't want to confuse the limitation in the child's graphic abilities with a lack of competence about the portrayed relationship, as we will explain later in greater detail.

Data coding

The description of the structure and function of the PAIR gives an idea of how our coding system is organized at a general level. For each relevant dimension we devised a scale (interval, ordinal or nominal) divided in subscales or categories, which allows the coder to focus each time on different aspects of the drawing. The indices to be considered in order to answer each of the questions of the PAIR are presented in detail, with graphic examples where necessary, in a coding manual, which is the result of our extended experience (overall we examined more than 10.000 drawings), as well as our empirical studies. To give the reader a better idea of the kind of instructions provided by the coding manual, the next section explains the indices to be considered in order to answer the question "Does the posture of one figure tend to reduce the space between oneself and the other?" and assign a score in the subscale C2 (*Moving towards*)[2].

Indices to be considered to assign the score in one of the subscales of Cohesion (Moving towards)

A figure receives a score in C2 when its position suggests a reduction of the space between itself and the other figure (without reaching contact with it) by (a) the act of walking towards the other or by (b) the act of stretching the upper limbs towards the other, without touching it.

(a) Walking may be indicated: by a raised foot (see pictorial scheme 1a in Figure 7.2) or by an outstretched leg (straight or bending) to an angle comprised between 30° and 90° with respect to the axis of the body (see pictorial scheme 1b in Figure 7.2)

(b) The outstretching of upper limbs may be indicated: in figures in profile, by one or both arms (straight or bending), forming with the body an angle comprised between 30° and 145° (see pictorial schemes 2a and 2b in Figure 7.2); in frontal figures, by both arms, more or less parallel, stretched (even slightly) towards the other figure; or by a lateral outstretching of a straight arm, forming with the body an angle comprised between 45° and 100° (see schemes 3a and 3b in Figure 7.2); or by a lateral outstretching of a bent arm, forming an angle of at least 90° between forearm and upper arm.

The examples illustrate the level of detail of the instructions provided, which is aimed at ensuring reliability, but is also a way to respect the freedom of the child to select one among the numerous pictorial options which could be adopted to show an increase of proximity between two figures. In this way, PAIR leaves space for stylistic

---

[2] Besides graphic examples of how to measure the angles, the manual also provides a list of cautions and special cases to take into consideration.

variations, which can arise from variations in the iconographic culture, individual taste, different graphic skills linked to the level of pictorial development reached by the child, as well as to his/her artistic talent (Gardner, 1980; Golomb, 1992; Milbrath, 1998; Tversky, Kugelmass, & Winter, 1991).

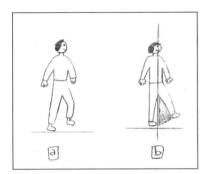

Pictorial schemes 1a - 1b

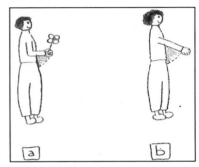

Pictorial schemes 2a - 2b

Pictorial schemes 3a - 3b

Figure 7.2 Illustrations of figure postures coded as *moving towards.*

We faced two more problems, arising from the variability of drawing both at a developmental and individual level. This should not surprise the reader: in fact our goal was not to measure drawing per se, as much as the ideas about relationships that children are conveying through it. The two main sources of "unwanted variation" are both linked to pictorial development: the larger number of details in the human figure and the increasing use of perspective in the organization of the space. The first problem was solved using weighted scores in several subscales of *Similarity* (*Body*, *Attributes* and *Colors*) and of *Value* (*Body detail*, *Number of attributes*, *Number of colors*). In other words, two figures are considered similar, e.g., for their body on the basis of the relative number of similar parts, not for the absolute number (which would create larger opportunities for a high score for those children who draw more detailed figures). The second problem was solved by distinguishing those drawings in perspective from the much more common drawings in which the figures are all aligned on the frontal-parallel plane, and giving separate coding instructions for each type of drawing.

Drawing and children's relationships across cultures

In the late 1980s, when we began to study friendship and siblinghood with PAIR, the need for studying children's social life from a cultural perspective was just beginning to be widely acknowledged. The anthropological and ethnographic studies of socialization were criticized as subjective (Clifford, 1986) and as biased by the researchers' perspective (Denzin, 1997). On the other hand, psychologists had studied children's relationships almost exclusively with Western middle class children, yet they had the ambition of describing universal trends (Cole, 1996). It's true that all children have the same basic relationships (with parents, siblings, other relatives, friends); however, psychological models of relational development should take into account also differences in these relational experiences, and not only the intra-cultural variations such as those linked to age, gender, social class, or life events, but the differences arising from the exposure to specific cultural backgrounds (Chen, French, & Schneider, 2006). When psychologists started to cross the cultural boundaries to investigate social development, they often employed methods developed within the framework of Western societies, which appeared insufficient to deal with the challenge of a wider application. The shortcomings of these methods were beginning to be noticed (Greenfield, Quiroz, & Raeff, 2000) but with very little concrete impact on the methodologies employed.

It was in this context that we realized the potential of PAIR for a cross-cultural study of children's representation of relationships. Drawing has been traditionally considered as a culture-free tool to assess the child's cognitive (Goodenough, 1926) or emotional development (Corman, 1967); but the question about the universal nature of graphic development is still not solved. Two main perspectives have been proposed in the literature about graphic development across cultures. One perspective supports the assumption of a relatively invariant succession of stages or phases in drawing development, based mainly on the fact that the same basic schemes can be observed in children's drawing at different ages, irrespective to their cultural background. The authors who identify themselves with this perspective recognize that cultural differences exist, but they are seen as "a limited set of variations on a common underlying structure, indicating that the same rules can generate alternative models that are representationally equivalent" (Golomb, 1992, p. 333). The other perspective does not dispute the overall trend in development from less to more complex structures, but suggests that what children are drawing has to be interpreted in the interactive context in which children's behavior is typically rooted (Vygotsky, 1978; Cole, 2002). According to this position, drawing is the product of culturally and socially transmitted conventions, which children come to know by seeing and reproducing the graphic models available in their life contexts (Sundberg & Ballinger, 1968; Wilson & Wilson, 1985; Van Meter & Garner, 2005).

These contrasting positions can be found also in the studies concerning the most crucial aspect for the cross-cultural use of PAIR, i.e., the depiction of the human figure. The critical question is: are there differences in the way children from various cultures would draw themselves and their social partners? And if differences exist, are they of such a nature as to prevent us from applying PAIR to assess children's representation of social relationships? Nobody could be so naïve as to think that there is a "natural" way of drawing a person; however, as Cox (1995) says "modern communication and advertising have helped to spread certain kinds of imagery all over the world. In addition, as more children world-wide receive schooling they become exposed to pictures and western imagery within the school context. Although we may still see local differences in the style of their pictures the gap begins to close" (p.75) A review of cross-cultural studies comparing the representation of the human figure in western and non-western populations does not support a view of graphic development as a rigid succession of stages, nor the opposite extreme position of drawing as composed of arbitrary signs (Cox, 2005).

In spite of this comforting consideration, we felt the necessity to examine some aspects of drawing development in contexts where the use of PAIR was planned, by ourselves or by other scholars. A series of studies were then conducted with the *Draw-a-Person Test* (Harris, 1963) in Bolivia (Fini, 2001), in Brazil (Zipoli, 2001; Tramonti, 2004), and in Cameroun (Prevete, 2004). These studies confirmed the above quoted conclusions of Cox (1998, 2005): in all the considered cultures, children's depiction of the human figure develops in a fairly regular, even predictable way, from scribbles, to simple forms, to more complex graphic structures; at the same time iconographic conventions within each culture play a role in orienting the selection of specific signs by means of which the mental representation of a person is transposed on the page, but the resulting differences are mainly stylistic and do not affect the structural characteristics of the human figure, as shown by the examples in Figure 7.3.

Stylistic differences, albeit evident, do not weight the scores assigned in the PAIR scales, as we presented our approach in the above paragraphs. These conclusions are supported also by the results of Tallandini and Dimitrova (2006) in a study with PAIR on Albanian, Serb and Italian families; the authors controlled the children's ability to represent human figures, finding equal access to the pictorial dimensions scored by our instrument.

We verified that children from 6 years of age were able to draw human figures in the Bolivian rural pre-technological environments. The Guaranì communities we had the opportunity to meet are social groups where there is no pictorial tradition apart from geometrical decoration, with virtually no access to the visual media and relatively limited exposure to schooling (Melià, 1988). In that context, when required to draw, children may be forced to construct their own solutions and can be hampered by technical limitations. We were particularly worried by the possibility that these children would have to draw non-canonical figures, which are especially difficult to execute. A study (Pinto & Bombi, 1995) was then conducted on the entire population of the village of Ipitacito which was comprised of 70 children between 6 to 11 years of age, and on two samples of middle-class children living in modern, technologically advanced environments: a group of Bolivian children living in the wealthy town of Camiri, and a group of Italian children from the town of Greve in Chianti (on the outskirts of Florence). In general, children's drawing is not greatly appreciated in the Bolivian culture, which places more emphasis on dance and music (Confalonieri, 1987).

Figure 7.3 Examples of stylistic differences in the human figures made by children from the Brazilian village and from the favela (Tramonti, 2004).

When drawing is taught at school (which rarely happens), teachers do not encourage children to try their own pictorial solution, and prefer to propose realistic drawings as models to be reproduced as "correctly" as possible. Italian children, on the contrary, enjoy a rich source of stimulation from illustrated books, which are as commonly available as in any other western country, and more than others they are exposed to the enormous pictorial patrimony found in public buildings and places of worship. In Italy, drawing activity is a relevant part of the curriculum in kindergarten (attended by almost all children), and is still present in the elementary school; the creation of personal pictorial solutions is always encouraged. In these very diverse cultural environments, differences are easy to forecast, but the results also show similarities. In fact, the older children in all three compared groups appeared to be able to represent human figures in profile, employing what we defined as a complex strategy, which includes displacement of elements, partial occlusions, shape variations of parts of the outlines (with respect to their canonical appearance) and concordant lateral orientation of body parts such as feet. On the other hand a simpler strategy, mainly based on the elimination of whole parts, appeared significantly influenced by culture, with young Italian children using it more frequently than their Bolivian age mates, and with no differences among these last. Figures 7.4 a and b present examples of the two strategies.

The access to this simple strategy could be explained – tentatively - by the opportunity provided to Italian preschoolers and elementary school children to experiment with pictorial signs as a free activity, for which even crude results are accepted and prized by the adults. Also the widely available models in illustrated books can play a role, providing some ready-made graphic solutions to the child, that are different from visually realistic pictures, and which are within the reach of non-skilled artist. In sum, this study shows that the capacity for representing figures in profile is present in the various cultures we looked at, even though the ability for doing so is not equal, particularly at early ages.

Figure 7.4a Example of simple strategy to draw a profile, combining elimination and displacement of parts; girl, 7 years old, Greve in Chianti, Italy (Pinto & Bombi, 1995).

Figure. *7.4b* Example of complex strategy to draw a profile, combining several displacement of parts, variations of their shapes and lateral orientation; girl, 10 years old, Guarani village, Bolivia (Pinto & Bombi, 1995).

Applications of PAIR to study friendship across cultures

Friendship has been the first close relationship we have studied with PAIR in Italy and the first we explored with this instrument in other countries (Pinto, Bombi, & Cordioli, 1997). Besides Bolivia, of whose iconic culture we have given some information above, we had the opportunity to collect data in Lebanon, a context rarely studied by psychologists in terms of socialization and never, as far as we know, adopting drawing as the research tool. Lebanon shares with the other Mediterranean countries a status of a Western technological culture, but has a different iconic tradition, much more interested in decoration than in figurative values. However, the main difference between Lebanon, and both Italy and Bolivia, is the war in which this nation has been recurrently involved, a condition which is still sadly a reality ten years after our research. All together, we had at hand groups of children whose cultural environment varied along the dimensions of war and peace (Lebanon vs. all the other countries), and collectivism and individualism (Bolivian Guaranì vs. all the other groups). Similarity between friends appeared the component of friendship most likely to be influenced by these dimensions. We then compared children's drawings of themselves with a friend, in order to determine whether children from two large cities (Rome and Beirut), two smaller towns (Camiri in Bolivia and Villafranca in Italy) and the rural pre-technological village of Ipitacito (Bolivia) would introduce the same amount of resemblance between the drawn characters. As we have seen above, pictorial similarity is an indication of psychological affinity, an important dimension of all close relationships, but especially of friendship, in which it constitutes one of the main conditions for reciprocity, and which in turn can be considered the basic deep feature of this relationship (Laursen & Hartup, 2002). In the study of adults, some authors have claimed that friendship is essentially the same in all cultures (Argyle, Henderson, Bond, Iizuka, & Contarello, 1986), while others have suggested just the opposite (Adamopoulos & Bontempo, 1986; Allan, 1989). Moreover, until the early 1990s, developmental studies about similarity between friends had been conducted in Western industrialized societies only. In short, the topic deserved attention, because one might legitimately question the universality of the models of children's friendship. To have richer information than the simple overall score in the Similarity scale, we also analyzed the scores in the subscales of which the scale was formed: *Dimensions*; *Position*; *Body*; *Attributes*[3].

The results indicated that there are more affinities than differences between the cultures considered. The children from all five groups illustrated friendship by endowing partners with similarities as well as differences in such a way that the resulting overall scores did not coincide either with the maximum possible similarity or with the maximum possible differences. It seems that in all environmental contexts a child would feel similar to a chosen partner "just enough" to be friends; at the same time he/she will feel the need to be different enough to maintain his/her personal uniqueness. Few differences emerged in the overall degree of similarity: only the Guaranì children, from the pre-technological rural community, endowed a greater degree of overall similarity to the drawn figures of the self and of the friend. However, other cultural variations emerged at the level of the Similarity subscales; in other words, the way in which the similarity was depicted was not the same even when its overall degree was comparable.

Both the Italian groups and the Bolivian children from Camiri expressed the affinity of friends mainly by putting them in the same position, which suggests a similarity of behavior, while the differences emerged mainly in the *Attributes*, i.e., the external signs of taste and resources which are so important in Western societies. Children from Beirut, while introducing as much overall similarity as their peers from Rome, Villafranca, and Camiri (with whom they also shared a preference for a similarity of *Position*) differentiated themselves from their friends much more in terms of *Dimensions*. These children often depicted one of the figures as taller and / or larger than the other, a type of representation that suggests a difference in age and / or strength between the partners. This in turn implies a lesser preoccupation for the egalitarian distribution of power between friends, and a preference for hierarchically organized relationships. Disparity, in fact, can turn into the opportunity of being protected or protecting the other, which might be psychologically important in critical situations, such as those experienced in a city where war is literally at the door. The fact that an increase

---

[3] In successive refinements of PAIR, we have separated the assessment of colors from the shape of *Body* and *Attributes* the scale of *Similarity* is now composed of five subscales.

in resemblance in the other parameters counterbalances the diversity in *Dimensions* supports the idea that a certain overall degree of affinity is necessary for expressing friendship independently of the circumstances in which it is created. Finally, let's consider the Guaranì children, whose figures were the only with markedly similar *Attributes*; in fact clothing and personal belonging are not used in their culture as elements that define individual identity as they are in the wealthier Western societies. To differentiate the partners, these children (in spite of their limited acquaintance with drawing) engaged in the difficult task of elaborating the body and facial features of each figure.

In sum, only the collectivist orientation appeared to carry weight on the amount of similarity between friends; the higher similarity introduced by the children of the pre-technological Bolivian villages can be a consequence of the emphasis placed by their communities on group identity over the individual self. On the other hand, the way in which similarity is achieved reflects the environmental circumstances in which children live.

Given the relevance of the collectivist organization for the children's representation of friendship, we conducted another study in Bolivia, comparing all the children of a Guaranì community with urban Bolivian children, all aged 6 to 11 years (Pinto & Bombi, 1997). This time, aspects of friendship under scrutiny were Cohesion and Distancing, which respectively express the existence of a link with the partner and the maintaining of one's own personal autonomy (Bombi & Pinto, 1995). Since to establish an interpersonal bond is the necessary condition for the existence itself of a relationship, we expected that all the children would include indices of Cohesion in their drawings of themselves with a friend. Nevertheless, in individualistic cultures, interpersonal bonding and autonomy are both considered important components of friendship, because the link which binds friends to each other should not be so exclusive as to hinder their goals as individuals. We thus expect that children from Camiri, with a prevalent individualistic orientation, will also include some Distancing in their drawings. The collectivist orientation of the Guaranì group should, on the contrary, be particularly effective in reducing the need for Distancing, which would appear to a lower degree than in the other samples. After assigning the scores in the two scales, we classified the drawings in six types, according to the combination of Cohesion and Distancing, ranging from drawings characterized by an exclusive or prevalent use of Distancing, to drawings in which Cohesion and Distancing are balanced, to drawings in which Cohesion prevails or is not combined with signs of Distancing. Balanced or cohesive solutions are overall preferred by children, but they are significantly more frequent in the Guaranì group. The children from Ipitacito are much more inclined than the children from Camiri to adopt pictorial solutions in which Cohesion is not combined with Distancing, that is drawings in which only the relatedness is shown. Moreover, in their group the two types of representation with Distancing only, or in which Distancing prevails over Cohesion, are extremely rare; this confirms our hypothesis about the reduced need, in this context, for individual autonomy. Here again to be members of a larger collective unit appears to affect social perception, supporting the value of intimacy and relatedness put on friendship: an interesting result, contradicting the expectation that a society characterized by a strong group commitment could impoverish personal close relationships (Raeff, Greenfield, & Quiroz, 2000).

Applications of PAIR to study family across cultures

Quite obviously, our further step in the study of the Guaranì culture was to analyze family relationships: in fact, little is known about how family is conceived by children in collectivist cultures. Although collectivist organization may not diminish children's basic needs for parental support, cultural differences may exist in terms of the degree of relatedness and autonomy expected among the family members. Studies on Cohesion and Distancing between children and their parents conducted in Italy (some of which are summarized in Bombi & Pinto, 2000) provided guidelines for the extension of PAIR beyond peer relationships. Pinto and Crispìn Arcienega (2001) however, were not interested in large scale differences, as would have been those between Italy and Bolivia, as much as the more in-depth comparison within two Bolivian environments; the 15 families of the Guaranì village of Chimeo (Santa Cruz Dept.) and the town of Villa Montes. In the Guaranì community the extended family plays a prominent role: grandparents, aunts, uncles provide a great deal of support and assistance for parents and their children. The 47 children in the age range between 5 and 11 years did not attend formal schooling. Villa Montes, instead, is a wealthy residential district, with a social organization very similar to other Western contexts. The authors asked children to draw "themselves with their family in order to show what a family is". Each drawing was scored separately for Cohesion and Distancing. Results show a higher degree of Cohesion in the drawings of the Guaranì children than those of Villa Montes. The Guarani children, however, did include Distancing in their relationships with parents, suggesting that the collectivist orientation of the community does not prevent children from perceiving their relationship with parents as both intimate and individuated, as shown by the examples in Figures 7.5 a and b.

Figure 7.5a Examples of high cohesion in drawing a family; boy, 10 years old, Guarani village, Bolivia (Pinto & Crispìn Arciénega, 2001).

Figure 7.5b Examples of low cohesion in drawing a family; boy, 10 years old, town, Bolivia (Pinto & Crispìn Arciénega, 2001).

Here support is given to the notion that the dichotomous conceptualization of individualism and collectivism has to be seen problematically and that independent and interdependent concerns coexist in the same culture (Killen & Wainryb, 2000).

Another interesting study on children's ideas about family relationships has been conducted in Brazil by Zipoli (2001), who used PAIR to compare children coming from the Igarassu favela (Pernambuco) and children from the village of Cruzeta (Rio Grande del Norte) from a population of middle and middle-low SES. All children were asked to produce four drawings, two representing a child with his/her mother in different situations ("when everything is OK" and "when things are not quite right"), and two representing the same situations between a child and his/her father. Here the source of possible cultural differences in the representations is the different composition of the families: extended, supportive families in the village, while in the favela there is a high incidence of mono-parental or disrupted families. The two groups of children did not differ in their representation of good relational moments with parents. The members of the portrayed dyads (child-mother and child-father) were similar (but not identical) to each other and the difference resulted in a larger value of the adult member of the dyad. The affective link between parent and child was shown by indices of Cohesion, which exceeded those of Distancing. When these drawings were compared with those of the "bad moments", the deterioration of the relationship was evident especially in terms of a significantly lower Cohesion, both between child and mother and between child and father, but only in the village children; the children from the favela, instead, did not modify this aspect of the drawing. Examples are given in Figure 7.6 a and b.

The author suggests that these children were unable to assume a critical view of the family, because they are extremely worried by the idea itself of a bad relationships between a child and his/her parents. In the favela, children don't have an extended family network to count on, in case of difficulties with parents; on the contrary, in a menacing situation of extreme poverty, mothers are the only practical and affective resource, while fathers are scarcely involved in children's education. The good or bad behavior of parents has to be forcibly accepted by children, who fear the risk of losing contact with their only support too much to indulge in any form of criticism. In considering Zipoli's (2001) explanations, we must keep in mind that other differences exist between the two groups (for instance, in the favela most of the children work, while in the village they live a much more typical children's life); even if the suggested interpretation appears reasonable, we cannot rule out the possibility that other factors would contribute to the obtained result.

Figure.7.6a Example of flexible use of Cohesion in drawings of the relationship with the parent in harmony vs. in conflict; girl, 8 years old, village, Brazil (Zipoli, 2001).

Figure 7.6b Example of less flexible use of Cohesion in drawings of the relationship with the parent in harmony vs. in conflict; girl, 8 years old, favela, Brazil (Zipoli, 2001).

The study of family relationships would not be complete without an analysis of siblinghood. Siblings share with friends the status of members of the new generation, and in this sense their relationship shares some analogy with friendship, in particular siblinghood is less *vertical* than adult-child relationships and allows for more equality, especially if the sibling ages are similar enough to moderate the status differences linked to birth order. Besides this, there are several important differences (Laursen & Bukowski, 1997): siblinghood is prescribed and permanent, as it is dictated by genetic and/or legal factors and is (at least in part) externally regulated by the adult members of the family; friendship, on the contrary, is voluntary and unstable. Children choose their friends and may lose them if the interaction rules they have negotiated fail to function in conflict solution. Are these notions about siblings and friends, based on Western societies, also valid in other cultures? Results from studies in different cultures suggest the relevance of the social rules applied to children's relations with their relatives and with their peers on their perception of close relationships (Schneider, 2000). And again, PAIR promised to be useful across cultures, as it was with Italian children to shed light on the distinctive features of sibling and friends relations (Bombi & Pinto, 1993; 2000; Lecce, Pinto, & Pagnin, 2003; Lecce, Pagnin, & Pinto, 2005). Fini (2001) and Prevete (2004) conducted two studies on this topic, co-operating with local researchers in order to have detailed accounts of the local social life: economy, living arrangements, social network, family composition, and child-rearing practices.

In the research performed by Fini (2001), Bolivian children from 6 to 11 years old were asked to draw themselves with a sibling and themselves with a friend. All the participants were recruited in Santa Cruz de la Sierra, but in three different educational environments. Two groups were children living in their families, and attending either a catholic state school or a private school; the third was a small group of orphans, living with their siblings in an orphanage and attending school within this institution. The first two groups represented friendship and siblinghood in different ways, which paralleled quite closely the representations that emerged in the Italian studies: friendship was characterized by higher levels of partners' Cohesion, Similarity and parity of Value than siblinghood, which instead more often presented signs of Conflict. The ability to recognize the different quality of the two relationships, however, did not appear in the group of orphans, as shown in Figure 7.7 a and b.

The author suggests that the life in the orphanage, with an over-emphasis on group interactions and rules, does not allow the children to experience dyadic relationships that are qualitatively specific, hence the tendency of these children to perceive their relationships with peers (siblings and friends) as undifferentiated. These considerations seem reasonable but, given the small number of the children, further evidence is required.

The Prevete's study (2004) aimed at comparing siblings' and friends' relationships across cultures. Prevete asked 120 children, aged 6 to 11, living in two areas of Cameroun, the city of Ebolowa and the forest village of Bimenguè, to draw themselves with the brother/sister nearest in age and to draw themselves with a friend. The study, performed in cooperation with local researchers, also contains detailed accounts of the local social life, which include descriptions of the living arrangements, economy, child-rearing practices, social network and family composition. Drawings were scored with four scales of PAIR (*Cohesion, Distancing, Similarity* and *Value*) and the results showed fewer differences between siblinghood and friendship as compared to the data on the Italian children reported by Lecce et al. (2003) and Lecce et al. (2005). In particular, in the two groups of Cameroun children the Cohesion with friends was not higher than that with the sibling (as it was in the drawings by Italian children); also the higher disparity of Value between the siblings, found in Italian children, was not evident in the drawings made in Ebolowa and Bimengué. Figure 7.8 presents examples of the typical representational strategies of Cohesion and Value in the participants from Cameroun.

Figure 7.7a Example of high differentiation in drawings of the relationship with the friend and with the sibling; girl, 8 years old, public school, town, Bolivia (Fini, 2001).

Figure 7.7b Example of low differentiation in drawings of the relationship with the friend and with the sibling; girl, 8 years old, orphanage, town, Bolivia (Fini, 2001).

 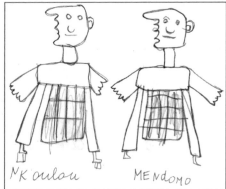

Figure 7.8 Example of low differentiation in drawings of the relationship with the friend and with the sibling; boy, 9 years old, village, Cameroun (Prevete, 2004).

These data on children from Cameroun call for a more careful consideration of the effect of the family composition on the perceived quality of the siblinghood, as suggested by Cannoni (2002). In particular, the high number of children, typical of Cameroun families, could weaken the links between siblings, which are – so to speak – "diluted" in the large group of children in the household. Also Prevete (2004) considers the lack of differentiation between friendship and siblinghood as an indication of a weaker relationship between the child and his/her siblings; but she suggests that the cause could lie more in the widespread practice which encourages an early independence from family in children, than in the family size *per se*.

Conclusions

Our (forcedly short) description of PAIR and of its applications in different environments gives an idea of what kind of contribution drawing could give in the debate about relationships and culture.

To consider children's drawing "culture free", without any restriction and in the absence of methodological cautions, would certainly be too naïve, given the current understanding of children's pictorial development. Too many studies have questioned the existence of universally valid stages, as well as the possibility of an immediate "reading" of a drawing in terms of a viewer's subjective impression. Drawing, and especially figurative drawing, is at least in part a cultural artifact, extremely sensitive to the conditions under which it is produced, and intrinsically complex, because of the large opportunity, for the person who is using it to represent something, to reach his/her representational goals in many different ways. Nevertheless, figurative drawing has its basis in some sort of visual correspondence between referent and symbol. When the possibility of obtaining this correspondence is acknowledged, drawing begins to be useful for communicative ends, because it also can be understood at least in part outside the boundaries of a given culture.

The heuristic potential of drawing is evident, in particular as a complement to verbal language in the study of "spontaneous concepts" ("spontaneous" in the sense of Vygotsky, 1978) such as those pertaining to social relationships: even when a child is unable to conceive explicit theories about social phenomena and to talk about them, he/she can have appropriate images that capture some basic properties of relationships and draw them. Children's drawings, in sum, can be seen as "an interesting mix of graphic and linguistic resources, in the service of a complex conceptualization" (Gardner, 1980, p. 154).

We hope to have demonstrated that it is possible to make clear to a child what a drawing should contain in order to communicate his/her ideas, and that this task can be afforded with success by children, even young and not especially skilled. The possibility of depicting the qualities of a given relationship with a variety of graphic devices, equally acceptable for the adult recipient of the pictorial message, is at the core of PAIR, the instrument we devised. From this to the cross-cultural use of this instrument the step is short, but with what hypothesis? To demonstrate that relationships are all the same world-wide, or to investigate their inevitable differences?

We feel that a "universal kernel" in children's interpersonal development should be acknowledged, namely the identification of the distinctive basic features of the principal relationships which form the social network of each child, within and outside of the family. This is a crucial developmental task, which allows the child to understand the rules which one has to follow in order to successfully relate to others. However, as Greenfield, Keller, Fuligni, and Maynard (2003) pointed out, this task may be addressed differently from group to group, and may be solved in different ways, adequate to each cultural group. The main merit of drawing, for us, has been precisely to be able to show, within a single product, both universal features of the child's relationships and their cultural variations. This is not a contradiction, because the information pertaining to each of these two broad aspects comes from different aspects of the drawings, separately coded by PAIR: the general features of the drawing, measured by the six scales forming PAIR (*Cohesion, Distancing, Similarity, Value, Emotions, Conflict*), seem to inform mostly on the universal aspects of relationships; the quantitative balance between these features, as well as the choice of the specific pictorial informants (scored at the level of the subscales or of the categories in each scale) seem to capture cultural variations. In short, to have broken down the complexity of the drawing in much finer aspects has proved useful not only as a means to avoid subjective interpretations, but also as a way to access a multiple level of analysis.

These conclusions come from a long research path, which reflects in some way a general trend of cultural research. As Garcia Coll, Akerman and Cicchetti (2000) have noted in reviewing this research, many earlier studies were conducted to compare one culture to another, or to test the possibility of generalizing some findings across cultures in order to develop universal models. Our first steps into a cultural examination of children's understanding of relationships did not make an exception in this regard. More recent studies tend to be more culturally relevant, in so far as they reflect the notion that "culture and psychology are mutually constitutive phenomena which cannot be reduced to each other" (Garcia Coll et al., 2000, p. 347). Our current research is more consistent with this second perspective (Pinto, 2006). Although it is impossible for an observer to be free of implicit or explicit models of development, we are trying to make our methodology culturally relevant in several ways. First, we have focused preferentially on differences within a country, taking a less generic stance, and looking for those aspects of the drawing which are sensitive to cultural variations. Second, we have deepened the co-operation with local investigators, who have an in-depth knowledge of culture, impossible to be matched by a foreigner. This first-hand acquaintance with social practices is necessary, on the one hand, to identify the relational phenomena that are relevant for children, and on the other hand to understand more accurately the way in which children would react to a drawing task. The problem here is not only to document the iconic culture of a place, but also to come to know in greater detail which rules children follow in making the transition from their implicit, tacit knowledge to the explicit expression included in a drawing. In order to understand the subtleties of children's drawings in their own cultural context, future research also should involve as much as possible parents and teachers. They are a unique source of information about the children's *pictorial socialization*: how much they are exposed to graphic materials, how much they are encouraged to draw, which styles are prized by adults, which scaffolding is provided, and so on. In short, we are trying more and more "to place cultural processes at the core and not at the periphery of our conceptualizations and investigations of developmental processes" (Garcia Coll & Magnusson, 1999, p. 2).

One aspect of our research, which has not been reviewed here, is the developmental pathway followed by children, in our country as well as in the other countries where we have had the opportunity to perform our studies. This is not to deny that the studied relationships change with age, as a result of a co-constructed process where individual and culture are intertwined: and in fact some differences between younger and older children were evident also in some of our studies. In this chapter, we have not focused our presentation on these differences, because the primary aim of PAIR has not been to capture the older children's progress, as much as to allow the younger children to manifest whichever competence about their social life is already present at an early age. This is why the very basic features of relationships have been discussed, leaving aside other aspects, which are more likely to change as children grow. Our choice has the merit, we hope, to demonstrate that even young children are not only able to behave in a socially appropriate way, but also to represent the relationships in which they are involved in a quite detailed and realistic fashion. A deeper appreciation of what changes across development remains one of the most compelling question of our agenda in the use of PAIR.

References

Adamopoulos, J., & Bontempo, R. N. (1986). Diachronic universals in interpersonal structures: Evidence from literary sources. *Journal of Cross-Cultural Psychology, 17*, 169-189.

Agnew, R. (1991). The interactive effects of peer variables on delinquency. *Criminology, 29*, 47-72.

Allan, G. (1989). *Friendship: A sociologic perspective.* London: Harvester Wheatsheaf.

Ambert, A. M. (1997). *Parents, children, and adolescents: Interactive relationships and development in context.* Binghamton: The Haworth Press.

Argyle, M., Henderson, M., Bond, M., Iizuka, Y., & Contarello, A. (1986). Cross-cultural variations in relationship rules. *International Journal of Psychology, 21*, 287-315.

Baumrind, D. (1991). Parenting styles and adolescent development. In: J. Brooks-Gunn, R. Lerner & A. C. Petersen (Eds.), *The encyclopedia of adolescence* (pp.746-758). New-York: Garland.

Beach, S. R. M., & Tesser, A. (1995). Self-esteem and the extended self-evaluation model: The self in social context. In: M. H. Kernis (Ed.), *Efficacy, agency and self-esteem* (pp. 145-170). New York: Plenum.

Berndt, T. J. (2004). Children's friendships: shifts over a half-century in perspectives on their development and their effects. *Merrill-Palmer Quarterly, 50*, 206-223.

Berscheid, E., & Reiss, H. T. (1998). Attraction and close relationships. In: D. T. Gilbert, S. T. Fiske & G. Lindzey (Eds.), *The handbook of social psychology* (pp. 193-281). New York: McGraw-Hill.

Bombi, A. S., & Pinto, G. (1993). *I colori dell'amicizia.* Bologna: Il Mulino.

Bombi, A. S., & Pinto, G. (1995). Making a dyad. Cohesion and distancing in children's representation of friendship. *British Journal of Developmental Psychology, 12*, 563-575.

Bombi, A. S., & Pinto, G. (1998). *Los colores de la amistad. Estudios sobre las representaciones pictoricas de la amistad entre los ninos.* Madrid: Visor. (Spanish traslation of: I colori dell'amicizia. Studi sulle rappresentazioni pittoriche dell'amicizia tra bambini. Bologna: Il Mulino, 1993).

Bombi, A. S., & Pinto, G. (2000). *Le relazioni interpersonali del bambino. Studiare la socialità infantile con il disegno.* Roma: Carocci.

Bombi, A. S., Pinto, G., & Cannoni, E. (2007). *Pictorial Assessment of Interpersonal Relationships. A quantitative system for evaluating children's drawing.* Florence: Florence University Press.

Bruner, J. S. (1964). The course of cognitive growth. *American Psychologist, 19*, 1-15.

Brussoni, M. J., & Boon, S. D. (1998). Grandparental impact in young adults' relationships with their closest grandparents: The role of relationship strength and emotional closeness. *International Journal of Aging & Human Development, 46*, 267-286.

Bukowski, W. M., (2003). Peer relationships. In: M. H. Bornstein, & L. Davidson (Eds.), *Wellbeing: Positive development across the life course. Crosscurrents in contemporary psychology* (pp. 221-233). Mahwah, NJ: Erlbaum.

Cannoni, E. (2002). Amici e fratelli. Effetti dell'esperienza fraterna sulla rappresentazione di relazioni interpersonali infantili. *Età Evolutiva, 73*, 70-78.

Chen, X., Rubin, K. H., & Li, B. (1995). Social and school adjustment of shy and aggressive children in China. *Developmental Psychopathology, 34*, 667-686.

Chen, X., French, D., & Schneider, B. (2006). *Peer relationships in cultural context.* New York: Cambridge University Press.

Clark, M. S., & Drewry, D. (1985). Similarity and reciprocity in the friendship of elementary school children, *Child Study Journal*, 15, 251-263.

Clifford, J. (1986). Partial truths. In J. Clifford & G. E. Marcus (Eds.), *Writing culture. The poetics and politics of ethnography* (pp. 1-29). Berkeley, CA: University of California Press.

Coie, J., Terry, R., Lenox, K., Lochman, J., & Hyman, C. (1995). Childhood peer rejection and aggression as predictors of stable patterns of adolescent disorder. *Development and Psychopathology, 7,* 697–713.

Cole, M. (1996). *Cultural Psychology: A once and future discipline.* Cambridge: Belknap- Harvard.

Cole, M. (2002). Culture and development. In: H. Keller, Y. H. Poortinga, & A. Schölmerich (Eds.), *Between culture and biology. Perspectives on ontogenetic development* (pp. 303-319). Cambridge, MA: Cambridge University Press.

Confalonieri, P. (1987). *Bolivia.* Roma: ASAL.

Corman, L. (1967). *Le test du dessin dans la pratique médico-pédagogique.* Paris: PUF.

Cox, M. (1998). Drawing of people by Australian Aboriginal children: The intermixing of cultural style. *Journal of Art and Design Education, 17,* 71-79.

Cox, M. (2005). *The pictorial world of the child.* Cambridge: Cambridge University Press.

Crutcher, R. J. (1994). Telling what we know: The use of verbal report methodologies in psychological research. *Psychological Science, 5,* 241-244.

Damon, W. (1977). *The social world of the child.* San Francisco: Jossey Bass.

Denzin, N. K. (1997). The standpoint epistemologies and social theory. *Current Perspectives in Social Theory, 17,* 39-76.

Doise, W. & Mugny, G. (1981). *Le développement social de l'intelligence.* Paris: Inter-Editions.

Duck, S., & Gilmour, R. (1986). *The emerging field of personal relationships.* Hillsdale, NJ: Erlbaum.

Dunn, J. (1993). *Young children's close relationship. Beyond attachment.* Newbury: Sage.

Feldman, S. S., & Weinberg, D.A. (1994). Self restraint as a mediator of family influences on boys' delinquent behavior: A longitudinal study. *Child Development, 65,* 195-211.

Fini, E. (2001). *La rappresentazione infantile del rapporto fraterno e amicale in uno studio transculturale.* Doctoral dissertation, University of Florence.

Fiske, A. P., (1992). The four elementary forms of sociality: Framework for a unified theory of social relations. *Psychological Review, 99,* 689-723.

Freeman, N. H. (1980). *Strategies of representation in young children: Analysis of spatial skills and drawing processes.* London: Academic Press.

Freeman, N. H. (1991). The theory of art that underpins children's naive realism. *Visual Arts Research, 17,* 65-75.

Freeman, N. H., & Cox, M. V. (1985). *Visual order: The nature and development of pictorial representation.* Cambridge: Cambridge University Press.

Furman, W. (1996). The measurement of friendship perceptions: Conceptual and methodological issues. In W. M. Bukowski, A. F. Newcomb, & W. W. Hartup (Eds.), *The company they keep: friendship in childhood and adolescence* (pp. 41-65). New York: Cambridge University Press.

Fury, G., Carlson, E. A., & Sroufe, L. A. (1997). Children's representations of attachment relationships in family drawings. *Child Development, 68,* 1154-1164.

Gallagher, T. M. (1993). Language skills and the competence in school-age children. *Language, speech and hearing services in the school, 24,* 199-205.

Garcia Coll, C., Akerman, H., & Cicchetti, R. (2000). Cultural influences on developmental processes and outcomes: Implication for the study of development and psychopathology. *Development and Psychopathology, 12,* 333-356.

García Coll, C., & Magnusson, K., (1999). Cultural influences on child development: Are we ready for a paradigm shift? In: A. S. Matsen (Ed.), *Cultural processes in child development. The Minnesota Symposia on Child Psychology.* (Vol. 29, pp. 1–24). Mahwah, NJ: Erlbaum.

Gardner, H. (1980). *Artful scribbles: The significance of children's drawings*. New York: Basic Books.

Golomb, C. (1981). Representation and reality: The origins and determinants of young children's drawings. *Review of Research in Visual Art Education, 14*, 31-48.

Golomb, C. (1992). *The child's creation of a pictorial world*. Berkeley, CA: University of California Press.

Goodenough, F. L. (1926). *Measurement of intelligence by drawings*. Chicago: World Book Company.

Goodnow, J. (1977). *Children drawing*. Cambridge, MA: Harvard University Press.

Greenfield, P. M., Quiroz, B., & Raeff, C. (2000). Cross-cultural conflict and harmony in the social construction of the child. In: S. Harkness, C. Raeff & C. R. Super (Eds.), *The social construction of the child: The nature of variability. New directions in child development*. (pp. 93-108). San Francisco: Jossey-Bass.

Greenfield, P. M., Keller, H., Fuligni, A., & Maynard, A. (2003). Cultural pathways through universal development. *Annual Review of Psychology, 54*, 461-490.

Grieve, R., (1990). Children's awareness. In R. Grieve & M. Hughes (Eds.), *Understanding children*. Oxford: Basil Blackwell.

Harris, D. B. (1963). *Children's drawings as measures of intellectual maturity*. New York: Harcourt, Brace & Court.

Harris, J. R. (1995). Where is the child's environment? A group socialization theory of development. *Psychological Review, 102*, 458-489.

Hinde, R. A. (1979). *Towards understanding relationships*. London: Academic Press.

Hinde, R. A. (1997). *Relationships: A dialectical perspective*. Hove: Psychology Press.

Kendrick, M., & McKay, R. (2004). Drawing as an alternative way of understanding young children's constructions of literacy. *Journal of Early Childhood Literacy, 4*, 109-128.

Kennedy, C. H., & Itkonen, T. (1996). Social relationships, influential variables, and change across the life span. In L. K. Koegel, R. L. Koegel & G. Dunlap (Eds), *Positive behavioral support: Including people with difficult behavior in the community* (pp. 287-304). Baltimore, MD: Paul H Brookes Publishing.

Killen, M., & Wainryb, C., (2000). Independence and interdependence in diverse cultural context. In: S. Harkness, C. Raeff, & C. Super, (Eds.), *Variability in social construction of the child: New directions in child and adolescent development*. (Vol.87, pp.5-21). San Francisco: Jossey-Bass.

Kramer, L., & Bank, L. (2005). Sibling relationship contributions to individual and family well-being: Introduction to the special issue. *Journal of Family Psychology, 19*, 483-485.

Lang, F. R., Reschke, F. S., & Neyer, F. J. (2006). Social relationships, transitions, and personality development across the life span. In D. K. Mroczek & T. Little (Eds), *Handbook of personality development* (pp. 445-466). Mahwah, NJ: Erlbaum.

Laursen, B., & Hartup, W. W. (2002). The origins of reciprocity and social exchange in friendships. In W. G. Graziano, & B. Laursen (Eds.), *Social exchange in development. New directions for child and adolescent development*. San Francisco: Jossey-Bass.

Laursen, B., & Bukowski, W. M. (1997). A developmental guide to the organization of close relationships. *International Journal of Behavioral Development, 21*, 747-770.

Lecce, S., Pinto, G., & Pagnin, A. (2003). *Children's evaluation of relationships: Congruence and incongruence into sibling's and friend's dyads*. Presented at the 11th Biennial Meeting ESDP. Milano, 27-31 August.

Lecce, S., & Pinto, G. (2004). The representation of sibling relationship: A comparison among MZ, DZ twins and singletons. *Twin Research, 7*, 362.

Lecce, S., Pagnin, A., & Pinto, G., (2005*). Me and You within siblings' and friends' relationship: A shared evaluation?* Presented at the 12th Biennial Meeting ESDP. La Laguna (Tenerife), 24-28 August.

Machover, K. (1949). *Personality projection in the drawings of the human figure.* Springfield: C.C. Thomas.

Melià, B. (1988). *Los Guarany-Chitiguano. Nande Reko, nuestro modo de ser.* Cuadernos de Investigation, 30, La Paz (Bolivia). Centro de Investigation y Promocion del Campesinado.

Milbrath, C. (1998). *Patterns of artistic development.* New York: Cambridge University Press.

Olweus, D. (1993). *Bullying at school: What we know and what we can do.* Oxford: Blackwell.

O'Mahoney, J. F. (1989). Development of thinking about things and people: Social and non-social cognition during adolescence. *Journal of Genetic Psychology, 150,* 217-224.

Patterson, G. (1995). Coercion – A basis for early age onset for arrest. In: J. McCord (Ed.), *Coercion and punishment in long-term perspective* (pp. 81-105). New York: Cambridge University Press.

Peterson, R. W. (1997). *Visual memory and language: A study of children's use of art and language to communicate their knowledge of science.* Presented at the Annual meeting of the National Association for Research in Science Teaching, Oak Brooks.

Piaget, J. (1932). *Le jugement moral chez l'enfant.* Paris: Alcan.

Pianta, R. (2006). Classroom management and relationships between children and teachers: Implications for research and practice. In C. Evertson & C. Weinstein (Eds.), *Handbook of Classroom Management: Research, Practice, & Contemporary Issues* (pp. 685-710). Mahwah, NJ: Erlbaum

Pinto, G. (2006). *Children's drawing of close relationship in different cultures.* Presented at the 36th Annual Meeting of the Jean Piaget Society, Baltimore, June, 1-3.

Pinto, G., & Bombi, A. S. (1995). *Children's drawing of the human figures in profile. A cross cultural study.* Presented at the VIIth European Conference on Developmental Psychology, Cracow, Poland.

Pinto, G., & Bombi, A. S., (1996). Drawing human figures in profile. A study of the development of representative strategies. *Journal of Genetic Psychology, 157,* 303-321.

Pinto, G., & Bombi, A. S. (1997). *Cohesion and distancing in children's friendship across cultures.* Presented at the International Council of Psychologists, Cross-cultural perspectives on human development. Padova, 21-24 July.

Pinto, G., Bombi, A. S., & Cordioli, A. (1997). Similarity of friends in three countries: A study of children's drawings. *International Journal of Behavioral Development, 20,* 453-469.

Pinto, G., & Crispìn Arciénega, R. (2001). Coesione e distanziamento tra genitori e figli: uno studio cross-culturale. *Rassegna di Psicologia, XVIII* (2), 51-72.

Povrzanovic, M. (1997). Children, war and nation: Croatia 1991. *Childhood, 4,* 81-102.

Prevete, S. (2004). *La rappresentazione infantile della relazione amicale e fraterna: Uno studio transculturale in Cameroun.* Doctoral dissertation, University of Florence.

Raeff, C., Greenfield, P. M., & Quiroz, B. (2000). Developing interpersonal relationships in the cultural contexts of individualism and collectivism. In: S. Harkness, C. Raeff & C..R. Super (Eds.), *The social construction of the child. New directions in child development.* (pp. 59-74). San Francisco: Jossey-Bass.

Rochat, P. (2001). *The infant's world. The developing child series.* Cambridge, MA: Harvard University Press.

Rogoff, B. (1990). *Apprenticeship in thinking: Cognitive development in social context.* New York: Oxford University Press.

Schneider, B. H. (2000). *Friends and enemies: Peer relations in childhood.* London: Arnold.

Schneider, B. H., Richard, J. F., Younger, A. J., & Freeman, P. (2000). A longitudinal exploration of the continuity of children's social participation and social withdrawal across socioeconomic status levels and social settings. *European Journal of Social Psychology, 30*, 497-519.

Selman, R. L. (1980). *The growth of interpersonal understanding*. Orlando: Academic Press.

Sroufe, L. A. (1995). *Emotional development*. New York: Cambridge University Press.

Stattin, H., & Magnusson, D. (1989). The role of early aggressive behavior in the frequency, seriousness and types of later crimes. *Journal of Consulting and Clinical Psychology, 57*, 710-718.

Sundberg, N., & Ballinger, T. (1968). Nepalese children's cognitive development as revealed by drawings of man, woman and self. *Child Development, 39*, 969-985.

Tallandini, M. A. (1991). Symbolic prototypes in children's drawings of school. *Journal of Genetic Psychology, 152*, 179-190.

Tallandini, M. A., & Dimitrova, R. (2006). *Modalità di rappresentazione della composizione familiare: un confronto tra bambini albanesi, serbi e italiani.* Presented at the XX Congresso Psicologia dello Sviluppo, Verona, 13-15 Settembre.

Tesser, A., Campbell, J., & Smith, M. (1984). Friendship choice and performance: Self-evaluation maintenance in children. *Journal of Personality and Social Psychology, 46*, 561-574.

Thomas, G. V., & Silk, A. M. J. (1990). *An introduction to the psychology of children's drawings*. New York: Harvester Wheatsheaf.

Tramonti, F. R. (2004). The evolution of children's representational capacities: A cross-cultural study. *Human Evolution, 20*, 47-54.

Trautner, H. M., & Campos-Ramirez, D. (2004). *The ideal woman and ideal man as depicted in drawings by young adolescents in Costa Rica and Germany.* Presented at the 18th Biennial Meeting of the ISSBD, Ghent, 2-5, July.

Tversky, B., Kugelmass, S., & Winter, A. (1991). Cross-cultural and developmental trends in graphic productions. *Cognitive Psychology, 23*, 515-557.

Van Meter, P., & Garner, J. (2005). The promise and practice of learner-generated drawing: literature review and synthesis. *Educational Psychology Review, 17*, 285-325.

Vygotsky, L. S. (1934). *Myslenie i rec' psichologiceskie issledovanija*. Gosudarstveennoe Social'no-Ekonomicskoe Izdatel'stvo, Moskva-Leningrad.

Vygotsky, L. S. (1978). *Mind in society. The development of higher psychological processes.* Cambridge, MA: Harvard University Press.

Walker, K., Myers-Bowman, K.S., & Myers-Wall, J.A. (2003). Understanding war, visualizing peace: Children draw what they know. *Art Therapy: Journal of the American Art Therapy Association, 20*, 112-123.

Waters, E., Merrick, S., Treboux, D., Crowell, J., & Albersheim, L. (2000). Attachment security in infancy and early adulthood: A twenty-year longitudinal study. *Child Development, 71*, 684-689.

Weber, S., & Mitchell, C. (1995*). That's funny, You don't look like a teacher.* Washington, DC: The Falmer Press.

Wetton, N. M., & McWhirter, J. M. (1998). Image based research and curriculum development in health education. In J. Prosser (Ed.), *Image based research: A source book for qualitative researchers.* Brighton: Falmer Press.

White, K. M., Speisman, J. C., Costos, D., & Smith, A. (1987). Relational maturity: A conceptual and empiric approach. In J. A. Meacham (Ed.), *Interpersonal relations: Family, peers, friends.* Basel: Karger.

Wilson, B., & Wilson, M. (1985). The artistic tower of Babel: Inextricable links between culture and graphic development. *Visual Arts Research, 11*, 90-104.

Youniss, J., & Smollar, J., (1989). Adolescents' interpersonal relationships in social context. In T. J. Berndt & G. W. Ladd (Eds.), *Peer relationships in child development* (pp. 300-316). New York: Wiley.

Zipoli, G. (2001). *La rappresentazione infantile delle relazioni familiari: uno studio transculturale in Brasile.* Doctoral dissertation, University of Florence.

Chapter 8

Developing Children's Appreciation of Photographs as Informative and Aesthetic Artifacts

Lynn S. Liben
The Pennsylvania State University

Photographs: What and why?

Photographs as pervasive and transparent

Photographs are everywhere. They appear in newspapers, in magazines, on television; they appear on art gallery walls, in academic lectures. They appear in family photo albums, on computer screens, and on cell phones. There is an ease to creating photographs that is unrivaled by any other representational medium. Assuming one has the necessary equipment, one need simply click a button, and an image is created.

The pervasiveness and simplicity of photography in contemporary culture undoubtedly contribute to the sense that photographs are an immediate (that is, un-mediated) representational genre. They are often assumed to be transparent; the viewer is presumed to be able to look through the representational surface to see the referent that lies beneath or beyond it (Barthes, 1981; Beilin, 1991; Liben, 2003; Sontag, 1977). However, as in any other graphic representational medium, the referent object and the photographic surface are neither equivalent nor interchangeable (Liben, 1999). As Szarkowski (1973) observed, "The simplicity of photography lies in the fact that it is very easy to make a picture. The staggering complexity of it lies in the fact that a thousand other pictures of the same subject would have been equally as easy" (p. 134). What, then, distinguishes photographs from their referents?

The photographic surface

Photographs are representations

First, as already implied, photographs are *representations*. As such, any particular representation is not some degraded re-presentation of the real world as it is, but rather is an intentional selection and instantiation of some referent that offers a vision that is not only different from – but in many ways richer than – the referent it depicts. As adults, we are poised to think about the interplay between representation and referent, as attested to by our response to Figure 8.1.

Figure 8.1 Photograph after Magritte's *Ceci n'est pas une pipe.*

As in the original Magritte painting on which this photograph is based, this image is amusing because it causes us to think about the automaticity with which we normally interpret representations as their referents rather than as representations. That is, when shown a painting or photograph of a pipe and asked to identify it, we are likely to name the referent, "a pipe," rather than its representational form, "a photograph." Yet this privileging of referential meaning does not imply that adults have lost sight of the representational nature of what appears in front of them. Adults see the humor in Magritte and Figure 8.1; they do not attempt to smoke the photograph. A full appreciation of a photograph requires understanding both referential meaning and surface form simultaneously.

Photographs are spatial representations

Second, photographs are *spatial* representations. Whereas referents themselves are encountered from multiple and ever-changing perspectives, photographs depict their referents in a *view-specific* way. As a consequence, they provide spatial information about the referents themselves and about the vantage point from which the representation was created (Liben, 2003). Specifically, a given referent has spatial qualities (e.g., shapes, locations, and relative sizes of its parts) and is depicted from a particular distance (e.g., a close-up vs. medium distance view), from a particular angle (e.g., looking straight ahead, straight down, straight up), and from a particular azimuth or orientation (e.g., showing the front, side, or back of an object). The photograph shown in Figure 8.1, for example, shows a pipe which has a relatively thin, elongated piece that is orthogonal to a rounded cylindrical piece; it is a close-up, eye-level, side-view of a pipe. Another photograph might show a pipe of a somewhat different shape, or it might show the same pipe from a greater distance, from an oblique angle, and facing toward the pipe's bowl. Spatial representations like these thus differ from verbal representations that can ignore spatial information entirely by denoting their referents in a non-spatial way (e.g., "a pipe"). Understanding photographs fully thus entails understanding both spatial content and spatial vantage point.

Photographs are media-specific representations

Third, photographs are *media-specific* representations that not only share qualities with all spatial-graphic media, but also have qualities that are unique. For example, photographs, like other static, two-dimensional graphic representations (e.g., paintings) are bounded such that the image-creator, not the image-user, controls what is seen. But each specific representational medium has different mechanisms for influencing the final appearance of the representation. In painting, for example, the final image is affected by factors such as the surface (e.g., paper, wood, canvas), the type of paint (e.g., acrylic, water color, oil paint), and the application device (e.g., a small or large brush, a stick, a palate knife). In film photography, the final image is affected not only by what was actually in the physical world when the film was exposed and not only by where the camera was held (at what distance, at what angle, and facing in what direction), but also by factors such as the kind of film (e.g., color or black and white, different light sensitivity, different color balance), the lens (e.g., normal vs. zoom), exposure speed (e.g., a 200th of a second vs. 2 seconds), the use of filters (e.g., polarizing filters, diffusion filters), developing processes (e.g., concentration of developing solution), and printing processes (e.g., selection of matte or glossy paper on which to print the negative). In digital photography, the final image is dependent on parallel factors including vantage point and choice of equipment during image-capture (e.g., image resolution, lens selection, exposure details, filters), processing decisions (e.g., color settings, cropping, inserting or deleting sections) and printing (e.g., paper quality, ink selections). Understanding the photographic image thus also involves an understanding of these media-specific qualities.

Summary and preview

I have used this introductory section (*Photographs: What and why?*) to argue that photographs carry more than transparent denotations of their referents and to identify their key qualities. In the second section (*Seeing the photographic surface*), I identify factors expected to influence viewers' appreciation of these photographic qualities. Included are factors related to the external stimulus or context as well as factors related to the developmentally changing internal qualities of the viewer. In the third section (*Illustrative empirical work*) I review research revealing age-linked differences in the way that individuals understand (in comprehension tasks) and make use of (in production tasks) photographs. I end (*Concluding comments*) by summarizing key points, and by urging the value of the arts both for developmental scholarship and for educational practice.

Seeing the photographic surface

Overview

The work that I and my collaborators have done has been driven by the general hypothesis that the ways in which photographs are understood and appreciated will be influenced by two kinds of factors: those related to the external stimulus and environment and those related to the internal qualities of the viewer. Before discussing each in turn, however, it is important to note that this division is based on the practical need to organize the discussion rather than on a conceptual belief that environment and organism can ever be split (Overton, 2006). Indeed, at the conceptual level we situate our work within the constructive, interactive theoretical positions of Piaget and Vygotsky. These positions deny the possibility of neatly partitioning human development and behavior into external versus internal influences, instead arguing for interactive, transactional mechanisms between individuals and the physical and social contexts in which they are embedded. We believe that such a characterization applies to the way that individuals interact with photographs at any given time, and applies to the way that individuals develop as a result of such interactions. From a Piagetian perspective, we presume that children's developing cognitive skills influence the ways they reach out to and make sense of (i.e., assimilate and accommodate) what is available in the social and physical environment, an environment that includes photographs and social interactions about photographs. From a Vygotskian perspective, we presume that children co-construct the referential and affective meaning of photographs with their collaborators, be they peers, parents, teachers, museum guides, or others who co-inhabit the environment.

The external stimulus and environment

Image qualities

I begin by suggesting that viewers will be increasingly likely to recognize and hence appreciate the photographic surface itself as the image becomes increasingly unlike the visual experiences obtained from moving around in the everyday, physical world. This point is a derivative of an earlier, more general argument (Liben, 1999) that the representational function of a graphic becomes increasingly salient as the physical similarity between referent and representation diminishes. Interestingly, the initial discussion of this point was made by contrasting non-photographic and photographic media: representations may also communicate some new insight or vision by presenting highly processed and transformed information about the referent. This revelation function of representations is generally recognized in painting and drawing, but is often overlooked for other art forms such as sculpture and photography. The latter are often naively assumed to show the world "as it is" (Liben, 1999, p. 14).

Extrapolating from this argument, I expect that attention to the photographic sur-face will be greatest when photographs are perceptually non-canonical in one or more ways. This non-canonical quality may be achieved by photographing a referent from an atypical perspective (non-canonical vantage point, e.g., photographing a tree from below); by photographing a referent that is not typically the focus of viewers' attention in the real world (a non-canonical referent, e.g., a close-up view of the texture of a brick or stone); or by photographing the referent in a way that transforms or modifies the visual experience of the unaided human eye (non-canonical visual experience). The latter might be realized by manipulating the optics in some way (e.g., using a dif-fusion filter to soften the entire image or using a prism filter to add refractions) or by capturing events that would otherwise occur too quickly or at too small a scale for the human eye and brain to process (as in the well-known photograph by Edgerton showing a drop of milk as it hits the table surface, see Jussim & Kayafas, 1987).

Display context

I hypothesize that a second factor that affects the viewer's attention to the photo-graphic surface is the context in which the photograph is displayed. Contexts vary from those in which photographs are presented as secondary or supplemental to an-other purpose (as when they appear in a textbook, newspaper article, or television news broadcast) to those in which photographs are presented as the *raison d'etre* (as when they appear on the walls of a museum or art gallery, illuminated by spotlights, accompanied by interpretive labels). I expect that viewers' attentiveness to photo-graphic surfaces – as contrasted to their referential meaning – will be greater in set-tings like the latter than the former (Liben, 2003). I would anticipate that when photo-graphs created for one purpose are displayed in another (e.g., snapshots initially in-tended to record family events or travel are collected, framed, and displayed in an art museum, e.g., Walther, 2000), viewers' responses will be modified accordingly.

A second way in which the display may affect viewers' attention to and apprecia-tion of the photographic surface concerns what contrasts are provided within the dis-play. To the degree that the variations within the display are defined primarily by con-tent (e.g., a series of landscape images in which the style stays roughly similar, and what differs is the particular landscape), attention is likely to be on the referential con-tent. To the degree that the referential content remains identical or nearly so and varia-tions are primarily related to photographic qualities such as vantage point (e.g., chang-ing angles) or technique (e.g., changes in lens filters or changes in the paper on which the negative is printed), attention is likely to be drawn to the photographic surface (see Liben, 2003).

Social context

In addition to being affected by the physical context in which photographs are encoun-tered, I propose that viewers' relative attention to the referential content versus the photographic surface will be affected by the social context in which they are viewed.

That is, I hypothesize that the degree to which viewers direct their attention to photographic surfaces (as opposed to referential content) will be influenced by the way that others steer the viewer to the photographic surface. This process goes beyond social mediation implicit in structuring the physical context (e.g., a curator's decision to frame photographs and place them on museum walls); it concerns explicit, concurrent interaction with another person or persons. Thus, it would be expected that a particular viewer in a particular setting (whether at home, looking at the family photograph album or at a museum, exploring a photographic exhibit) will attend differentially to photographic surfaces versus content as a result of the social dynamic between or among collaborative viewers.

The viewer inside

Overview

At any given moment in any given context, an individual approaches any given stimulus object or event – such as a particular photograph – with a complex assortment of characteristics and personal history. No one chapter can begin to list, much less to discuss, all the potentially relevant viewer qualities. Here I focus on three domains of viewer qualities that appear to be particularly relevant to interpreting photographs, and that have been shown to undergo normative age-linked change.

Representational development

One arena of normative cognitive development relevant to the present discussion concerns children's growing understanding and use of representations, both mental and physical (e.g., Piaget, 1951; Sigel, 1999). There is considerable theory and empirical work suggesting that representational development is a complex and extended process. Major stages in understanding external spatial representations such as maps and photographs have been detailed elsewhere (Liben, 1999); here I provide highlights of the progression.

During infancy and early toddlerhood, children evidence difficulty distinguishing between referent and representation altogether. For example, a number of investigators have reported toddlers' tendencies to attempt to grasp objects depicted in drawings or photographs as if they were real objects (Church, 1961; DeLoache, Pierroutsakos, Uttal, Rosengren, & Gottlieb, 1998; Liben & Downs, 1989; Ninio & Bruner, 1978). By the later preschool years, children are rarely confusing representations with their referents at the global level, but they continue to confuse specific qualities of the representation and specific qualities of the referent. For example, research on children's understanding of maps (Liben & Downs, 1991, 2001) has shown that preschoolers often assume that a feature of the map symbol necessarily implies something about a referential feature. Some young preschool children, for example, interpreted a red line on a road map to mean that the road it stood for was itself red. Others interpreted irregular yellow regions on the map (used to show built up population areas) as eggs or fire-crackers, presumably because they were seeking a referent that would match the color and shape of the symbols. Children as old as 8 years have difficulty accepting that green marks stand for the locations of toy (red) fire trucks on a map; they presume that red marks stand for red referents, even if they have seen that those red dots were applied without any intent to symbolize location (Myers & Liben, in press).

Relevant to the challenge of understanding the media-specific qualities of photo-graphs, it is still later that children "come to understand how the correspondences be-tween referent and representation work for various types of representational media (e.g., maps, photographs) and for various instances within each (e.g., this particular map or this particular photograph)" (Liben, 1999, p. 312). The final competency, typi-cally not achieved until adolescence, is meta-representational understanding which involves the viewer being "able to understand representations not simply as convenient substitutions for referents, but rather as cognitive tools that enrich understanding of the referent, and to select among them appropriately for particular purposes" (Liben, 1999, p. 308).

In short, given that representational status is a fundamental quality of photographs, viewers' understanding of photographs may be expected to deepen well into adoles-cence as their representational understanding more generally progresses from an ability to identify the referent through to meta-representational competency.

Spatial development

A second relevant area of normative development is in the domain of spatial concepts. One useful conceptualization of spatial development was formulated over half a cen-tury ago by Piaget and Inhelder (1956). They argued that when representing space, young preschoolers can call on only *topological* concepts which refer to spatial quali-ties that are conserved even with changes in distance and direction. Illustrative topo-logical concepts are *on, next to, between, open,* and *closed.* Thus, for example, a young child using topological concepts would be able to distinguish an open figure from a closed one (e.g., the letters "u" vs. "o"), but not two figures that differ in only metric proportions (e.g., a circle vs. an ellipse).

Piaget and Inhelder further suggested that over the course of childhood, children gradually develop an understanding of both *projective* and *Euclidean* concepts. Projec-tive concepts are those that take viewpoint into account. Projective spatial concepts would, for example, allow the child to understand that locations such as right versus left, up versus down, or in front of versus behind have meaning only in relation to a specified viewpoint. Supporting the later-emerging nature of projective concepts is children's difficulty solving the classic three-mountains task (in which children are asked to determine what a scene looks like to someone viewing it from a different van-tage point) or difficulty in giving "turn right" versus "turn left" directions to someone facing them. Projective spatial concepts also involve understanding the effects of viewing direction on the appearance of individual objects. For example, projective concepts are needed to calculate the shadow cast on a flat surface (e.g., understanding that when flashlight is directed toward a tilted round dinner plate, the cast shadow is elliptical rather than round); they are needed to draw objects from different vantage points (e.g., drawing the dinner plate from directly overhead [circular] vs. from an oblique angle [elliptical]).

The third family of spatial concepts identified by Piaget and Inhelder, Euclidean concepts, underlies the ability to conceptualize and quantify space with an abstract system such as Cartesian coordinate system of horizontal and vertical axes. By specifying a point of origin and fixing a spatial system, it becomes possible to measure and conserve distances across locations. Again, Piagetian paradigms used to study children's developing metric concepts, including the calculation and conservation of size, distance, angles, and proportions (Piaget & Inhelder, 1956; Piaget, Inhelder, & Szeminska, 1960), suggest that these concepts develop over childhood (although rudimentary competencies appear even in infancy, see Newcombe & Huttenlocher, 2000).

In summary, there are important progressions in children's understanding of spatial concepts. Given that each photograph carries information about the spatial qualities of the referent and about the vantage point, it is reasonable to expect that children's growing general spatial competencies will support their growing specific photographic competencies.

Other-mindedness

A third relevant arena in which there is well-established evidence of normative cognitive development is what I have labeled here *other-mindedness*. I use this term to mean the individual's understanding and awareness of others' minds, that is, others' perspectives, thoughts, intentions, vantage points, and so on. I thus intend it to be a broad umbrella term that covers developmental progressions studied under the headings of egocentrism (e.g., Piaget, 1926), perspective-taking (e.g., Newcombe, 1989), communication and joint attention (e.g., Krauss & Glucksberg, 1969; Tomasello, Carpenter, Call, Behne, & Moll, 2005), theory of mind (e.g., Wellman, Cross, & Watson, 2001), and interpretive theory of mind (e.g., Carpendale & Chandler, 1996).

The richness of extant work in each of these topics and their embedded controversies with respect to early versus late emergence preclude reviewing even one, much less all of the relevant theoretical and empirical literatures. It is possible, however, to characterize development in the other-mindedness domain in broad terms. Despite some specific controversies about the details of development, most researchers would agree that infants and young preschool children are unable or at least limited in their ability to acknowledge, calculate and act on others' affects, intentions, and cognitions, particularly when these differ from the child's own concurrent cognitive, visual, or affective experiences. In later preschool years, children begin to recognize that others' beliefs may differ both from one another and from reality, and still later they come to understand and communicate nuances of different peoples' alternative cognitions, perceptual experiences, emotions, and interpretations. Most adolescents and adults may be expected to have achieved competence in these domains, although they may not necessarily implement those competencies with perfect consistency or accuracy.

Viewers who approach photographs with limited other-mindedness may be expected to see through the surface largely with respect to the referential *object* rather than the representational *creator*. To the degree that one is unaware of the creator, one is less likely to consider and hence appreciate the creator's role in producing the photograph (e.g., selection of boundaries, vantage point, use of media-specific techniques) or the creator's intentions in making these choices. Such a viewer would be more likely to focus on the denoted content rather than to attend to the photographer's vision, thus perhaps missing the deeper message that the photographer may have been attempting to convey. Similarly, when the photograph depicts sentient beings, viewers with limited other-mindedness might find it difficult to project themselves into the depicted being's experience. An illustration of the potential relevance of both the photographer and the depicted subject is found in a comment about the unsettling family portraits by Diane Arbus. In writing about an exhibition of her work, Kimmelman (2004, p. E-44) commented:

> In the photograph, the 11-year-old girl stands stiffly before a plain wall in her sleeveless, white crocheted dress, arms leaden, mouth shut. Her grave face is tightly framed by long hair and bangs, which almost conceal her eyes. She stares back at us from the shadow cast by the bangs, with a look that I might register as fear, although who is to say for sure? The heavy formality of the transaction between photographer and subject announces itself. The girl is clearly responding to the person making this portrait, whose presence we sense. By its nature the picture tells us who this photographer is. She makes sure that we know.

As Kimmelman continues later, "Arbus did not celebrate things as they are, as her fans like to say, but as she willfully conceived them. The frontal gaze she favored only implied, as it always does, honesty, directness and cooperation" (p. E-44). It would take considerable other-mindedness to appreciate both the photographer's presence and the girl's responses, and thus sensitivity to features like these are likely to undergo age-linked change as individuals' skill in taking others' perspectives develops.

Having presented the rationale for why one would anticipate age-linked differences in the way that children understand and respond to photographs, in the next section I review illustrative empirical work documenting such differences.

Illustrative empirical work

Overview

The first section of this chapter was devoted to identifying and discussing qualities of photographs themselves, and the second to identifying external and internal factors hypothesized to influence viewers' sensitivity to photographic qualities. In the current section I turn to empirical research that my colleagues and I have conducted to examine photographic understanding in individuals ranging from preschoolers to adults (e.g., Liben & Szechter, 1999, 2001, 2002, 2007; Szechter & Liben, 2007; Szechter, Liben, & Rogers, 1998). I have organized this section by the type of task rather than by type of phenomenon largely because findings from any given task bear on more than one phenomenon simultaneously. I end the section by commenting briefly on links between the empirical findings and more general developmental progressions.

Understanding similarities and differences between photograph pairs

Overview

Based on the argument that attention to photographic surfaces is enhanced when alternative photographs of the same referent are displayed simultaneously (see earlier section on *Display context*), one paradigm we have used in our empirical work asks participants to contrast pairs of photographs. Questions are designed to explore the participant's sensitivity to – and explanations of – differences between the two images. We have used these photograph-pair tasks to focus on photographic qualities related to vantage point and on qualities related to media-specific photographic technique. Each is discussed in turn.

Spatial contrasts

Based on the normative developmental progressions in spatial concepts described earlier, we expected that young children would find it challenging to appreciate the contrasts between pairs of photographs that differed because of a changed vantage point. Understanding the photographic effect of a changed vantage point should draw on projective concepts (point of view) and Euclidean concepts (measurement; distance), both of which (as discussed earlier) evolve gradually from the preschool through the elementary school years.

To test this prediction, we prepared photograph pairs that differed with respect to one of the three spatial qualities defined earlier, and, to insure that all possible responses were sometimes correct, we also prepared pairs in which the same photograph was simply printed twice and some in which something in the scene had, in fact, changed.

For each pair, we asked participants to begin by judging whether the two images were the same or different. For "different" responses, the participant was then queried about whether the difference resulted from something that the photographer did or something that changed in the scene that had been photographed. If the former, the participant was asked to explain what the photographer had done; if the latter, the participant was asked to explain what changed in the place or object photographed. Illustrative pairs of all but the identical-pair type are shown in Figure 8.2.

Figure 8.2 Examples of the photograph-pairs tasks including (a) viewing distance, (b) viewing angle, (c) viewing azimuth, and (d) referent-change items.

We have given these spatial photograph-pair tasks to children aged 3, 5, and 7 years and to college students who were participants in studies examining understanding of various kinds of graphic images (Liben, 2002), effects of photography lessons (Liben, 2003; Liben & Szechter, 2002; Szechter, Liben, & Rogers, 1998) and the association between different parental picture-book reading strategies and children's spatial understanding (Szechter & Liben, 2004).

All types of spatial pair items proved difficult for the youngest children and most were solved easily by adults, although there were differences among the various spatial challenges at both ends of the spectrum.

Specifically, the distance pairs were solved earliest, but still, only about 25% of 3-year-olds ever were able to explain that the photographer had moved closer or farther away. Even these children were successful on only a single one of the five items. By the age of 5 years, about 50% responded correctly on all or most of the distance items. Errors were rare by the age of 7, and were virtually non-existent by adulthood. Given the highly verbal nature of the procedure, it is always possible that some of the younger children understood, but could not explain what the photographer had done, or that we interpreted the intent of the child's response incorrectly. An example of a somewhat ambiguous response comes from a 3-year-old child who, when given a pair showing a statue of a man from two distances, responded: "This man is smaller and this man is bigger." This child was not credited with understanding that the photographer had changed distance. It is possible that the response reflected that the child recognized a change in the image rather than the more primitive inference that there had been a change in referent (a different man). In either case, though, it did not provide clear evidence that the child understood the change in viewing distance, evidence that in contrast was routinely apparent in the explanations given by older children and adults who said that the photographer "got closer" or "moved further back."

Pairs that differed by viewing angle provided an even greater challenge to participants. Among the 3-year-olds, none was able to provide a correct explanation on even a single item. Indeed, children this age seemed to have difficulty even noticing anything was different between the photographs. A compelling illustration is this 3-year-old's response to the tulip photographs: "They're both the same." When the investigator probed "Well, they're both of tulips, but is there anything different about the pictures?" the child responded: "Nope this one [points] has the same stuff." Among the 5-year-olds, the responses were more mixed. Unlike the younger children, they did routinely recognize that the photographs were different. Many, however, attributed the difference to a change in the referential scene. Illustrative was a child who said that the photographer "took this one when they were all curled up and those ones when they were all blooming," another who explained "First, in the spring they were closed and then in the summer they came out again," and another who said "This one is closed and this one is open" and then when asked how the photographer had done that said "He took one sometime when they were closed and one sometime when they were open." There were, however, some children at this age who were able to articulate the role of viewing angle as in a child who explained: "Um, that one you're looking that way [points straight ahead] and that one you're looking down, this way [bends over the picture]"; or another child who answered: "Oh I like these. He [the photographer] went sort of on the side of them and then like up above them to get the middle [points hand down on top of the tulips and rises in chair] because um, like this one is like straight across and this one's like you're looking down" [flexes hand to point all fingers down onto the tulips]. By the age of 7 years, responses of this kind were common, and by adulthood, virtually universal.

Among children, the azimuth pairs elicited patterns of performance that were generally similar to those of the angle pairs. Again, 3-year-olds often failed to notice that the two photographs differed, and when they did, they typically assumed that there had been a change in the referent. For example, in the pair shown in Figure 8.2, a few children asserted that the referent had been changed (e.g., "Hey, that's not the same rooster! There he's putting his head up and he's not the same!"), with many more asserting that the tile had been turned (a possibility that can be ruled out by noting the fixed relation between the orientation of the tile and the wood-grain direction of the table).

Among adults, the azimuth pairs elicited lower performance than the angle pairs. Like the children, the adults commonly attributed the difference between the two photographs to movement of the referent rather than to movement of the photographer, a finding consistent with other research showing adults' difficulty in understanding azimuth in relation to one's own orientation (e.g., in the difficulty adults face when using misaligned "You Are Here" maps, see Levine, Marchon, & Hanley, 1984). Taken together with the other data on the photo-pair tasks described above, the data are consistent with the notion of gradual mastery of projective and Euclidean concepts and of their relevance for understanding the spatial information provided by view-specific photographs.

Technique contrasts

The second photograph-pair task we have used employed images that differed either because of a change in vantage point or because of a change in some media-specific technique (e.g., the use of a polarizing filter). Our goal was to explore participants' sensitivity to surface features of photographs and their understanding that the photographer played a role in determining those features, not to examine knowledge of particular photographic techniques. Thus, participants were credited with success if their responses demonstrated understanding that the photographer had effected a change even if their responses were silent or incorrect about the particular technique used. The 10 pairs used in this task were reproduced from a technical guide to photography (Feininger, 1973), and included pairs that differed because of techniques such as different filters, lighting, shutter speed, and aperture size. Participants were children ranging in age from 7 to 13 years and their parents (N = 40 dyads) engaged in a study on children's aesthetic understanding of photographic art (Szechter & Liben, 2007).

Participants were explicitly told that the photographs in each pair showed the same thing, and were asked to explain how the photographs differed (probing for reasons as necessary). A point was assigned for each response that identified a difference and attributed that difference to something related to the photographic process rather than the referent. For example, in one pair, a woman wearing a head scarf had been photographed using either a blue or a red filter. Most participants easily noted that the scarf looked light in one photograph and dark in the other. For each of the 10 pairs, a point was awarded for responses that offered a photographer action (e.g., changing the lighting, using a flash, using a filter, or changing the film) but not for referent-based responses (most commonly that the woman had changed her scarf). Scores ranged from 0 to 6 among children and from 2 to 8 among parents, with mean scores increasing significantly with each age group (1.7, 2.4, 3.4, and 4.8 for middle childhood, late childhood, early adolescence, and adulthood, respectively). Thus, the data from the pairs that differed by implementing various media-specific photographic techniques are consistent with the data from the spatial pairs in demonstrating individuals' developing success in going beyond the referential meaning of photographs and coming to appreciate and understand qualities of the photographic surface.

Reproducing photographic models

A second paradigm that we have used to explore individuals' developing sensitivity to the photographer's vantage point is one in which participants are asked to reproduce model photographs as precisely as possible. Compared to the photographic-pairs task, this task places few verbal demands on participants, and, in addition, provides the participants with the motivation and opportunity to experience the visual consequences of moving around in the environment. Thus, even if they had not already paid attention to the view-specific nature of images in the past, they might be led to appreciate them in the course of the activity.

Specifically, 8-year-olds and college students were taken to a campus building, and once inside, shown four photographs of scenes within that building (reproduced in Liben, 2003). After seeing each, participants were asked to create another photograph that would match the model as exactly as possible, using the same digital camera that had been used to create the original. They were asked to frame their picture through the view finder, and after capturing the image, to look at the display. They were then asked to compare their photograph to the model, and then to take a second picture that would match the model even more precisely.

The four model photographs included images showing a café scene with a table and two chairs, a decorative flag of a sports team hanging from the ceiling, a large sign at the entry to the café, and a mailbox against a wall. In all cases, the vantage points used in the model photographs were intentionally selected to be non-canonical in some way (e.g., photographing the table slightly from below). This was done first, to minimize the likelihood that a participant's photograph would match the model by chance, and second, to increase the salience of vantage point (see earlier discussion of the role of non-canonical views in enhancing attention to the photographic surface).

As would be anticipated from the hypothesized centrality of referential content in photographs, all but one image reproduced the focal content of the models. Vantage point, however, was not always matched so precisely. To score the degree to which participants reproduced the correct vantage point, photographs were awarded points according to qualities that were associated with viewing distance, viewing angle, and viewing azimuth. For example, to receive credit for viewing angle in the photograph of the chair and tables, at least some of the table's underside had to show. Combining over the four photographs, the scores could range between 0 and 46. Distributions may be found in Figure 8.3. On average, adults did significantly better than children (29.0 vs. 18.7 points, respectively). Photographs taken second were better than those taken first (25.8 vs. 22.0), although the improvement was accounted for by the children (i.e., there was a significant interaction between age group and trial number). The data from this task are thus consistent with the general notion that children attend readily to what is "in" the photograph, but only gradually develop their understanding of the spatial effects of vantage point.

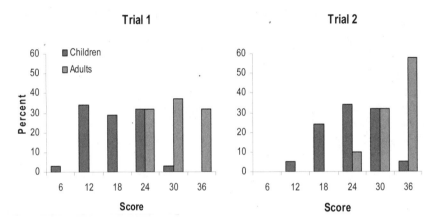

Figure 8.3 Distributions of total scores (maximum score = 46) on photographic model task by age and trial.

Creating original photographs

The task just described involved the creation of photographs by participants, but it was a highly constrained task insofar as it required simply that participants re-create model images. Thus it allowed no room for creativity in vantage point. In the tasks described next, participants were also asked to create photographs, but this time in a way that allowed personal choice. Participants (8-year-old children and college students; N = 40) were introduced to the digital camera they would be using, then led on a walk through a university campus. At four locations along the way, participants were asked to produce photographs that fulfilled some verbal description. Given that participants could control only vantage point (that is, the digital camera being used had a fixed focus, and neither filters, nor alternative lenses, nor lighting accessories were available), of interest was how participants would use vantage point to satisfy the photographic challenges.

The first request was given as participants approached a large, circular water fountain containing a spherical sculpture through which the water flowed (see Liben, 2003). Participants were simply asked to take a picture of the fountain, and then to view the resulting image on the camera display. If the resulting image included most or the entire fountain (true for all but a few participants), the participant was asked "What if you only wanted to see that spiral shaped part on top [gesturing a sphere up in the air] in your picture? What could you do to make that part take up most of the picture?" The two participants whose first image contained only part of the fountain were asked to include all of it (including the base) in their second image.

To measure success, photographs were printed to a fixed size, and the diameter of the sphere was measured. With only two exceptions, participants' first photographs were taken from a considerable distance. Thus, the entire fountain was almost always depicted, and the spheres in the initial photographs were quite small, and almost identical in size for children and adults. Because all but two participants (both adults) had begun with a long viewing distance, all but these two were asked to take the second photograph so that the sphere would take up most of the picture. Here the patterns from children and adults differed considerably. Among adults who were asked to have the sphere take up more of the image in their second image, 100% did so successfully. On average, the spheres in the second photograph were 3.2 times larger than those in the first. Among children, only 65% had larger sphere in the second photograph, and some of these (8%) were only trivially larger (less than 10% change in size). The remaining 35% were made up of some whose second sphere was identical to or trivially smaller (11%) and some whose second sphere was considerably smaller than the first (24%). On average, the spheres in the second photograph were only 1.02 times larger than the first. The conclusion from these findings is that adults, but only some children, were able to create a specified effect by controlling viewing distance. (Other solutions to the problem – such as a drastic change in viewing angle – also occurred extremely rarely, and again, were confined to adults.)

The second request was given as participants arrived at an art museum which had sculptures of lion paws on either side of the main entrance to the building. Participants were asked to take a photograph so that there would be "just one paw in the picture." Again, adults were more successful than children, with 90% creating images that satisfied the request. Furthermore, the remaining cases (10%) were pictures in which the second paw showed at the very edge of the image, an edge that would have been out of sight through the view finder (which shows slightly less of the scene than what is recorded on the digital image). Hence, given the visual information available to them, 100% of the adults met the request successfully. Among children, 68% created images with only a single paw, and importantly, the errors were not accounted for by the imperfect match between the view finder and digital image. Children found a variety of strategies for effecting the one-paw outcome. Although the majority of children simply changed viewing azimuth so that the second paw was beyond the edge of the image, some children changed viewing distance (taking extreme close-up photographs of a single paw) and some changed viewing angle. Among the latter, most photographed a single paw from below, tilting the camera toward the sky, although one child climbed on the paw statue and photographed it from above. Interestingly, one child reported a different strategy, saying he "waited for people walking by to block one of the paws from view."

The remaining two requests were given at a statue of a mountain lion, the school mascot. One request asked participants to take a photograph so that "it looks like we're seeing the lion peeking out from behind a tree." All participants except one (a child) positioned themselves so that a tree would be in front of the lion's side, thus producing images in which the lion's head was indeed emerging from behind a tree. The only noticeable age difference was that more adults than children (58% vs. 34%) selected a vantage point such that the only visible part of the lion was its head, yielding a more compelling sense of "peeking" than when the entire lion's body was visible except for the section obscured by the tree.

The second was a request to photograph the lion so that he would look "kind of scary." Again, we examined the resulting photographs with respect to viewing distance, angle, and azimuth. To assess viewing distance, we printed the images at a fixed size and measured the diameter of the lions' heads. On average, adults tended to move in closer to the lion statue than did children, creating heads of roughly twice the size, as illustrated in Figure 8.4.

Although close-up shots were taken by both children and adults, photographs from a very great distance (thus with very small images of the lion) were found only among children. Different patterns were also evident with respect to viewing angle. Among children, a viewing angle that was straight ahead was more common than a viewing angle in which the camera was tilted up (65% vs. 35%) whereas among adults, this pattern was reversed (22% vs. 61%). (Adults' remaining photographs were taken with the camera angled slightly downward, a viewing angle more easily used given their greater height.) Finally, there were also age-group differences with respect to viewing azimuth. Among children, photographs were less likely to be facing directly toward the lion's face than not (35% vs. 65%) whereas for adults, this pattern was reversed (67% vs. 33%).

Figure 8.4 Illustrative responses to the verbal request to make the lion look "kind of scary." Sample photographs approximate the average head size in photographs taken by children (left) and by adults (right).

Interestingly, anecdotal data from the scary lion request also provided support for the generalization that when judging the emotion conveyed by a representation, children are especially focused on the *referent* of the image rather than on the means used to depict it. In a spontaneous response to the scary-lion request, one child commented that "If you want to make it look scary you can't take a picture of the face because the face isn't scary at all. The eyes are just circles and the mouth isn't growling. You have to take other angles to make it look scary." Although this comment might have implied a sophisticated understanding of the need to change the vantage point (viewing angle) to make the face look scary, the fact that the child went on to avoid the face entirely by photographing the lion from the side suggests that the child thought that different portions of the lion were inherently differentially scary, rather than that camera angle could make an otherwise tame lion face look frightening. Another child also spontaneously protested that she could not make the lion look scary and, after taking her own picture, asked the interviewer to take a picture while she climbed up on the lion to "give him horns to make him scary."

To provide an independent assessment of whether the various differences in vantage points were effective in creating photographs that rendered the lion more or less scary, we asked another group of college students who had not participated in the lessons to rate the photographs for "scariness" using a 7-point scale ranging from "not scary at all" to "very scary." Data showed that, on average, the photographs taken by children were rated as significantly less scary than those taken by adults (with mean ratings of 3.1 vs. 3.7, respectively). Although these data are consistent with the suggestion that adults are better able to manipulate the spatial qualities for the emotional impact of photographs, they are by no means definitive. For example, children and adults may find different characteristics scary, and thus it is possible that data from child raters would have led to the reverse conclusion. Furthermore, many non-spatial factors may also have influenced the emotional tone of the children's and adults' photographs in this study (e.g., different framing to include or exclude background referents such as buildings or flowers; patterns of shadows).

Reflecting on photographs

Overview

The final group of tasks discussed here are those that ask participants to reflect in some way on photographs that they or others have created. Included are tasks in which participants were asked to examine a series of photographs and answer a number open-ended questions about them, to sort photographs into groups and explain the basis for their grouping, to examine identify their most- and least-liked photographs from among a set of photographs that they had produced, and finally, to provide numerical ratings of their responses to others' photographs and to explain a selection of their ratings.

Open-ended responses to photographs

As one method for exploring the way individuals think about and respond to photographs, we (Szechter & Liben, 2007) showed five professional photographs to participants (those given the technique-pair tasks described earlier, i.e., 7- to 13-year-old children and their parents). Drawing on methods developed by Barrett (1997) to help viewers critique photographs, we asked (a) "What do you see?" (b) "What does it mean?" and (c) "How do you know?" We selected photographs for this task that we judged to be non-canonical in some way, and hence more likely to draw attention to the photographs themselves rather than merely to their on content (see earlier discussion about the role of non-canonical qualities). For example, one photograph by Eggleston, entitled "Memphis," shows a tricycle but from a vantage point that dwarfs the suburban home behind it.

The qualitative difference in responses between prototypical children and adults is best conveyed by examples reported in Szechter and Liben (2007, p. 887, section letters added). The first example is from an 8-year-old child:

(a) "I see a little like bike. It has three wheels. Um, there's houses behind it and a car. And, um, there are no clouds in the sky." (b) "Um, I think it means someone left their bicycle out and it got a lot [mumbles]." (c) "Because it looks flat there [points to bike]. That's all."

The second is from a 10-year-old child:

(a) "A trike." (b) "The person who owns this is not very good at putting away his toys." (c) "Well he left his trike out in the middle of the street!"

And finally, although some adults responded similarly with respect to the tricycle itself (e.g., commenting on its condition and the neighborhood), adults generally reflected far more broadly on the more metaphorical meaning of the photograph, and of the role of the photographer in creating it. Illustrative is the following quote (pp. 887-888, section letters added) from one of the adults in the study:

(a) "I see a tricycle on the sidewalk in front of a house." (b) "I guess in some ways I think about how normally kids are little, and houses and people and parents are big, and so it's like they're kind of turning that on its head and saying this is the kid's world and of course it's at a kid's eye level, it's not taken down this way [gestures], but it's taken at kind of a level where the kid's at, so it's like this is what would be important to a kid." (c) "Um, I know because he took the trouble to get down, it's obviously, nobody's ya know, this tall, so he's taken the trouble to lie on his stomach and compose it just so ... Maybe causing adults to see things from a child's perspective."

To provide a quantitative analysis, responses were coded for whether or not they explicitly commented in some way on the role of the photographer. As would be expected from the illustrative responses above, comments about the photographer were significantly more common among adults than among children.

Sorting photographs

As a somewhat more structured means of exploring how individuals think about photographs, participants in the study just described (Szechter & Liben, 2007) were also given a sorting task. Participants were asked to group 12 photographs into two or more piles in as many different ways as they could. After each grouping, participants were asked to explain the basis of their piles, and then asked if they could think of a different way to group them. The photographs were selected to provide variation along lines of referential content (e.g., animals; buildings) and of media-specific and vantage point qualities (e.g., black-and-white vs. color; close-up vs. distant views). In addition, they were selected to sample across photographic styles and tone, achieved by selecting photographs from professional photographers' work rather than using canonical, picture postcard images. Although this approach did not allow some universal, *a priori* categorization of the materials against which participants' categorizations could be judged, it did provide the grist for participants' use of their own emotional or aesthetic responses to the images as a basis for categorization.

In general, the data from this sorting task showed that children had a tendency to sort (and provide rationales) primarily on the basis of multiple details of referential content. Illustrative is an 11-year-old who after some of the more common divisions (e.g., humans/animals/buildings; black-and-white/color) continued to sort on the basis of content divisions such as inside/outside; with windows and doors/without windows and doors; with houses/without houses; with a wall/without a wall and so on (see Szechter & Liben, 2007). Adults had a greater tendency to go beyond referential content and also sort on the basis of photographic qualities. Illustrative were the groupings of one adult which included: black-and-white versus color; people versus animals versus places; full subject versus close-up; and happy versus sad. When groupings were credited according to whether or not they were based on aesthetic features (including composition, color, emotion), children received significantly fewer points than adults.

Responses to one's own photographs

A third method that we have used for learning more about how individuals think about photographs involves asking them to select and explain photographs they liked and disliked. Data on "best-liked" and "least-liked" photographs were collected as part of the study described earlier in which 8-year-old children and college students had taken a range of photographs while walking on campus (Liben & Szechter, 2002). Following the walks, photographs were downloaded and displayed on the computer screen. Participants were asked to select their three most favorite and three least favorite pictures, and to explain the reasons for their choices.

Samples of best- and least-liked photographs selected by children and adults are given in Figures 8.5 and 8.6 Apart from the interesting nature of the selections themselves, the quality of children's and adults' explanations differed. As illustrated by the sample explanations reproduced in the figure captions, children tended to emphasize the degree to which they liked or disliked the *referent* depicted in the photograph, rather than the photograph itself. A particularly amusing example is the explanation given by one young boy (#23) who selected a photograph of a poster as his least-liked image "Because it has the word *love* on it." In contrast, adults tended to offer explanations directed to the qualities of the photographs themselves. Illustrative is the explanation given by #48 who refers to "The way the sun beats down, it kind of distorts the image. You can see like spectrum colors."

Figure 8.5 Illustrations of children's most-liked (top row) and least-liked (bottom row) images. Explanations for the most-liked (top row) selections were:

#4 "Because it was my favorite team's mascot, because there is my favorite summer sport in it...planting flowers"; #6 "Cause it shows a pretty sign and pretty flowers", and #11 "I love beetles, and plus it is a yellow beetle and yellow is one of my favorite colors." Explanations for least-liked (bottom row) were: #7 "It doesn't have that many artistic things"; #15 "Mom and dad don't like flags... they like the pointy flags more than square ones"; and #23 "Because it has the word *love* on it."

Figure 8.6 Illustrations of adults' most-liked (top row) and least-liked (bottom row) images. Explanations for the most-liked (top row) selections were:

#44 "Cause it just makes him look really cool. The close up of it. Just the effect of it"; #48 "The way the sun beats down, it kind of distorts the image. You can see like spectrum colors"; and #57 "It just reminds me of something I would do; lie on the ground and stare up at a tree and a really blue sky. Also I like the colors. Also usually you look at pictures straight on [gestures straight ahead], but you're looking up." Explanations for the least-liked (bottom row) selections were: #42 "No depth to it. Kind of took it at a bad angle. Should've gotten a side angle to see more depth to it"; #52 "It's kind of hard to look at. You don't know where your eye's supposed to be focused, and the water fountain is just not that exciting from that point of view"; and #58 "Because with the colors you can't see what it is very easily... the metal blends in with the concrete of the building."

To quantify the patterns of explanations, we coded all comments into one of four categories. *Referent* comments were those focused on the referent itself (e.g., "I like flowers"), memories of the referent (e.g., "it reminds me of my dog"), or qualities of the referent (e.g., "it shows how pretty the lake is"). *Surface* comments were those focused on the appearance of the image (e.g., "you can see...spectrum colors"). *Technique* comments were those addressing the way that the image was created (e.g., "kind of took it at a bad angle"). The fourth category, *uncodable*, was used when it was impossible to decide whether the comment referred to the photograph or to the referent (e.g., "it's beautiful"). When a single explanation contained more than one type of explanation, the coders judged which type appeared to be most central.

The pattern of results that emerges is consistent with the impressions from sample comments. Specifically, and as may be seen in Figure 8.7, for best-liked images, children's comments were overwhelmingly focused on the referents whereas adults' comments were roughly evenly divided between comments about the referent and those about the photographic surface. Both age groups offered relatively few (and roughly equivalent) comments about technique.

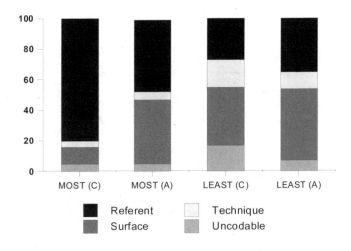

Figure 8.7 Types of explanations given by children (C) and adults (A) in selecting their most- and least-liked photographs.

For least-liked images, the pattern of explanations differed: the modal category for both children and adults was the photographic surface. Interestingly, for these least-liked images, children commented more on technique and less on referents than did adults (see Figure 8.7). It is important to remember, however, that the corpus of photographs that participants were judging in this study included those that were taken in response to the request to reproduce photographic models and to fulfill verbal requests (e.g., to make the lion look scary). Thus, the tendency to comment on surface and technique rather than referent may have been inflated beyond what might have occurred if all photographs had been created freely. At least some participants included among their "least liked" choices photographs that did not succeed on one of those requests, a response that is presumably unrelated to more general aesthetic judgments.

Responses to others' photographs

The final method discussed here was one in which we showed participants photographs and asked them to indicate their personal responses to each by using a 7-point scale in which the highest end (a "7" for older children and adults, an extreme "happy face" for younger children) indicated a really positive response to the photograph and the lowest end ("1" or an extreme "frown face") indicated a really negative response. After completing numerical ratings of 25 photographs, college students were asked to explain the reasons for their ratings on 8 items; children were asked to explain their ratings for 3 items.

Because data from children are not yet analyzed, only adults' responses are described here. We have obtained ratings from college students with (a) generally limited experience with photography (students enrolled in introductory psychology classes); (b) considerable academic familiarity with photography (students enrolled in a photography appreciation course that covers the history, major figures, and techniques of photography), and (c) extensive "hands-on" experience with photography (students enrolled in studio photography courses).

The rating data from adults with different levels of photography experience allow two clear conclusions. First, there is considerable variability: Virtually any photograph elicits the full range of ratings in each of the samples. Second, though, despite this variability, there are some systematic differences among samples. Such differences appear to reflect respondents' differential weighting of qualities of the referent (i.e., a response to the object depicted) versus qualities of the photograph (i.e., a response to the abstract, emotional, expressive, or technical aspects of the photographic surface).

An illustration of this point may be found in the pattern of responses to two photographs that were intentionally selected to contrast these two sets of qualities. One was an amateur's canonical snapshot of the Eiffel Tower that was expected to elicit generally positive ratings by those with relatively little photography experience and less positive ratings by those with greater levels of photography experience. The reverse pattern of ratings was expected for a professional photograph by Sean Kernan entitled *Man and Kitten, West Virginia Penitentiary*. This photograph allows a less definitive verbal description precisely because it is a non-canonical image of a non-canonical referent, but it might be described as showing a man (homeless? troubled? sad? concerned? frightening?) cradling a cat (that he is saving? protecting? loving? stealing?), apparently walking away from a building (burning? derelict?) in a hazy (smoky? misty?) background. Indeed, as predicted, mean ratings for the *Eiffel Tower* photograph decreased significantly with each level of experience whereas the mean ratings for the *Man and Kitten* increased with each level of experience.

Although these numerical ratings allow only inferences about what qualities are responsible for respondents' reactions to the photographs, participants' explanations for their ratings provide more direct access to what qualities individuals themselves believe are important. Coding systems for these open-ended responses are still under development, but the verbatim examples from both children and adults that are given below provide a flavor of the data.

Illustrative explanations given by participants for their ratings of Sean Kernan's *Man with Kitten, West Virginia Penitentiary* photograph.

Grades 1 and 2

Rating 7: I liked it because he's saving the cat. Because he's saving the cat and it's nice of him to do it.

Rating 3: Because I thought it was on fire and I don't like people being on fire and picking out animals who might be injured. I don't like it when it looks like a poor town. Like a poor town where people can get something to eat. I don't think that's very good.

Rating 5: Because it has a little kitten, a sorta happy and sad picture. Because he saved a kitten from a fire. That was the only reason why.

Grade 5

Rating 1: I thought this photograph looked really sad. I don't really like sad photos. It looks like the man has saved a cat from smoke. The environment looks very sad to live in! If this photo was in color, I might rate it different because I might be able to actually tell what is going on!

Rating 4: It was ok because the man in the picture looks evil. That's the downside. The upside is that I think he rescued the cat from all the smoke in the background. There also is a lot of pollution in the picture which is not good. Maybe the man started it. That's why I gave it in the middle because he could've created the smoke or he could have saved the cat from dying. So since I didn't know that much and it doesn't have any beauty but it could be a nice thing that he did.

Rating 7: I love cats and it reminded me of my cat when I first got her and because that guy saved that cat from a fire. It looks like he really likes the cat too.

Psychology Class

Rating 2: This photo scared me actually. I don't like the alley that the man is in or the smoke lingering behind him. A dirty image.

Rating 5: The steam in the background makes the figure of the man stand out. Yet, a building can also be seen in the back. I think it's a decent photograph.

Rating 5: Is an okay photo, but could have more contrast; not enough detail of man, can't see what he is carrying.

Photography Appreciation Class

Rating 2: I see poverty and depression in this picture. The man looks homeless and looks like he is in run-down area. It actually makes me sad.

Rating 5: I liked the way it looked like a man was trying to save/protect the kitten from the fog and dark surroundings.

Rating 6: Good composition and framing, subject matter; this is unique and appealing contrast.

Studio Photography Class

Rating 4: This photo seemed to be interesting. There is a variety of tones and shading. And the old man, his surroundings (mist in background) and facial expression made me think about the photo more.

Rating 5: I like the way the picture is kind of divided in half, one half with the smoky background, and the other half a dark alley, or street of some kind. This photo keeps my attention because it keeps my eye moving.

Rating 5: This photograph is very eye-catching. I immediately like the image. The sharp contrasts add a heightened emotion and feeling to the scene and it is very balanced compositionally.

Our tentative impression from responses like these is that the younger participants and those with relatively little photography experience focus more on the depicted referent and less on expressive impact and technique. Older participants and those with greater photography experience more commonly show attention to both.

Irrespective of whether these impressions about age- and experience-linked associations are born out once coding and analyses are completed, the specific examples shown before provide compelling demonstrations that some people focus on the referential content (e.g., "I like cats, since I like cats, I like the picture"), others on the expressivity conveyed (e.g., "The man in the picture looks like his kitten is one of the only good things in his life. I really like his expression and the cat's expression"), and still others on the photographic technique (e.g., "This photograph is very eye-catching. I immediately like the image. The sharp contrasts add a heightened emotion and feeling to the scene and it is very balanced compositionally").

Conclusions and future empirical directions

The empirical data just described show age-linked differences in understanding and appreciating photographs that fit expectations derived from the corpus of literature showing normative cognitive development in mastering representation, space, and other-mindedness. Results from the full range of tasks speak to children's growing sensitivity to the fact that the content and appearance of any given photograph is determined not only by what referents had been present when the picture was taken, but also by a variety of decisions and actions made by the photographer. With age, there is a greater tendency to talk about expressive emotions, photographer's intent, and photographic actions rather than merely about the content of what is depicted. Children are better able to understand the consequences of vantage point in distinguishing between pairs of photographs (photographic pairs task), in producing view-specific images (as in reproducing model photographs or as in photographing only a single paw), and in effecting particular impressions or emotions (as in creating photographs of the lion statue to show him peeking from behind a tree or looking scary). The observation concerning the emerging shift from initially focusing almost exclusively on content to gradually coming to focus on higher level meaning and style is consistent with what has been noted about developmental progressions in other visual arts (e.g., Freeman & Parsons, 2001; Gardner, 1970; Gardner & Gardner, 1970; Parsons, 1987; Winner, 1982).

In the discussion of empirical work thus far, I have approached developmental changes in children's understanding and appreciation of photographs as normative, attributing age-linked changes in children's photographic sensitivity to normative age-linked changes in cognitive development that may be expected in all cognitively intact individuals. Although at the level of group analysis the data described in the prior section are consistent with the broad sweep description of normative age-linked progression, embedded within this overarching trajectory are striking individual differences.

First, some children show sensitivity to photographic qualities and are able to profit from specific experiences far better than their peers. For example, the data from the reproducing photographic models task shown in Figure 8.3 reveal that even on the first trial, one child's performance surpassed that of all other children and rivaled (and even surpassed) the performance of many adults. On trial 2, over 30% of the children met or surpassed many adults' performance. Second, there is also striking variability at the other end of the developmental spectrum. For example, although (as reported earlier) adults asked about the Eggleston photograph of the tricycle tended to provide interpretations that went beyond description, some did talk almost exclusively about the objects in the photograph and about their characteristics (see Szechter & Liben, 2007). Even the less interpretive tasks revealed adults who seemed to be struggling (e.g., errors made by adults on some of the azimuth items in the photographic pairs task). In short, there are individual differences both with respect to the rate of change as well as the ultimate level that is reached by individuals. Core developmental questions thus include identifying the mechanisms that are responsible for both speed and level of outcomes.

Our recent and ongoing empirical work has been addressed to these questions. One approach has been to study the ways in which parents guide discussions of photographs with their children (Szechter & Liben, 2007). Another has been to study the effects of photography curriculum. In one study with college students, for example, we obtained students' ratings of others' photographs at the beginning and end of the semester. Students were enrolled in either a course in studio photography, a course on the history of photography, or a course in introductory psychology. Of interest was whether ratings change differentially as a function of the difference in the intervening curriculum (see Liben & Szechter, 2007). In another study with children in grades 1, 2, and 5 (Liben, 2007), we obtained ratings before and after one of three randomly assigned curricula given in the school art class. Curricula varied with respect to whether photography was specifically discussed and, if so, whether children were given an opportunity to take their own photographs). Although it is not possible to include details of these studies both because of space constraints and because the work is still in progress, it is mentioned here to provide some concrete ideas about the ways in which developmental mechanisms may be studied empirically. As a field, our ultimate goal is to do more than catalogue developmental and individual differences: It is also to understand where they arise and how they may be influenced.

Concluding comments

To close, I return full circle to the title of this chapter. The first two words (*Developing Children*) were intentionally chosen to imply two ideas. One is that children *themselves* develop and thereby become increasingly able to appreciate photographs in various ways. That is, as a consequence of general developmental growth in a range of arenas, children bring ever more advanced skills to bear on their interactions with photographs. The other implied idea is that there are experiences available via the social world that help *to* develop children's appreciation. That is, children's experiences with photography and other visual arts may be influenced by more knowledgeable others who introduce, guide, and mediate children's experiences. I have suggested that we need to look to both internally-motivated, child-driven mechanisms as well as to externally-motivated, socially-driven mechanisms to identify how photographic appreciation is facilitated. The former involve the various cognitive-developmental progressions (e.g., in spatial concepts) that emerge more or less universally as a result of normative constructive interactions children initiate with their physical environments. The latter involve the various kinds of experiences that children "receive" (even if moderated by the child's own constructive processes) from informal interactions with others (e.g., parents in the course of looking at a photograph album or book) and from formal educational experiences (e.g., participation in art classes).

The second part of the chapter title, which modifies photographs by both *informative* and *aesthetic*, is meant to highlight the idea that photographs carry referential meaning about the depicted object, scene, or event while simultaneously functioning as aesthetic objects in their own right. Too often photographs are thought about merely as record-keeping archives. Indeed, in earlier times photographs were considered to lie outside the realm of art, and they were not routinely collected or exhibited in art museums. The emphasis on practical over aesthetic is not unique to the graphic medium of photography. For example, a parallel point may be made about maps, aerial photographs, and satellite images, all of which are typically designed and used for some functional purpose despite the fact that they can also serve in aesthetic roles (Liben, 2001).

This point segues to the final word of the chapter title, *artifacts*. Photographs are indeed artifacts. They do not occur naturally; they are human-made. Their particular forms and the technologies that create them have undergone many changes from the days of daguerreotypes of the 1800s to the digital images of today. And although the etymology of the "art" in "artifact" refers to skill rather than to aesthetic beauty, I close with the thought that there is, indeed, art in photographic artifacts if the viewer is prepared to see it.

Even while the experience of producing, manipulating, and viewing photographs offers potential cognitive gains in a variety of domains, it also offers children the chance to discover new beauties, emotions, feelings, and insights that are valuable in and of themselves. It is helpful to recall Ellen Winner's observation that despite no obvious contribution to survival, some form of artistry has been practiced by all known human societies. Its production continues even in circumstances that require focusing most of one's energy on the sheer act of survival, as the art of concentration camp inmates attests (Winner, 1982). I believe that the current volume is a testament to art's growing centrality to the academic community; I can only hope that its centrality to children's lives will grow as well.

References

Barrett, T. (1997). *Talking about student art*. Worchester: Davis.

Barthes, R. (1981). *Camera lucida: Reflections on photography*. New York: Hill and Wang.

Beilin, H. (1991). Developmental aesthetics and the psychology of photography. In R. M. Downs, L. S. Liben & D. S. Palermo (Eds.), *Visions of aesthetics, the environment, and development: The legacy of Joachim F. Wohlwill* (pp. 45-86). Hillsdale, NJ: Erlbaum.

Carpendale, J. I. M., & Chandler, M. J. (1996). On the distinction between false belief understanding and subscribing to an interpretive theory of mind. *Child Development, 67*, 1686-1706.

Church, J. (1961). *Language and the discovery of reality*. New York: Random House.

DeLoache, J. S., Pierroutsakos, S. L., Uttal, D. H., Rosengren, K.S., & Gottlieb, A. (1998). Grasping the nature of pictures. *Psychological Science, 9*, 205-210.

Feininger, A. (1973). *Photographic seeing*. Englewood Cliffs, NJ: Prentice Hall.

Freeman, N. H., & Parsons, M. J. (2001). Children's intuitive understanding of pictures. In B. Torff & R. J. Sternberg (Eds.), *Understanding and teaching the intuitive mind: Student and teacher learning* (pp. 73-91). London: Erlbaum.

Gardner, H. (1970). Children's sensitivity to painting styles. *Child Development, 41*, 813-821.

Gardner, H., & Gardner, J. (1970). Developmental trends in sensitivity to painting style and subject matter. *Studies in Art Education, 12*, 11-16.

Jussim, E., & Kayafas, G. (1987). *Stopping time: The photographs of Harold Edgerton*. New York: Abrams.

Kimmelman, M. (January 9, 2004). *Photography review: Diane Arbus, a hunter wielding a lens*. New York Times, E-44.

Krauss, R. M., & Glucksberg, S. (1969). The development of communication: Competence as a function of age. *Child Development, 40*, 255-266.

Levine, M., Marchon, I., & Hanley, G. (1984). The placement and misplacement of You-Are-Here maps. *Environment and Behavior, 16*, 139-158.

Liben, L. S. (1999). Developing an understanding of external spatial representations. In I. E. Sigel (Ed.), *Development of mental representation: Theories and applications,* (pp. 297-321). Mahwah, NJ: Erlbaum.

Liben, L. S. (2001). Thinking through maps. In M. Gattis (Ed.). *Spatial schemas and abstract thought* (pp. 45-77). Cambridge, MA: MIT Press.

Liben, L. S. (2002). Spatial development in children: Where are we now? In U. Goswami (Ed.), *Blackwell handbook of childhood cognitive development* (pp. 326-348). Oxford: Blackwell Publishers.

Liben, L. S. (2003). Beyond point and shoot: Children's developing understanding of photographs as spatial and expressive representations. In R. Kail (Ed.), *Advances in Child Development and Behavior* (Vol. 31, pp. 1-42). San Diego: Elsevier.

Liben, L. S. (2007, June). *Children's developing appreciation of photography as an artistic medium of representation.* Symposium presentation at the annual meeting of the Jean Piaget Society, Amsterdam.

Liben, L. S., & Downs, R. M. (1989). Understanding maps as symbols: The development of map concepts in children. In H.W. Reese (Ed.), *Advances in child development and behavior:* (Vol. 22, pp. 145-201). San Diego: Academic Press.

Liben, L. S., & Downs, R. M. (1991). The role of graphic representations in understanding the world. In R. M. Downs, L. S. Liben & D. S. Palermo (Eds.), *Visions of aesthetics, the environment, and development: The legacy of Joachim Wohlwill* (pp. 139-180). Hillsdale, NJ: Erlbaum.

Liben, L. S., & Downs, R. M. (2001). Geography for young children: Maps as tools for learning environments. In S. L. Golbeck (Ed.), *Psychological perspectives on early childhood education* (pp. 220-252). Mahwah, NJ: Erlbaum.

Liben, L. S., & Szechter, L. E. (1999, October). *Teaching children photography.* Poster presented at the biennial meeting of the Cognitive Development Society, Chapel Hill, NY.

Liben, L. S., & Szechter, L. E. (2001, October). *Understanding the spatial qualitites of photographs. In L. S. Liben (Chair). Cognitive development: A photographic view.* Symposium conducted at the biennial meeting of the Cognitive Development Society. Virginia Beach, VA.

Liben, L. S., & Szechter, L. E. (2002). A social science of the arts: An emerging organizational initiative and an illustrative investigation of photography. *Qualitative Sociology, 25,* 385-408.

Liben, L. S., & Szechter, L. E. (2007). Children's photographic eyes: A view from developmental psychology. *Visual Arts Research, 33*(2).

Myers, L. J., & Liben, L. S. (in press). The role of intentionality and iconicity in children's developing comprehension and production of cartographic symbols. *Child Development.*

Ninio, A., & Bruner, J. (1978). The achievements and antecedents of labeling. *Journal of Child Language, 5,* 1-15.

Newcombe, N. (1989). The development of spatial perspective taking. In H. W. Reese (Ed.), *Advances in child development and behavior* (Vol. 22, pp. 203-247). New York: Academic Press.

Newcombe, N., & Huttenlocher, J. (2000). *Making space.* Cambridge, MA: MIT Press.

Overton, W. F. (2006). Developmental psychology: Philosophy, concepts, methodology. In R. M. Lerner (Ed.), *Theoretical models of human development. Volume 1 of the Handbook of child psychology* (pp. 18-88, 6th ed. Editors-in-Chief: William Damon; Richard M. Lerner). New York: Wiley.

Parsons, M. J. (1987). *How we understand art: A cognitive developmental account of aesthetic experience.* Cambridge, MA: Cambridge University Press.

Piaget, J. (1926). *The language and thought of the child.* London: Routledge and Kegan Paul.

Piaget, J. (1951). *Play, dreams and imitation in childhood.* New York: Norton

Piaget, J., & Inhelder, B. (1956). *The child's conception of space.* London: Routledge and Kegan Paul.

Piaget, J., Inhelder, B., & Szeminska, A. (1960). *The child's conception of geometry.* New York: Basic Books.

Sigel, I. E. (1999), *Development of mental representation: Theories and applications.* Mahwah, NJ: Erlbaum.

Sontag, S. (1977). *On photography.* New York: Anchor Books.

Szarkowski, J. (1973). *Looking at photographs: 100 pictures from the collection of the Museum of Modern Art*. New York: Museum of Modern Art.

Szechter, L. E., & Liben, L. S. (2004). Parental guidance in preschoolers' understanding of spatial-graphic representations. *Child Development, 75*, 869-885.

Szechter, L. E., & Liben, L. S. (2007). Children's aesthetic understanding of photographic art and the quality of art-related parent-child interactions. *Child Development, 78*, 879-894.

Szechter, L.E., Liben, L.S., & Rogers, J.D. (1998, August) *Children's understanding of photographs: Interventions and implications.* Paper presented at the 106th Annual Convention of the American Psychological Association, San Francisco.

Tomasello, M., Carpenter, M., Call, J., Behne, T., & Moll, H. (2005). Understanding and sharing intentions: The origins of cultural cognition. *Brain and Behavioral Sciences, 28*, 675-735.

Walther, T. (2000). *Other pictures: Anonymous photographs from the collection of Thomas Walther*. Santa Fe, NM: Twin Palms Press.

Wellman, H. M., Cross, D., & Watson, J. (2001). A meta-analysis of false belief reasoning: The truth about false belief. *Child Development, 72*, 655-684.

Winner, E. (1982). *Invented worlds: The psychology of the arts*. Cambridge, MA: Harvard University Press.

Part IV

Developing a Theory of Pictures and Aesthetic Preferences

Children's Understanding of Artist-Picture Relations: Implications for Their Theories of Pictures

Tara C. Callaghan
St. Francis Xavier University

Philippe Rochat
Emory University

Introduction

The ultimate human social-cognitive behavior is communicating with others through culturally shared symbols (Deacon, 1997; Tomasello, 1999; Wittgenstein, 1953). Just as all roads lead to Rome, much of early infant perceptual, cognitive, and social cognitive development converges upon this behavior dawning toward the end of infancy. The foundations that are built from the development of these basic processes prepare the infant for inclusion in this central social-cognitive goal: intentional communicative exchanges with others. The exquisite design of the human infant goes beyond the perceptual and cognitive abilities that enable independent interaction with the world of objects and events to encompass the unique ability to learn through others (Tomasello, Kruger, & Ratner, 1993). This social cognitive ability includes not only the capacity to reproduce the actions of others, but also the capacity to infer, and then adopt, the mental stance of others. It is ultimately these social cognitive abilities that enable infants to become symbol users.

Tomasello (1999, 2003) presents a cultural learning view of language acquisition that stresses the central importance to this development of understanding others as intentional agents like the self. He provides evidence to suggest that intentional understanding begins to develop during the period of 9-12 months, and it eventually enables infants to understand the communicative intentions of others as these intentions are directed toward them. Intentional understanding also positions infants to be able to interact with others in new ways such as in the establishment of joint attentional frames, which provide an intersubjective framework for communication, or in the ability to engage in role reversal imitation, which allows infants to acquire the symbolic conventions that others are using toward them.

Tomasello (2003) argues that it is the development of these foundations in intentional understanding that accounts for the particular timing of the onset of language toward the end of the first year.

Intentional understanding serves as a foundation in other symbolic domains as well. Tomasello and Rakoczy (2003; Rakoczy & Tomasello, 2006) argue that understanding of the intentions behind others' actions is critical for the development of pretense, which emerges around the second birthday and develops late due to its having the additional requirement that the child understand that pretense involves counterfactual actions. In this chapter and elsewhere, we explore the idea that intentional understanding is the core process that accounts for the onset of functioning with pictorial symbols (see also Callaghan, Chap. 2; 2003; 2004; Rochat & Callaghan, 2005). Thus, it appears that the foundation of intentional understanding, which emerges during the first year, positions infants to become true partners in communicative exchanges across a number of symbolic domains. That this ability develops first in the domain of language, and later in the domains of pretense and pictorial symbols attests to both the additional cognitive demands that these other domains may require, and to the relative importance the culture may place on the symbol systems (Callaghan, Chap. 2; 2003, 2004; Rochat & Callaghan, 2005).

Intentional understanding in the context of symbolic interactions amounts to the child coming to understand both that the communicative partner is using symbols to share meaning, and what the message means. Pictures, like words, are not transparent in their symbolic function. Infants need to learn about that function in some way, and we propose that the way they learn is through others, using the social cognitive skills of intention reading and imitation. In particular, the developmental story we propose is that children's intentional understanding enables them to acquire increasingly sophisticated knowledge about the nature of pictorial symbols from interacting with others who use those symbols in exchanges with them. As children gain communicative experience with the symbols that others have created, they build a theory of what a picture is for and come to be able to produce their own pictorial symbols. Thus, the child's theory of pictures is initially built through an inference of what goes on in the mind of others who use pictorial symbols. Once the child understands the referential function of pictures and begins to produce representational drawings, his theory of pictures can be further refined through symbolic interaction that can now be self-initiated.

Freeman (1995, see also Freeman, Chap. 3) proposes a theory of picture processing that captures the importance of intentional understanding with its claim that mature understanding of the referential function of pictures involves an appreciation of the complex intentional network that links the picture to three other components in the pictorial symbol communication process: The real world referent, the artist, and the viewer. Much of the theory and research on pictorial symbol understanding focuses on the first of these three links; that is, explaining how the picture comes to be linked to the referent by the child (DeLoache, 1995, 2002; DeLoache & Smith, 1999; Liben, 1999). What children understand, or misunderstand, about this symbol-referent relation at various stages of development, and the situational factors that can influence this understanding, occupies a significant portion of these research efforts. Very little research has focused on the question of the processes through which children come to understand the link. We have explored the question of process in our own research (Callaghan, 1999; Callaghan & Anton, under review; Callaghan & Rankin, 2002; Callaghan & Rochat, 2003, under review; Callaghan, Rochat, MacGillivray, & MacLellan, 2004; Callaghan, Rochat, Lerikos, MacDougall, & Corbit, under review; Rochat & Callaghan, 2005), and will argue in this chapter that the question of *how* children come to understand the referential link between pictures and their referents has to be answered by an exploration of children's understanding of the intentional link between the artist and the picture.

Specifically, we argue that children come to understand the referential function of pictures through others, especially through joint attentional episodes where others are using pictures as symbols in communicative exchanges with children. Through observing the referential actions of others, through inferring their communicative intentions, and through the reproduction of those actions and intentions, children enter the world of pictorial symbols. They come to understand what others use pictures for, thereby achieving referential understanding, and only then can they take on the role of artist. Production of a pictorial symbol is grounded in intention; symbols are intentional artifacts (Goodman, 1968; Wittgenstein, 1953). Children who do not understand the referential function of pictures cannot intend to have their graphic productions function as a symbol. In what follows we provide evidence from our own and others' research for the claim that children's understanding of referential intent is built from their understanding of the referential intentions of others, and that this understanding is initially implicit and only later develops into explicit understanding.

In middle class Western culture even very young infants are exposed to a rich array of pictorial symbols in their home environment. Baby board books, colorful wall decorations, family photo albums, visually attractive packaging, and other assorted pictorial symbols are typically made available for infants' direct sensorimotor interaction. We propose that the active exploration of this world of pictures through visual perception, cognition, and motor action has little impact on the building of referential understanding until it is linked to the exploration of those pictures through others (Szechter & Liben, 2004). Thus, in all of our tasks we present infants and young children with experts using pictorial symbols, challenge them to respond to that symbolic act, and infer through their actions what they take the expert's action to mean. We look for evidence of what infants and children understand about the symbolic behavior of those who produce pictorial symbols in their responses to others' symbolic behavior. These include tendencies to reproduce the actions of the experimenters, to find the pictorial products that the experimenters made, or to make predictions about what actions the experimenter will take next. Rarely do we use a language-based assessment of this understanding because we want to tap into the earliest dawning of the ability to understand pictorial symbols, and language terms for symbolic concepts may be difficult for young children to understand. Learning through others begins in infancy.

Infants: action-based knowledge of intentions

Before infants truly understand the referential function of pictures, there is a phase where they will nevertheless model the symbolic actions of others (Callaghan et al., 2004). In this study an experimenter presented infants with two types of items (photos of infant toys and the infant toys depicted in the photos) and demonstrated for eight trials one of two types of actions on the items: one that was referential (i.e., looking and pointing to the picture or object while shifting gaze between infant and item) and another that was manipulative (i.e., flexibly jiggling the picture or object while shifting gaze between infant and item). Following the demonstration trials, the infants were given four test trials that began with another demonstration of the target stance and ended by giving the infant the photo or object of the items. The first action that the infant took toward the item was coded as either referential (i.e., pausing manual action for at least 3 sec to look at the item), or manipulative (i.e., manually exploring the item). On the basis of prior social referencing research (e.g., Campos & Stenberg, 1981), we reasoned that infants would model the experimenter's actions only when the item was novel and they were unsure of what to do with it, and not in cases where the item was of a familiar type and they were confident of what to do with it. Thus, we expected them to model what the adult did with our high fidelity photos (novel stimuli for all children) but not with the infant toys that were depicted in those photos (similar to toys they had in their own environments). Our results confirmed that regardless of what the experimenter did with the toys, the 6- to 18-month-old infants manually explored them (see Figure 9.1). In contrast, beginning at 12 months of age, infants emulated what the experimenter did with photos – they looked at them significantly more following a referential, contemplative demonstration and they manually explored them more following a manipulative demonstration (see Figure 9.2). On the basis of these findings, we proposed that an early stage in developing an understanding of the symbolic function of pictures occurs between 6- to 12-months, wherein infants are acting toward pictures as others do, but without a conceptual understanding of the symbolic function.

Action-based knowledge is a first step in the construction of the more sophisticated knowledge that pictures are symbols; first infants act toward them as others do, later they understand why others act that way toward them. In order to conclude that infants both act on pictures as though they were symbols and also know that they are symbols, we would need to have converging evidence showing that infants can use pictures to cue their behavior in other symbolic tasks. We have completed a great number of these tasks in our lab and find no evidence that children can use pictures as symbols to guide their behavior before 30 months of age (Callaghan, 1999; Callaghan, 2000; Callaghan & Rankin, 2002).

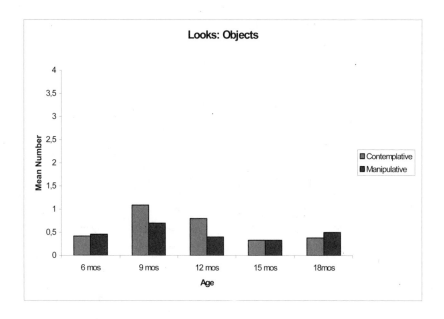

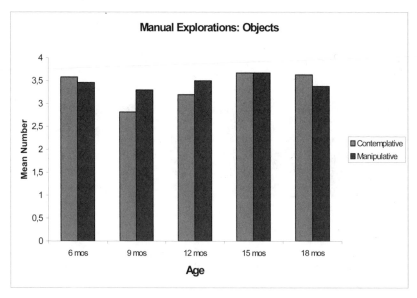

Figure 9.1 Findings from Callaghan et al. (2004) showing that infants do not imitate actions on objects.

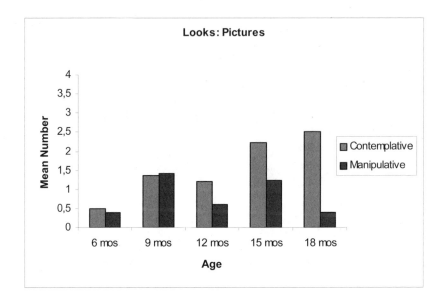

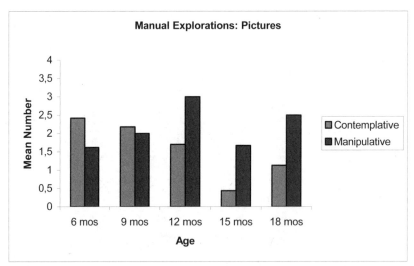

Figure 9.2 Findings from Callaghan et al. (2004) showing that infants imitate actions on pictures, beginning at 12 months.

Toddlers: perceptually-based knowledge of symbol-referent links

A number of studies investigate children's sensitivity to artists' intent by describing scenarios involving hypothetical artists rather than by having children watch others draw, and then asking children to name the drawing. In one such study, Gelman and Ebeling (1998) asked children between 2.5 and 4 years and adults to name line drawings that were drawn intentionally or happened by accident (spilled paint). They reported that children and adults used shape cues to name pictures they thought were intentionally created, but used these cues less so when they thought the picture was created by accident. In a second study with 4- and 7-year-olds, Browne and Woolley (2001) pitted the drawing's resemblance to an object (i.e., perceptual similarity of form cues) against the intention to draw a particular object and reported that children named on the basis of intention if the resemblance to the object was ambiguous, but on the basis of resemblance if it unambiguously resembled the object. Thus, they ignored intention when the drawing looked unambiguously like a particular referent that was different from the referent cued by intention (e.g., a drawing looks like a rabbit but, according to the story, was 'intended' to represent a dog).

In a study that asked children to name pictures that they had drawn, Bloom and Markson (1998) presented results to suggest that children can name drawings on the basis of intention, even when form cues cannot distinguish those intentions (e.g., drawings of a balloon and lollipop, or of self and the experimenter). In a replication and extension of this study, we uncovered a problem in the original study: Children were given a different color pencil to make each drawing, which introduces the potential confound of naming on the basis of color, and not intention, as the researchers claimed. In our study (Callaghan & Rochat, under review, Study 1), we asked children to draw the four pictures either using four different colors for each picture, or using a single color. We reasoned that children would successfully read their intention (i.e., correctly label their drawings of balloons and lollipops) only when there was a form or color difference between the items in the pair (see sample drawings of self and experimenter in Figure 9.3). Our results confirmed this prediction (see Figure 9.4).

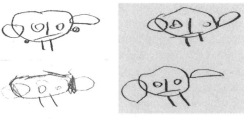

Form Difference   No Form Difference

Figure 9.3 Sample children's drawings of self and experimenter, one pair with form differences and another pair without form differences.

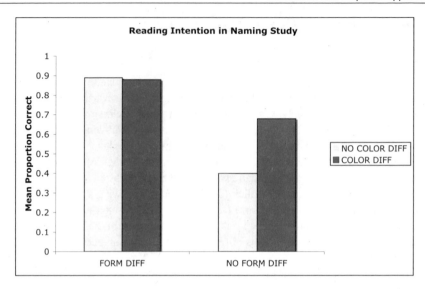

Figure 9.4 Data from Callaghan & Rochat (under review, Study 1) indicating that children utilize form and color differences between drawings to help them infer intent, and can not name drawings when neither of these types of differences appear across the pair.

Children were best at naming their drawings (i.e., reading intentions) when there were form differences between the items of the pair, but were also able to name drawings with color differences. They were unable to name drawings if there were neither form nor color differences to draw on. Thus, when reading their intentions post hoc from their own productions, children need to have a perceptual cue of that intention, and form seems to be an especially effective one. This conclusion was supported in a second study, where we had 3- to 5-year-old children make their own drawings, or watch an adult draw, and then find these drawings when they were embedded in backgrounds of other people's drawings of the same object or different objects (Callaghan & Rochat, under review, Study 2). When searching for the pictures they had intentionally made a few minutes before in a background of distractors that were drawings of different objects, the difference in form attributes did help to cue intention for children of both ages (see Figure 9.5). Form cues also helped them to infer intention when searching for drawings an adult had just made.

Taken together, what these studies suggest is that by the age of 3 years children can infer intention from hearing about scenarios that describe artists' drawing, by making their own drawings, or by watching an adult draw. For the most part children judge the relation between the picture and the referent when they make this inference; in particular, the resemblance of form cues. What we need to know is whether children can use this knowledge gained from judging the symbolic intentions of others to influence their own symbolic functioning.

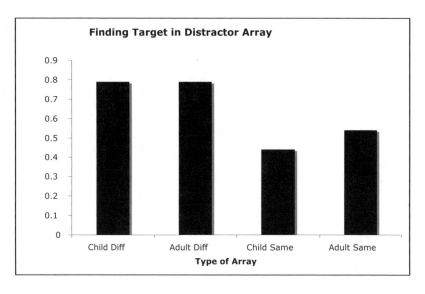

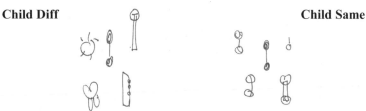

Figure 9.5 Data from Callaghan & Rochat (under review, Study 2) indicating that children more easily find drawings in distractors depicting different objects than in those depicting the same object.

In a longitudinal training study from our lab (Callaghan & Rankin, 2002), we exposed children to an artist producing pictures and examined whether this experience would facilitate the emergence of symbolic processing in children who were not yet using pictures as symbols or producing their own pictorial symbols. We found that within 2 months of the beginning of training, 2.5-year-old children who had been exposed in weekly sessions to an adult producing and then using pictorial symbols over 24 trials performed better on picture symbol comprehension and production tasks than children who had weekly sessions interacting with the experimenter and the same objects used in the training group, but who never saw pictures produced or used by the experimenter. These control children did not show the same level of performance as the training group until after they received training in the 5th month of the study (see Figure 9.6). Thus, repeated exposure to an expert who makes pictorial symbols and then highlights the symbol-referent link was enough to accelerate the onset of comprehension and production of pictorial symbols in these young children.

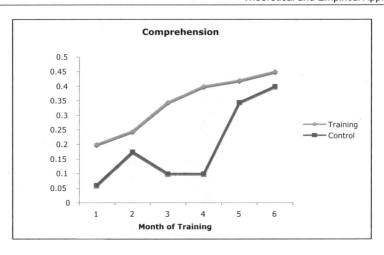

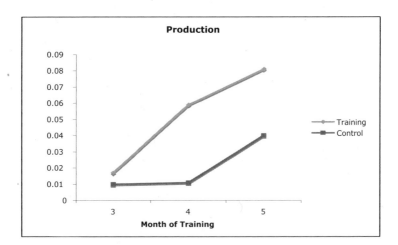

Figure 9.6 Data from Callaghan & Rankin (2002) showing positive effects of training on comprehension and production of representational pictures.

DeLoache and her colleagues have also tried to accelerate the symbolic functioning of young children in another symbol task using 3D scale models as symbols of rooms where items are hidden. The typical task for the child in her studies is to use the model as a cue to where a toy is hidden in the life-sized room. DeLoache (2002) summarized the findings from a variety of techniques used to try to improve young children's performance through highlighting the referential intention of the experimenter. Although not directly relevant to the study of pictorial symbol use, what is interesting is that most of these interventions using scale models that aimed to highlight referential intent were unsuccessful. In one of their few studies with pictorial symbols, DeLoache and Burns (1994) reported that extensive instructions that focused on the high level of perceptual correspondence between the symbol of the hiding place and the corresponding place in the room (i.e., the picture-referent link) were necessary for 2.5-year-olds to do well on the task. Recently, Salsa and Peralta de Mendoza (2007) replicated this finding but report that highlighting the representational intention of pictures facilitated performance of children far more than highlighting the perceptual correspondence between pictures and referents. In addition to the picture-referent link, children in both of these studies may have been able to support their performance by using the verbal label for the hiding place. Callaghan (2000) has demonstrated that young children will use verbal labels when they can to scaffold their performance in picture symbol tasks, and when they cannot, they typically do not show evidence that they can use pictures as symbols until closer to 3 years. It was also not until 3 years that children who received no informational support about intentions or perceptual correspondence in Salsa and Peralta de Mendoza's study were able to perform the symbolic retrieval task.

With the exception of the production measures in Callaghan and Rankin's (2002) study, the studies discussed so far focus on symbolic comprehension tasks; typically search tasks. While this measures children's understanding of how to use a pictorial symbol made by someone else, it does not illuminate how their symbolic understanding that comes from knowledge of how others use pictorial symbols is applied to their own production of symbols. The evidence from Callaghan and Rankin (2002) suggests that there is an impact, and we explored this question more fully in a recent study that spans the ages of 3- to 7-years.

Callaghan and Anton (under review) assessed 3- to 7-year-old children's ability to infer intent from artist's actions, and then act on that inference, under conditions where the intention to symbolize was more or less directly evident in the artist's actions. We measured imitative responses, reasoning that children's use of the artist as a source of information about what to do in a picture symbol task would be evidenced by their tendency to reproduce the actions of the artists. Children first engaged in a sorting game in which they played with, and then categorized, two types of toys. When they had sorted each type into one of two identical boxes, they were presented with one of four scenarios. In the Control condition they sorted a group of balls and sticks into two boxes, with balls in one and sticks in the other, and then were given a pencil and pad of post-it-notes to see whether they would spontaneously draw a picture to symbolize the contents of the boxes. For all remaining conditions the same procedure and stimuli were used on the test trial. Before the test trials on these other conditions, children watched artists as they produced, or tried to produce, visual symbols using different props than those used on the test trial. There were three experimental conditions; Demo (artist drew 2 quick pencil sketches on post-it-notes and placed them on the appropriate box to indicate the contents, see Figure 9.7), Multi-Symbol (artist sequentially made 3 types of symbols to indicate the contents of 3 pairs of boxes; playdough model, photo, replica object, see Figure 9.8), and Failed Attempt (artist tried to make a sketch to label boxes but failed because the pencil was broken).

Figure 9.7 Sample stimuli used in Callaghan and Anton's (under review) Demo condition.

Playdough model   **Replica object**

Photo

Figure 9.8 Sample stimuli used in Callaghan and Anton's (under review) Multi Symbol condition.

The results are summarized in Figure 9.9. Children of all ages inferred the intention to make a symbol in the Demo condition, where the intention to symbolize was directly given, readily making drawings to indicate the contents of boxes on the test trial. 5- and 7-year-olds were able to infer the intention to symbolize in the Multi-Symbol condition, where the intention to symbolize with a picture had to be abstracted from actions of the artist making other types of visual symbols. When the intention to symbolize was most obscure, no young children, but about half of the 7-year-olds, were able to infer the intention to symbolize from the Failed Attempt condition. Only two 7-year-olds spontaneously produced pictures in the Control condition, where there was no intention to symbolize evident in the experimenter's actions. What these results suggest is that children can make an inference about what pictures are for from watching an artist producing pictorial symbols, and they can then translate that knowledge into symbolic actions of their own. They can do this by 3 years when the intention can be imitated from a direct demonstration (Demo), and by 5 years if it the intention has to be inferred from related symbolic actions (Multi-Symbol). Together with the production study of Callaghan and Rankin (2002), this experiment provides support for the claim that children can apply what they learn from an artist who is engaging in symbolic actions with the child to symbolic actions of their own. Toward the end of the preschool period children begin to mirror an artist's symbolic intent.

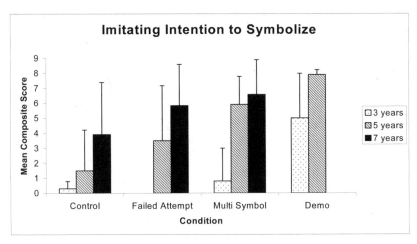

Figure 9.9 Findings from Callaghan & Anton (under review).

School age children: conceptually-based understanding of the symbolic function

There have been a number of interview studies that explored children's understanding of the artist-picture link. Freeman and Sanger (1993) interviewed 7- to 12-year-olds about the impact that the artist would have on the quality of pictorial representations. Their questions included such themes as what made for a beautiful or an ugly picture and whether the feelings or skills of an artist would have an impact on the quality of the product. Young children (7 to 10 years) focused on the picture-referent link suggesting that the only thing that mattered was how beautiful or ugly the referent was. Later on (11-14 years) children believed that qualities of the artist, such as emotional state or skill level, could affect the product. In a related interview study, Parsons

(1987) also found that children in this age range believe that artist's mood would be directly displayed on the canvas. The more mature realization that an artist could transcend felt mood and create an imagined world on the canvas was only rarely reported in these studies among the oldest children (late adolescence) and so may be an insight of the symbolic process that is rarely achieved without specific training. However, the interview task, which may only reveal children's relatively late-developing explicit knowledge (Karmiloff-Smith, 1992) of the factors that affect the picture making process, may be underestimating children's implicit knowledge about how attributes of the artist may have an impact on the picture.

In a series of three studies we explored children's implicit knowledge of the artist-picture link by asking children to identify pictures made by artists who varied in age, sentience, affective style, and emotional state (Callaghan & Rochat, 2003). Only in the last study did we interview children about how the factor of emotion influenced artists' drawings. Using a forced choice procedure in the first study, we presented children between the ages of 2 to 5 years with pairs of drawings that had been done by artists who varied in age (adult vs. older child vs. younger child) and sentience (person vs. machine). Beginning at 4 years, children chose the drawing that was appropriate to the age of the artists and at 5 years children could make machine-person distinctions. In the second study, 3- and 5-year-olds watched videotapes of artists who varied in affective style (agitated or calm) engage in a painting process and then judged which of two drawings were done by a given artist. Five-year-olds were successful at this task. In the third study, we showed 3- to 7-year-olds photographs of artists who differed in expressed emotion (happy vs. sad) and asked them to identify which artist painted each of 12 paintings. In this study we also interviewed children about whether an artist would make a picture that matched the artist's mood, whether an artist could do a picture that was opposite to their mood, and whether an artist could make a picture opposite in emotion of a theme that was personally relevant to the child (e.g., Could an artist make a sad picture of something that made the child happy?). The results of this study indicated that 5- and 7-year-olds successfully matched the emotion expressed in the painting to the emotion of the artist, corroborating earlier findings in this area (Callaghan, 1997; Callaghan & MacFarlane, 1998). In response to the interview questions, most of these children felt that to go against one's felt emotion when creating a picture would be difficult for the artist, and they found that especially unlikely if the theme was personally relevant to the child. We also included a battery of theory of mind tasks in this study to determine whether reasoning about how the attributes of the artist relate to the picture that artist produced would correlate with mental state reasoning. Our false contents task asked children to predict what an experimenter would think was in a crayon box that they had just learned had candles in it. Performance on the false contents task did correlate with performance on the picture judgment task, suggesting that the reasoning that underlies judgments of the mind behind the visual symbol may be linked to onset of basic mental state reasoning.

In a final study, we took our exploration of the link between mental state reasoning and children's conceptual understanding of pictorial symbols one step further. In this study, we asked children to make judgments about what an adult would do when a picture symbolizing the contents of identical boxes had been surreptitiously switched (Callaghan et al., under review). The study was designed to measure children's understanding about what a picture is for, but we tapped into this by asking them to judge how another person would respond to a pictorial symbol. Thus, we investigated children's understanding of the artist-picture link as a means of measuring the depth of their conceptual understanding of the picture-referent relation. To do this we designed a pictorial analog of the false belief task.

In the picture false belief task two adults and a child played with some toys and then one experimenter sorted them into two categories and placed them in identical boxes. Before leaving the room, he highlighted one of the contents and said he would play with these toys later because they were his favorites. When that experimenter left the room, the second experimenter announced she had a good idea and then labeled the boxes with a quick sketch to indicate the contents (see Figure 9.10).

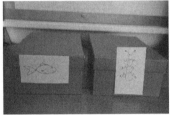 

Generic Symbols   **Familiar Logo Symbols**

Figure 9.10 Sample stimuli used in Callaghan et al. (2006) in the picture false belief task with familiar and unfamiliar logos.

Following this, she asked if the child wanted to play a trick on the other experimenter and then switched the pictures on the front of the boxes. The child was then asked to predict where the experimenter would look for his favorite toys when he returned. The level of understanding measured in this task goes beyond that found for the traditional false belief task in that it requires the child to form a representation of another person's representation of a representation (picture) of reality (contents of the box). Children found this additional level of complexity difficult; it was not until 7 years of age that children correctly predicted that the experimenter would look in the box with the picture of his favorite toys (see Figure 9.11). In a follow-up study we found that when we used more familiar logos (e.g., *Shrek* vs. *Lion King*) as labels for the contents of boxes, then 5-year-olds did well on the task.

Taken together, the results of these studies with older children suggest that when implicit knowledge of the picture-referent relation is measured in tasks that expose children to an artist in the process of making and using pictorial symbols, children fare well beginning around 5 years of age (Callaghan, 1997; Callaghan & Anton, under review; Callaghan & MacFarlane, 1998; Callaghan & Rochat, 2003; Callaghan et al., under review). When explicit knowledge is measured in language-based tasks (Freeman, 1997; Freeman & Sanger, 1993; Parsons, 1987), children's accessible knowledge of the artist-picture relation appears to emerge later in childhood, and becomes more sophisticated by adolescence. There has been relatively little work completed on the forces that are necessary to move children, and indeed most adults, toward the more mature understanding of the artist-referent relation that would allow, for example, for understanding that an artist could hide his felt emotion at the time of the making process and still complete a masterpiece of an imagined world.

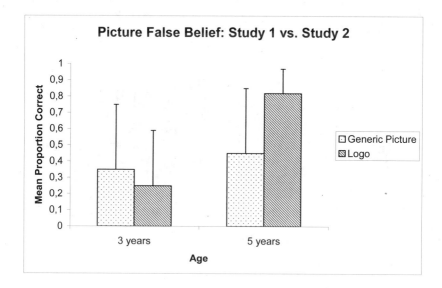

Figure 9.11 Findings from Studies 1 and 2 (Callaghan et al., under review).

Conclusions

We have reviewed a number of studies that examined what children know about the picture-referent relation in situations where children have to infer this knowledge from an artist using or producing pictorial symbols. What is clear from these studies is that reading intentions from artists' symbolic actions is a process that begins in infancy. Children's knowledge of symbols is manifested differently depending on the stage of development, giving us some insight into the understanding the child has of the picture symbol process at various points in development. Infants act on pictures as they see adults act on pictures, but we have no converging evidence that they have knowledge that pictures have a symbolic function (Callaghan et al., 2004). Three-year-olds can readily use the pictorial symbols of others to find the referent, implying implicit knowledge of the picture-referent link (Callaghan, 1999; Callaghan & Rankin, 2002; DeLoache & Burns, 1994). Their ability to do this can be facilitated by concentrated exposure to an adult producing pictorial symbols (modeling the symbolic act) and highlighting the symbol-referent link (Callaghan & Rankin, 2002), as well as by giving them information about the intention to represent with pictures (Salsa & Peralta de Mendoza, 2007). Three-year-olds can also reproduce the act of making a pictorial symbol, thereby making their own symbols, under conditions where the artist has just explicitly demonstrated that action (Callaghan & Anton, under review). When the inference of a symbolic intention is more difficult to infer from the artist's actions, only older children reproduce the symbolic act. The ability to conceptualize how the artist's concept of a pictorial symbol will influence that artist's belief system also takes some time to develop. However, when familiar pictorial symbols are used as props, even 5-year-olds accomplish this complex cognitive leap (Callaghan et al., under review), revealing that they do have a sophisticated, albeit implicit, understanding of the symbolic function of pictures. Also relatively late to develop is explicit knowledge of the artist-referent relation. When children are interviewed about the link between the referent and artists' skills or mental states they typically do not clearly communicate about this link until late in childhood (Freeman, 1995; Freeman & Sanger, 1993; Parsons, 1987). This may be due to language demands or lack of experience with aesthetic concepts and needs to be further explored, especially given the finding that even 4-year-old children readily make a link between artist and pictorial symbol in matching tasks (Callaghan & Rochat, 2003).

Many of the studies reviewed here have a common goal of understanding how children infer referential function from engaging with others who are using pictorial symbols. The responses of children to adults engaging with them in such symbolic acts are used as a window on what children know about the function of pictorial symbols. That children can build this knowledge through observations of other people is clear from the studies we have reviewed here, and suggests that cultural learning plays a lead role in the development of symbolic functioning with pictures. But is cultural learning necessary? We have recently begun to explore this question in cross-cultural studies of children's picture symbol understanding. These studies are not yet complete, but what the preliminary findings do indicate is that in our field sites (traditional villages in southeastern India and central highlands Peru), where there are very few pictorial symbols in the environments of children and very few interactions between adults and children that center around pictorial symbols, using pictures as symbols or producing pictures are relatively late-developing skills. Thus, the central importance in symbolic development of the ability to understand communicative intentions in others appears to be supported. Ultimately, it is this understanding that children acquire through others that will allow the child to fly on their own, using pictorial symbols intentionally in communicative exchanges that they initiate.

References

Bloom, P., & Markson, L. (1998). Intention and analogy in children's naming of pictorial representations. *Psychological Science, 9*, 200-204.

Browne, C. A., & Woolley, J. D. (2001). Theory of mind in children's naming of drawings. *Journal of Cognition and Development, 2*, 389-412.

Callaghan, T. C. (1997). Children's judgements of emotions portrayed in museum art. *British Journal of Developmental Psychology, 15*, 515-529.

Callaghan, T. C. (1999). Early understanding and production of graphic symbols. *Child Development, 70*, 1314-1324.

Callaghan, T. C. (2000). Factors affecting graphic symbol understanding in the third year: Language, similarity and iconicity. *Cognitive Development, 15*, 206-236.

Callaghan, T. C. (2003). Nascita e primo sviluppo della rappresentazione grafica. [The birth and early development of graphic representation]. *Età Evolutiva, 76*, 51-63.

Callaghan, T. C. (2004). Developing an intention to communicate through drawing. *Enfance, 1*, 45-56.

Callaghan, T. C. (2008). The origins and development of pictorial symbol functioning. In C. Milbrath & H. M. Trautner (Eds.), *Children's understanding and production of pictures, drawing, and art (pp. 21-32)*. Cambridge, MA: Hogrefe & Huber.

Callaghan, T. C., & Anton, F. (under review). *Three- to seven-year-olds imitate referential intentions with pictures.*

Callaghan, T. C., & MacFarlane, M. (1998). An attentional analysis of children's sensitivity to artistic style in paintings. *Developmental Science, 1*, 307-313.

Callaghan, T. C., & Rankin, M. (2002). Evidence of graphic symbol functioning and the question of domain specificity: A longitudinal training study. *Child Development, 73*, 359-376.

Callaghan, T. C., & Rochat, P. (2003). Traces of the artist: Sensitivity to the role of the artist in children's pictorial reasoning. *British Journal of Developmental Psychology, 21*, 415-445.

Callaghan, T. C., & Rochat, P. (under review). *Intention to represent in the drawings of children aged 2 to 5 years.*

Callaghan, T. C., Rochat, P., MacGillivray, T., & MacLellan, C. (2004). Modeling referential actions in 6-to 18-month-old infants: A precursor to symbolic understanding. *Child Development, 75*, 1733-1744.

Callaghan, T. C., Rochat, P., Lerikos, M., MacDougall, D., & Corbit, J. (under review). *Conceptual understanding of pictures and logos in 2.5- to 7-year-olds.*

Campos, J. J., & Stenberg, C. (1981). Perception, appraisal and emotion: The onset of social referencing. In M. E. Lamb & R. Sherrod (Eds.), *Infants' social cognition: Empirical and social considerations* (pp. 273-314). Hillsdale, NJ: Erlbaum.

Deacon, T. W. (1997). The symbolic species: *The co-evolution of language and the brain*. New York: WW Norton.

DeLoache, J. S. (1995). Early symbolic understanding and use. In D. Medin (Ed.), *The psychology of learning and motivation* (Vol. 33, pp. 65-114*).* New York: Academic Press.

DeLoache, J. S., (2002). Early development of the understanding and use of symbolic artifacts. In U. Goswami (Ed.), *Blackwell handbook of childhood cognitive development* (pp. 206-226). Oxford: Blackwell Publishers.

DeLoache, J. S., & Burns, N. M. (1994). Early understanding of the representational function of pictures. *Cognition, 52*, 83-110.

DeLoache, J. S., & Smith, C. M. (1999). Early symbolic representation. In I. E. Sigel (Ed.), *Development of mental representations: Theory and applications*. Mahwah, NJ: Erlbaum.

Freeman, N. H. (1995). The emergence of a framework theory of pictorial reasoning. In C. Lange-Küttner & G. V. Thomas (Eds.), *Drawing and looking: Theoretical approaches to pictorial representation in children* (pp. 135-146). New York: Harvester Wheatsheaf.

Freeman, N. H. (2008). Pictorial competence generated from crosstalk between domains. In C. Milbrath & H. M. Trautner (Eds.), *Children's understanding and production of pictures, drawings, and art: theoretical and empirical approaches* (pp. 33-52). Cambridge, MA: Hogrefe & Huber

Freeman, N. H., & Sanger, D. (1993). Language and belief in critical thinking: Emerging explanations of pictures. *Exceptionality Education in Canada, 3,* 43-58.

Gelman, S. A., & Ebeling, K. S. (1998). Shape and representational status in children's early naming. *Cognition, 66,* 35-47.

Goodman, N. (1968). *Languages of art.* Indianapolis: Bobbs-Merrill.

Karmiloff-Smith, A. (1992). *Beyond modularity: A developmental perspective on cognitive science.* Cambridge, MA: MIT Press.

Liben, L. S. (1999). Developing an understanding of external spatial representations. In I. E. Sigel (Ed.), *Development of mental representation: Theory and applications.* Mahwah, NJ: Erlbaum.

Parsons, M. J. (1987). *How we understand art.* Cambridge, MA: Cambridge University Press.

Rakoczy, H., & Tomasello, M. (2006). Two-year-olds grasp the intentional structure of pretense acts. *Developmental Science, 9,* 557-564.

Rochat, P., & Callaghan, T. C. (2005). What drives symbolic development?: The case of pictorial comprehension and production. In L. Namy (Ed.), *The development of symbolic use and comprehension.* Mahwah, NJ: Erlbaum.

Salsa, A., & Peralta de Mendoza, O. (2007). Routes to symbolization: Intentionality and correspondence in early understanding of pictures. *Journal of Cognition and Development, 8,* 79-92.

Szechter, L. E., & Liben, L. S. (2004). Parental guidance in preschooler's understanding of spatial-graphic representations. *Child Development, 75,* 869-885.

Tomasello, M. (1999). *The cultural origins of human cognition.* Cambridge, MA: Harvard University Press.

Tomasello, M. (2003). *Constructing a language: A usage-based theory of language acquisition.* Cambridge, MA: Harvard University Press.

Tomasello, M., Kruger, A. C., & Ratner, H. H. (1993). Cultural learning. *Brain and Behavioral Sciences, 16,* 495-552.

Tomasello, M., & Rakoczy, H. (2003). What makes human cognition unique? From individual to shared to collective intentionality. *Mind and Language, 18,* 121-147.

Wittgenstein, L. (1953). *Philosophical investigations.* New York: MacMillan.

Chapter 10

The Relationship Between Production and Comprehension of Representational Drawing

Richard P. Jolley
Staffordshire University

Sarah E. Rose
Staffordshire University

Introduction

In this chapter we consider a range of approaches to investigating the relationship between children's production and comprehension of representational drawing. First, we present studies that examine whether children's production lags their cognitive and affective comprehension of drawings, or if the two develop concurrently. Second, we report on the developmental shift in children's estimation and self-efficacy of their own drawings. Third, we explore the relationship between children's understanding of the developmental sequence in children's drawing development, and the causes of its development, with their own production level. We interpret these findings in terms of the varying graphic models children represent both graphically and mentally. Finally, we suggest future lines of enquiry that will build upon both empirical knowledge and theoretical understanding of the interaction in development between production and comprehension in the drawing domain.

In order to explore the relationship between children's production and comprehension of representational drawing we first need to consider what we mean by production and comprehension, and also to understand their underlying processes and elements. Picture production refers to the creation of the picture, and involves a number of cognitive, graphic and motor demands placed upon the child. For instance, when producing a representational drawing from memory the child may hold in mind a mental image of their chosen drawing topic or scene, and decide which features of this image they want to represent and how to depict them. Graphic schemas need to be chosen to reflect the child's choices, the execution of which depends upon the child's drawing skill and motor control of wrist and fingers. Furthermore, the child needs not only to attend to the line currently being drawn but also to its placement relative to other lines drawn or planned to be drawn, so that the finished drawing presents a coherent and spatially organized set of lines for the topic depicted.

Picture comprehension, in contrast to picture production, appears on the surface to be more straightforward. In the classic Hochberg and Brooks (1962) study the authors report a 19-month-old boy brought up since birth in an environment that provided only minimal exposure to pictures. Line drawings and photographs of objects and toys familiar to the boy were then prepared and presented to him. Despite the lack of experience with pictures he was able to name many of the pictures' contents when presented with them for the first time at 19 months of age. There is evidence from habituation studies that even babies in the first months of life can notice a similarity between a three-dimensional object and its picture (DeLoache, Strauss, & Maynard, 1979). Such an early ability to recognize depictions of referents (a referent being the three-dimensional object that the picture refers to) is no doubt due to the iconic similarity that representational pictures have with their referents. The apparently simpler process of recognition compared to the processes of production is borne out by the developmental delay in children producing representational drawings compared to when they appear to recognize them. Even the most rudimentary representational drawing is not typically created by children until around 3 years of age.

Nevertheless, recognizing a referent from its symbolic representation does not mean that the child fully understands its meaning. For example, in the case of language a young child may recognize sounds and words but not necessarily understand their full meaning or significance. Similarly, in the case of pictures there is much more to learn about a picture than merely recognizing its contents. In the world of adult art an art critic may comment about a painting on a number of aspects of pictorial comprehension. For instance, the materials and processes used to create it, the intention and interpretations of the picture, its expression of mood or concepts, the style in which it has been painted, and the art tradition it falls under. Furthermore, these cognitive responses may be supplemented by the art critic's affective and personal evaluation of the painting, such as whether he or she likes it or not, and how the picture affects the art critic's feelings. These different facets of understanding a painting (both cognitive and affective) form a framework for the comprehension of pictures.

Although children are not expected to understand the deep complexities of adult art and the art culture that surrounds works of art, they nevertheless are able to cognitively and affectively respond to pictures beyond the level of mere recognition (see Trautner, Chap. 11). In the next section we will discuss some of the key responses children make to pictures from a developmental perspective, as well as outlining the developing progression of their own picture production.

Development of children's production and comprehension of pictures

Since the latter part of the 19th century when children's drawings were first being subjected to scientific study there has been a wealth of literature on the developmental changes in the representational forms children use. Considering the work derived from natural observations of children drawing as well as experimental studies (for reviews, see Cox, 2005; Golomb, 2004; Jolley, in press) there is a general consensus that children's drawing production develops from disorganized scribbles to representational forms of increasing visual realism. But a statement of shift from non-representation to visual realism is too simplistic as the development of realistic drawing in childhood does not follow a linear pattern of steady incremental shifts with age. For instance, in Luquet's (1927/2001) account of drawing development he argued that children produce different styles of realism before embarking upon a desire to capture the visual likeness of topics. In particular, he discussed a graphic system of intellectual realism that children adopt prior to visual realism. In intellectual realism the child is concerned with depicting what they regard as the most salient or significant features of the subject matter as well as drawing the features in their generic shape. In effect this means that a drawing shows more features than could be seen from any single perspective, and that features tend to be drawn in their full shape rather than the partial shapes more typically observed when viewing an object or scene (e.g., because another feature in the foreground blocks one's view of the whole shape of a behind feature). The child uses certain techniques to create this desired effect, such as separation of details, transparency, drawing some features from an air-view plan, and folding out certain parts of the topic.

Luquet observed that there then comes a point in the child's drawing development that they begin to notice that their multi-perspective drawings do not reflect how objects actually look in reality. Consequently, they begin to try to draw only those elements of a scene that can be seen from one vantage point and in the shape that they appear from that perspective. Accordingly, they start to drop the aforementioned techniques of intellectual realism in preference of occlusion, suppression of some details and perspective. Children are in essence moving away from drawing an internal model of the subject matter towards a visual model (for further details see Jolley, in press).

Research on children's comprehension of pictures has adopted a variety of different methodological approaches (picture selection tasks to semi-structured interviews) and pictorial forms (colored line drawings to adult paintings). Machotka (1966) asked children to select from artists' paintings the ones they preferred and to justify their selections. Children younger than 7 years tended to focus on color and subject matter, while the most frequent responses made by 7- to 11-year-olds referred to the realism of the subject matter depicted. Parsons (1987) carried out semi-structured interviews with children and adults, asking them to comment on a selection of works of art. Color was a prominent feature among the younger children's comments, whereas older children focused on the subject matter and preferred pictures of topics depicted realistically (see Trautner, Chap. 11). Furthermore, Parsons' (1987) analysis of children's interest in subject matter in paintings, developing from a preference for the depiction of *schematic realism* to *photographic realism*, seems to correspond closely with Luquet's shift from intellectual to visual realism in children's own productions.

Overall, there appears to be a broadly similar developmental path in production and comprehension from an initial interest in non-representation to a shift of attention to subject matter and its graphic systems of realism. But does production and comprehension of drawing develop at the same rate, that is, concurrently? Or does the child's comprehension of pictures develop quicker than for their production (as is the case for recognition), presumably because of the increased demands in the production process? In the next two sections we shall review research that is supportive of one or the other position.

Concurrent development of production and comprehension

In our discussion of Luquet's (1927/2001) notion of intellectual realism in the previous section we commented that according to Luquet the child is drawing from their internal model of the topic. Although the specific nature of the internal model is difficult to define (e.g., see Freeman, 1972; Cox, 1993; Golomb, 2002; Kosslyn, Heldmeyer, & Locklear, 1977; Piaget & Inhelder, 1956) for Luquet it appears that it contains what the child believes are the criterial features of a topic that help to define it, assisted by showing the features in their full shape and not diminished by being partially occluded by other features. One argument that has been presented in the literature for production and comprehension developing concurrently is that the child's internal model (or metaknowledge) drives their choice of drawing, whether it is one that they make themselves or select from an array of pictures presented to them (Brooks, Glen, & Crozier, 1988; Moore, 1986; Taylor, & Bacharach, 1981). If one extends this argument further then production and comprehension develop concurrently due to the child's changing conception of the salient features of the topic and how they should be depicted. Indeed, this case can be extended even further to include the child's subsequent shift in preference to a visually realistic style, as mentioned above in terms of children's own drawings (Luquet, 1927/2001) and children's attitudes to pictures made by others (Parsons, 1987).

Studies comparing children's attitudes to pictures with their own productions have typically asked the child to draw a topic (the measure of production) and to select a picture of that topic (the measure of comprehension). For the selection task an array of pictures are presented to reflect the developmental range of forms that children produce of the topic. Taylor and Bacharach (1981) showed 3- to 5-year-old children three representational drawings of a man: a *tadpole* form (arms and legs protruding from the head with no body shown), a transitional figure (as in the tadpole form but with a suggestion of a body drawn between the head and the legs), and a complete figure (clearly defined separate areas of the head and body, with arms and legs protruding from the body). Children were asked to select from these three drawings the drawing that most looked like a picture of a real man. The children were then asked to draw their own picture of a man while the complete drawing of a man from the selection task was left in front of them to serve as a model. The findings indicated that the most frequent choice in the selection task made by the tadpole drawers and those children who drew a complete figure was the figure similar to their own level of drawing. We must be cautious, however, in interpreting this as strong evidence for production and comprehension developing concurrently. First, there were many tadpole and *complete* drawers who did not select a similar form of drawing that they drew themselves. Second, the data from the scribblers are difficult to interpret as there was no similar (i.e., scribbled) drawing available to them in the selection task. Furthermore, the scribblers tended to pick the complete figure rather than the (developmentally closer) tadpole version.

Moore (1986) presented children with an array of drawings of houses which had chimneys and windows in each of two alternative positions, which also showed either one or two sides of the house (see Figure 10.1). The 4- to 9-year-olds tested were asked to select the best drawing from multiple paired drawings from this array, and also to draw their own picture of a house in a separate session where no drawing model was shown (the order in which the children participated in the two sessions was counterbalanced). Moore concluded from her data that children of all ages preferred those drawings which had the most features in common with their own productions. Brooks et al. (1988) extended Moore's (1986) study by testing younger children (who are likely to suffer from production problems), and by comparing children's production and selections of the human figure as well as houses. Three- to four-year-olds were asked to draw a man and a house, and then in a later session instructed to choose the best drawing from pairs of man drawings and pairs of house drawings (see Figure 10.2 for complete array of drawings). Consistent with Moore's (1986) data and interpretations Brooks et al. (1988) reported that the children significantly preferred representations which were most in common with their own drawings, and that children's drawings are not inferior forms of their ideal because of any production difficulties.

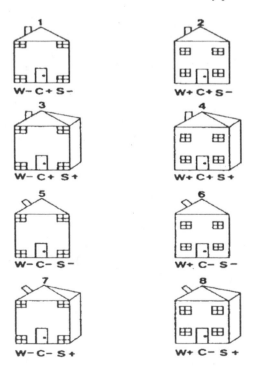

Figure 10.1 Drawings of a house used as stimuli in Moore's (1986) selection task.

Figure 10.2 Drawings of a person and house used as stimuli in Brooks et al. (1988) selection task.

A fundamental problem with both Moore's (1986) and Brooks et al.'s (1988) studies is the formulaic representations the children saw in the selections tasks. Moore's (1986) drawings varied only on the placement of windows and chimneys, and whether an additional side of the house was shown. Such variations reflect poorly the range of house drawings that children typically produce (see Barrouillet, Fayol, & Chevrot, 1994). A similar problem is evident in the drawings of houses and people presented in Brooks et al.'s study. The drawings only varied in number of details and so did not take into account other distinguishing properties of children's drawings such as placement, spatial relationships and proportion.

In conclusion, although Taylor and Bacharach (1981), Moore (1986) and Brooks et al. (1988) found some evidence that children may select drawings for the *best* or most *real* that have a similar developmental level to their own drawing, the evidence is not wholly convincing. We shall now consider whether the evidence for children's production of drawing lagging behind their comprehension of drawings is more persuasive.

Production lagging comprehension

We commented earlier in this chapter on the extensive cognitive, graphic and motor demands on producing a representational drawing. These demands lie at the core of the argument that production of drawing lags comprehension. Thus, although children have an intention of what to draw and how to draw it, they struggle to translate this on to the paper. Such an account is supported by the observation made by many researchers that drawing activity declines in the pre-adolescent period (e.g., Cox, 1989; Gardner, 1980; Golomb, 2002; Jolley, in press; Kellogg, 1969; Luquet, 1927; Mathews, 2003; Mortensen, 1991; Thomas & Silk, 1990; Winner, 1982). One of the reasons suggested for this decline in older children is that they become increasingly frustrated at producing drawings of less visual realism than they would like. A variation of this view is that children are aware they cannot produce what they regard as an ideal image of a topic, and therefore construct a simplified form that they are content with for their drawings. In contrast, their choices in selection tasks reveal a more accurate reflection of their preferred form of the topic. Further support for the production deficit hypothesis comes from other domains in the child's development where comprehension develops faster than production. In the case of language, for example, there appear to be similar production demands as found in drawing production. For instance, in order to convey an oral message the child has to consider what needs to be said, translate this mental conception into words, and pronounce these words appropriately and in the correct order. Even babies and young infants have some level of understanding of what is being said to them a long time before they can vocalize words and construct sentences (see Jusczyk, 1997, for a discussion on the relationship between production and comprehension in language). Given the similarity between the production demands of language and drawing one would expect that production lags comprehension in the drawing domain too.

An early study that compared children's drawings and selections was reported
by Kosslyn et al. (1977). They presented 4- to 11-year-olds with the following
three-dimensional objects: a cube, a flat surface with sticks protruding out of it, a
house (although it was shaped more like a warehouse or barn!), and a prism. All
four objects were presented at an angle so that the depth of the object was visible
to the child. The children were then shown an array of drawings that represented a
range of graphic forms of each of the presented objects, such as the front face
only, a diagrammatic or fold out drawing, or different types of perspective drawing (see Figure 10.3). Within each topic drawings were presented in pairs from
which the children were asked to pick the best drawing of what they saw of each
object (on half of the trials the object remained in view). Additionally, the children
were asked to draw each object themselves, with the objects in front of the child
as models.

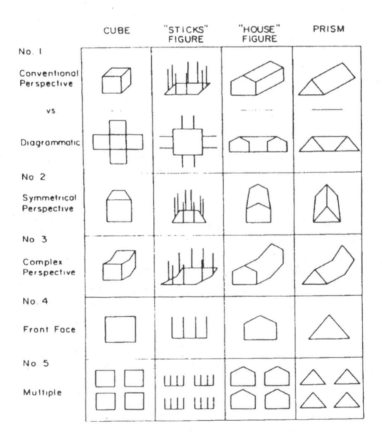

Figure 10.3 Drawings of a *cube*, *sticks* figure, *house* figure and a *prism* used as stimuli
in Kosslyn et al. (1977) selection task.

The authors reported that whereas many children drew diagrammatic pictures (which displayed all the components of the object but was deficient in visual accuracy as the drawings lacked perspective) few children preferred them. Instead, they often selected perspective drawings as the best representation of each object. Kosslyn et al. (1977) commented that many children who consistently picked the perspective drawings seemed frustrated in their failed attempts to draw what they had preferred. These anecdotal reports are consistent with the view that children's internal representations of an object are subjected to production difficulties when children try to draw them, and provide further supporting evidence that children's production lags behind their comprehension of drawing. We should be careful, however, not to apply this conclusion to all levels of drawing ability found in children. For instance, a closer examination of Kosslyn's et al.'s (1977) data reveals that many older children both drew and chose drawings showing conventional perspective. Could it be possible that any lag between production and comprehension may diminish with age?

This was the claim made by Fayol, Barrouillet, and Chevrot (1995). They asked 3- to 10-year-olds to draw a house and a man, and in a later session to choose the drawing from pairs of other children's drawings of houses and men the one they considered was made by an older child. They aimed to test two hypotheses. First, that children's internal models are similar to those held by adults but that difficulties with production lead the child's own drawings to be inferior to those which they prefer. This hypothesis predicted that the child's tendency to select more advanced drawings declines with age as children's own production skills increase. The alternative hypothesis was that if children's own drawings and selections are both dictated by their internal model of the topic, then there would be no lag in production compared to comprehension. These two hypotheses Fayol et al. (1995) entertained are particularly interesting as they are directly derived from the opposing theoretical positions in this literature. Fayol et al. (1995) found that children did choose more advanced drawings than they drew themselves but this production gap decreased with age, a finding consistent with their first hypothesis. Both Kosslyn et al.'s (1977) and Fayol et al.'s (1995) findings, therefore, appear to support the view that although production lags comprehension, this lag diminishes in older children as they become more accomplished in producing drawings which reflect their visually realistic internal model.

As is the case for the studies reported in the previous section that support production and comprehension developing concurrently, there are methodological problems also inherent in Kosslyn et al.'s (1977) and Fayol et al.'s (1995) studies. In the case of Kosslyn et al.'s (1977) study children made their drawing with the three-dimensional object in view. Giving a child a model to draw from is likely to influence what the child draws, compared to how the child would choose to draw the topic if given no direction (a similar problem applied to Taylor and Bacharach's (1981) selection task where children were presented with a drawing of a complete figure of a man while they drew). A more serious problem in Kosslyn et al.'s (1977) study is the choice of unfamiliar topics. One has to look at many children's drawings before one finds a drawing of a cube, prism, or a flat surface with protruding sticks! Such unusual subject matter is likely to lead to production difficulties for children due to their inexperience of drawing them (see Jolley, in press). Indeed, as we noted above, Kosslyn et al. (1977) observed that many children made frequent revisions as they struggled to draw a representation of the presented model which they felt satisfied with.

In contrast, Fayol et al. (1995) used the more common topics of the human figure and house as the basis of their investigation. The human figure in particular is not only the most common topic children draw, but also there has been much research on it facilitating our knowledge of its developmental pattern in children's drawings (see Cox, 1993). Although Fayol et al. (1995) presented actual children's human figure drawings in the selection task (and not adult-generated stereotype drawings that plagues much of the research in this area), the drawings did not reflect the full developmental range of forms that would be expected from the age range of the children they tested. For instance, all drawings included a body. The youngest children tested (from 2 ½ years of age) were therefore only given forms to choose from that were far in advance of the drawings they could produce. This artifact of the experiment would no doubt have contributed to the overall effect of children drawing inferior forms to those they selected. At the other end of the developmental scale the oldest participants were not presented with drawings made by those older than themselves. Consequently, Fayol et al.'s (1995) finding that the lag between production and comprehension reduces with age is compromised by the very real possibility that the older children may have chosen a more advanced drawing compared to their own production level if they had been presented with such an option.

Separating out cognitive and affective responses

It is clear that making sense of the conflicting evidence is problematic due to concerns of methodology and interpretation of data. Another notable methodological issue in this literature is the variety and ambiguity of the instructions in the selection tasks, particularly in respect of the basis in which children are asked to make their selection. Brooks et al. (1988), Kosslyn et al. (1977) and Moore (1986) asked children to choose the *best* drawing. Taylor and Bacharach (1981) asked their participants to pick the most realistic drawing, and Fayol et al. (1995) asked children to pick the drawing made by the oldest child. The instruction to pick the *best* drawing is somewhat ambiguous. Brooks et al. (1988) and Moore (1986) appear to interpret *best* as the one which the child likes the best as they conclude from their data that children are satisfied with their drawings. An alternative interpretation of *best*, however, is the drawing that is the most visually realistic. Whereas one interpretation of the best drawing seems to be based on an affective response to the pictures, the other interpretation is grounded in a cognitive understanding of the respective levels of realism among the drawings. Consequently, we should not assume that these two alternative interpretations would lead children to selecting the same drawing from the array. Recall our earlier discussion regarding the complexity of measuring comprehension, and in particular that a viewer can respond cognitively and affectively to a picture. It is clear, therefore, that any methodological refinements to the existing body of work should separate out children's cognitive and affective comprehension responses to drawings.

In our own work carried out at Staffordshire University we have conducted a number of studies with this aim in mind. In two studies reported by Jolley, Knox, and Foster (2000) children produced human figure drawings which were categorized as either a scribble, pre-conventional, simple conventional or an advanced conventional drawing. We used the term conventional in the sense that conventional figures included the main criterial features of person that are found in older children's drawings (i.e., head with facial features, body, arms and legs), and corresponds with Taylor and Bacharach's (1981) term *complete*. Drawings considered to be non-representational were assigned to the scribbling category. Pre-conventional drawings were representations of the human figure in which only some of the main parts were included, and those parts that were represented were on some level displaying an inadequate spatial relationship between them. A typical example of this category is the tadpole form, with the body apparently omitted and the arms and legs protruding from the head. In simple conventional drawings all the salient body parts were depicted (head, facial features, body, arms and legs). Although the spatial arrangement of these features was accurate the features were drawn simply, and out of proportion to each other. In the fourth category, the advanced conventional drawings portrayed more details, a higher standard of proportion, and showed evidence of being drawn from a single perspective. The overall impression of the advanced conventional drawings was that they could represent a particular person, rather than the basic generic form of the simple conventional drawings. In both studies the reliability of the production measure was checked by having each drawing rated by two independent raters.

In the standard presentation of the selection task each child saw four drawings made by other children, each drawing representing one of the aforementioned drawing categories (see Figure 10.4 for one set used in Study 2). For each set of four drawings children were required to make three choices: "Which picture looks most like a real man?" (eliciting a cognitive response), "Which picture do you like the best?" (affective response) and "Which picture looks most like how you draw a man?" (estimation response). The estimation question was included to gain insight into how children comprehend their own drawing ability.

Sixty-one 2- to 9-year-olds participated in both the production and comprehension task in the first study. All but one child selected a conventional drawing in response to the realism question. More importantly, almost all the scribblers, pre-conventional and simple conventional drawers chose a drawing from a higher category than their own drawing. This was also true for these three categories of drawers in their preference responses to the "like the best" question, although there was a small minority who preferred a similar standard of drawing to the one they produced. The advanced conventional drawers preferred and considered most realistic the advanced conventional drawing. In respect of the estimation data, scribblers and pre-conventional drawers generally overestimated the level of their own human figure drawings. Simple conventional drawers showed some improvement with approximately half successfully estimating their own drawing level. It was only the advanced conventional drawers where the majority estimated their drawing level correctly.

(a) Scribble

(b) Pre-Conventional

(c) Simple Conventional

(d) Advanced Conventional

Figure 10.4 One example set of four children's drawings of a man used in the selection task reported by Jolley et al. (2000, Study 2).

Children's responses to all three questions clearly indicated that production lagged comprehension for most developmental points of drawing behavior, the exception being children who drew at the most advanced level. It would appear, therefore, that our findings were consistent with that of Fayol et al. (1995). But a significant methodological weakness of our first study, as was the case in Fayol et al.'s (1995) study, was that the most advanced drawers were not presented with a drawing of a higher standard in the selection task compared to the level of their own human figure drawing performance. Accordingly, it would be wrong to concur with Fayol et al.'s (1995) interpretation that the lag between production and comprehension declines with age.

One of the amendments of our second study reported in Jolley et al. (2000), therefore, was to present the advanced conventional drawers with a set of four children's drawings that included an additional drawing depicting a higher visual realism standard (made by an artist, see Figure 10.5 for an example). There were a number of other methodological refinements adopted in our second study. Children were asked to draw a man in two sessions to gain a more reliable measure of children's own level of production. Similarly, the reliability of the comprehension measures was improved by asking all the children the three comprehension questions (realism, preference and estimation) to each of three sets of drawings instead of just one set. The upper age range of children tested was extended to 14 years old to examine the relationship between production and comprehension in drawing up to early adolescence.

One hundred and three children aged between 3 and 14 years participated in Study 2. The realism data supported the findings from Study 1. Almost all the scribblers, pre-conventional and simple conventional drawers chose a drawing from a higher category than their own drawing, while the advanced conventional drawers chose a figure from the same category as they drew themselves. However, when the advanced conventional drawers were presented with the set that included the artist's drawing almost all of them chose the artist's drawing. A similar pattern of responding was observed for the preference data: Children preferred drawings in advance of those which they themselves produced, with all but one of the advanced conventional drawers selecting the artist's drawing. Accordingly, a more advanced human figure depiction was preferred and considered more realistic by all levels of drawers. The estimation data was also broadly in concordance with Study 1. The scribblers and pre-conventional drawers often overestimated their own drawing ability. A majority of the simple conventional drawers estimated correctly and all of the advanced conventional drawers did so (even in the set that included the artist's drawing).

In our two studies reported in Jolley et al. (2000), therefore, there was a strong indication that production lags comprehension for all drawing levels of children. In a further series of studies (Jolley, Knox, & Wainwright, 2001) we sought to replicate and extend Jolley et al.'s (2000) findings. In our first study we included three methodological amendments to our earlier work in relation to the selection task.

Figure 10.5 An example of one of the adult artist's drawings of a man used in the
selection task reported by Jolley, Knox, and Foster (2000, Study 2).

It is possible that asking children to respond to the realism, preference and estimation
questions within each set of drawings may result in children's selected drawings not being independent from one another. This is not desirable as the rationale of unpacking the
cognitive and affective responses to pictures is to tap into potentially different forms of
comprehension. Therefore, Jolley et al. (2001) asked only one comprehension question
to any given set. Each child saw nine sets of four children's drawings (from a pool of 15
sets), and each form of question (realism, preference or estimation) was asked for three
sets each (consecutively). Children were allocated to six order of presentation groups so
that the order in which they answered the forms of questions was counterbalanced.

The second amendment to the selection task was to show all the children sets that included an artist's (visually realistic) drawing of a man. In Jolley et al. (2000) only the
advanced conventional drawers had seen such a set. This amendment allowed us to examine how the presence of an artist's drawing affected the comprehension responses
from other levels of drawer. Three sets of five drawings (four children's drawings plus
an artist's drawing) were shown one at a time after the child has responded to the nine
sets of children's drawings. Each of these three *artist* sets was assigned one of the three
comprehension questions. The children's drawings for these three sets were taken from
the pool of fifteen sets, but they varied for each child and were always different from the
nine sets they had been shown earlier in the selection task. The artist's drawing was
randomly chosen by the experimenter from a pool of five artist's drawings.

The third amendment in the selection task related to an additional measurement of children's ability to estimate their own human figure drawing standard. It is possible that children's poor estimation ability reported by us in Jolley et al. (2000) was partly contributed by the child not being able to see one of his or her own drawings to compare to the other children's drawings presented. In Jolley et al. (2001) we tested children in a second comprehension session approximately six to eight weeks after the selection task session. After responding to a developmental seriation task in this second session (to be reported in the next section) children were asked to draw a man with no children's drawings in view. Then the three sets of four children's drawings that had been used for the developmental seriation task were presented again one at a time, with each child asked for each set the estimation question, "which one looks most like your drawing?".

In this first study reported in Jolley et al. (2001) we categorized 128 children aged between 18 months and 12 years of age as either a scribbler (30), pre-conventional (29), simple conventional (35), or advanced conventional drawer (34). The child's classifications were based on two human figure drawings they provided for us in two production sessions.

Findings from the first nine selection trials (the sets with four children's drawings only) replicated Jolley et al. (2000) with scribblers, pre-conventional and simple conventional drawers typically selecting a more advanced drawing in response to the realism and preference questions than they produced themselves (see Table 10.1). Also consistent with Jolley et al.'s (2000) findings for the estimation data was that very poor performance was observed for scribblers (3% accuracy), and pre-conventional drawers (10%), while the percentage of estimation accuracy of the simple conventional drawers was below half (42%). Of the many children who estimated incorrectly all but five of them over-estimated. In respect of children's responses to the sets of drawings that included the artist's drawing most advanced conventional drawers chose the artist's drawing as the most realistic and preferred, but resisted picking it for the estimation question (the majority correctly choosing the advanced conventional drawing). This pattern of responses for the advanced conventional drawers replicated the findings reported in Jolley et al. (2000).

The data for the selections made by the other levels of drawer to the artist sets revealed some unexpected findings. The scribblers infrequently chose the artist's drawing for the realism and preference questions. Although more pre-conventional drawers did so the numbers were still under 50% of them for both realism and preference question. Even the 60% of the simple conventional drawers who considered the artist's drawing the most realistic seems a low proportion considering that the artist's drawing was so much more realistic than even the presented (child's) advanced conventional drawing. Furthermore, under half of the simple conventional drawers preferred the artist's drawings. For the estimation question the previously reported pattern of estimations was replicated with a considerable majority of scribblers and pre-conventional drawers over-estimating, and more than half of the simple conventional drawers doing so. However, it was reassuring that most of these three categories of drawers resisted picking the artist's drawing, which at least indicates there is a limit to how deluded they are in their perception of their human figure drawing ability!

Table 10.1 Numbers of Children Selecting Four Levels of Human Figure Drawings to the Realism, Preference and Estimation Questions by the Category of the Children's Own Human Figure Drawings (Jolley, Knox, & Wainwright, 2001; Study 1)

Comprehension Performance	Production Performance				
	Scribblers	Pre-Conventional	Simple Conventional	Advanced Conventional	
Realism					Σ
Scribble	1	-	-	-	1
Pre-Conventional	2	-	-	-	2
Simple Conventional	7	2	2	-	11
Advanced Conventional	15	26	33	34	108
Inconsistent Responders	5	1	-	-	6
Σ	30	29	35	34	128
Preference					Σ
Scribble	-	-	-	1	1
Pre-Conventional	5	2	1	-	8
Simple Conventional	12	5	4	1	22
Advanced Conventional	10	20	29	32	91
Inconsistent Responders	3	2	1	-	6
Σ	30	29	35	34	128
Estimation of own drawing level					Σ
Scribble	1	-	-	-	1
Pre-Conventional	3	3	1	-	7
Simple Conventional	11	12	14	3	40
Advanced Conventional	7	12	19	31	69
Inconsistent Responders	8	2	1	-	11
Σ	30	29	35	34	128

But were children more able to accurately estimate their own drawing standard when they had one of their drawings they had just produced in front of them to compare? Sadly, no! In the second comprehension session children's production level was categorized according to the human figure drawing they drew in that session. Their drawing level was compared to which drawing from three sets of children's drawings they had estimated as being most like their drawing. The pattern of estimation responding was very similar to the estimation selections they had made in the earlier comprehension session where they did not have one of their own drawings present. That is, most of the scribblers and pre-conventional drawers estimated inaccurately, over half of the simple conventional drawers also did so, with most of the advanced conventional drawers estimating correctly. Again, the vast majority of inaccurate estimations were over-estimations. Our previously reported findings of over-estimations made by children cannot be attributed therefore to a difficulty trying to recall how they draw a man.

The data collected in the three selection tasks reported by us (Jolley et al., 2000; Jolley et al., 2001) had clearly shown that children of all drawing levels understand

and prefer higher levels of drawing than they produce themselves. However, because we had not asked children to explain their selections we could not be sure about children's rationale for making their selections. In Study 2 reported in Jolley et al. (2001) we explored the reasons children gave for their selections. A pilot study indicated that the verbal demands of the task would be too much for very young children, and accordingly there were no scribblers assessed in the second study. Children aged from 4 to 13 years participated in two sessions within a fortnight of each other. In the first session children were asked to draw a man. In the second session they were again asked to draw a man, and on the basis of these two drawings a sample of 76 children were categorized as either pre- (24), simple (34) or advanced conventional (18) drawers. Following their second drawing they were asked a number of questions in a mini-interview about their drawing, and then the children were shown nine sets of five drawings one set at a time. These sets included four children's human figure drawings (scribble, pre-, simple and advanced conventional drawing) and one artist's drawing. The sets had been used in Jolley et al.'s (2001) first study. As in Study 1 children were asked only one question per set, with each form of question (realism, preference or estimation) asked for three sets each (consecutively). The human figure drawing the child had produced earlier in the session was presented for the estimation question to facilitate comparison. Children were asked to explain each selection they made.

In respect of their selections children once more predominantly selected a more advanced version for the realism and preference question compared to their own developmental level. The children's explanation for their realism and preference selections revealed a similar developmental shift. In each case there was a shift away from merely stating a body part or clothing feature in their chosen drawing (pre-conventional drawers), to more holistic responses related to detail, realism and the use of formal properties to portray realism (advanced conventional drawers). The realism-based justifications provided by the advanced conventional drawers, and some of the simple conventional drawers, confirmed therefore that these children were recognizing the visual realism in the drawings they selected. Realism-based explanations in the justifications provided by the children for their preferred drawings also grew to be more common with higher levels of drawing ability. This confirmed that children's preferences for more developmentally advanced drawings were based on an interest in realism, at least among older and more experienced drawers.

Children's estimation data again replicated our previous findings. The majority of the pre-conventional and simple conventional drawers over-estimated their drawing ability, while most of the advanced conventional drawers correctly selected the same standard of drawing. The explanations given by all three categories of drawer were dominated by comments referring to a particular part or feature of the selected drawing (a body part or article of clothing). The developmental change we did observe in the comments was that there were an increasing number of references to formal properties, detail, proportion and movement/posture made by children of higher drawing categories. Nevertheless, it was not readily apparent from children's justifications why more accurate selections were a function of drawing standard. For instance, many of the advanced conventional drawers justified their choice of drawing by referring to a perceived likeness to a particular body part, clothing or formal property (e.g., size, shading and color), rather than a holistic comment on a similar overall structure and realistic detail of their chosen figure. It appears, therefore, that the shift toward accurate estimations of drawing standard relied on an implicit understanding, rather than an understanding they were able to explicitly verbalize.

Children's understanding of what develops and why in children's drawings

The literature we have cited so far has limited children's comprehension responses to the selection of a single drawing from an array. In this section we will extend our consideration of children's comprehension of representational drawing by examining their knowledge of the developmental sequence of children's drawings and the factors that stimulate developmental change. Continuing our focus on the relationship between comprehension and production we shall compare children's knowledge of what develops and why in children's drawings with their own drawing production level.

Children's knowledge of the developmental pattern in children's drawings

Asking children to choose the most realistic drawing from a developmental sequence of children's drawings not only taps into their awareness of visual realism but also represents a measure of their understanding of the end-point of children's drawing development. But what about their knowledge of earlier points in the developmental sequence? When are children able to differentiate between standards of drawing ability, and is this skill related to the child's own production performance? Goodnow, Wilkins, and Dawes (1986) tested children aged between 4 and 11 years on whether they could distinguish between a younger and older child's drawing, and investigated if this ability was related to the child's own drawing skill. From a total of eight drawings representative of drawings made by 4- to 10-year-olds according to the Goodenough-Harris Scale (Harris, 1963), the authors presented the children with all possible pairs of human figure drawings. In a previous session the participating children had drawn their own human figure to enable their own drawing level to be assessed. Goodnow et al. (1986) reported that the 4- and 5-year-olds' ability to distinguish between the younger and older children's drawings was not above the level of chance. In contrast, the 7-year-olds' judgments were well above the chance level, and all the 9- and 10-year-olds were successful with all pairs of drawings. What is most interesting for the present discussion was that the children's own drawing level was significantly and positively correlated with their ability to distinguish between the pairs of older and younger children's drawings. A possible explanation of this correlation is that as a child progresses in their own drawing ability they gain knowledge of the developmental pattern up to their own level, but remain uncertain of future developments (see Jolley, in press; Trautner, Lohaus, Sahm, & Helbing, 1989). Consistent with this suggestion, the correlation reported by Goodnow et al. (1986) for the 7- and 9-year-olds ($r = 0.36$) was stronger than that for the 4- and 5-year-olds ($r = 0.13$). However, Goodnow et al. did not report where the developmental errors in children's judgments occurred, so we do not know whether they tended to relate to differences above the child's own production level or not.

Trautner et al. (1989) carried out a study designed to examine the possibility that children's knowledge of the developmental sequence was constrained to those levels which they had already achieved in their own drawing development. Children aged between 5 and 10 years of age were presented with sets of five drawings where each set had each been made by a child longitudinally once a year between the ages of 5 and 9 years (i.e., a similar age span to the children tested in their study). Each child was asked to arrange the sets in the correct age-related sequence. Contrary to Goodnow et al.'s (1986) findings the authors reported that even the youngest group of children (5-year-olds) ordered the drawings with an accuracy above chance levels, and that the skill improved progressively with age. Further, Trautner et al.'s (1989) data provided no evidence for errors in the seriation task predominantly occurring for developmental points in advance of the child's own production level. Judgment errors for the youngest children were as high for drawings around their own age level as they were for the drawings beyond their own drawing level. However, one difficulty with this interpretation from Trautner et al.'s (1989) study is that the drawing level of the participating children was not assessed.

This limitation was addressed in our second study reported in Jolley et al. (2000). Recall from our earlier discussion of this study the production level of 103 children (3- to 14-year-olds) was assessed by asking each child to make two human figure drawings over two production sessions. In a further comprehension session the children were administered a developmental seriation task (after they had participated in the selection task). Children were presented with four portrait photographs of children aged 2, 4, 6 and 10 years of age. The photographs were presented horizontally in chronological order of age. The names and ages of the children depicted were written below each picture and were read out to the participating children in the task. The particular ages of the children depicted had been chosen to represent the typical ages in which the four forms of human figure drawing presented to the children in this task (a scribble, pre-conventional, simple conventional and advanced conventional drawing) are drawn. Children were told, "Each of these children has drawn a picture. Can you tell me which picture they have drawn?" The procedure was repeated for two further sets of four children's drawings (where two further sets of children's photographs were shown).

In accordance with Goodnow et al.'s (1986) correlations our results indicated that children's level of awareness of the drawing sequence was positively related to their own ability within the sequence. Additionally, performance on this developmental sequence task was significantly correlated with the child's production level when age was statistically partialed out. This significant positive correlation was replicated by a further developmental seriation task we conducted in Jolley et al. (2001) first study (also with age partialed out). Removing likely age effects was important to assessing the direct relationship between production and comprehension. Both Goodnow et al. (1986) and Trautner et al. (1989) found that the ability to order the drawings developmentally was an age related skill, and of course children improve their drawing skill with age.

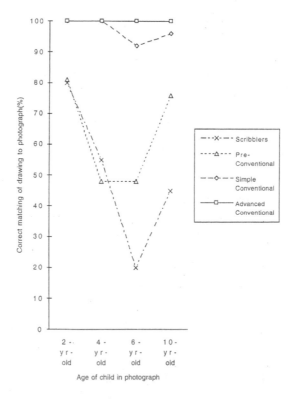

Figure 10.6 Percentage responses of matching each category of drawing to its appropriate position in the developmental seriation task by the four levels of drawers (Jolley et al. 2000, Study 2).

Consequently, our data showing a relationship between children's understanding of the developmental sequence in children's drawings and their own production level confirmed and extended the earlier studies of Goodnow et al. (1986) and Trautner et al. (1989).

In Jolley et al. (2000) we analyzed where children's errors were occurring in the developmental pattern by the child's own drawing level. Our analysis of the errors supported Trautner et al.'s data that children's ability to understand the developmental sequence was not constrained to the levels which they had achieved in their own drawing productions. From Figure 10.6 one can see that the only group of drawers which displayed any indication of being restricted in their knowledge to their own production level was the scribblers. They showed a high degree of accuracy for matching the scribbled drawings to the picture of the two year old, but performed less well on matching the three representational drawings. Very young children may be more inclined to focus on the colors and the lines for their own sake (Luquet, 1927/2001; Parsons, 1987) rather than as potential representations. Nevertheless, there were still many scribblers who accurately matched the representational drawings to the correct photographs.

It appears, therefore, that children's understanding of the developmental sequence in children's human figure drawing is related to their production level, but that their understanding relates to points both prior and beyond their own drawing ability.

Children's knowledge of causation in developmental change in children's drawing

A further extension of our examination into the relationship between children's production and comprehension of representational drawing was to examine children's knowledge of why children's drawing develops, and whether such understanding is related to children's own production level. In Jolley et al. (2001) we investigated just this in our third study. Sixty seven children were initially assessed for their own human figure drawing level (pre-conventional, simple conventional and advanced conventional). Additionally, each child participated individually in a semi-structured interview in which questions were asked concerning the child's own picture making, their preferences/dislikes about drawing, what they believed were difficult or easy things to draw, what made a good picture, and how drawing skill is improved. Content analysis was used to identify themes of responses to these questions, but for the purpose of the present discussion we shall focus on the different reasons children gave on developmental change in drawing. The most popular themes mentioned were maturation (e.g., age, getting bigger, intelligence, inheritance), application/enjoyment (e.g., practice, concentration, trying hard, more experience, motivation) and teaching/learning (e.g., watching and being shown by others, seeing other drawings, education). A full list of themes and a breakdown of the number of children by drawing level who cited them is described in Table 10.2.

Table 10.2 Numbers of Children Citing Each Theme of Change by Production Level
(Jolley, Knox, & Wainwright, 2001; Study 3)

Prod. Level	Theme of Change						
	Matu- ration	Applic./ Enjoym.	Teach./ Learn.	Knowled.	Motor Develop.	Draw.- Related	Miscel- laneous
Pre- Convent. (n = 22)	13	8	5	-	-	4	4
Simple Convent. (n = 22)	20	10	15	3	3	2	1
Ad- vanced Convent. (n = 23)	23	18	20	4	5	4	-
Σ	56	36	40	7	8	10	5

To examine the relationship between the child's production level and understanding of developmental change we initially gave each child a score depending upon the number of themes of developmental change they cited (excluding *miscellaneous*) in their interview (i.e. a score between zero and six). The positive correlation between the child's production level and the number of themes which they referred to was highly significant, even with age partialed out. To examine this relationship further we investigated which themes differentiated the levels of drawer. We found that the numbers of children citing reasons categorized as *application/enjoyment* and *teaching/learning* increased significantly with more advanced production levels. In other words higher drawing levels of the children were associated with a recognition of both internal (e.g., practice and motivation) and external (e.g., observation and demonstration of drawing from others, education) resources in drawing development.

Interpretations and future directions

Evidence assimilated by Jolley and his colleagues (Jolley et al., 2000; Jolley et al., 2001) strongly supports the argument that production lags comprehension among children of all drawing standards, from scribblers to experienced representational drawers. It is likely that the cognitive, motor and graphic demands involved in producing a drawing play a significant role in the developmental delay of production, and that these demands continue to exert their influence throughout children's drawing experience. Although much of the supportive evidence for the production lag has been derived from studying human figure drawings, there is no reason to suppose that different findings would be obtained from using other topics. Indeed, it is likely that due to the demands of production the lag between production and comprehension would be enhanced for topics less practiced in the drawing activity of children. Furthermore, the gap may be expected to widen during adolescence and adulthood where drawing is practiced minimally for most people, and hence drawing performance would be expected to be in stagnation or decline.

The alternative account that production and comprehension of drawing develop concurrently must be rejected. The theoretical underpinning for concurrent development is that the child's current conception of how a topic should best be graphically represented dictates both their comprehension and production of that topic. Researchers who have held this view have tended to adopt Luquet's (1927/2001) internal model, broadly defined as the child's notion of the important features of any given topic and represented in such a way so that the individual features are displayed unambiguously. It has long since been accepted in the children's drawings literature, however, that children's drawings are not simply print outs of their mental images. The way in which children comprehend drawings and produce them is more dynamic than being dictated by a single unitary source. The research carried out by ourselves, as well as other independent work, has conclusively shown that the drawings children choose as the most realistic and preferred are developmentally different from those they produce themselves. Even within children's comprehension and production there is evidence of varying graphic models. In our research we have noticed that children do not always pick the same drawings for the most realistic and most preferred. Where different selections have been made there is a tendency for children to prefer a drawing that is not as developmentally advanced as the one they recognize as the most realistic. Such choices indicate that some children hold different cognitive and affective comprehension models in selection tasks. In respect of children's own productions we only need look at children's drawings to see examples of children depicting different developmental versions of the same topic (see Jolley, in press). Furthermore, children may produce diverse drawings depending upon the audience, such as drawings they produce for themselves, their teachers or an experimenter (Anning, 2002; Goodnow et al., 1986).

The different production and comprehension graphic models children hold raises the question of whether children are aware of, and are satisfied with, the developmental inferiority of their productions. In terms of awareness the estimation data we have reported from our own studies clearly identifies many children who over-estimate their drawing ability. When asked to choose a drawing similar to how they themselves draw very few scribblers and pre-conventional human figure drawers select a drawing similar to their own standard, choosing instead a more developmentally advanced drawing. Around half of simple conventional human figures drawers over-estimate, while almost all advanced conventional human figure drawers accurately estimate their own drawing ability. Although the advanced drawers appear to be at ceiling it would be interesting to include among the drawings in the selection task a drawing depicting a level of realism someway between their own standard and that portrayed by an adult's drawing. The adult artist's drawings that we have used in our studies communicate a level of visual realism far beyond that shown in children's advanced conventional drawings, and therefore may be relatively easy to discriminate.

Whether children are satisfied with their drawing products appears to be a function of development. In our second study reported in Jolley et al. (2001) we asked children whether they liked, disliked or considered okay/alright their human figure drawing they had just made. Whereas all of the pre-conventional drawers (n = 27) and most of the simple conventional drawers (27/34) liked their drawings, only 4 of the 18 advanced conventional drawers did so. The common complaint made by the advanced conventional drawers was that their drawing was insufficiently detailed and visually realistic. It appears, therefore, that the production lag may only become a disconcerting issue for older children.

A combination of graphic intention and cognitive factors may account for this development shift in self-efficacy. Arnheim (1974) has argued that children invent a graphic representation of topics in their drawings that *stand for* the referents in their environment. For Arnheim (1974) children's drawings are symbolic and not an attempt to capture a visual likeness. Such a view takes a more positive view of children's drawings rather than the production lag hypothesis (see also Golomb, 2002), and implies that for at least for younger and more inexperienced drawers children may be satisfied with their inventions. For older drawers many authors have acknowledged that children become more critical of their drawing performance (e.g., see Cox, 2005). Furthermore, this shift in self-efficacy in the drawing domain is consistent with a more general developmental shift in children becoming more self critical of their abilities (Blatchford, 1997; Plumert, 1995; Stipek, 1984). In contrast, there is a general tendency for younger children to overestimate their abilities (Schuster, Ruble, & Weinert, 1998). Cognitive factors and engaging in wishful thinking have been suggested to account for young children's over estimations (Hungerige, Trautner, Uredat, & Wagner, 2000; Schuster et al., 1998; Stipek & MacIver, 1989; Stipek, 1984). Furthermore, it is possible that there is an interaction between children's estimation ability and self-efficacy. Younger and more inexperienced drawers may be content with their drawings because they are deluded in thinking they are better than they are!

Our studies investigating children's understanding of deeper levels of picture comprehension revealed a potentially interesting link with production performance. We found that children's understanding of what develops and why in children's drawings is related to their own production level, and that the relationship could not be accounted for solely by a third variable of age improvements in both production and comprehension. An understanding of developmental change is derived from Piaget's interest in diachronic thinking (Piaget, 1969). Previous research on diachronic thinking has shown that children's ability to explain a present situation from past events, and to predict future events from the present, is age-related (see Montangero, 1996; Tryphon & Montangero, 1992). Our data in the drawing domain suggests that production performance also is related to comprehension.

Nonetheless, any causal nature of this relationship is not straightforward, nor as yet adequately understood. The simple explanation that children understand developments in drawing only up to the point of their own production level can be dismissed. The data shows a spread of errors in matching drawings to age-related developmental points in seriation tasks that includes errors both prior to, as well as beyond, the child's own production level. In respect of the relationship between understanding the causes of developmental change and the child's own production level, we found that children citing more casual factors were more advanced drawers. Again this relationship was independent of the age of the child. In particular, an awareness of the external and internal resources to drawing development was differentiated between the three levels of representational drawer we tested (Jolley et al., 2001). How may this be explained? On the one hand children who have an explicit awareness of these internal and external resources may be more motivated to use them, leading to advances in their own drawing level. Conversely, improvements in the child's own drawing might provide them with insights as to why this might have occurred, and potentially give the child a clearer understanding of developmental change in representational drawing.

The evidence we have found for a relationship between the child's own production level and their understanding of what develops and why in drawing development suggests further work. For instance, is there a relationship between children's understanding of other aspects of pictures and their production level? We know that children of different representational drawing standards vary in respect of self-efficacy in their own drawing behavior (Jolley, Knox, & Wainwright, 2001, study 2) but do they also systematically vary in other attitudes towards their own drawings and pictures in general? Rose, Jolley, and Burkitt (2006) asked 260 5- to 14-year-olds about their drawing behavior and attitudes to their own drawing activity and to other pictures. This survey included questions about what they liked/disliked about drawing, their attitudes to the decline of drawing activity among older children, and what they thought made a good/bad picture. Although we did not ask children to draw themselves, it would be useful to explore in future work children's answers to these and other similar questions in relation to the child's own production level. An interesting and more holistic approach to studying the potential links between production and comprehension would be to study Norman Freeman's model on the child's developing framework theory of pictures (see Freeman, 1995, 2000, 2004; Freeman & Parsons, 2001; Freeman, Chap. 3) in relation to the child's production performance. Freeman argues that children develop their theory of pictures based on their understanding of the relationships between the referent, picture, artist and viewer. How such understanding develops in relation to their own production performance is unknown, but studying such a relationship may highlight some interesting links.

Another line of enquiry is to investigate the role of seen drawing models on children's own drawing development. Some years ago now a preliminary investigation was carried out by Wilson and Wilson (1977) who asked children about where their ideas had come from for their current and past drawings. Children were asked a number of questions including: "Did the drawing originate with you?", "Is it a copy of something?", "Did someone show you how to do it that way?" The authors concluded that nearly all drawing could be traced back to an existing graphic source; however, they provided no data in their paper. As far as we are aware this promising line of enquiry has not been developed. If pursued it might prove fruitful in providing insight into the extent to which comprehension of drawing models influences production in children's drawings. However, we must be a little cautious and refrain from conceiving that any casual relationship between production and comprehension is necessarily uni-directional.

Many of the approaches to studying the relation between production and comprehension would benefit from longitudinal studies. These should provide us with a more precise outline of how the development of production and comprehension in drawing interact with each other. In addition to the empirical work there is also the need for theories to explain the developing interaction between production and comprehension of drawing. The development of our empirical and theoretical knowledge of picture production and comprehension would not be complete without including the growing body of literature into children's making and understanding of expressive drawing (e.g., Carothers & Gardner, 1979; Davis, 1997; Jolley, in press; Jolley, Cox, & Barlow, 2003; Jolley, Fenn, & Jones, 2004; Jolley & Thomas, 1995; Jolley, Zhi, & Thomas, 1998; Lin & Thomas, 2002; Winston, Kenyon, Stewardson, & Lepine, 1995; see also Burkitt, Chap. 6).

Summary

In this chapter we have considered the relation between children's production and comprehension of representational drawing on a number of levels. First, we have shown that children of all drawing standards understand and prefer more developmentally advanced drawings than they produce themselves. Second, the child's estimation of their own drawing ability and self-efficacy is a function of their own drawing level. While over-estimation and satisfaction with one's own drawing ability is associated strongly with the more inexperienced drawers, the most advanced drawers are aware of their own drawing ability but are much less content with it. Third, we found that understanding what develops and why in children's representational drawers is related to the child's own production level. The different graphic models children use for production and comprehension have been discussed in terms of the extent to which children are aware and satisfied with their own drawings. A number of lines of enquiry are suggested to develop our understanding of children's developing and interacting relationship between production and comprehension in the drawing domain.

References

Anning, A. (2002). A conversation around young children's drawing: The impact of the beliefs of significant others at home and at school. *International Journal of Art and Design Education, 21*, 197-208.

Arnheim, R. (1974). *Art and visual perception: A psychology of the creative eye.* London: Faber & Faber.

Barrouillet, P., Fayol, M., & Chevrot, C. (1994). Le dessin d'une maison. Construction d'une echelle de developpement [The drawing of a house: Construction of a developmental scale]. *Annee Psychologique, 94*, 81-98.

Blatchford, P. (1997). Pupils self assessments of academic attainment at 7, 11 and 16 years: effects of sex and ethnic group. *British Journal of Educational Psychology, 67,* 169-184.

Brooks, M. R., Glenn, S. M., & Crozier, W. R. (1988). Pre-school children's preferences for drawings of a similar complexity to their own. *British Journal of Educational Psychology, 58,* 165–171.

Burkitt, E. (2008). Children's choice of color to depict metaphorical and affective information. In: C. Milbrath & H. M. Trautner. (Eds.), *Children's understanding and production of pictures, drawing, and art.* (pp. 109-123) Cambridge, MA: Hogrefe & Huber.

Carothers, T., & Gardner, H. (1979). When children's drawings become art: The emergence of aesthetic production and perception. *Developmental Psychology, 15,* 570-580.

Cox, M. V. (1989). Children's drawings. In D. J. Hargreaves (Ed.), *Children and the arts* (pp. 43-58). Milton Keynes: Open University Press.

Cox, M. V. (1993). *Children's drawings of the human figure.* Hove, England: Erlbaum.

Cox, M. V. (2005). *The pictorial world of the child.* Cambridge: Cambridge University Press.

Davis, J. H. (1997). Drawing's demise: U-shaped development in graphic symbolization. *Studies in Art Education: A Journal of Issues and Research, 38,* 132-157.

DeLoache, J. S., Strauss, M. S., & Maynard, J. (1979). Picture perception in infancy. *Infant Behavior and Development, 2,* 77-89.

Fayol, M., Barrouillet, P., & Chevrot, C. (1995). Judgement and production of drawings by 3–10-year-olds: Comparison of declarative and procedural drawing knowledge. *European Journal of Psychology of Education, 10,* 303–313.

Freeman, N. H. (1972). Process and product in children's drawing. *Perception, 1,* 123-140.

Freeman, N. H. (1995). The emergence of a framework theory of pictorial reasoning. In C. Lange-Küttner & G. V. Thomas (Eds.), *Drawing and looking* (pp. 135-146). New York: Harvester Wheatsheaf.

Freeman, N. H. (2000) Communication and representation: Why mentalistic reasoning is a life-long endeavour. In P. Mitchell & K. Riggs (Eds.), *Children's reasoning and the mind* (pp. 349-366). Hove, England: Psychology Press.

Freeman, N. H. (2004). Aesthetic judgement and reasoning. In E. W. Eisner & M. D. Day (Eds.), *Handbook of research and policy in art education* (pp. 359-377). Mahwah, NJ: Erlbaum.

Freeman, N. H. (2008). Pictorial competence generated from crosstalk between domains. In: C. Milbrath & H. M. Trautner. (Eds.), *Children's understanding and production of pictures, drawing, and art.* (pp. 33-52) Cambridge, MA: Hogrefe & Huber.

Freeman, N. H. & Parsons, M. J. (2001). Children's intuitive understanding of pictures. In B. Torff & R. J. Sternberg (Eds.), *Understanding and teaching the intuitive mind* (pp.73-91). Mahwah, NJ: Erlbaum.

Gardner, H. (1980). *Artful scribbles.* New York: Basic Books.

Golomb, C. (2002). *Child art in context: A cultural and comparative perspective.* Washington, DC: American Psychological Association.

Golomb, C. (2004). *The child's creation of a pictorial world (2nd Edition).* Mahwah, NJ: Erlbaum.

Goodnow, J. J., Wilkins, P., & Dawes, L. (1986). Acquiring cultural forms: Cognitive aspects of socialization illustrated by children's drawings and judgments of drawings. *International Journal of Behavioural Development, 9,* 485–505.

Harris, D. B. (1963). *Children's drawings as measures of intellectual maturity.* New York: Harcourt, Brace ,World.

Hochberg, J., & Brooks, V. (1962). Pictorial recognition as an unlearned ability. *American Journal of Psychology, 75,* 624-628.

Hungerige, H., Trautner, H. M., Uredat, A., & Wagner, C. (2000). *Awareness of variation in graphic level and complexity of human figure drawings, drawing performance, and evaluation of own drawing ability.* Paper presented at the 30th Annual Meeting of the Jean Piaget Society, Montreal, June 1-3.

Jolley, R. P. (in press). *Children and pictures: Drawing and understanding.* Oxford: Blackwell.

Jolley, R. P., Cox, M. V., & Barlow, C. M. (2003). *What develops and why in British children's expressive drawings.* Paper presented at the British Psychological Society Developmental Section Conference, Coventry, UK. September

Jolley, R.P., Fenn, K., & Jones, L. (2004). The development of children's expressive drawing. *British Journal of Developmental Psychology, 22,* 545-567.

Jolley, R. P., Knox, E., & Foster, S. (2000). The relationship between children's production and comprehension of realism in drawing. *British Journal of Developmental Psychology, 18,* 557-582.

Jolley, R. P., Knox, E., & Wainwright, R. L. (2001). *The relationship between production and comprehension in drawing.* Paper presented at British Psychological Society Developmental and Education Sections' Joint Annual Conference. Worcester, UK, September.

Jolley, R. P., & Thomas, G. V. (1995). Children's sensitivity to metaphorical expression of mood in line drawings. *British Journal of Developmental Psychology, 12,* 335-346.

Jolley, R. P., Zhi, Z., & Thomas, G. V. (1998). How focus of interest in pictures changes with age: A cross-cultural comparison. *International Journal of Behavioral Development, 22,* 127-149.

Jusczyk, P. (1997). *The discovery of spoken language.* Cambridge, MA: MIT Press.

Kellogg, R. (1969), *Analyzing Children's Art.* Palo Alto: National Press.

Kosslyn, S. M., Heldmeyer, K. H., & Locklear, E. P. (1977). Children's drawings as data about internal representations. *Journal of Experimental Child Psychology, 23,* 191–211.

Lin, S. F., & Thomas, G. V. (2002). Development of understanding of popular graphic art: A study of everyday aesthetics in children, adolescents and young adults. *International Journal of Behavioral Development, 26,* 278-286.

Luquet, G. H. (1927). *Le Dessin Enfantin* [Children's drawings]. Paris: Alcan.

Luquet, G. H. (2001). *Children's Drawings.* (A. Costell, Trans.) London: Free Association Books (Original work published 1927).

Machotka, P. (1966). Aesthetic criteria in childhood: Justifications of preference. *Child Development, 37,* 877-885.

Matthews, J. (2003). *Drawing and painting: Children and visual representation.* London: Paul Chapman.

Montangero, J. (1996). *Understanding changes in time.* London: Taylor & Francis.

Mortensen, K. V. (1991). Form and content in children's human figure drawings: Development, sex differences, and body experience. New York: New York University Press.

Moore, V. (1986). The relationship between children's drawings and preferences for alternative depictions of a familiar object. *Journal of Experimental Child Psychology, 42,* 187–198.

Parsons, M. J. (1987). *How we understand art: A cognitive developmental account of aesthetic experience.* Cambridge, MA: Cambridge University Press.

Piaget, J. (1969). *Psychologie et pédagogie* [Psychology and pedagogy]. Paris: Denoël.

Piaget, J., & Inhelder, B. (1956). *The child's conception of space.* London: Routledge & Kegan Paul.

Plumert, J. M. (1995). Relations between children's overestimation of their physical abilities and accident proneness. *Developmental Psychology, 31,* 866-876.

Rose, S. E., Jolley, R. P., & Burkitt, E. (2006). A review of children's, teachers' and parents' influences on children's drawing experience. *International Journal of Art and Design Education, 25,* 341–349.

Schuster, B., Ruble, D. N., & Weinert, F. E. (1998). Causal inferences and the positivity bias in children: The role of the covariation principle. *Child Development, 69*, 1577-1596.

Stipek, D. J. & MacIver, D. (1989). Developmental change in children's assessment of intellectual competence. *Child Development, 60*, 521-538.

Stipek, D. J. (1984). Young children's performance expectations: Logical analysis or wishful thinking? In J. G. Nicholls (Ed.), *Advances in motivation and achievement. Vol. 3: The development of achievement motivation* (pp. 33-56). Greenwich: JAI Press.

Taylor, M., & Bacharach, V. R. (1981). The development of drawing rules: Metaknowledge about drawing influences performance on non-drawing tasks. *Child Development, 52*, 373-375.

Thomas, G. V., & Silk, A. M. J. (1990). *An introduction to the psychology of children's drawings.* New York: Harvester Wheatsheaf.

Trautner, H. M. (2008). Children's developing understanding and evaluation of aesthetic properties of drawings and art work. In C. Milbrath & H. M. Trautner (Eds.), *Children's understanding and production of pictures, drawing, and art.* (pp. 241-264) Cambridge, MA: Hogrefe & Huber.

Trautner, H. M., Lohaus, A., Sahm, W. B., & Helbing, N. (1989). Age-graded judgments of children's drawings by children and adults. *International Journal of Behavioral Development, 12*, 421–431.

Tryphon, A., & Montangero, J. (1992). The development of diachronic thinking in children: Children's ideas about changes in drawings skills. *International Journal of Behavioral Development, 15*, 411-424.

Wilson, B., & Wilson, M. (1977). An iconoclastic view of the imagery sources in the drawings of young people. *Art Education, 30*, 4-12.

Winner, E. (1982). *Invented worlds: The psychology of the arts.* Cambridge, MA: Harvard University Press.

Winston, A. S., Kenyon, B., Stewardson, J., & Lepine, T. (1995). Children's sensitivity to expression of emotion in drawings. *Visual Arts Research, 21*, 1-15.

Chapter 11

Children's Developing Understanding and Evaluation of Aesthetic Properties of Drawings and Art Work

Hanns M. Trautner
University of Wuppertal

"More than meets the eye"

When we read a picture as a work of art, we do not solely, or primarily, attend to the subject matter of a picture, but also to non-representational, aesthetic properties, in particular to what the picture expresses, the style of the work, and its composition (Winner, 2006). Children not only produce drawings and paintings themselves that can be judged according to their aesthetic properties, but they also perceive aesthetic properties and express likes and dislikes of art work that has been produced by others. Assuming that production lags behind comprehension (see Jolley and Rose, Chap. 10), it can be expected that children are sensitive to aesthetic properties in drawings and paintings made by others before they are able to produce these properties in their own work. It may be assumed further that the comprehension and evaluation of aesthetic properties in art work changes significantly over age.

There is a long standing debate from which age on children are sensitive to aesthetic properties in drawings and art work of others, and, in particular, how far children's sensitivity to formal properties and artistic style may be underestimated when it is in conflict with subject matter. Features of drawings and art work studied under these aspects were, e.g., the subject matter or theme depicted, color, expression, formal properties like line quality, number of details, composition, realism vs. abstractness, and individual style. Besides the question which aesthetic properties can be perceived and are used for classification and evaluation of art work by children, it is also of interest to explore what characteristics predispose one art work to be preferred over another. A further question is, what relations exist between a child's judgments and preferences and her own drawing abilities.

After a short outline of the extant models of aesthetic development, the empirical research dealing with the developmental changes of the attributes used for classification and evaluation of art work is presented and critically evaluated. Addressed are children's judgments about age of artist and developmental level of drawings, their understanding of the expression of emotions in pictures, their sensitivity to formal and stylistic properties of art work, and their reasoning about aesthetic properties of liked and disliked pictures. The research findings are discussed as to their meaning for children's aesthetic development.

Models of aesthetic development

The U-curved aesthetic development hypothesis by Gardner and Winner

Gardner and Winner (1976, 1982), noting some similarities between young children's drawings and modern artists' abstract work (e.g., regarding authenticity, directness, formal creativity, expressiveness) and, at the same time, noting the poor aesthetic performance of young adolescents, concluded that graphic development is not linear but U-curved. Although their non-linear model of artistic development was originally based upon observations of children's and adolescents' graphic productions it was also applied to children's perception and understanding of art (Gardner & Winner, 1982, Winner, 2006). Further, it is important to note that the basic framework for the model is the aesthetic value of pictures, not necessarily its realism or technical mastery (see Pariser and Kindler, Chap. 13).

Gardner and Winner (1976, 1982) interviewed children between four and sixteen years of age on their understanding of pictures, poems, and music. The questions concerned such matters as the way in which art is produced (*"Where do you think this came from?" "What does it take to make something like this?"*), sensitivity of style (*"How can you tell if two paintings were done by two different artists?"*), the relation of a picture to the topic depicted (*"What is the difference between a real shell and a painting of a shell?"*), formal properties of art (*"How can an artist tell if a painting is finished?"*), and evaluation (*"Do you like it? How can you decide if it is good?"*). Based upon these interviews, they concluded that, irrespective of social class, children pass through three distinctive stages in their understanding of art.

Between four and seven, the children concentrated on the concrete and mechanistic aspects of art, and they emphasized its technical aspects and limitations. Asked, for example, where a painting by Goya came from, they were likely to say "a factory". A painting, for them, was finished when the artist "fills up the paper" or "when the paint is dry". They usually confused the picture with the thing it depicts. They had no idea that it takes talent and training to produce a great work of art. In general, they did not express opinions about the quality of a picture and did not agree on what makes a painting good. Gardner and Winner were intrigued to find that the four- and five-year-olds liked abstract paintings more than realistic ones, and that they were also more likely than older children to tell what the abstract work was about. In a similar vein, McGhee & Dziuban (1993) observed that children in the scribble stage preferred abstract depictions.

Starting with six and seven years realistic paintings were preferred. Around the age of ten, in the intermediate stage, the criterion of judging a work as good or bad was the degree of visual realism achieved. The children were now more aware of differences between a picture and the topic depicted. Although they were sensitive to style (e.g., able to recognize that a landscape by Poussin and one by Corot were by two different artists), they considered that the main purpose of art was to copy the details of the external world. The ten-year-olds were less able than the five-year-olds to conjure up imaginary worlds. Gardner and Winner assume that the meticulous realism of the intermediate stage is necessary for progressing to more complex, abstract forms of aesthetic understanding.

By adolescence, it was recognized that there are many different ways and styles of creating art and that evaluation of art may be viewed as relative, i.e., as a matter of taste. However, most adolescents still preferred realistic works to abstract ones. Adolescents knew that an artist needs talent and imagination. Like the younger children, however, adolescents were not concerned with the aesthetic standards that could be used to evaluate art.

Parsons' model of aesthetic development

As an outgrowth of Harvard's Project Zero in which Gardner and his associates were engaged since the early 1970s, Parsons interviewed children, adolescents and adults about their responses to color reproductions of paintings by well-known artists, for example, Chagall, Picasso and Renoir (Parsons, 1987; Parsons, Johnston, & Durham, 1978). In the first instance (Parsons et al., 1978), the authors showed three large reproductions of well-known paintings to individual students from grades one through twelve. Based upon the responses of the students on questions relating to six topics (semblance, subject matter, feeling, artist's properties, color, appraisal) they identified three developmental levels for each topic. In his later work, in order to find out how children's thinking about pictures proceeds, Parsons (1987) interviewed children and adults extensively about their responses to color reproductions of eight paintings by well-known artists. Subjects had to describe and evaluate each painting and to reason about their evaluations generally, and with respect to emotions, colors, forms, textures, and level of technical skill necessary to execute the painting. Analysis of the interview data resulted in a five-stage model of aesthetic development that "explicitly drew on Kohlberg's stages of moral development and on neo-Piagetian theories of mind related to taking the perspective of others." (Milbrath, 1998, p. 275). The stages are not rigidly tied to age, and people are likely to reach the higher stages only with serious schooling in arts.

During stage one (preschool age) children express a more or less uncritical delight for all paintings. They take pleasure in paintings that have strong, bright colors and contain favored subject matter. Thus, a child might say she liked a picture because it was predominantly blue and her favorite color was blue, or because it had a dog in it and she had a dog.

In stage two (elementary school children), the beauty of a painting is mainly judged by the content of the subject matter and its realistic depiction. A happy event or something nice to look at is judged beautiful. Realistic depiction renders that the subject matter can be clearly recognized. Now, with the emergence of concrete operations, the understanding of formal features of realism like overlap, relative size and perspective is growing. Children are also able to "infer that what they judge as good can be judged that way by others, even when they don't personally like the painting." (Milbrath, 1998, p. 276).

In stage three (from about 10 to 14 years), expressive qualities of paintings, i.e., paintings that express an emotion or an idea, are valued. The child is now aware of the subjectivity of aesthetic experience. "Previous criteria such as subject matter or realism are separated from the experience of a painting so that abstract paintings or those representing ugly events can be appreciated for their expressiveness." (Milbrath, 1998, p. 276). In addition, the children are not only aware that an artist has motives, but they try to connect what is represented with the artist's motives to convey his feeling or idea to the viewer.

In stage four, "Expressiveness moves from the private world of the viewer to the public space of the canvas" (Parsons, 1987, p. 110). While in stage two children ignored the formal properties of a painting, such as its composition or style, and concentrated on thematic content as justification for preferences, and in stage three, although being aware of such formal properties, noticed them only in their relation to a painting's expressiveness, in stage four, the formal properties of a painting are used for the first time as justifications for preferences. The viewer becomes aware of the subjectivity of his role in relation to art. Whereas before, an interpretation was based upon one's own internal response, it is now recognized that what is seen in a painting is constructed by a community of viewers.

In stage five, called the *post-conventional* stage, in analogy to Kohlberg's moral stages, the viewer no longer accepts the "authority of tradition". The traditional canons to understand and interpret paintings are still used but critically examined. The viewer is confronted with the difficulty of making his/her own response that, at the same time, may be regarded as an objective judgment, i.e., a judgment that is validated by reasons that in principle are available to others and not by its agreement with others. "Thus, for example, the value of a particular painting's style becomes a personal choice that is consistent with a valued artistic direction that both is personal and can be argued as having value for everyone, and not just because it is a good exemplar of a valued style" (Milbrath, 1998, p. 277).

Parsons' model of aesthetic development is based upon a lengthy semi-structured interview that gathered qualitative data on how children can reason about paintings. Therefore, as Milbrath (1998) notes, he assessed children's and adults' ability to understand and interpret art, a process that clearly relies on their capacity to analyze and elaborate conceptually what they see, rather than studying the subjects' sensitivity to specific aesthetic properties of paintings. Further, there is not necessarily a steady progression through the later stages. Where someone ends up is influenced by the personal experiences with artworks.

Freeman's theory of pictorial reasoning

Although the role of the artist and, in Parsons' higher stages, also the role of the viewer are considered in the two models of aesthetic development described before, the understanding, appreciation, and aesthetic properties of a picture itself is still at the centre of analysis. This is in accordance with the traditional view that pictorial meaning is there to be discovered in the picture and the task of the beholder is to retrieve it. However, pictures are objects that are usually made intentionally by an artist. To perceive and to evaluate a picture, you also need a viewer or beholder. According to this alternative view, pictorial meaning is constructed and imposed by an act of judgment (Wollheim, 1993).

What do children know about the role of the artist in the making of a picture and what do they know about the role of the viewer in perceiving and evaluating a picture? In contrast to the modernist view of aesthetics, which maintains that the meaning is there *in the picture*, the postmodern view postulates that the understanding and aesthetic appreciation of a picture cannot be grasped directly through perceptual observation, but only by taking the context in which the picture was created and the experiences of the observer with such work into account (Cox, 2005).

With this contemporary view in mind, Freeman (1995) developed his framework theory of pictorial reasoning that links the picture with the artist, the beholder, and the world (see Freeman, Chap. 3). Linked to the picture at the centre of the assumed net of relationships and to each other, are the world (i.e., the object(s) that the picture represents or refers to), the artist, and the beholder or observer. The problem of the beginning learner is "to forget about the artist and the viewer and to look for a simple match between the appearance of the picture and the appearance of the scene. [However], the match must be filtered first through the mind of the artist and then through that of the viewer." (Freeman & Parsons, 2001, p. 75) These distinctions allow one to study children's beliefs in how far the beauty of a picture or painting passes from world to picture (a picture as a mirror of the beauty in a scene), from artist to picture (the artist as beautifier), and from beholder to picture (beauty seen as being in the eye of the beholder).

Of interest for the developmental psychologist is how children gradually enrich their knowledge and progress from considering a picture solely in terms of its representation of something in the real world to considering the artist's role in making this representation, and, finally, to acknowledging the contribution of the beholder in perceiving and interpreting the picture, i.e., to realize that people can have different interpretations of the same picture. This includes the ability to separate judgments like, for instance, that a picture showing something ugly, at the same time, can be a good and beautiful picture. Freeman (1995) argued that children normally seem to acquire sufficient insight into the relation among these four elements somewhere around middle childhood. Now, the child comes to see that pictures are vehicles of representation, mediating communication from one mind (the artist) to another (the beholder) about a state of affairs (the world), real or imaginable.

In continuation of the model suggested by Freeman (1995), Freeman and Parsons (2001) elaborated and integrated their ideas on children's understanding and appreciation of the sources of aesthetic properties attributed to pictures. Whereas Parsons (1987) emphasized the increasingly reflective character of intuitive theories as they develop and postulated a basic pattern of first, focus on the subject matter of the pictures (the world), then on the artist, and finally on the self as viewer, Freeman (1995) emphasized the domain involved and the elements that the learner has to coordinate in a theory of art. "In summary, where Freeman (1995) tended to focus on the breadth of the domain to be learned, Parsons (1987) tended to focus on the depth of thinking involving in learning about art." (Freeman & Parsons, 2001, pp. 74-75).

When children are not yet able to coordinate one or more of the four terms of the net of relationships, they face difficulties. Freeman and Parsons (2001) illustrate this by taking abstract expressionism and the *objet trouvé* as examples. If one does not understand the basic idea of abstract expressionism, namely to remove the world element from the net, it is difficult to see why this should be called a work of art. The objet trouvé that eliminates the artist by starting with the natural world, makes it hard to believe that there is a representation at all (Freeman & Parsons, 2001).

The tendency to focus on the picture-world relation, that is characteristic particularly for young children, results in the preference for realistic depictions and the location of the beauty of a picture in its subject matter. When Freeman and Sanger (1995) asked rural 11-year-olds that had little art training whether an ugly thing would make an uglier picture than a pretty thing, 10 out of 12 said that if you painted something ugly the picture would be an ugly picture. Also, when asked whether depending on painting a pretty or an ugly thing a picture would turn out better or worse, the children argued that an ugly thing would be worse. Thus, the children conflated quality with beauty. The 14-year-olds had a different answer. They acknowledged that the artist, i.e., her/his skill and enthusiasm, is the responsible agent for beautifying a picture, and that the artist's intentionally expressed thoughts and feelings are the key to understanding the work. But still, they were not aware of what shaped their own attitudes and influenced their interpretations. Only at the highest level, does one become aware of one's own interpretative activity and realize that to abandon "the belief that one can get the meaning of a picture simply by seeing what there is to be seen or consulting the intentions of the artist" (Freeman & Parsons, 2001, p. 85). One is further able to consider that different people may make different interpretations of a picture, depending on their individual character and experiences. Although taking into account that the rural children in their views of art were some three years behind metropolitan children that were interviewed by Freeman (1995), the ordering of phases of comprehension of the four elements of pictorial reasoning remains a productive starting point for any analysis (Freeman & Parsons, 2001).

Properties of drawings and paintings used for classification and evaluation

Aesthetic responses to pictures depend on what is perceived in pictures. Research on children's classification and evaluation of pictures has dealt with a variety of problems that were investigated by employing different methodological approaches (ranging from picture selection and matching tasks to semi-structured interviews) and various kinds of pictorial forms (ranging from line drawings to paintings of contemporary artists). Research questions studied were children's understanding of age-graded drawings or drawings of different developmental level, their understanding and preferences for expressive qualities, formal features, or artistic style of drawings and paintings, including concepts of a good artist, or the relationship between children's comprehension and evaluation of art work and their own production level. In the following, research dealing with these questions is presented.

Judgments about age of artist and developmental level of drawing

A way to examine children's knowledge of drawing norms independent of their own drawing ability is to have them chronologically order a series of drawings according to the age at which they were drawn. Several such studies have established that about age 6, children are able to discriminate between drawings of different developmental levels above chance, i.e., to order a series of drawings according to the chronological age or the developmental drawing level of the artist (Goodnow, Wilkins, & Dawes, 1986; Lewis, 1963; Trautner, 1992; Trautner, Lohaus, Sahm, & Helbing, 1989; Tryphon & Montangero, 1992; see also Jolley and Rose, Chap. 10).

Goodnow et al. (1986) presented children aged between 4 and 11 years with pairs of human figure drawings representative of drawings made by 4- to 10-year-olds and asked them which of the two drawings had been made by the younger and by the older child. While the 4- and 5-year-olds were not able to distinguish between the younger and older children's drawings above chance level, children aged 6 and older, with increasing success, were able to discriminate between *younger* and *older* drawings. The correlation between judgmental ability and the developmental level of the child's own drawing performance was low, but positive. A similar methodological procedure was used by Lewis (1963) who asked children about their preferences by allowing them to choose between drawings of different developmental levels. She found that children preferred drawings slightly above their own drawing level.

The previous studies could not determine if children are limited in their judgmental skill to drawings produced by other children close to their own age. In a study with 185 children aged between five and ten years (89 boys and 96 girls) Trautner et al. (1989) examined if children's knowledge of the age-grading of human figure drawings is constrained to their own age level, or if, alternatively, children also are able to judge drawings beyond their own age level. Participants were asked to rank five drawings for eight different sets of drawings according to the age in which they were drawn by the child artist. The sets were made up from human figure drawings that had been produced by individual children tested longitudinally from age 5 until age 9. Although the youngest children made more errors than the older children, they ordered the drawings with an accuracy above chance level. As errors were as high for drawings around the subject's own age level as for *older* drawings, judgmental ability seems not to be constrained to the child's own drawing level.

When looking at 24 possible features of human figure drawings that accurate and inaccurate judges used in ranking the drawings on an age-graded scale, Trautner et al. (1989) observed that the younger children overestimated considerably the size of the figure (indicating the erroneous conception that older children draw figures of larger size) and underestimated the contribution to age changes of nearly all other features .

Since in the longitudinal stimulus material of Trautner et al. (1989) the correlation between age of artist and drawing level of r = .64 was far from perfect, and the relevant information that allowed to distinguish drawings by younger and older children was only to retrieve from the drawing level, Trautner (1992) carried out another study with children ages 5, 7, and 9, and a group of adults, in which the influence of age of artist and of drawing score on judgments about the drawing level of stimuli could be independently assessed. For that reason, two kinds of series of human figure drawings were created (see Figure 11.1): three series of five drawings each that varied in drawing score (11, 13, 15, 17, 19) while holding age of artist (5, 7, or 9 years) constant (condition A), and three series of five drawings each that varied in age of artist (5, 6, 7, 8, or 9 years) while holding drawing score (11, 15, 19) constant (condition B).

Figure 11.1 Examples of drawing series for condition A (variation of drawing score with constant artist age 5) and for condition B (variation of age of artist with constant drawing score 11). Examples shown about 30% of original size.

Using the method of paired comparison, subjects had to decide for each ten pairs of a drawing series which of the two drawings had been produced by the older child. As expected, it was only under condition A (variation of drawing score holding age constant) that subjects were able to rank the drawing level correctly. The accuracy of judgments (correlation between real drawing score and individual ranking) increased from around $r = .45$ at age 5 to $r = .80$ at age 9. Judgments under condition B were random in all age groups. Thus, only if drawings of younger and older children vary in their drawing score, they can be judged according to age of artist, and differences in drawing level of drawers of the same age can be discerned when drawing scores vary. The results of our two studies indicate that children base their judgments about age of artist of human figure drawings on their knowledge about age-graded normative changes of such drawings, assuming that the drawing level conforms to the age of the artist.

More interested in children's development of diachronic thinking (i.e., to put a present state into temporal perspective) than in children's knowledge about changes in drawing skills, Tryphon and Montangero (1992) asked children aged 6 to 12 years to draw a human figure, inquired if they have always drawn in the same way, requested them to make another drawing in the way they used to draw when they were younger, and, finally, asked them to produce as many drawings of the human figure as necessary to show how their drawings have changed over the years. Besides age changes in varying quantitative and qualitative criteria (e.g., size of figure, number of details, perspective, or style) to illustrate changes in drawing abilities, the authors noticed differences in the way time was used to date the drawings and in the number of drawings representing past stages. While the younger children ordered different stages to distinct ages, without conceptualizing the continuity of changes, the older children conceived change rather as connected stages of an evolution process.

Also related to diachronic thinking, Cox and Hodsoll (2000) compared the current human figure drawings of 5- and 7-year-olds with the figures they drew when asked to draw as if they were 3 and 9 years old. The figures were examined for changes in height, detail, and schema complexity. When projecting backwards in time, 5-year-olds made quantitative changes (e.g., height of figure, number of details) and some made qualitative changes (complexitiy of schema). When projecting forwards in time, however, only quantitative changes were made by 5-year-olds, and it was only at age 7 that children began to make qualitative changes.

Summarizing the research on children's understanding of the developmental changes in children's drawings (mainly tested in analyzing human figure drawings), it appears that even young children are able to allocate drawings according to age of artist above chance provided that the variation of the drawing level conforms to normative age changes. Moreover, children's understanding is not limited to their own drawing level or prior to their own drawing ability, but relates also to points beyond their own drawing ability. However, judgments of younger children are less accurate than those of older children, and they are based on quantitative features (e.g., size of figure) rather than on qualitative features (e.g., complexity).

Understanding of the literal and metaphorical expression of emotions in pictures

There are literal and non-literal (symbolic or metaphorical) ways to express emotions in pictures. A literal way would be, for example, to depict a smiling or a crying person to suggest happiness or sadness. A non-literal way to express emotions would be to depict, for example, a sunny day or to use bright colors to suggest happiness, and a withered tree or the use of dull colors to suggest sadness. At what age do children perceive these expressive properties of pictures?

Research on the understanding of literal expressive properties of pictures has concentrated on facial expressions of emotion. The face is the most expressive part of the human body. From infancy on, children tend to look at human faces and are responsive to its expression (Fantz, 1963). Since Darwin (1872) happiness, sadness, fear, anger, surprise and disgust are regarded as the six basic emotions (Ekman & Friesen, 1986). Studies using photographs or drawings of these basic emotions concur in the finding that by age 4 to 5 years children's judgments of the facial expressions are similar to those of adults, although older children's and adults' performance is better than the performance of the younger children (Cox, 2005; Russel & Bullock, 1986; Trautner & Wagenschütz, 2005). Children focus also on facial features rather than other bodily features when they themselves draw persons with different kinds of emotions (Golomb, 1992; Morra, Caloni, & d'Amico, 1994).

There are systematic differences according to which expressions can be recognized earlier and later. Russel and Bullock (1986) found that even 2-year-olds could differentiate between positive and negative emotions (happy versus angry), but had more difficulty in differentiating between different kinds of negative emotions, like angry and sad, or fear and disgust. In general, happiness and sadness were the most easily recognized, whereas anger, fear, disgust and surprise were more difficult to differentiate, varying with the kind of task and stimulus material (Cox, 2005).

Trautner and Wagenschütz (2005) tested 409 4- to 11-year-old children for their understanding of the four facial expressions of *happy*, *sad*, *surprised* and *angry*. More than 90% of the children at all ages were able to identify correctly the happy, sad and angry face from photographs and cartoon-like drawn faces and 80% and 65% identified the surprised face from the photograph and the cartoon drawing, respectively.

There are different explanations why happy and sad are more easily recognized than anger, fear and surprise. One reason may be that happiness and sadness are simpler emotions and more often experienced by children, whereas anger, fear and surprise are more complex emotions and less frequently experienced. Another explanation may be that happy and sad can be largely understood from the shape of the mouth (up-curved or down-curved), whereas anger, fear and surprise involve a combination both of the mouth and the eyes or eyebrows. In particular, eyebrows may be an area of the face that children pay less attention to.

Since the non-literal or metaphorical expression of emotion in a picture is less obvious than a literal expression, it can be assumed that an understanding of non-literal (abstract) expressive properties (e.g., color, line, or composition) will develop later. However, there are controversial findings regarding at what age children begin to grasp non-literal expressive properties in pictures. While some studies found that sensitivity to visual metaphor does not develop until about age 7 or later (Carothers & Gardner, 1979; Jolley & Thomas, 1994; Jolley, Zhi, & Thomas, 1998), others observed metaphorical understanding in 6-year-olds or even in younger children (Callaghan, 1997, 2000; Morra, Caloni, & D'Amico, 1994; Winston, Kenyon, Stewardson, & Lepine, 1995).

Jolley and Thomas (1994) examined the development of understanding of metaphorical expression of positive and negative moods in abstract paintings. In a sample of subjects aged 5, 7, 10, and 17 years, sensitivity to the expression of mood developed at different rates for the moods happy, sad, angry and calm. Happiness was easiest to detect, followed by calm and angry, and sadness was the most difficult to detect. By age 7, children recognized the appropriate mood for 3 of the 4 moods. More positive than negative feelings were read into the mood-equivocal works across all ages. Jolley, Zhi and Thomas (1998) compared Chinese subjects, ranging in age from 4 years to adult, with British participants on the same tasks tested by Jolley and Thomas (1995). While recognition of mood in pictures could be shown at an early age in both cultures, performance on completion tasks and reported justifications indicated that Chinese children attended to mood metaphors in pictures at an earlier age than the British children. The cultural difference is explained by the authors as a greater emphasis on teaching technique within the Chinese art program for children.

Callaghan (1997) showed 5- to 11-year-old children sixteen paintings of contemporary artists that 15 experts had rated to express four emotions (happy, sad, excited and calm). None of the stimuli contained any human figures that may directly cue through facial or postural expression the emotion portrayed. Instead, the emotional mood was conveyed by both the subject matter and abstract properties of the pictures. The subjects had to match each painting with a photograph of an actress portraying the appropriate emotion. Between 5 and 11 years there was an increase in the level of agreement between children's matches and experts' ratings, but even the 5-year-olds performed above chance. For children of all age groups, there were more reasons given that referred to subject matter than to formal properties to justify choices. As for when reasons were given based on formal properties, they referred mainly to color. (For a discussion of the role of colors in identifying expressive properties in pictures, see Burkitt, Chap. 6).

Considering that language-based tasks and presenting abstract pictures may impede young children's performance, Callaghan (2000) used representational pictures in a non-verbal matching task. Here, not only the 5-year-olds performed above chance, but also the 3-year-olds were able to match a picture to an emotion, when the task was embedded in the context of a game, i.e., when paintings were chosen to match the emotion of a teddy bear.

Summarizing the research on children's understanding of the literal and non-literal expression of emotions in pictures, one can say that at least some research shows that even 2-year-olds can recognize some depicted facial expressions of emotion, and that at about the age of 5, they are beginning to understand non-literal or metaphorical ways of picturing emotion.

According to the general relationship between comprehension and production, children's ability to depict emotion in their own pictures should lag behind their understanding. The question remains, irrespective of this lag, whether or not the sequence of developmental changes in their own drawings is the same as the sequence of their understanding of expressions in pictures. Concerning the order of difficulty to draw different facial expressions, as in recognizing the emotions in the drawings of others, happy and sad are more successfully drawn than other emotions. With regard to using non-literal means of conveying emotions in their drawings, results vary depending on the tasks and on the means of expression analyzed (e.g., color, line, or composition).

Trautner and Wagenschütz (2005) did an experiment to find out if the lag between comprehension and production of facial expressions gets smaller if the difficulty of the drawing task is reduced. 409 children aged 4- to 11 years were distributed to three groups: (1) drawing from memory, (2) copying drawings, and (3) drawing from memory following copying drawings. For drawing from memory, only the verbal labels of the emotions were given, and the child had to draw into a cartoon-like outline of a face the respective lines indicating each emotion. Under the copying condition children had to identify the particular expressions of cartoon-like faces which, then, had to be copied onto the paper with the standard outline face. The model drawings used are shown in Figure 11.2. The four emotions to be drawn were *happy, sad, surprised* and *angry*. Four adult experts rated the drawings of the children according to correctness of the facial expression shown and the use of relevant facial features.

happy   sad   surprised   angry

Figure 11.2 Model drawings of four facial expressions (happy, sad, surprised, angry).

While most children of all ages were able to recognize the expression in the photographs as well as in the cartoon-like stimuli, successful depictions of the requested emotions were only observed in the copying task (> 90% hits for a happy, sad and surprised face; 80% correct for the angry face). When drawing from memory, there were significant differences between emotions (happy and sad easier than surprised and angry) and a significant interaction between difficulty of expression and age. Copying first had some positive effect on the subsequent memory drawing. But the remarkable finding was that the correlation between age and drawing performance was much higher for the copying tasks than for drawing from memory. This may indicate that the copying task is a more valid method to assess a child's competence level than drawing from memory. The difficulties children have in depicting facial expressions in their drawings seem to be caused by deficits in procedural skills rather than by deficits in understanding facial expressions or their depictions.

Sensitivity to formal and stylistic properties of drawings and art

Gardner (1972) and Parsons (1987) concluded from their research that before adolescence, children base their judgments and preferences on the subject or theme portrayed in a work and only later on a range of more formal properties, like composition, contrast, or artistic style. The dominant responsiveness of younger children to subject matter in art work has also been replicated in recent studies (Cox, 2005; Golomb, 1992; Winner, 2006).

Carothers and Gardner (1979) assessed children's sensitivity to perception and production of repleteness (e.g., line variation in thickness, brightness, and shading) and expression (e.g., conveying happy or sad feelings) of pictures by asking them to complete unfinished line drawings with distinctive features relating to repleteness and expression, and then to match drawings on the basis of these properties. First-grade children showed little capacity either to detect or produce repleteness and expression in drawings. Fourth-grade children were able to perceive these characteristics in drawings made by others and showed some capacity to complete the pictures consistent with features of expression and some aspects of repleteness. Only the sixth grade children demonstrated considerable capacities to exhibit these artistic characteristics in their own drawings.

O'Hare and Westwood (1984) investigated the sensitivity of 6- to 11-year-old children to the formal properties of line drawings by asking them to judge the similarity of twelve line drawings, all representing the same scene (houses in a street) but varying along three dimensions which were shown to be salient in adults' discriminations: thickness of lines, amount of shading, and expressiveness. Detailed analyses of children's classifications through the use of multidimensional scaling and multiple-regression analyses revealed that the youngest subjects (6-year-olds) were able to make systematic comparisons utilizing the three dimensions of line variation contained in the drawings. The contrast to the findings of Carothers and Gardner (1979), who did not find a spontaneous sensitivity to line variations until the ages of 7 to 12, may be explained by differences in the task demands of the two studies. While Carothers and Gardner (1979) varied depicted scenes, assessment methods, and performance measures, O'Hare and Westwood (1984) held the content of the pictures constant and asked only for similarity judgments using the method of paired comparisons. Another reason for the difference in results was addressed by the latter authors based on findings of Smith and Kemler (1977) that younger children seem to treat multidimensional stimuli as unitary wholes and tend to categorize them on the basis of overall similarity, whereas older children are able to classify such stimuli on any one dimension separately. Therefore, tasks such as those used by Carothers and Gardner (1979) that require the child to respond to a single dimension may underestimate younger children's aesthetic sensitivity, whereas direct measures of similarity classification may be better suited to the judgmental abilities of the younger child.

Similar findings concerning young children's awareness of dimensions such as line quality in their judgments of drawings were presented by Itskowitz, Glaubman, and Hoffman (1988). Artistically inexperienced children aged 4-, 5-, 10-, and 13 years, and a comparison group of 13-year-olds with artistic inclination were presented pairs of nine human figure drawings each differing on three levels of articulation (few details to many details) and line quality (smooth to sketchy). For all thirty-six possible pairings of the drawings children were asked to say how similar they thought each pair of drawings was, and, subsequently, to indicate which member of each pair they liked best. Multidimensional scaling analyses revealed that in similarity judgments children of all age groups employed articulation as the primary criterion, with the older children tending to give somewhat greater weight to this dimension than the younger children. The role of line quality appeared to vary as a function of both age group and task. The younger children and the artistically inclined group gave greater weight to line quality than the older children, and the impact of this dimension was more pronounced in the preference task than in the sorting task. Thus, even the 4-year-olds were able to systematically sort stimuli that varied in articulation and line quality into classes of similarity or difference and express preferences on the basis of these dimensions. An interesting further result was that relatively limited individual differences appeared in the similarity judgments, whereas major individual differences appeared in the preference judgments, in particular among the young children and the artistically inclined. According to the authors, this indicates that the sorting task reflects more objective cognitive dimensions, while the preferences are more related to subjective and varying affective elements.

Studies that tested children's sensitivity to formal and stylistic properties against subject matter of the picture more directly indicate that the former may be underestimated when they are in conflict with content. Steinberg and DeLoache (1986) in a study with 3- to 5-year-olds observed a strong preference for subject over style only when the latter conflicted with subject matter cues. The preschool children preferred matching paintings on the basis of subject matter only as long as subject matter cues were available. If those cues were unavailable the children matched the paintings correctly on the basis of style (varied by composition, texture, coloring, or affective tone). In a similar vein, O'Hare and Westwood (1984) had observed that 6-year-olds were sensitive to formal properties of line variation if subject matter was held constant across stimuli and the task was given as classification task.

However, Callaghan and MacFarlane (1998) challenged the claim that (younger) children are not able to judge artistic style when it conflicts with subject matter cues in paintings. In their study with 6-year-olds, 9-year-olds, and adults, the participants had to choose from a pair of pictures the one that looked like it was painted by the same artist who painted the target picture. The paintings shown were by artists such as van Gogh, Gauguin, or Magritte. While style choices were always possible, choices based on subject matter were either not possible (e.g., all portraits or landscapes), or possible (e.g., portrait vs. landscape) but in conflict with style choices. The level of discriminability of style and subject matter differences were varied. The authors found that the youngest children were able to make style matches, provided the styles were highly discriminable, even when a subject matter match also was possible, suggesting that they are sensitive to artistic style and can focus on that dimension in the face of irrelevant variation on other dimensions.

In the studies described before, children's sensitivity to the aesthetic properties of the picture itself was at the centre of analysis. However, as explicitly elaborated in Freeman's theory of pictorial reasoning (see pp. 240-242; see also, Freeman, Chap. 3), pictures are usually made intentionally by an artist. While Freeman and Sanger (1993) concluded from interviews that it is not until 11-14 years that children consider the skill, intentions, or mood of the artist when evaluating the quality of pictorial representations, other studies (Bloom & Markson, 1998; Browne & Woolley, 2001; Callaghan, 1997) have reported a much earlier sensitivity to how attributes of the artist (e.g., intentions, emotions) have an impact on pictures. From studies by Callaghan and Rochat (2003) it can be concluded that children's consideration of attributes of an artist begins around 5 years (see Callaghan and Rochat, Chap. 9). Variability of findings seems to be due to different task demands. Interviews may underestimate children's understanding compared to the simpler naming tasks used by Bloom and Markson (1998) and by Browne and Woolley (2001), or matching tasks as used by Callaghan and Rochat (2003). The findings from the latter studies suggest that even children of 3 years of age will use intentions of the artist as a cue to name the picture when there are no other conflicting cues, whereas even adults may fail to use intentions as a cue when there is a conflict between, for instance, the name cued by intentions and the name cued by resemblance.

Aesthetic properties of preferred art and reasoning about likes and dislikes in children

Besides research on children's developing ability to *perceive* aesthetic properties of art work, there are also studies that explored what kinds of aesthetic properties pictures have that are *preferred* by children of different ages (Winner, 2006). In a pioneering study, Machotka (1966) asked 6- to 18-year-old boys to choose the paintings they liked best and liked least from an array of fifteen color reproductions of paintings (grouped in sets of three) representing a wide range of content, style, and use of color from the Western tradition since the Renaissance. The boys also had to give reasons for their choice. It was found that subject matter and color accounted for 87% of the preference justifications at age 6, while only 7-year old and older children referred to realism as preference criterion. He also identified a range of more sophisticated criteria (e.g., contrast, harmony, style, composition) that were only addressed by children aged 9 and older. Based upon these results, Machotka distinguished between three developmental levels which he saw related to Piaget's theory: (1) appreciation based on subject matter and color (until age 7), requiring preoperational functioning; (2) evaluation based upon realistic representation, contrast and harmony of colors, and clarity of presentation (ages 7 to 11), requiring operational thought; and (3) interest in style, composition, affective tone, and luminosity (from about age 12), necessitating formal thinking.

The pictorial preferences of 7-, 11- and 15-year-old children were investigated by Rump and Southgate (1967) in the natural context of visiting an exhibition of paintings in an art gallery. The 7- and 11-year-olds strongly preferred pictures realistically depicting familiar objects. Brightly colored paintings were preferred by all age groups. Color was also the prime criterion for those older subjects who appreciated abstract paintings. Verbal comments mainly referred to objects represented, decreasing from 71% (7 year-olds) and 60% (11-year-olds) to 45% (15-year-olds). Color and composition were second and third as stated reasons for preferences, both increasing between 7 and 15 years (color from 19 to 27%; composition from 4 to 24%). Gardner et al. (1975) and Rosenstiel et al. (1978) interviewed children about their response to reproductions of paintings by well-known artists and found also that younger children used subject matter and color as their primary aesthetic criteria.

The studies described before are characterized by using a great number of paintings representing a wide range of content, color, and stylistic properties without exact definition or controlled variation of the relevant stimulus dimensions. Also, conclusions about the criteria of participants' picture preferences are based only on subjects' verbal reasoning. However, later studies by Bell and Bell (1979) and by Golomb (1992) that were more controlled in presenting the stimuli or in the statistical analysis of the data concur with the earlier studies demonstrating the primary importance of subject matter and color for picture preferences in younger children, and, though to a lesser extent, in older children and adolescents as well.

Bell and Bell (1979) reported a multidimensional scaling analysis of preference judgments by 10 to 16-year-olds for a number of paintings of 20th century modern art. The subjects were found to construe their preferences for these paintings in terms of representation, color, and complexity, thus corroborating earlier findings. However, preference for representational over non-representational paintings was not found for these modern paintings. While younger children and girls preferred the more sombre tones, the older children and boys preferred the brighter colors. No significant differences between grades were found in appreciation of complexity, but girls were found to prefer the simple geometric paintings, and boys the more complex paintings.

In studies reported by Golomb (1992) children's preferences for pictures drawn by children or pictures drawn by the researchers in the style of such pictures were investigated. Four- to eleven-year-old children were shown pairs of drawings in which color, detail, proportion, or depth were varied and pitted against each other. When asked to choose the best picture, 4-year-olds were very inconsistent in their responses, but those who were consistent preferred colored pictures over detailed ones. From 7 years onwards children preferred detailed pictures, even if they were uncolored. Only later, did proportion and depth play some role in children's preferences.

To test if the findings of the former studies can be replicated when varying more systematically the relevant stimulus dimensions and using rating scales in addition to the interview method, Trautner (2007) investigated the picture preferences of 88 boys and girls of 1st, 4th, 8th, and 11th grade, aged between 6 and 18 years.[1]

---

[1] I am grateful to Frauke Becker, who collected the data in the context of her thesis project.

Assessed were participants' preferences for subject matter, color and artistic style. As stimulus material three series of colored postcard reproductions of established contemporary artists' paintings or painted in the style of such artists were used. The six paintings of series A contained a Teddy Bear as constant subject matter, but varied in coloring (many-colored, bright vs. monochrome, dark) and in artistic style (realistic vs. abstract depiction). The six paintings of series B were all painted in a more or less abstract style, but varied in coloring (contrast vs. blending of colors) and in subject matter (representational vs. non-representational). The six paintings of series C were all painted by Kandinsky in a non-representational style, but varied in coloring (many colors vs. few colors) and in picture composition (simple vs. complex).

The six postcards of each series were placed in a random arrangement on the table in front of the subject, and for each series subjects were asked: *"Which of the paintings do you like best?" "What do you like of this painting?" "Which of the paintings do you like least?" "What don't you like of this painting?"* The responses of the subjects were later grouped into three categories: subject matter (e.g., object / parts of object or scene depicted; attributes associated with object or scene, like nice, happy, sad, interesting), coloring (e.g., naming of colors, kind of coloring, impression of painting associated with colors), and style (e.g., composition, contrast, line quality, realism). For individuals' most liked (preferred) and least liked (rejected) painting of each series, subjects were then asked to rate the painting on fifteen 3-point Likert scales concerning attributes that refer to subject matter (SM), color (CO), style (ST), or overall evaluation (OV) (see Table 11.1).

Table 11.1 Rating scales for evaluating most liked and least liked paintings

1	2	3	Categ.
boring	-	interesting	(SM)
dark	-	light	(CO)
good	-	bad	(OV)
beautiful	-	ugly	(SM)
bright	-	dim	(CO)
sad	-	happy	(SM)
many colors	-	monochrome	(CO)
irregular	-	regular	(ST)
fitting colors	-	colors not fitting	(CO)
accurate	-	inaccurate	(ST)
easy to make	-	difficult to make	(OV)
cruel	-	peaceful	(SM)
articulate	-	inarticulate	(SM)
complex	-	simple	(ST)
good artist	-	bad artist	(OV)

As in earlier studies, we observed a strong preference for realistic depictions with bright colors, in particular for children in 1st and 4th grade. But even some of the youngest children addressed also stylistic features in reasoning about preferred and rejected paintings. With increasing age, the importance of subject matter decreased and the importance of artistic style increased, whereas there was no significant age difference for consideration of color in likes and dislikes (see Figure 11.3). The observed age trends were more pronounced for rejected paintings than for preferred paintings.

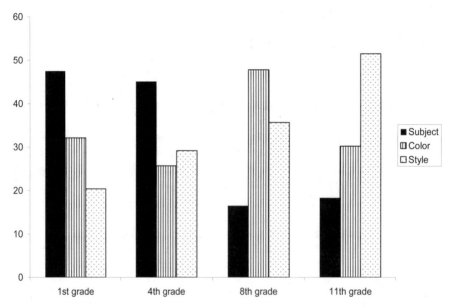

Figure 11.3 Relative weights (%) of subject matter, color, and style in reasoning about most liked and least liked pictures in four age groups

For children in 1st and 4th grade the relative weights of subject matter, color, and style varied depending on which combinations of properties of paintings were presented in a series. The strongest reference to subject matter in younger children was observed when interviewed about the best liked painting in the one series with constant content (the Teddy Bear), that is, where other, varying criteria (for instance, realistic or abstract depiction) must have been the basis for the stated preference. This suggests that these children were sensitive to an aesthetic property of a painting, but were either unaware or unable to verbalize what led them to select a painting.

The age differences shown in Figure 11.3 that are based upon subjects' free responses when explaining their picture preferences and rejections, in particular, the systematic increase of stylistic properties over subject matter, could not be found in the analysis of ratings of the fifteen aesthetic properties listed in Table 11.1 Further, the ratings for liked paintings were more intense than those for disliked paintings, and the ratings of rejected paintings by adolescents showed a striking change in that neutral or even positive ratings of style features appeared in evaluations of disliked paintings.

The absence of an increase in rating stylistic properties over subject matter with age may be explained by differences in what is measured by the free responses when contrasted with the ratings. While the free responses reflect an individual's hierarchy of relevant evaluative criteria, the ratings measure standardized criteria independent of their relevance for the individual. In addition, there seems to be a confounding of age and general response tendencies leading to a steady decrease with age of the rating intensity for all categories except overall evaluation. This decrease was associated with a stronger weighing of subject matter and color over style in all age groups, in particular in reasoning about preferred pictures.

Although boys and girls of all age groups differed in *what paintings* they liked, there were no systematic sex differences in children's and adolescents' *reasoning* about what they liked and disliked regarding preferred and rejected paintings. This was valid for free responses as well as for ratings on the Likert scales.

Concluding remarks

Summarizing the research on children's understanding and evaluation of the aesthetic properties of drawings and art work, how can we answer our two main questions: 1. From which age on are children sensitive to aesthetic properties of drawings and art work and what developmental changes are observed in the aesthetic sensitivity of children? 2. What characteristics of drawings and art work influence children's evaluative judgments of pictures and how do children's picture preferences change with age?

Although several studies of children's aesthetic responses, including our own study, have found that children under age 8 to 10 years tend to base their judgments about art work primarily on subject matter and color, there is sound evidence that sensitivity to formal and stylistic properties of art work, such as line quality, expressiveness, composition, or artistic style is present well before that age. As could be shown by O'Hare and Westwood (1984) and by Itskowitz et al. (1988) children by age 6 were able to attend to formal properties of line drawings if subject matter was held constant. At the same age, children were able to match paintings on the basis of artistic style if subject matter cues were not available (Steinberg & deLoache, 1986), or provided the different styles were highly discriminable, even when subject matter matches were also possible (Callaghan & MacFarlane, 1998). Around age 5 children were also able to allocate human figure drawings according to the age of artist or drawing level (Cox, 2005; Trautner, 1992), and they were beginning to understand non-literal ways of depicting emotion.

The discrepancy between the findings that accord with assumptions by Gardner's (1972) and Parsons' (1987) models of aesthetic development expecting sensitivity to formal and stylistic properties of art work not before early adolescence on the one hand, and those of research observing such sensitivity at age 6, or even earlier, can be explained by differences in the methodologies of the two lines of research. While studies in the tradition of the models of Gardner and Parsons assessed children's sensitivity to aesthetic properties of art work mainly by interviewing the children and gathering qualitative data on how children reason about pictures, the other line of research asked for similarity judgments in matching tasks and used paired comparisons of well defined stimuli that allowed for quantitative statistical analyses. The latter assessment methods put lesser demand on children's ability to verbalize and, thus, seem to be better suited to detecting the criteria on which children's judgments are based. By using a nonverbal matching task that was embedded in the context of a game (to match the emotion of a teddy bear), Callaghan (2000) could show that even 3-year-olds were able to match a picture to an emotion. Thus, one can conclude that young children are sensitive to aesthetic properties of art work beyond attending to subject matter and color, but that they do not address these properties in their spontaneous judgments or reasoning about pictures.

Turning now to our second question, children's developing picture preferences. In contrast to the observation of young children's ability to refer to aesthetic properties of art work, when evaluating picture *preferences* there seems to be a marked orientation to depicted content and color that persists well beyond childhood. Also, visual realism of representational drawings, in general, seems to be more valued than abstract non-representational pictures. This was not only found for spontaneous responses of subjects in interview studies, but also in more controlled studies using more indirect measures of judgments and reasoning (Cox, 2005; Golomb, 1992; Trautner, 2007).

Like the studies that tested what properties are perceived, studies investigating what is preferred differ in their findings, depending on the pictures used and the assessment methods administered. However, the differences between the preference studies concerning the observed relative weight of subject matter, color and style features depending on methodology were not as pronounced as in the sensitivity studies. Over a wide range of stimuli and with different methods of assessment we observed in our own study (Trautner, 2007), for instance, a strong preference for realistic depictions with bright colors throughout childhood. Only in a minority of 1st grade children were likes and dislikes of paintings associated with stylistic properties such as accuracy, articulation, or complexity.

In conclusion one can summarize the results of the preference studies to confirm more to the models of aesthetic development as proposed by Gardner and Parsons than is the case for the studies testing children's ability to perceive aesthetic properties.

The discussion of the research on children's developing understanding and evaluation of aesthetic properties of drawings and art work so far has concentrated on characteristics of pictures as self-contained entities. However, as elaborated in Freeman's theory of pictorial reasoning (Freeman, 1995; Freeman, Chap. 3), pictures are not only a medium of representation but also a medium of communication. As such, pictures are usually made intentionally by an artist and are perceived by a viewer, both, artist and viewer having distinct characteristics. On the side of the artist as well as on the side of the viewer, it would be premature to assume that a picture, in any case and solely, was made with the intention to *represent* something of the world. A representational intention is only one among different possible intentions. The artist as well as the viewer may alternatively take an approach to the picture that is guided by an expressive, decorative, or narrative intention (Reith, 1996). Depending on what participants of a study understand as what is expected from them, i.e., what aspects of a picture are to be judged and evaluated, their responses may vary considerably. The ability to conceptualize and to distinguish between the world, the artist and the beholder, and their relationships, as sources of the beauty of a picture is itself something that develops (Freeman and Parsons, 2001; see also Freeman, Chap. 3). Future research on children's aesthetic sensitivity in perceiving and evaluating art work that aims to put children's minds in the centre of analysis should include the network of relationships that connects pictures, artists and viewers with the world.

References

Bell, R., & Bell, G. (1979). Individual differences in children's preferences among recent paintings. *British Journal of Educational Psychology, 49*, 182-187.

Bloom, P., & Markson, L. (1998). Intention and analogy in children's naming of pictorial representations. *Psychological Science, 9*, 200-204.

Browne, C. A., & Woolley, J. D. (2001). Theory of mind in children's naming of drawings. *Journal of Cognition and Development, 2*, 389-412.

Burkitt, E. (2008). Children's choice of color to depict metaphorical and affective information. In C. Milbrath & H. M. Trautner (Eds.), *Children's understanding and production of pictures, drawings, and art: Theoretical and empirical approaches* (pp. 107-120). Cambridge, MA: Hogrefe & Huber.

Callaghan, T. C. (1997). Children's judgments of emotions portrayed in museum art. *British Journal of Developmental Psychology, 15*, 515-529.

Callaghan, T. C. (2000). The role of context in preschoolers' judgments of emotion in art. *British Journal of Developmental Psychology, 18*, 465-474.

Callaghan, T. C., & MacFarlane, J. M. (1998). An attentional analysis of children's sensitivity to artistic style in paintings. *Developmental Science, 1*, 307-313.

Callaghan, T. C., & Rochat, P. (2008). Children's understanding of artist-picture relations: Implications for their theories of pictures. In C. Milbrath & H. M. Trautner (Eds.), *Children's understanding and production of pictures, drawings, and art: Theoretical and empirical approaches* (pp. 187-205). Cambridge, MA: Hogrefe & Huber.

Carothers, T., & Gardner, H. (1979). When children's drawings become art: The emergence of aesthetic production and perception. *Developmental Psychology, 15*, 570-580.

Cox, M. V. (2005). *The pictorial world of the child*. Cambridge: Cambridge University Press.

Cox, M. V., & Hodsoll, J. (2000). Children's diachronic thinking in relation to developmental changes in their drawings of the human figure. *British Journal of Developmental Psychology, 18*, 13-24.

Darwin, C. (1872). *The expression of the emotions in man and animals*. London: Murray.

Ekman, P., & Friesen, W. V. (1986). A new pan-cultural facial expression of emotion. *Motivation and Emotion, 10,* 159-168.

Fantz, R. L. (1963). Pattern vision in newborn infants. *Science, 140,* 296-297.

Freeman, N. H. (1995). The emergence of a framework theory of pictorial reasoning. In C. Lange-Küttner & G. V. Thomas (Eds.), *Drawing and looking* (pp. 135-146). New York: Harvester Wheatsheaf.

Freeman, N. H. (2008). Pictorial competence generated from crosstalk between core domains. In C. Milbrath & H. M. Trautner (Eds.), *Children's understanding and production of pictures, drawings, and art: Theoretical and empirical approaches* (pp. 33-52). Cambridge, MA: Hogrefe & Huber.

Freeman, N. H., & Sanger, D. (1993). Language and belief in critical thinking: Emerging explanations of pictures. *Exceptionality Education Canada, 3,* 43-58.

Freeman, N. H., & Sanger, D. (1995). The commonsense aesthetics of rural children. *Visual Arts Research, 21,* 1-10.

Gardner, H. (1972). The development of sensitivity to figural and stylistic aspects of paintings. *British Journal of Psychology, 63,* 605-615.

Gardner, H., & Winner, E. (1976). Three stages of understanding art. *Psychology Today, 9,* 42-45.

Gardner, H., & Winner E. (1982). First intimations of artistry. In S. Strauss (Ed.), *U-shaped behavioral growth* (pp. 147-168). New York: Academic Press.

Golomb, C. (1992). *The child's creation of a pictorial world.* Berkeley: University of California Press.

Goodnow, J. J., Wilkins, P., & Dawes, L. (1986). Acquiring cultural forms: Cognitive aspects of socialization illustrated by children's drawings and judgments of drawings. *International Journal of Behavioral Development, 9,* 485-505.

Itskowitz, R., Glaubman, H., & Hoffman, M. (1988). The impact of age and artistic inclination on the use of articulation and line quality in similarity and preference judgments. *Journal of Experimental Child Psychology, 46,* 21-34.

Jolley, R. P., & Rose, S. (2008). The relationship between production and comprehension of representational drawing. In C. Milbrath & H. M. Trautner (Eds.), *Children's understanding and production of pictures, drawings, and art: Theoretical and empirical approaches* (pp. 207-235). Cambridge, MA: Hogrefe & Huber.

Jolley, R. P., & Thomas, G. V. (1994). The development of sensitivity to metaphorical expression of moods in abstract art. *Educational Psychology, 14,* 437-450.

Jolley, R. P., & Thomas, G. V. (1995). Children's sensitivity to metaphorical expression of mood in line drawings. *British Journal of Developmental Psychology, 13,* 335-346.

Jolley, R. P., Zhi, Z., & Thomas, G. V. (1998). The development of understanding moods metaphorically expressed in pictures. *Journal of Cross-Cultural Psychology, 29,* 358-376.

Lewis, H. P. (1963). The relationship of picture preference to developmental status in drawing. *Journal of Educational Research, 57,* 43-46.

Machotka, P. (1966). Aesthetic criteria in childhood: justifications of preference. *Child Development, 37,* 877-885.

McGhee, K., & Dziuban, C. D. (1993). Visual preferences of preschool children for abstract and realistic paintings. *Perceptual and Motor Skills, 76,* 155-158.

Milbrath, C. (1998). *Patterns of artistic development in children.* New York: Cambridge University Press.

Morra, S., Caloni, B., & d'Amico, M. R. (1994). Working memory and the intentional depiction of emotions. *Archives de Psychologie, 62,* 71-87.

O'Hare, D., & Westwood, H. (1984). Features of style classification: A multivariate experimental analysis of children's responses to drawings. *Developmental Psychology, 20*, 150-158.

Parsons, M. J. (1987). *How we understand art: A cognitive developmental account of aesthetic experience.* New York: Cambridge University Press.

Rump, E. E., & Southgate, V. (1967). Variables affecting aesthetic appreciation in relation to age. *British Journal of Educational Psychology, 37*, 58-72.

Russell, J. A., & Bullock, M. (1985). Multidimensional scaling of emotional facial expressions: Similarity from preschoolers to adults. *Journal of Personality and Social Psychology, 48*, 1290-1298.

Steinberg, D., & DeLoache, J. S. (1986). Preschool children's sensitivity to artistic style in paintings. *Visual Arts Research, 12*, 1-10.

Trautner, H. M. (1992). *Judgments about the quality of children's man drawings based upon age of artist and drawing score.* Paper presented at the 5th European Conference on Developmental Psychology, Sevilla, September.

Trautner, H. M. (2007). *Children's and adolescents' aesthetic judgments and reasoning about likes and dislikes of art work.* Paper presented at the Annual Conference of the Jean Piaget Society, Amsterdam, June, 1-3.

Trautner, H. M., Lohaus, A., Sahm, W. B., & Helbing, N. (1989). Age-graded judgments of children's drawings by children and adults. *International Journal of Behavioral Development, 12*, 421-431.

Trautner, H. M. & Wagenschütz, P. (2005). *Four- to eleven-year-old children's understanding and portrayal of facial expressions.* Paper presented at the 12th European Conference on Developmental Psychology, Tenerife, August, 24-28.

Tryphon, A., & Montangero, J. (1992). The development of diachronic thinking in children: Children's ideas about changes in drawing skills. *International Journal of Behavioral Development, 15*, 411-424.

Winner, E. (2006). Development in the arts: Drawing and music. In D. Kuhn & R. Siegler (Eds.), *Handbook of child psychology* (6th ed.), Vol. 2: *Cognition, perception, and language* (pp. 859-904). New York: Wiley

Winston, A. S., Kenyon, B., Stewardson, J., & Lepine, T. (1995). Children's sensitivity to expression of emotion in drawings. *Visual Arts Research, 21*, 1-14.

Wollheim, R. (1993). *The mind and its depth.* Cambridge, MA: Harvard University Press.

Chapter 12

Developmental Preferences and Strategies for Visual Balance in Aesthetic Compositions

Constance Milbrath
University of British Columbia

> *"...a work of art is more than an artistic equilibrium; but it is always committed to being at least that. A work which achieves less is artistically incomplete. A work which is committed to achieving less has not the status of art at all" (Taylor, 1964, p. 28).*

When an adult artist composes a work of art, decisions are complex and multidimensional; color, size, shape and location of forms are considered in a complex perceptual equation that is regulated by artistic decisions about the statement and impact the artist wishes to make. One of the most significant aims of this artistic effort is to create a coherent piece that engages the viewer on different levels. Crucial to this objective is the creation of a visually well balanced piece because when a work of art is well balanced it gains stability and coherence allowing the eyes of the viewer to explore the whole before settling on "a determined average path" that takes in all parts of the work (Arnheim, 1988; Molnar, 1992). Adult viewers appreciate artistic properties of artwork such as balance, symmetry, complexity, and structural features of the composition within the first 50 ms of viewing (Cupchik & Berlyne, 1979; Locher & Nagy, 1996). Among these, visual balance appears to be the most fundamental (Nodien, Locher, & Krupinsky, 1993). In fact, the perceptual appreciation times noted for visual balance alone regardless of viewer sophistication in the visual arts, led Locher (2006) to conclude that the visual system is "hard-wired" to respond to visual balance. While this conclusion seems well warranted when considering responses of the adult viewer, the absence of confirming research on children and especially young children, make it premature to presume that infants and young children automatically apprehend visual balance. In this chapter, I consider the question of the artistic appreciation and production of visual balance by children. First, I define what visual balance means in a work of art and examine the plausibility of a "hard-wired" response to visual balance using studies of infant perception that demonstrate their capabilities for perceptual organization. Second, I review existing research on children's aesthetic sensitivity and present some observations on the artwork of young but highly talented child artists. Finally, I review a series of studies that I conducted that point to both a protracted period for normative development of compositional skills and the capacity for early appreciation and production of visual balance.

Visual balance and the development of perceptual capacities

Critical to visual balance in a work of art is the organizing framework imposed by the boundaries of the piece (Arnheim, 1974). This bounding frame, dictates the structural skeleton around which the work is built. The greatest visual stability is achieved when elements are located along the major structural axes. As elements move away from this defining internal structure, they interrupt the stability of the piece and become perceptually heavier. Therefore, if visual balance is to be maintained these errant elements must be made "lighter." Elements that are larger in size, brighter in color, regular in form or shape, and more complex or interesting in content are perceived as visually heavier than their contrasts and like the pull of gravity, they "attract" other elements in the composition. Likewise forms that are visually isolated and regions that are enclosed are perceived as heavier than embedded forms or surround areas (Arnheim, 1974). Force is also exerted by centric properties of a work; a center focal area that can both issue and exert "gravitational" pull and which Arnheim (1988) described as an "indispensable structural property of any composition." Such considerations point toward weighing scales as an apt metaphor for visual balance. Metaphorically elements with visual weight correspond to those with physical weight.

In the simplest case, artists achieve visual balance by rigid adherence to the hidden internal structure, aligning elements of equal visual weight along the horizontal and/or vertical axes, resulting in a static equilibrium. Use of symmetry lends itself easily to static balance but also can yield a dynamic tension if the primary organizing axes are the diagonals rather than the vertical and horizontal axes. Visual balance also can be accomplished by an asymmetrical counterbalancing of compositional dimensions around the structural skeleton, creating a dynamic but equilibrated tension (Klee, 1978). Asymmetrical balance results when the artist counterbalances the composition with non-identical pictorial properties. One example of a simple asymmetrical form involves equalizing mass organized around a central axis by distributing the mass across a different number of elements (i.e., 2 smaller and 1 larger; called complex symmetry by Golomb, 1992). A more complex and dynamic balance can be achieved by counterbalancing across quite different compositional properties. For example, a *dark mass* (tonality) shifted slightly off center can be visually balanced by a much "lighter" element placed *in the periphery* (location) of the picture. In this case distance (location) is used to equalize the heavier dark mass. In addition, artists use the anisotropy of visual space to create dynamic tension. Visual anisotropy is experienced most strongly on the vertical axis of a picture where elements in the upper part of the frame are perceived as 'heavier' than those in the lower portion (cf. Kandinsky, 1982 pg. 639-640). While less compelling, along the horizontal axis greater visual weight is given to the elements on the left than the right, an effect that may result from our training in reading or from compensatory attention mechanisms in the brain that initially overcome the dominance of the right visual field (left brain dominance) by orienting to the left visual field (Arnheim, 1974).

Perceptual theory

These stabilizing properties of relationships among visual elements are easily identified as "field effects" resulting from the operation of primary organizational principles of visual perception recognized and first researched by Gestalt psychologists (Kohler, 1947; Koffka, 1963; Wertheimer, 1924/1950). These early pioneers argued that visual weight is in large part determined by relational laws built into the visual system, such as the *eye's* insistence on visually grouping by proximity, similarity, continuity, or common fate of elements, the perceptual privilege or weight the *eye* ascribes to regular forms over irregular forms, and the tendency to complete open figures and regroup patterns toward "prägnanz" and stability. Gestalt psychologists maintained that form perception was based on an unlearned built-in perceptual organizational processes capable of extrapolating 3-D forms of unfamiliar objects from a single viewpoint. This organizational process was thought to operate as soon as underlying brain mechanisms became mature.

Gestaltists were reacting against Structuralism, the prevailing theory of perception, which argued that complex percepts were built from *atoms* of sensory experience as associations based on spatial and temporal contiguity of experiences (Palmer, 1999). More recent theories utilize some of the ideas proposed by the early Gestalt psychologists. Gibson's ecological optics (1966; 1979; E. Gibson, 1969) put an emphasis on perceptual analysis of the whole. But rather than a focus on the "emergent properties" of the Gestalten as some critics would have (see Ash, 1998 cited in Cupchik, 2007), Gibson made the more radical proposal that neural mechanisms evolved specifically to extract and process information available in the environment from real life transformations in an object's optical projection as an object or observer moves in the world. This form of dynamic information utilization of optical transformations appears in infants as early as it can be tested, at 2 months, whereas information about form from other sources appears unusable by infants until the 2nd half of the first year (Kellman & Arterberry, 2006).

Modern constructivism, an elaboration of Helmholz' earlier perceptual inference theory, combines many of the best facets of these earlier theories, acknowledging that while some aspects of perception are innate, others are learned through experience (Palmer, 1999). Based on their research, these modern constructivists have proposed three new grouping principles; synchrony, common region, and element connectedness (Palmer, 1999). Synchrony is related to the classical principle of common fate, but visual events that occur at the same time are grouped (e.g., the flicker of illuminated dots is coincident) rather than visual events that change toward the same fate (e.g., all dots flicker to same level of brightness). Common region refers to grouping of elements located within the same enclosed region and element connectedness refers to grouping of connected elements. Both can be shown to be stronger than grouping by proximity. The result is that in some cases, the principles of grouping, such as by proximity, similarity, common region, (and in some instances common fate) result in perceptual organizations of loosely aggregated elements, while in others, such as grouping by element connectedness, good continuation, and common fate, the result is stable unit formation (Palmer, 1999). Accordingly, this modern movement accepts and extends the Gestalt principles of perceptual organization but further seeks to understand the "emergent properties" of percepts as mechanisms by which perceptual organization unfolds during the act of perception.

Infant visual sensitivity

The paradigms for studying what newborns and young infants see are limited. At birth, visual sensitivity is far from complete so researchers are hard-pressed to demonstrate any newborn competencies. Use of animals with precocial visual sensitivity, neural imaging techniques, and studying the developmental linkages between visual sensitivity and perceptual organization as infants mature are suggested methods to circumvent the newborns limitations (Condry, Smith, & Spelke, 2001). Research on newborn visual sensitivity indicates considerable deficiency in acuity, contrast, color sensitivity, and pattern discrimination (phase sensitivity), most of which undoubtedly rests on the immaturity of the eye's optics and photoreceptors (Kellman & Arterberry, 2006). Initially infants' processing of basic perceptual properties such as unity, size, shape and texture are dependent on processing phase information or the relative position of spatial frequency components of which a pattern is composed. Sensitivity functions improve quickly, and in most areas adult levels are reached in the first half year of life. Nevertheless, and this remains a puzzle (Kellman & Arterberry, 2006), newborns appear able to respond to the configuration of faces and show some face recognition within days of life (Bushnell, 2001). Research on size perception suggests further that newborns perceive size constancy since they respond to the novelty of physical size not projective size (Slater, Mattock ,& Brown, 1990).

Perceptual organization in infancy

Perceptual organization in infants has been most effectively studied with the classic habituation paradigm. Infants of 4 months presented with a display of a rod occluded by a rectangle across its center do not perceive the rod's unity unless common motion (common fate) of each visible part is used as the cue (Kellman & Spelke, 1983; Kellman, Gleitman, & Spelke, 1987). More limited capacities to discriminate certain types of motion are found in younger infants but newborns are unable to use common motion and instead appear to make perceptual judgments based on visible parts (Kellman & Arterberry, 2006). Grouping based on static features of the display are not apparent until around the 7th month of life when unity of an occluded stimulus is perceived based on good continuation and similarity of color (Spelke, 1990). Kellman and Arterberry (2006) conclude that the late onset of perceiving continuity of edge or "relatability" makes it possible that experience with an object's view under occlusion contributes to this ability. Further while infants under 6 months can transfer object recognition from kinetic to static displays they cannot do the reverse until about 9 months suggesting this as the age for the appearance of true form perception.

The body of research on infant perception is quite coherent in demonstrating that during the first year of life, perception becomes increasing organized toward perceiving the form and unity of objects and capable of grouping visual displays into homogeneous units based on principles of Gestalt grouping. Such evidence has led Condry, Smith, and Spelke (2001, p. 22) to argue "…that perceptual organization is responsive to the same types of perceptual information at all ages," and what changes with development is simply the sensitivity to visual information. Kellman and Arterberry (2006) while acknowledging that some perceptual learning operates throughout life, also conclude that the evidence on infant's capacities affirms that "meaningful perception" operates from birth and is not initially learned through visual experiences. On the other hand, Palmer (1999), a modern constructivist, proposes a role for both innate and learned percepts, arguing that newborns are born with innate mechanisms that allow certain kinds of perceptual organization but that the rest is quickly learned through interactions with the world during the first 8 months of life. What is particularly compelling about the infancy research, is that the "field effects" noted by the pioneering Gestaltists to organize perception in adults, also have been shown to be active components of perceptual organization in very young infants; just as the Gestaltists surmised. One might conclude, therefore, that by end of the first year of life infants respond to effects in the visual field such that they demonstrate perceptual organizational capacities that would allow for appreciation of "prägnant" forms, those presumed to be organized as the most visually stable by the Gestaltists.

Children's aesthetic appreciation of pictures

Our knowledge of children's aesthetic responsiveness has been significantly informed by Parsons' influential book, *How we understand art: A cognitive developmental account of aesthetic experience*. An outgrowth of Harvard's Project Zero collaborative enterprise with art educators to study artistic development, Parsons modeled aesthetic development as a five stage process that drew heavily on the 19th century aesthetic philosophy of Baldwin, wherein response to art constituted an exploration of the self, and on Kohlberg's stages of moral development, which evolve from dependency through conventionalism to autonomy. Parsons based his model on interviews with children and adults that assessed their ability to understand and interpret the experience of viewing color reproductions of eight well know paintings; a process that clearly relied on the viewer's capacity to analyze and elaborate conceptually on what they saw. It is therefore, not surprising that Parsons obtained a quite protracted period for the full development of these analytical skills. Despite this aspect, Parsons' theory has played a major role in our thinking about aesthetic development (see Trautner, Chap. 11).

Parsons' initial stages were typical of the younger children, beginning with the uncritical and intuitive delight of preschoolers for strong bright colors and sympathetic subject matter and graduating to the more critical assessment by elementary school age children that privileges realism and *beautiful* content of a painting's subject matter. Appreciation for the expressiveness of a painting and its ability to evoke emotion in the viewer comes about in Stage 3, as previous criteria such as subject matter and realism are distinguished as separate from the experience of a painting. At this point, abstract paintings or those representing *ugly* events can be appreciated for their expressiveness. What is distinctive as well about this stage is a newly developed ability for the child to appreciate the communicative relationship between artist and viewer. There is now an artist on one side of the painting who is trying to express a feeling or idea to a viewer who is on the other side of the painting.

In stage 4, "[e]xpressiveness moves from the private world of the viewer to the public space of the canvas" (Parsons, 1987, p. 110). This marks an awareness of the subjectivity of the viewer's role in relation to art. For the first time, formal properties of a painting such as style and composition are critically evaluated and the interaction of the artist with the medium is understood as a collaboration that helps to define these formal aspects. Further, whereas in the previous stage an interpretation of a painting was checked against one's own reaction, one's interpretation is now checked against the *facts* of a painting which are understood to be constructed by a community of viewers. At the culminating stage 5, called the 'post-conventional' stage, the "authority of tradition" is no longer a given. While the viewer may still use conventions to understand and interpret a painting, these canons are critically examined in relation to the viewer's own responses. A judgment is validated by reasons that in principle are available to others and not by its agreement with others. The dialogue with the community of viewers that was begun at stage 4 is opened up allowing for a reinterpretation of one's experience.

Empirical research on children's aesthetic sensitivity dates back at least 60 years (Taunton, 1982). Earlier researchers who studied children (Gardner, Winner, & Kircher, 1975; Lark-Horovitz, 1973; Machotka, 1966; Rosenstiel, Morrison, Silverman, & Gardner, 1978) found results surprisingly similar to Parsons' later study; young children based their preferences for reproductions of paintings primarily on subject matter and color. Realism became a consistent criteria after age 7, increasing thereafter up until preadolescence (Machotka, 1966; Trautner, Chap. 11). Those who used an explicitly cognitive framework to explain children's aesthetic development, invoked Piaget's stage of Formal Operations to explain the appearance of sensitivity to formal properties of composition and style and the objective stance of the art critic (Gardner, 1983; Machotka, 1966). Studies which utilized simpler performance tasks found that although young children ages 4 to 6 show some sensitivity to artistic style (Callaghan & MacFarlane, 1998; O'Hare & Westwood, 1984; Steinberg & DeLoache, 1986; Walk, Karusaitos, Lebowitz, & Falbo, 1971; Winner, Blank, Massey, & Gardner, 1983) and expressiveness (Cox, 2005; Gebotys & Cupchik, 1989; Taunton, 1980), they generally were unable to explain their choices. However, even a few early studies at Project Zero were more successful in demonstrating that some children as young as age 5 could give appropriate reasons for their preferences, particularly in relation to the mood conveyed by a painting (Blank, Massey, Gardner, & Winner, 1984). The review by Callaghan and Rochat (Chap. 9) suggests as well that studies which rely on explicit knowledge typically find a later developmental course than those which tap children's tacit knowledge of the artist-picture relationship. Callaghan and Rochat demonstrate that even very young children understand some of the functions of pictures and some aspects of the artist's intention in producing a picture. More recently Freeman (Freeman & Parsons, 2001; Freeman & Sanger, 1995) has engaged children in general discussions about art rather than focusing on specific reproductions of masterpieces. Nevertheless, overall his results describe a progression remarkable similar to that summarized by Parsons albeit with variations in focal content and more specific age data; the realist reasoning of younger children is transformed in the pre-adolescent to an appreciation of the relationships between artist, picture, and viewer.

Children's ability to produce aesthetic pictures

It seems only reasonable that children's cognitive reflections on art would rely on conceptual development for their elaboration. Their artistic productions, however, might depend on sensitivity to aesthetic properties upon which young children cannot yet reflect. That is, even if a young child's explicit intention is simply to make a communicative picture, aesthetic considerations could implicitly come into play. One cannot claim that this capacity would resemble the intentional awareness of the adult artist. Nevertheless, young children could potentially exploit a much simpler compositional strategy, by using their eyes to group elements toward "what looks good, where" as they execute a drawing (see review below of Barnhart, 1942). In this case composing a drawing becomes a sequence of two-dimensional perceptual decisions dissociated from either the graphic problems raised by constructing and representing three dimensional spatial relationships or the cognitive complexity of planning an entire piece prior to its execution (see Morra, Chap. 4). Our observations of the drawings of young gifted child artists suggests that they might well have been sensitive to the laws of *prägnanz* when drawing. The drawings produced by these gifted child artists presented visually balanced wholes that depended on surprisingly complex field effects (Milbrath,

1998). I illustrate the capacity talented children have to produce visually balanced pictures with two examples below. Other examples are discussed in Milbrath (1998) and Winner and Martino (2002).

Figure 12.1 Talented child artist; Kate, age 4. Source Milbrath (1998).

At age 4, Kate uses symmetry of form and color to balance the frontal pose of *The Juggler* in Figure 12.1. But the composition also contains an interesting asymmetry. The juggler holds a tall stack of pineapples in his left hand that is beautifully counterbalanced by the density of colored lines applied to the otherwise near symmetry of the form behind the juggler to the right. The composition therefore achieves its balance not only from symmetrical placement of like forms but also from a balance across two different dimensions, that of height (size) and color density (weight).

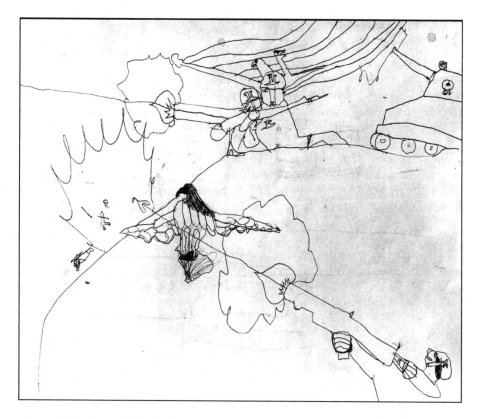

Figure 12.2 Talented child artist, Hondo, age 7. Source: Milbrath (1998).

A second example, Figure 12.2, was produced by a seven year old boy, Hondo. In this drawing, balance is achieved by counterbalancing weight and location with the directional path the eye takes. A chevron shape is used to organize the drawing such that the eye fixes the large figure and gun on the lower right. The direction in which the gun points and the shot trace guides the eye up the hill to the left toward the eagle. As the shot meets the contour of the hill, directional biases of the eye (up and to the right) and the outline of the hill converge to further direct the viewers gaze to the soldier, his cat, and the tank grouped on the top right of the picture. The weight of these end elements is held in check by a cannon which shoots off to the left behind the soldier and his cat.

These two remarkable examples of sophisticated compositional strategies were not unique in the artwork of these two talented children when they were young or in the artwork of other talented children studied (Milbrath, 1998). It cannot be claimed that these children planned such compositions apriori, the way an adult artist might, but rather that these talented children were visually sensitive to compositional properties, taking the design of the two-dimensional picture surface into account during the execution of a drawing. Despite these achievements by very young gifted child artists, research that has examined children's normative drawings has generally found a protracted developmental period for the appearance of advanced compositional forms.

Golomb (1992) calls attention to the fact that at the very least, an "intuitive understanding of part-whole relations and their mutual regulation" (Golomb, 1992, p. 166), is required for children to produce coherent compositions. This may ring even truer if one considers the visual relationships in a well balanced composition. In order to compose a balanced whole, children could use a strategy in which they relate each part to the larger composition while deciding on its location, size, and color. In some sense this is similar to the problems faced by children in constructing a coherent spatial referent within a picture, but it is not as difficult because it does not require the construction and coordination of the depth plane. In addition, more complex forms of visual balance that use dynamic and asymmetrical balancing could involve more advanced conceptual understandings. For example, establishing an equivalency of visual weights in different parts of a picture could require understanding that greater size can be compensated for by placing smaller objects at greater distances from the central axis of a picture. Similarly compensatory relationships between size and color or tone, or shape could require the ability to establish equivalency while coordinating the compensatory relationships across several dimensions at once. One caveat, however is that in order to construct these compensatory relationships, children must first either spontaneously perceive or learn to perceive that certain dimensions (e.g., color, tone, shape) carry visual weight. Although the above review of infants perceptual capacities concluded that very young children organize their perceptions according to Gestalt principles of perceptual organization, there are no studies that have specifically set out to study how young children respond to these properties as aesthetic dimensions.

Golomb (1992) is strongly influenced by Arnheim's framework which combined the law of differentiation with the Gestalt law of *prägnanz* as guiding principles in children's graphic development. Her studies of children's composition abilities began with the classification of close to 1500 drawings by children aged 3 to 13 years of age, after they had been asked to draw pictures of six different themes. Two major organizational strategies emerged. The majority of younger subjects aligned elements in grid-like fashion along the horizontal and vertical axes of the picture. A second strategy, observed in drawings of children at all ages, was to organize elements around a pictorial center. Golomb noted that whereas the centering approach led to well balanced pictures often by stimulating symmetry, alignment strategies in general did not appear to promote symmetry or intentionally balanced compositions. Older children between the ages of 7 and 13 combined the two strategies, aligning groups of figures by size, color, form or activity within an overall centric composition. Older children with more artistic skill sometimes used complex symmetry strategies, organizing elements of equal visual weights around a center. Analyzing drawings by theme, however, revealed that composition strategies were frequently dictated by the theme. For example, the theme of a family was often drawn using alignment strategies as if the family had posed for a photograph, whereas the theme of 3 children playing ball pulled for centric and symmetry strategies (see Pinto & Bombi, Chap. 7). Between the ages of 9 and 13, compositional competence leveled off, apparently as children became preoccupied with other graphic aspects of drawing, such as drawing detail or movement. Overall, however, Golomb noted that it was rare to find drawings that achieved a well integrated compositional balance. At best, this was achieved in local parts of a picture. Dynamic principles of balance that relied on asymmetrical balance by weight, direction, or locations of forms were never observed.

Earlier studies of children ages 5 to 15 enrolled at the Cleveland Museum art school (Barnhart, 1942; Munro, Lark-Horovitz, & Barnhart, 1942) found the same general compositional progression with age as Golomb with younger children aligning elements in a row in either an organized or disorganized fashion and older children organizing multiplanar compositions by a general symmetry or asymmetry along a diagonal axis. It was only after the age of 7 that children's drawings became increasingly organized as coherent compositions. Significantly, few children below the age of 11 in this sample were identified as talented by their art teachers. A detailed analysis of drawings by 52 of the children age 5 through 16, showed the influence on compositional forms of representational skill and drawing order (Barnhart, 1942). In this case, compositional forms were classified at six levels beginning with two levels of disorganized alignment strategies, a third more organized alignment type, and a fourth and a fifth in which dispersed elements were organized locally or holistically. At level 6, three organizational strategies appeared; a tri-fold arrangement in which elements were arranged symmetrically around a center, a diagonal arrangement in which the picture plane could be bisected around a diagonal line, and a rare type in which elements were organized to make a shape such as a circle or triangle[1]. Representational types were classified as either *schematic, transitional,* or *true to visual appearance.* Three drawing orders were observed; a spotting procedure in which individual elements were placed in the "empty spaces" without apparent order, a serial procedure in which the elements were placed in a sequential order across the page one after another, and a constructive procedure in which the child worked from group to group or section to section.

Schematic drawings were almost all composed using alignment strategies and most had elements aligned along a ground line. Transitional drawings (only 12%) fell within the first four levels while true to appearance drawings (50%) were split between compositional levels 5 and 6. The relationship between representational type and compositional form led Barnhart to conclude that older children's interest in representing a spatial scene, leads them away from alignment strategies toward the more organized forms. The relationship observed between drawing order and compositional forms showed that generally, spotting and serial orders were used to produce alignment forms whereas constructive procedures, tended to result in the more advanced compositional forms. For example, two well balanced compositions were produced by two children who had worked on their pictures in a balanced fashion, first completing a

---

[1] Note that the drawing by the talented seven year old Hondo organized as a chevron shape would constitute this level.

group of elements on one side of the drawing, then in the center, and then on the other side before returning to different locations to add elements. This is interesting because it implies that these children could have been monitoring placements with implicit intention of achieving a well balanced composition. At the most advanced compositional form, level six, 82% of the children used a constructive procedure.

The results from these studies suggest that compositions that meet our adult standards of visual balance are rarely produced by young children. Older children are more capable in this regard, primarily using simple forms of symmetry to effect visual balance. A developmental progression from simple alignment strategies to symmetrical and later to asymmetrical balancing strategies is indicated. But only talented children utilize dynamic and asymmetrical compositional strategies to achieve visual balance in their drawings. Some serious confounds also were brought out. Thematic content and representational skill have an impact on a child's compositional strategy. Some themes, such as drawing one's family, pull for alignment strategies while others such as, a birthday party, provoke symmetry. For a child still at the schematic representational level and/or who draws by filling in the available space, alignment strategies prevail. The dependency between representational skill and compositional forms also hints at one reason why compositional balance is observed most often in the artwork of young talented children. Talented children reach a higher level of representational skill at younger ages than less talented children. Therefore, if a child has not gone beyond the level of schematic representation, it may be difficult to estimate compositional competence from her drawings.

In subsequent studies, Golomb designed tasks that were less heavily dependent on a child's graphic competence. In one study that employed a picture completion task, children 6 to 13 years were asked to complete six unfinished pictures in a "pleasing" manner (Golomb, cited in 1992). Use of symmetry increased with age but only the older subjects used complex symmetry balancing strategies. In a more recent study (Gallo, Golomb, & Barosso, 2003), children ages 5 to 9 were asked to represent three themes in drawings, on a felt board with prepared pieces, and on a wooden board with solid 3-D representational pieces. Compositional strategies across the three media were contrasted using a scoring procedure that went from partial alignments to complex symmetry. Results for the drawings were similar to those found in earlier work. Alignment strategies prevailed in younger children while some older children began to organize their drawings around a pictorial center. Compositional strategies with the felt board were generally judged as more advanced at all ages and older children received higher compositional scores than younger children. When the 3-D representational pieces were judged, no statistical developmental differences emerged, with all children achieving higher scores suggestive of more coherent organizational strategies. In general, the range of all scores was restricted and as the authors state "the variability of symmetry scores was low so it was not analyzed." Unfortunately, the task for all three media, instructed children to "recreate the scene" after a thematic vignette was read to them. While this task context undoubtedly influenced compositional strategies in all three media, the lack of variability in the composition scores for the three-dimensional medium suggests further that the instructions positioned the task as widely divergent from one that instructs children to use aesthetic considerations. Related is Gebotys' and Cupchik's (1989) finding of an inverse relationship between children's attention to the storytelling aspects of pictures and sculptures and their consideration of the composition, style, line, and color of the artworks. When children age 6 to 12 were asked to order a triad of paintings or sculptures as to "meaningfulness," they generally attended to either the narrative qualities of the presented artworks or the aesthetic dimensions but not to both.

The influence of drawing theme and result that compositional competence is masked by a child's representational skill appear salient in the studies reviewed. But the review also points to the compositional advantage talented children accrue as a result of their graphic skill in that more advanced balancing strategies such as complex symmetry or intentional asymmetry are rarely observed in normative samples. Tellingly, visual balance in artworks is used as one criteria for identifying children gifted in the visual arts (Clark, 1989). These considerations become important when deciding how to study children's competence to produce visually balanced compositions. When drawings are studied, the compositional strategies observed are likely to be confounded with factors extrinsic to purely aesthetic considerations.

The composition studies

The results of these decisive studies led to the design of composition tasks that would not depend on a child's drawing skill or be confounded with a requested drawing theme but would use simple abstract shapes that a child could arrange and rearrange purely to please the *eye* (Milbrath, 1998). Initially both a two- and three- dimensional composition task were piloted with elementary school children using either flat shapes on a form board or the same shapes made three-dimensional out of wood. Children performed both tasks with ease, but were much more responsive to the three-dimensional task. The first study of elementary school aged children, therefore, used two different sets of 3 solid blocks. In one, only the shapes of the forms differed, 2 "L" and 1 "T" block, such that the two "L"s could be put together to make the "T" shape; all were painted blue (see blocks in Figure 12.5b on p. 277). Balanced compositions could be produced, therefore, by symmetry (e.g., 2 "T"s) or by asymmetries that either maintained equalities in total mass or that employed distance to compensate for inequalities of mass. In the second block set, both color and size of the same shaped forms differed, 1 white and 1 gray large square block and 1 small black square block; the gray value was subjectively matched to equal the white and black value (see blocks in Figure 12.5a on p. 277). Achieving balance with this set, therefore, posed a more complex problem than the former. Balanced compositions could be produced by symmetry (e.g., stacking) or by asymmetry; for example, placing the small black cube adjacent to the large white cube and opposing them with the large gray cube on the other side of a central open space. This latter constitutes asymmetrical balancing across two dimensions, size and tonality. These forms were presented to the children in a *free* composition task in which children were asked to make an arrangement with the blocks on a table from which they might draw a still life picture that would be pleasing to them. Time was spent to assure the children understood what a still life picture was. The *free* task structure, allowed children an opportunity to be creative and unreservedly compose the forms relying on their own aesthetic values and standards. Even the young kindergarten children seemed to understand the demands of this task, although their compositions were often intended to be representational.

The *free* composition task was later elaborated in a second study with middle school children who were not only asked to produce a pleasing arrangement of the three blocks, but also to respond to two- *(picture selection task)* and three-dimensional *(prepared task)* compositions produced by artists using 5 rather than 3 blocks (see below on pp. 279-282). These students were interviewed as well about their views on what was important in judging a work of art. All composition problems were presented to the middle school children at eye level on the top of a white rectangular box against a white backboard meant to represent a canvas or paper on which such a composition might appear as a two-dimensional picture. Four years later, when the youngest middle school child had reached tenth grade, a subset of the original middle school sample (N=40) participated a second time. But this time, the adolescents were given the 5 block sets for the *free* composition task presented on the same rectangular box with white backboard. One block set contained 3 "L" and 2 "T" blocks and the other had 1 large white and 1 large gray block and 3 small equal size black blocks. These are referred to below as the blue block set and gray block set respectively (see Figures 12.4 – 6, pp. 276-278).

Free compositions

Because the number of elements differed, *free* compositions for elementary and middle school children were evaluated separately from the high school students compositions. Photographs of the compositions were judged by 24 students at a local art college with four independent Q-sorts using the dimensions of visual balance, static to dynamic, symmetry to asymmetry, and originality. The students were enrolled in two design classes which had just completed class work covering the first three of these Q-sort dimensions. Prior to making their judgments, students were presented with a 20 minute introduction to the study that covered the anchors for each of the 4 dimensions (see details in Milbrath, 1998). Separate Q-sets were made for the 3 and 5 blue and gray block sets (4 Q-sets in all) and all judgments were relative to others in a Q-set. Therefore, the art students sorted a single Q-set 4 times, once on each dimension using a 7 point scale. On average, each Q-set was judged by 8 students on each dimension. Compositions from 32 elementary school children and the 40 middle school children, who were retested in high school, from both their middle and high school performance were judged.

Results from the 3-block *free* composition task were somewhat surprising. Compositions produced by the younger children were judged by the "experts in training" as better visually balanced, more symmetrical, and static than those produced by the older children. The older children's 3 block compositions were judged as less well visually balanced, but more asymmetrical, dynamic and original than the younger children. Figure 12.3 shows the results (see Milbrath, 1998, for details of analysis). What becomes clear is that the younger children were achieving visual balance by using symmetry and horizontal and vertical alignments that were judged as static. Older children, on the other hand, attempted more sophisticated compositions that relied on asymmetry and dynamic placements of the blocks but at the expense of achieving visual balance.

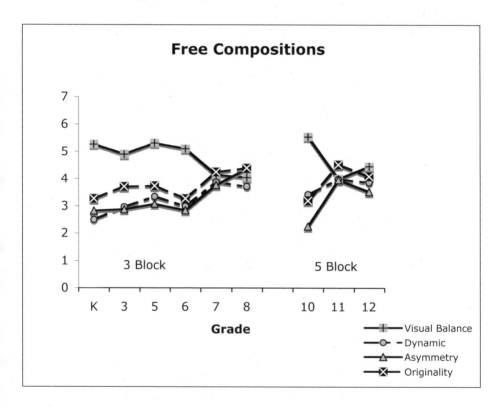

Figure 12.3 Q-sort ratings of free compositions.

Figure 12.4 a and b and 12.5 a and b show four arrangements composed by the grammar and middle school children that exemplify these relationships. Arrangements in Figure 12.4 a and b were composed by kindergarten and fifth grade students, respectively. Average ratings of visual balance were 6.4 and 6.5 respectively whereas average ratings for static-dynamic and symmetry-asymmetry ranged from 1.4 to 1.9.

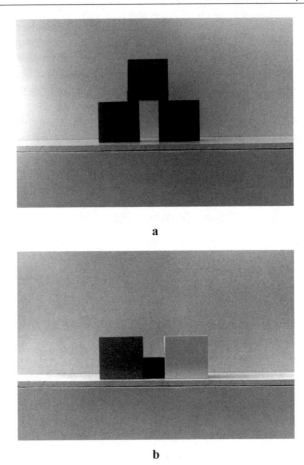

Figure 12.4 Free compositions by (a) kindergarten and (b) fifth grade students.

These can be contrasted with compositions by a seventh and eight grader in Figure 12.5 a and b, respectively. Average ratings on visual balance for these compositions fell between 3 and 4, while average ratings on static-dynamic and symmetry-asymmetry dimensions ranged between 4.5 and 6.

When the middle school children reached high school and arrangements were with 5 instead of the 3 blocks, the younger adolescents again relied on symmetry to produce compositions that were judged as highly visually balanced. By eleventh grade, adolescents concentrated on producing more original composition by experimenting with asymmetrical compositions but again somewhat sacrificing visual balance. The oldest adolescent, however, began to use dynamic and asymmetric arrangements more successfully to achieve compositions that were judged to be better visually balanced than those of their younger high school peers.

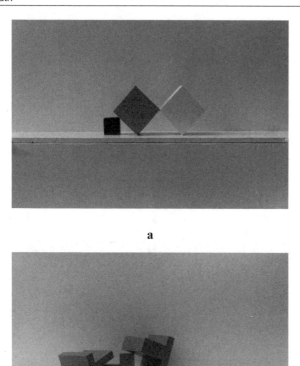

a

b

Figure 12.5 Free compositions by (a) 7th and (b) 8th grade students.

The compositions in Figure 12.6 a –c demonstrate these developments. Visual balance was rated on average as 6.7 in the composition of the tenth grader (12.6 a) with static and symmetry as 3.5 and 1 respectively and originality as 3.8. The compositions of the older students are more typical of the inverse relationship found between visual balance and asymmetry. In Figure 12.6 b the composition of the eleventh grader rated lower on average for visual balance (3.5) but dynamic, asymmetry and originality average ratings were between 4.5 and 5.9. The composition of the twelfth grader in Figure 12.6 c was rated lower on average for visual balance (3.2) but higher on dynamic, asymmetry and originality with average ratings ranging between 5 and 5.7.

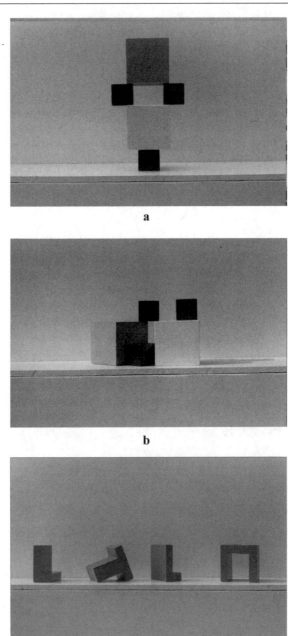

Figure 12.6 Free compositions by (a) 10th, (b) 11th and (c) 12th grade students.

Prepared compositions

In a second series, the same 5 block sets were used to make *prepared* compositions that were presented to 67 middle school students and the 40 high school students who comprised part of the middle school sample after they had completed their *free* compositions. The *prepared* compositions were chosen from a number originally produced by two artists and an architect with these blocks. Choices were based on which compositions were most amenable to the removal of one block and its replacement into the composition to either make a truly symmetrical or nearly symmetrical composition and a clearly unbalanced composition.

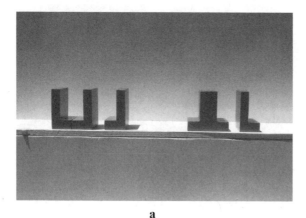

a

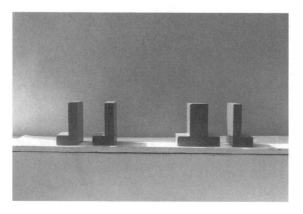

b

Figure 12.7 Artists' composition with blue block set and same composition for Prepared task.

Two alternative solutions besides the artists' original compositions were identified for each composition, a "symmetrically" balanced (true symmetry of form or symmetry of mass) and an unbalanced solution. The artists' originals were all asymmetrically balanced. Two of the four compositions were with the blue blocks and two were with the gray block set. Figures 12.7 a and 12.8 a, show two of the four artists' compositions selected for the study. Figures 12.7 b and 12.8 b, show how these same 2 compositions appeared as presented with the removal of one block.

a

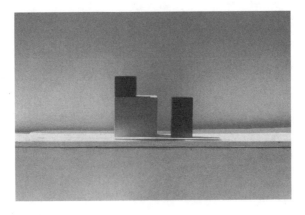

b

Figure 12.8 Artists' composition with gray block set and same composition for Prepared task.

The prepared composition task was scored categorically based on a logic extended from the definitions for types of visual balance presented earlier. This resulted in a general classificatory scheme that included an unbalanced category, a true symmetry or near symmetry balanced category, and an asymmetrically balanced category that either relied on balancing across one (e.g., mass) or two dimensions (e.g., color and distance). In addition, a centering category, was added because many children attempted to place the block in a center position within the composition.

Analysis of the *prepared* compositions across 8 trial presentations (2 choice trials for each of the 2 blue block compositions and 2 for each of the 2 gray block compositions) showed that when true symmetry placements were possible, it was preferred over all others regardless of age (approx. 32% of placements). These types of placements were possible placements in only two of the four compositions (see below). One-dimensional asymmetrical balancing strategies were almost as high (approx. 29% of placements). Many children, particularly those in high school, however, also used centering strategies (approx. 27% of placements). The percentage of unbalanced placements (approx. 20% regardless of age) declined from middle (approx. 23% of placements) to high school (approx. 16% of placements). A strategy of asymmetrically balancing across two dimensions was much less frequent (approx. 9% of placements), but high school students, principally the older students, were more likely to use this successfully (approx. 16% of placements by 11th and 12th grade).

Analysis at the level of the individual compositions suggested differences according to the organization of the composition presented. One composition for each block set (blue and gray) included greater presentation of unfilled space (e.g., Figure 12.7 b) while the other was grouped more tightly together (e.g., Figure 12.8 b). Both middle and high school students used a symmetry strategy to complete those compositions that presented with greater unfilled space (approx. MS = 31%, HS = 33% of placements) whereas this strategy was not really possible with the grouped organizations. Centering strategies were just as prevalent (approx. MS = 26%, HS = 36% of placements) for the composition types that presented with unfilled space. In contrast, those compositions that were organized in a tighter group, provoked greater use of balanced asymmetry (placements balanced asymmetrically in one dimension, approx. Grouped = 36% vs. Spaced = 23% of placements), and particularly in the high school students' use of two dimensional asymmetrical balancing strategies (approx. HS Grouped = 19% vs. HS Spaced = 9% and MS Grouped = 11% vs. MS Spaced = 8% of placements).

Composition picture selection

After completing their responses on the prepared compositions, the middle and high school children were asked to select the "best" solution from three artist rendered tempera colored drawings that included the artist's original, a true symmetry or near symmetry solution, and an unbalanced solution (see Figure 8.4 and 8.5 in Milbrath, 1998). In a final study, a new group of high school students and young adult college students were presented with slides of the two-dimensional artist rendered tempera colored drawings using the method of paired comparisons. Since each alternative composition for the picture selection task had been assigned a category prior to presentation, each composition simply received a preference score of 1 to 3 depending on the rank order a child gave it. In the paired comparison studies, each alternative composition was given a score based on the proportion of times it was chosen on its paired presentations. If an alternative was always chosen, its score was 1 whereas if it was never chosen its score was 0.

Students in both the middle school and high school showed very similar patterns of responding to the *picture selection* task, patterns that more clearly differed according to the organization of the composition presented. As with the potential placements for the prepared compositions, the alternative pictured solutions for the compositions that were more tightly grouped or included more unfilled space differed in the degree of true symmetry possible. Those with more unfilled space had an alternative solution that was true symmetry of form whereas the symmetry solutions for the grouped compositions constituted a near symmetry of mass. When the composition arrangements were closely grouped, 70% of the students chose the artists' original asymmetrically balanced composition (Figure 12.9 a). When the composition arrangements included unfilled space and a true symmetry of form solution was offered, most students preferred the symmetry solution (Figure 12.9 b). In middle school this preference was strongest for the eighth graders whereas by twelfth grade, 42% of the high school students preferred the artists' original asymmetrical composition. Overall, however, when a true symmetry of form was an option, preferences were for the symmetrically balanced alternative compositions, whereas the asymmetry of the artists' original composition was always preferred when the alternatives were complex symmetry. Nevertheless, by twelfth grade many more of the students preferred the artists' asymmetrical compositions, even when a symmetry of form solution was available. The results from the *paired comparison* picture task carried out with a different group of high school students confirmed these results. Unbalanced compositions were always least preferred, symmetry was clearly preferred when a symmetry of form option was offered, and otherwise the artists' asymmetrical compositions were favored. The college sample of young adults showed the same preferences as the high school students.

Summary of results

These studies on largely normative samples of children and adolescents demonstrate clearly that visual balance is always the preferred aesthetic choice regardless of age. The composition strategies to achieve visual balance, however, differ as children develop and their thinking and experience grows more complex. When aesthetic preferences were assessed with methods that demanded little more than visual inspection, preferences for compositions balanced by symmetry of form dominated over those balanced by asymmetry. But, by the end of High School, this preference

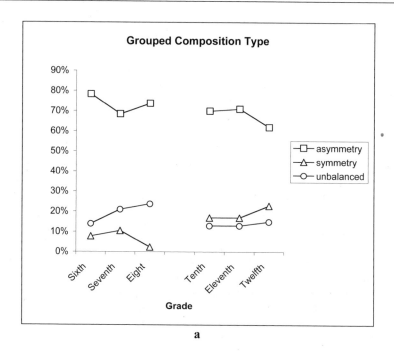

a

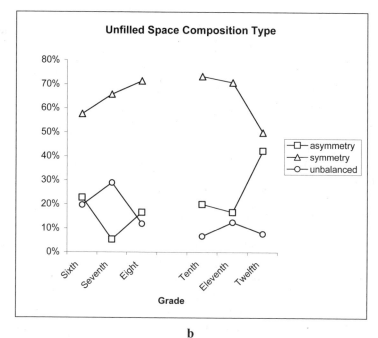

b

Figure 12.9 Picture selection responses to grouped or greater unfilled space compositions.

pattern had begun to reverse, as many more of the 12th graders chose the artists' asymmetrical composition over the symmetry of form alternatives. Near symmetry alternatives, however, offered for compositions that did not have a true symmetry solution were generally rejected in favor of compositions that were balanced by asymmetry. When a more active response was required, as in the *prepared* compositions, both middle and high school students preferred to attempt asymmetrical balancing using one dimension such as mass, unless true symmetry was possible. When it was possible, symmetry was generally preferred. By high school, students began to expand their aesthetic placements to include more complex asymmetrical compositional forms, attempting to balance compositions across two dimensions (i.e., color and size).

Arguably the most demanding of the composition tasks was the free composition task. In this task, students had to organize a composition with no prompts. These spontaneous productions showed a clear shift away from symmetry to more dynamic and asymmetrical compositions as children matured. Children in elementary school produced highly symmetrical and static visually balanced compositions whereas older middle school children shifted away from these symmetrical forms toward asymmetrical and more original compositional forms. A similar shift appeared in high school between 10th and 11th grade, when the composition task was more difficult; composing 5 blocks instead of 3. Older high school students favored dynamic asymmetry producing compositions of greater originality but not always achieving visual balance with these more complex strategies. Overall, therefore, school children of all ages in these studies appeared aware and appreciative of visual balance with symmetry as the most compelling of the compositional forms studied. Nevertheless, older high school students began to appreciate and elaborate more complex compositional forms, while still maintaining strong preferences for visual balance. In simple picture preference tests, symmetry was still favored but less so by the oldest students who chose balanced asymmetrical composition almost as often. When older high school students had to produce a composition they also utilized more complex asymmetrical compositional forms. Therefore, the results from these studies suggest that the ability to produce visual balance using dynamic and asymmetrical compositional forms is a relatively late developmental achievement.

Compositionally sophisticated students

Although the preference for and production of visual balance appeared early, the normative model for realizing visual balance with more complex compositional strategies appears to be one of slow growth. But a question that remained across these studies was whether any of the students studied were aesthetically sensitive in the manner ascribed to our young gifted child artists. Although, I was unable to collect drawings from these students, it was possible to use the *free* compositions as an index of compositional competence. The earlier discussion of visual balance emphasized dynamic asymmetry as a more complex composition strategy. The assumption here is not that this strategy has greater aesthetic value, but only that it is a more difficult strategy to effectively use. Clearly, symmetry is given a higher value in the artwork of some cultures, for example the Haida (see Pariser & Kindler, Chap. 13). Accordingly, the ratings for visual balance, symmetry to asymmetry, and static to dynamic Q-sort ratings were summed for the middle school and high school students separately. Approximately 11 students in each sample could be identified in the top 25% of their distributions and designated as "compositionally sophisticated." It is worth remembering that visual balance was negatively related to asymmetry and dynamism in this study, that is, dynamic asymmetry resulted in compositions that for most students regardless of age, were judged as poorly balanced. This suggested that students whose *free* compositions combined these three elements were indeed unique when compared to the others. These "sophisticated" students were then contrasted with their peers on the *prepared* composition and *picture selection* tasks, statistically controlling for their grade since this sophisticated group was slightly more advanced in grade level. No differences in picture selection were found for the composition groups but placements in the *prepared* compositions did differ. Compositionally sophisticated students in both the middle and high school were more likely to make balanced placements than less sophisticated students. Although compositionally sophisticated high school students were not more likely to use a particular type of balanced placement strategy than their peers, those identified in the middle school balanced the *prepared* compositions more often by using one dimensionally balanced placements.

While some degree of consistency in the performance of these sophisticated and less sophisticated students is suggested by their performance across the composition tasks, it still might be asked whether or not their performance was stable from middle to high school. The correlations between the summed Q-sort rankings used to identify the compositionally sophisticated students in middle and high school suggested there was modest stability over the four intervening years (rho = .36, p = .01). When the middle school summed Q-sort rankings were regressed on the high school Q-sort rankings, the middle school *free* composition scores predicted an additional 13% of the variance after the high school students performance on the *prepared* compositions was accounted for; the total model accounted for 29% of the variance. Neither age nor grade entered into these equations. Consequently, while current performance on the prepared compositions was the best predictor of students' performance on the free compositions, students' performance on the free composition task in middle school appeared to be a reasonably good predictor of their high school performance four years later. In addition, examination of the individuals and their scores showed that five of the 11 sophisticated middle school students were still in the top 25% four years later, 1 had dropped out of the study, and another 3 were within a half point of the cutoff score. Of the high school students who had not been identified in middle school but were now, 4 had middle school scores a half point below the cutoff for the compositionally sophisticated middle school group; therefore, approximately 70% of those identified as compositionally sophisticated either in middle or high school performed consistently across the two points in time.

Reasoning about art work

After they had completed their *free* compositions, the middle and high school students also were interviewed about the criteria they used in judging a work of art. The interview began by asking the students which artistic dimensions they thought were important when looking at a painting and what it was about paintings that generally caught their attention. Once students had responded, they were probed about other artistic dimensions they had left out from a list that included subject matter, color, realism, the three-dimensional qualities of a painting, originality, and visual balance. The interview was an attempt to obtain information related to Parson's original study but also to probe specifically about children's understanding of visual balance.

Regardless of grade level, middle school children mentioned color, subject matter, and realism, in that order with the majority indicating that it was the colors used in a painting that drew them to a work or art (see Trautner, Chap. 11). Preferred subject matter varied greatly and was somewhat gender specific with boys mentioning pictures about sports or with action. Realism was almost always favored over abstract pictures except by several children in each grade who mentioned abstract art. Few children mentioned other dimensions spontaneously but balance and originality were almost three times as likely to be mentioned by eighth graders than children in the lower middle school grades. Those in the lower grades were more likely to cite the three dimensional attributes of a picture. When children were asked specifically about each of the dimensions, originality appeared to be the most important, followed by the three-dimensional qualities of a painting. Visual balance appeared to be less important to these students and a number could not explain what it was. Nevertheless, some students gave convincing definitions, usually by examples.

High school students were more comfortable addressing the topic of art and appeared to be more engaged and better understand the topic of the interview. The criteria these students mentioned also went beyond the interview list. For example, a small percentage, largely 12th graders, mentioned the feeling or mood a picture conveyed or the meaning the artist intended to convey as being one of their primary criteria. Nevertheless, for most students the primary criteria were the same as for the middle school students, color, followed by subject matter and realism. Very few students favored abstract art, although two mentioned liking surrealism. Almost none of the students spontaneously mentioned the other criteria including visual balance. When probed, about half the students acknowledged the importance of visual balance and even those who did not think it was an important artistic element were able to give convincing definitions. Many defined it as symmetry or as one tenth grade student, an "evenness ... not necessarily symmetry. ... uneven feels awkward." As many students in middle school, some high school students still defined visual balance by saying what it was not and only a few older students seemed aware that visual balance was important in the effectiveness of a piece. For example, an 11th grader noted that a painting is "... easier to look at for long periods of time if it is balanced, easier to concentrate on the whole thing." Another 12th grade student said, "if [a painting] is not balanced it won't please the eye ...any artist won't want to do that."

Engaging the middle and high school students who participated in the composition studies in a general discussion about how they judge a work of art appeared to spontaneously elicit few discussions that could be assigned Parson's higher level stages of aesthetic development. When criteria approximating Parson's stage 3 were discussed (e.g., discussion of artist's communicated mood), it was always by high school students. Parson's found that artistic training was critical to scoring at the higher stages of aesthetic development. The number of art classes a student had taken was obtained for a few students, but the majority of students in this study had not had classes beyond a required semester in sixth grade. Nevertheless, a few high school students who had more training in the arts showed more complex evaluative thoughts, such as the importance of the mood a painting conveyed and the role color has in evoking feeling's in a viewer. With the noted exceptions, however, none of the students could discuss the formal elements such as style in relation to the artists' communicative intentions. This could suggest that the absence of exposure and training in the arts threatens the ability of students to engage meaningfully with art.

Conclusions

This chapter began with a discussion of whether or not we could reasonably expect very young children to be sensitive to visual balance in a painting or work of art. The Gestalt psychologists predicted that as soon as underlying visual sensitivities matured, the primary principles of perceptual organization, such as grouping toward prägnanz and stability, would operate. Locher (2006) also noted that the appreciation of visual balance in a work of art was so immediate as to suggest this capacity was hard-wired in the brain. However, without evidence that young children are sensitive to visual balance, Locher's conclusion appeared premature. A review of the research on the capacity for perceptual organization in young infants made it clear that by the end of the first year of life, infants were subject to the Gestalt laws of perceptual organization that would allow grouping toward stability and perception of unity. This supported the idea that very young children could well be sensitive to visual balance but there are few if any studies that have looked at this issue in children apart from those that ask young children to respond to pictures or drawings or that study the composition strategies in children's drawings. Several problems with these latter two approaches were noted. Young children's responses to art appear conditioned by their preferences for certain subject matter and colors and reflective discussions of the formal properties of a picture appear beyond them. In addition, when young children draw, their composition strategies are confounded with their representational skill level and by the theme they wish to depict. There are young children, however, for whom representational skill is not an issue. Drawings from these artistically talented children give us every reason to believe that young children can be sensitive to visual balance. When these talented children are able to flexibly produce a drawing from their imagination, they are capable of using quite advanced compositional strategies.

These considerations led to the formulation of a series of composition tasks that were designed to look at whether or not children appreciated visual balance and, if so, what kinds of composition strategies evolved in relation to children's developmental level. Taking grade in school as an index of developmental level, children between the ages of 5 and 17 years of age were asked to participate in some or all of the composition tasks. In general the results were clear as regards visual balance. Most children at all developmental levels, showed a marked preference for producing or selecting well balanced compositions. Locher's suspicion that this perceptual preference is organized very early appears tenable within the limits of this study. Composition strategies, however, appear to undergo noticeable changes as children develop. As children mature, they begin to use more complex strategies and to some degree prefer compositions that attain visual balance with these more advanced compositional forms. The preferences for symmetry of form in the picture selection task were true for all students regardless of age, although by 12th grade the preference for an asymmetrically balanced alternative was almost on par with symmetry. Even in the *prepared* task, when true symmetry was a potential solution students of all ages favored it over asymmetrical balancing. When true symmetry was not an option, however, asymmetrical balancing using one and two dimensional strategies were more frequently used to complete prepared compositions by high school students and preferred by all students in the picture selection task. It is curious, however, that the older high school students still retained a distinct preference for symmetry in the *picture selection* task and even in responses to the *prepared* task, yet when they produced their own compositions they favored more complex asymmetrical and original compositional forms. It suggests that the act of producing a *free* composition de novo was more progressive than the perceptual preference; these older students appeared to 'know how' before they actually began to demonstrate a preference for the more dynamic asymmetrical compositional forms. It is recognized that the aesthetic value that is put on one compositional form over another can best be thought of as culturally determined. Nevertheless, effecting visual balance with dynamic asymmetry is considerably more difficult than with symmetry and presumably requires more of children.

This conclusion is at stark odds with the more typical finding in studies of young children's pictorial reasoning where production lags behind comprehension (see Jolley & Rose, Chap. 10). Several major differences between those studies and the series reported here are worth considering. Those studies typically ask young children to produce drawings and to reason about and select pictures. The production demands in these studies were reduced considerably by requiring simple 3-D arrangements, where drawing skill was not a factor. Therefore, the difficulties inherent in pictorial production were eliminated yet the task itself still required the productive act of creating a composition. The children responding to the composition completion and preference tasks also were older than many of children typically used in the pictorial studies. Under these conditions, the lag between production and comprehension appears to shift in favor of production leading visual preferences for the more difficult compositional forms. That children's comprehension can be 'educated' by their own productive acts has been found for reasoning in other domains. For example, in a study of problem solving in physics, older children began to grasp the nature of the problem posed to them only after at length engaging through their actions (Milbrath, 2005; see also Piaget, 1987a; 1987b). Future studies looking at aesthetic competence could consider engaging children's actions in tasks that are not limited by graphic skill, as well as using more diverse methods to inquire about their reasoning.

References

Arnheim, R. (1974). *Art and visual perception. A psychology of the creative eye.* Berkeley, CA: University of California Press.

Arnheim, R. (1988). *The power of the center.* Berkeley, CA: University of California.

Ash, G. M. (1998). *Gestalt psychology in German culture, 1890-1967: Holism and the quest for objectivity.* New York: Cambridge University Press.

Barnhart, E. N. (1942). Developmental stages in compositional construction in children's drawings. *Journal of Experimental Education, 11*, 156-184.

Blank, P., Massey, C., Gardner, H., & Winner, E. (1984). Perceiving what paintings express. In R. Crozier & A. Chapman (Eds.), *Cognitive processes in the perception of art* (pp. 127-143). Amsterdam: North-Holland.

Bushnell, I. W. R. (2001). Mother's face recognition in newborn infants: Learning and memory. *Infant and Child Development, 10*, 67-74.

Callaghan, T. C., & MacFarlane, J. M. (1998). An attentional analysis of children's sensitivity to artistic style in paintings. *Developmental Science, 1*, 307-313.

Clark, G. (1989). Screening and identifying student talented in the visual arts: Clark's drawing abilities test. *Gifted Child Quarterly, 33*, 98-105.

Condry, K. F., Smith W. C., & Spelke, E. S., (2001). Development of perceptual organization. In F. Lacerda, C. von Hofsten, & M. Helmann (Eds.), *Emerging cognitive abilities in early infancy* (pp. 1-28), Mahwah, NJ: Erlbaum.

Cox, M. (2005). *The pictorial world of the child.* Cambridge: Cambridge University Press.

Cupchik, G. C. (2007). Arnheim: Critical reflections. *Psychology of Aesthetics, Creativity, and the Arts, 1*, 16-24.

Cupchik, G. C., & Berlyne, D. E. (1979). The perception of collative properties in visual stimuli. *Scandinavian Journal of Psychology, 20*, 93-104.

Freeman, N. H., & Parsons, M. J. (2001). Children's intuitive understanding of pictures. In B. Torff & R. J. Sternberg (Eds.), *Understanding and teaching the intuitive mind,* (pp. 73-92). Mahwah, NJ: Erlbaum.

Freeman, N. H., & Sanger, D. (1995). The commonsense aesthetics of rural children. *Visual Arts Research, 21*, 1-10.

Gallo, F., Golomb, C., & Barosso, A. (2003). Compositional strategies in drawing: The effects of two- and three-dimensional media. *Visual Arts Research, 1*, 2-23.

Gardner, H. (1983). *The arts and human development.* New York: Wiley.

Gardner, H., Winner, E., & Kircher, M. (1975). Children's conceptions of the arts. *Journal of Aesthetic Education, 9*, 60-77

Gebotys, R. J., & Cupchik, G. C. (1989). Perception and production in children's art. *Visual Arts Research 15*, 55-67.

Gibson, E. J. (1969). *Principles of perceptual learning and development.* New York: Appleton-Century-Crofts.

Gibson, J. (1966). *The senses considered as perceptual systems.* Boston: Houghton Mifflin.

Gibson, J. (1979). *The ecological approach to visual perception.* Boston: Houghton Mifflin.

Golomb, C. (1992). *The creation of a pictorial world.* Berkeley, CA: University of California Press.

Kandinsky, W. (1982). *Kandinsky; complete writings on art. Volume 2* (1922-1943). K.C. Lindsay, & P. Vergo (Eds). Boston, MA: G. Hall & Co.

Kellman, P. J., & Arterberry, M. E. (2006) Infant visual perception. In D. Kuhn & R. S. Siegler (Eds.), *Handbook of child psychology: Vol. 2, Cognition, perception and Language,* (pp. 109-160). New York: Wiley.

Kellman, P. J., Gleitman, H., & Spelke, E. S. (1987). Objects and observer motion in the perception of objects by infants. The ontogenesis of perception (Special issue). *Journal of Experimental Psychology: Human Perception & Performance, 13,* 586-593.

Kellman P. J. & Spelke, E. S. (1983). Perception of partially occluded objects in infancy. *Cognitive Psychology, 15,* 483-524.

Klee, P. (1978). *Paul Klee notebooks, Volume 1: The thinking eye.* J. Spiller (Ed.). London: Lund Humphries.

Koffka, K. (1963). *Principles of Gestalt psychology.* New York: Harcourt Brace & Worlds, Inc.

Köhler, W. (1947). *Gestalt psychology: An introduction to new concepts in modern psychology.* New York: Liveright.

Lark-Horovitz, B., Lewis, H., & Luca, M. (1973*). Understanding children's art for better teaching.* Columbus Ohio: Charles F. Merrill.

Locher, P. (2006). Experimental scrutiny of the role of balance in the visual arts. In P. Locher, C. Martindale & L. Dorfman (Eds.), *New directions in aesthetics, creativity, and the arts,* (pp. 19-32). Amityville, NY: Baywood Publishing co.

Locher, P., & Nagy, Y. (1996). Vision spontaneously establishes the percept of pictorial balance. *Empirical Studies of the Arts, 14,* 17-31.

Machotka, P. (1966). Aesthetic criteria in childhood: Justifications of preference. *Child Development, 37,* 877-885.

Milbrath, C. (2005). Epistemology and creative invention. *Journal of Cultural and Evolutionary Psychology, 3,* 119–140.

Milbrath, C. (1998). *Patterns of artistic development in children: Comparative studies of talent.* New York: Cambridge University Press.

Molnar, F. (1992). A science of vision for visual arts. In G. C. Cupchik & J. Laszlo (Eds.), *Emerging visions of the aesthetic process,* (pp. 100-117). New York: Cambridge University Press.

Munro, T., Lark-Horovitz, B., & Barnhart, E. N. (1942). Children's art abilities: Studies at the Cleveland Museum of Art. *Journal of Experimental Psychology, 11,* 97-160.

Nodien, C., Locher, P., & Krupinsky, E. (1993). The role of formal art training on the perception and aesthetic evaluation of art compositions. *Leonardo, 26,* 219-227.

O'Hare, D., & Westwood, H. (1984). Features of style classification: a multivariate experimental analysis of children's responses to drawings. *Developmental Psychology, 20,* 150-158.

Palmer, S. E. (1999). *Vision science: Photons to phenomenology.* Cambridge, MA: MIT Press.

Parsons, F. (1987). *How we understand art: A cognitive developmental account of aesthetic experience.* New York: Cambridge University Press.

Piaget, J. (1987a) *Possibility and necessity: Volume 1, The role of possibility in cognitive development.* Minneapolis, MN: University of Minnesota Press.

Piaget, J. (1987b) *Possibility and necessity: Volume 2, The role of necessity in cognitive development.* Minneapolis, MN: University of Minnesota Press.

Rosenstiel, A. K., Morrison, P., Silverman, J., & Gardner, H. (1978). Critical judgment: A developmental study. *Journal of Aesthetic Education, 12*, 95-100.

Slater, A., Mattock, A., & Brown, E. (1990). Size constancy at birth: Newborn infants' responses to retinal and real size. *Journal of Experimental Child Psychology, 49*, 314-322.

Spelke, E. (1990). Principles of object perception. *Cognitive Science, 14*, 29-56.

Steinberg, D., & DeLoache, H. S. (1986). Preschool children's sensitivity to artistic style in paintings. *Visual Arts Research, 12*, 1-10.

Taunton, M. (1980). The influence of age on preferences for subject matter, realism, and spatial depth in painting reproductions. *Studies in Art Education, 21*, 40-52.

Taunton, M. (1982). Aesthetic responses of young children to the visual arts: A review of the literature. *Journal of Aesthetic Education, 16*, 93-107.

Taylor, J. (1964). *Design and expression in the visual arts.* New York: Dover.

Walk, R. D., Karusaitos, K., Lebowitz, C., & Falbo, T. (1971). Artistic style as concept formation for children and adults. *Merrill-Palmer Quarterly, 17*, 347-356.

Wertheimer, M. (1924/1950). Gestalt theory. In W. D. Ellis (Ed.), *A sourcebook of Gestalt psychology* (pp. 1-11). New York: Humanities Press.

Winner, E., Blank, P., Massey, C., & Gardner, H. (1983). Children's sensitivity to aesthetic properties of line drawings. In D. Rogers & J. A. Sloboda (Eds.), *The acquisition of symbolic skills* (pp. 97-104). New York: Plenum.

Winner, E., & Martino, G. (2002). Artistic giftedness. In N. Colangelo & G. Davis (Eds.), *Handbook of gifted education*, 3rd edition, (pp. 335-349). Needham Heights, MA: Allyn and Bacon.

Chapter 13

Drawing and Aesthetic Judgments Across Cultures: Diverse Pathways to Graphic Development

David A. Pariser
Concordia University

Anna M. Kindler
University of British Columbia

Axel van den Berg
McGill University

Background

The emergence of the *artist* and the emergence of *art* are things that social psychologists, art historians and others have long pondered. Csikszentmihalyi (1988, 1999) and Abu-hamdeh and Csikszentmihalyi (2004) offer us a conceptual framework for addressing this problem. They say that three components must be considered if one is to account for the emergence and recognition of significant creativity and, by extension, significant art: 1) the individual, which is where the germ of innovation takes hold; 2) the domain, which is the discipline(s) in which the individual works, i.e., the visual arts; and 3) the field, which consists of the social organizations that teach, regulate and evaluate the people who exercise the discipline in question, that is, teachers, mentors, journals and art critics. Csikszentmihalyi claims that it is only when one has taken these three elements into account that one can begin to address the question of where *big C* Creativity comes from. Csikszentmihalyi's model applies just as well to the question of where Art (with a *big A*) comes from. Art and aesthetic performance, like Creativity, have to be understood as largely contextual phenomena. The systems approach to Creativity can be successfully extended to the concept of Artistic development (e.g., Kindler, 2004, 2007).

In addition to extending the use of the systems approach to the visual arts, we will also be using a multiple-terminus model to study the development of visual representation. This model (as formulated by Kindler and Darras, 1998) provides us not only with insights about the nature of graphic development, but also suggests some explanations for the *disconnect* which famously exists between the expectations and needs

'ents studying the visual arts, and the art educators, who with
il to deliver what it is their students expect. Much discussion
‿ation literature on the *slump* in enthusiasm and performance in
‿at marks the transition from childhood to (and through) adolescence. This
‿ump has been attributed to teachers' reluctance to convey basic graphic skills to
students who crave mastery of these basic drawing competencies. However, with
Kindler and Darras's model in mind, we find another reason for this slump. Middle-
school decline may also be due to the fact that, whereas the students are anxious to
acquire mastery of several different kinds of visual repertoire, the teachers focus
(mostly) on one visual repertoire alone – the mastery of naturalism – as opposed to
other repertoires.

In the discussion that follows, care must be taken to distinguish between the development of graphic competence and the development of artistic competence. All
too often, drawing development and mastery of skills are conflated with the question
of developing artistry. These are two distinct questions and we intend to keep them
separate. At the same time, we acknowledge that appraising the quality of drawings
may – and often does – involve considerations of skill which, historically, has also
been tied to determinations of artistic merit.

The difference between artistic development and graphic development is one of
degree, if not kind. The distinction depends on the extent to which activities associated with *Art* and *drawing* share socially contextualized criteria. *Art* is a highly contextualized category whose definition is an endless and thankless task. Art is best
grasped as a concept rooted in cultural practice (Freeland, 2001). The same cannot
be said of graphic development, a term that simply refers to the regularities that one
observes in beginners as they acquire mastery of culturally preferred images and
representational styles. Even here, some would argue that graphic development is
also an illusion (Hagen, 1985). But we do not share Hagen's somewhat narrow rationale for debunking the existence of graphic development in toto. We grant that
the notion of graphic development has a cultural component, but the activities and
media that pertain to this process are far better defined than those associated with
the more general category of *Art*. The symbol systems relevant to graphic development are generally based on mark-making tools that function mostly in the two-
dimensional medium and that are sanctioned by the relevant cultural milieu, be it
traditional Chinese brush painting as codified in the Mustard Seed Garden book
(Sze, 1977) or the conventions and norms of comic book narrative (Wilson, 2004).
For our purposes, we will consider graphic development as the gradual acquisition
of certain forms, conventions and technical skills – either through spontaneous experimentation or deliberate instruction – in the service of what Willats (2005) calls
effective representation.

It is important to note that these skills may be used for, but are not the same thing
as *artistry*. Willats (2005) defines an *effective representation* as one in which "…
something specific can be seen and recognized clearly and unambiguously" (p. 14).
Note that Willats does not insist that the representation looks *realistic*, but only that it
be *recognizable*. We claim that in many of their pictorial efforts, even those which

are unrecognizable to other viewers, children the world over seek to attain *effective representations*. Such representations run the gamut from naturalistic images of people, places and animals; images that resemble maps and charts; highly stylized images from the popular media, such as cartoons, comic-strip figures and caricatures; to those that in abstracted ways allow the representations to stand efficiently for their referents. Further, we would claim that effective graphic representations may well exploit auditory and gestural symbols as adjuncts to the more conventional marks and signs committed to a two-dimensional surface. (See Kindler & Darras's notion of *plurimedia*.) This is especially true in early childhood years where the culturally mediated separation of the gestural, vocal and graphic means of representation becomes internalized.

As we suggested, the main factor that raises questions in these developmental scenarios is that the endpoint of graphic development is very much determined by the culturally selected forms that are considered as models of *accomplished graphic work*. This, of course, varies from one era to another, from one culture to another, and from one class to another (Bourdieu, 1984). One has only to compare the formulaic imagery of classical Chinese landscape painting with the austere abstraction of a Giacometti sketch or the meticulous naturalism of a Norman Rockwell study in order to recognize this.

Two questions attach to the issue of graphic (rather than *artistic*) development. The first asks what is the structure of graphic development, i.e., what are the common sequences and elements in the acquisition of graphic competence? In other words, what are the pan-human or universal features that mark the process of learning to make drawings? What happens when we think about it as an *objective* natural process, like the acquisition and development of linguistic abilities?

The second and focal question for us is: how do people (children, art-novice adults and artists) conceive of graphic development? That is, how do people's models of graphic development differ as a function of cultural background, age, and education? In our research to date, we will present some initial answers to these questions.

Models of graphic development

Classic linear models: Luquet (1927/2001), Piaget and Inhelder (1956), and Lowenfeld (1957)

Graphic-developmental pathways have been studied and speculative models have been proposed since the *discovery* of children's drawings in the late 19th century (Costal, 1997). Most of these early models, with the exception of Luquet (1927/2001), were linear in conception, and used the achievement of perspectival rendering as the benchmark against which to measure all graphic attempts. The key features of these models were that they presented development as passage through a series of stages, each one being the prerequisite for what followed. In the case of Piaget (Piaget & Inhelder, 1956) and Lowenfeld (1957), there was a shared belief in the linear and unique pathway that all neophyte draughtsmen/women must follow in order to reach the *natural* terminus for graphic development, that is, visual realism and its highest manifestation, perspectival rendering. For Piaget, this achievement dovetailed nicely with his more general notions about the achievement of abstract, formal thought. In Lowenfeld's case, the achievement of visual realism can be seen as a prerequisite for *modern* artistic forms such as abstract expressionism and pure modernism.

These two models of graphic development proposed that children's graphic apprenticeship was a narrowly confined and culturally invariant process, one in which the child followed a single path that led eventually to the achievement of naturalistic imagery. Although Piaget's notions of stages of graphic development owe much to Luquet, there is one area in which Luquet differed significantly from Piaget (Costal, 1997). He observed that children learning to draw can focus their representations on concerns other than visual resemblances based on observation of the world. Luquet was among the first to note the child's fascination with other forms of visual representation, based on pre-existing visual imagery, popular, casual, and utilitarian. Moreover, Luquet noted that his own daughters (whom he used as subjects of study) were concerned not only with rendering space and form, but also time, and that their graphic inventions were not aimed solely at creating a three-dimensional illusion. Young children, noted Luquet, seemed more concerned with economic solutions to visual problems of all sorts, rather than just achieving verisimilitude.

These researchers also assume that development proceeds along a single road toward the goal of accomplished representation. With the exception of Luquet, they hardly consider excursions along side-paths and meanderings along other roads. Within these two points, an embedded assumption is that as one moves to the next stage, forms of pictorial representation that characterized the previous stage are absorbed into those of later stages.

With the models that we will sketch below, non-linear possibilities are invoked, and realism is no longer identified as the necessary or even the highest attainment of graphic development. Some of these approaches recognize that as development proceeds in a multi-linear fashion, there is a resulting growth in pictorial repertoires, and that aspects of earlier forms are not lost.

Among those who reject the notion of a simple and steady linear ascent from incoherent scribbling to realistic image-making are Davis (1991, 1997a, 1997b), Gardner and Winner (1982), Kindler and Darras (1997, 1998), and Wolf and Perry (1988). Gardner and Winner, and Davis invoke aesthetic/expressive accomplishment rather than realism as a criterion for assessing drawings and as a possible endpoint for graphic development. Building on Luquet's insights, Darras and Kindler and Wolf and Perry explore in earnest the possibilities of a set of multiple pathways for graphic development. It is to this latter approach that we have adapted our research stance.

U-curved aesthetic development hypothesis: Gardner and Winner (1982)

More than two decades ago Gardner and Winner (1982) made a claim about artistic development. They noted that the visual art work of young children and mature artists seem to share certain important features: authenticity, directness, formal inventiveness, and expressive force. The Gardner and Winner theory of graphic development posits a developmental path that is not linear, but U-curved, such that its beginnings in early childhood and its end (in artistic adulthood) are at the same level. That is, Gardner and Winner make much of the aesthetic similarities between young children's graphics and Modernist artists' abstract work. They also bemoan the much discussed aesthetic slump that characterizes the work of older children and adolescents: the tightness and rule-oriented graphics that many adolescent neophytes produce.

Therefore, graphic development, when calibrated against a Modernist appreciation for abstract expressionist art, yields an assessment that places the work of young children and adult artists at the same aesthetic level. In between these two endpoints is the poor aesthetic performance typical of late childhood and early adolescence, hence a U-curve. Davis (1991, 1997a, 1997b) provided an empirical basis for the theory by demonstrating that, under the right experimental conditions and with the right judges, children's work and that of adult artists are indeed seen as equally aesthetic. It is important to note that the basic framework for this non-linear model of artistic development is the aesthetic value of the graphic image, not necessarily its realism or technical mastery. The theory was challenged from the start because of its clear Modernist bias in favor of abstract, expressive work (Wilson & Wilson, 1981; Duncum, 1986; Korzenik, 1995).

Network models of graphic development: Kindler and Darras (1998)

Except for Luquet's early ruminations about the multiple graphic interests and exploration of the young draughtsman/woman, all of the other models we have mentioned propose a linear-developmental path for graphic mastery. However, Kindler and Darras (1998) propose a network model of graphic development, one that emphasizes the many uses which drawings serve and the possibility that, even though there may be *stages* in the development of graphic competence, there are a multiplicity of graphic repertoires, and thus a multiplicity of paths. Other researchers such as Golomb (2002) concur that "...one has to reject a unilinear view of developmental progression towards realism in artistic development" (p. 48). Using the semiotics of Pierce (1931-1935), Kindler and Darras built on the speculations of Wolf and Perry (1988), who suggested that graphic development involves the exploration of different drawing repertoires.

The Kindler and Darras model suggests that one consider an individual's graphic development as an exploration of one of many paths in the acquisition of graphic symbolism. This model acknowledges that there are different impulses, reasons, aims and purposes behind pictorial acts and it claims that they lead to experimentation with, and development of multiple pictorial repertoires. Kindler and Darras propose that one should conceive of graphic development as "...an increase in pictorial repertoires rather than as a cumulative linear growth within a system that has a single endpoint." (Kindler, 2004, p. 234) They claim that this new perspective on development allows one to "...incorporate or account for a vast universe of pictorial imagery that may or may not be classified as art" (p. 235). Integral to the Kindler and Darras model is a noted distinction between *visual art* and *graphic communication*, with an understanding that the boundaries of this divide are culturally shaped and shift over time. Because we wished to avoid the confusion between *artistic development* and *graphic development*, we adopted this model as the basis for the empirical research we initiated.

Previous studies that examine the U-curve claim

Davis (1991)

Davis (1991) made an empirical demonstration of the proposed U-curved graphic developmental trajectory. She asked 5-, 8- and 11-year-old children as well as artistic and non-artistic 14-year-olds and adults to make three *emotion* drawings of *happy, sad* and *angry*. (For examples of these types of drawings, see Figures 13.2-13.6). The drawings were evaluated by two judges trained in fine arts who used a scoring protocol developed by Davis. The scoring procedure incorporated elements of Goodman's (1976) *symptoms of the aesthetic* and formal visual concepts from Arnheim (1974). Davis's cross-sectional research provided positive support for the Gardner-Winner hypothesis. There were indeed strong and measurable parallels between the aesthetic qualities of drawings by the youngest children and drawings by adult artists.

Pariser and van den Berg (1997)

With Davis's cooperation, Pariser and van den Berg (1997) replicated Davis's study, using two Montreal judges who had been trained in art in China, and two judges trained in Western art that were chosen by Davis from the Boston area. One hundred and sixty-four drawings were requested from adults and children of the Montreal Chinese community and these drawings were evaluated by both sets of judges.

Pariser and van den Berg made two key findings. First, the Western-trained judges from Boston did not rank the drawings in the same way as the Chinese-art-trained judges. In fact, the Boston-based judges ranked the drawings in such a way that they created a U-curve, once again equating the aesthetic merits of the youngest children's drawings with those of the adult artists. One of the Boston judges said that even though she couldn't tell what the image was all about, she knew it was the work of a young child and was thus hugely original and expressive (Pariser & van den Berg, 1997). The Chinese-Canadian judges did not find a similar aesthetic equivalence between the youngest children's work and that done by the artists. Instead of creating a U-curve, the Chinese judges' rankings created an ascending line that attributed higher value to the drawings of older participants. In later work we refer to this pattern as *traditionalist*.

It became clear that when the two sets of judges looked at the same drawings, their assessments differed markedly. The Western art-trained judges found equivalences between adult artists and children's work, while the Chinese artist-judges did not. In their conversations with us, the Chinese judges freely admitted the charm of the youngsters' work, but they were unwilling to grant that the effects that the children achieved were the results of intention coupled with skill, which is how these judges conceived of a *good drawing*. For these judges, children's drawings were in the same category as *found natural art,* i.e., aesthetically pleasing driftwood, rocks, etc.

An underlying reason Western-art-educated judges (and others like Gardner and Winner, 1982) find the work of the youngest children so aesthetically strong is a legacy of Modernism, best explained by Fineberg (1997). He has documented the way in which major Modernists such as Klee, Miró, Picasso, Munter and others collected young children's drawings and paintings, and deliberately referenced the style and syntax of these images. In their quest for non-academic and authentic forms, these Modernists saw the work of children as a rich source of potential imagery (Fransiscono, 1998). No less a figure than Robert Motherwell (1970) (no psychologist, but a Modernist artist of high standing) commented on the significant relationship between the *universal visual language* of children and Modernist art. This, then, explains the apparent similarity in aesthetic impact of the work of very young children and that of some mature artists. The mature artists have been using the work of the children as their inspiration. This also explains why the notion of the U-curve had currency in 1982 and still has (Eisner, 2002) despite the evidence to the contrary.

The Pariser and van den Berg (1997) study highlighted the need to consider the cultural background of the judges as well as to consider the qualities of the drawings themselves. The study also revealed that it was not necessary to use Davis' elaborate scoring protocol. One arrived at exactly the same rankings if one used a simple three-way sort asking the judges to place the drawings in one of three piles: one for poor drawings, another for average or mediocre, and one for excellent drawings.

The Pariser and van den Berg replication of the Davis study resulted in the following insights: 1) The U-curved trajectory was largely a function of judges' culturally-determined aesthetic responses; 2) a three-way sorting procedure for the drawings provides the same assessment information as the more elaborate Davis scoring protocol; and 3) research revealed that Modernism idealized young children's graphic productions, identifying them as authentic, expressive and full of *naturally aesthetic qualities*, which resulted in their becoming sources of influence and inspiration for artists (Fineberg, 1997; Wilson, 2004).

Kindler (2000)

In 2000, Kindler replicated a part of the Pariser and van den Berg (1997) study in Taiwan, using the same 165 drawings collected for the Montreal study and the same three-way sort to elicit the judges' aesthetic rankings. She asked eight judges from Taiwan (two artists, two 14-year-olds, two 11-year-olds and two 8-year-olds) to rank the drawings. When average scores were calculated for the various draughtsman/woman groups, the same ranking pattern emerged for the drawings. Taken as a group, the eight judges created an upward-sloping line, with the highest scores awarded to the adolescent artists and adult artists, and all other drawing groups, comprising the younger age-groups, ranked below. In other words, the *developmental* path suggested by the judges from Taiwan was the same as the path suggested by the Montreal-Chinese judges. With the exception of one of the adult expert judges, all of the Taiwan judges ranked images made by 5-year-olds as the least successful.

Having used judges of different ages, this study began to explore the ways in which children, adolescents and adults construe the aesthetic value of drawings. In the second part of her study, Kindler asked the same eight Taiwanese judges to evaluate different sets of drawings that children, adolescents and adults in Taiwan had produced in response to tasks designed to elicit pictorial representations reflective of different kinds of graphic repertoires. Her findings suggested that the aesthetic value of different types of drawing may be assessed in different ways by judges who belong to different groups, according to age and schooling. In other words, the ranking patterns created by children, adolescents and adults may differ not only as a result of varying levels of maturity among the judges, but also because of the pictorial repertoires being considered. For example, the youngest judges showed a clear preference for cartoon drawings, while the adult judges showed a preference for *expressive* drawings. In other words, when faced with a range of pictorial repertoires, the *endpoints* of graphic development were not consistently identified with demonstrations of realistic drawing.

To recapitulate, the significance of Kindler's Taiwan study was that it: 1) reinforced our earlier findings of cultural differences between the Western judges from Boston and judges from the Montreal-Chinese community; 2) it alerted us to the fact that there were multiple sorting patterns – even among judges from the same educational and cultural background – and that these different patterns were a function of the judges' maturity and experience; and 3) it suggested the need to look more closely at the relationships between pictorial repertoires and notions of pictorial development that formed at different stages of a person's life.

The three-country study (Kindler, Pariser, and van den Berg, 2000)

With the accumulated data that we gathered from these smaller studies we organized a large three-country study to extend the scope of these earlier investigations. The judges in this large study included children, adolescents, and non-art-trained adults, as well as art experts. It also requested drawings from children of different ages and from art-trained and art-naïve adults in all the three countries.

Using this study, we addressed two outstanding questions. The first examined the impact of the age, education and cultural background of the judges themselves. We had previously accumulated limited evidence that the characteristics of the judges more than of the drawings determined the outcomes that we observed, and that there was no consensus on the direction of development in drawing. We increased the number of judges from the handful with whom we had been working, to a total of 192 (64 from each of the 3 countries). The judge-sample in each country consisted of 8-year-olds, 14-year-olds, adult artists, and adult non-artists.

The second question examined the way the judges responded to different repertoires presented for their judgment. Even though it may be the case that the aim of drawing is to arrive at an *adequate representation*, diverse symbol systems and graphic conventions, each with different criteria, can be employed to arrive at such representations. In addition, the different aims of drawing, ranging from naturalistic depiction, to orientation in an environment, or a mnemonic for action, will call for different visual repertoires, according to which will be best suited to the task. The Kindler and Darras model (1997, 1998; Kindler, 2004) focuses on the nature of these different sorts of visual tasks. In effect, we were looking at the *multiple paths* that characterize non-linear models of graphic development.

With this vast universe of pictorial imagery in mind, we asked half of our subjects to produce four types of representational imagery, each having different functions. The first type was figure drawings. These are spontaneously made by young children who want to represent people and they account for much of the pictorial imagery that young children produce without systematic teaching or encouragement. Such drawings often call for the use of pictorial devices that capture some physical characteristics of the human figure. The second type comprised images that require a very different kind of cognitive abstraction: images that convey information about how to get from point *A* to *B*. In order to make effective images of this sort, the draughtsman/woman has to focus on spatial relationships, orientations, and simplified visual symbols rather than detailed and naturalistic renditions. Rudimentary maps have been studied for their developmental patterns by other researchers (Liben, 2001). The third type consisted of images of the sort produced in the original Davis (1991) study. These drawings were supposed to convey emotions and thus called for the use of visual devices that emphasized expressive qualities. These we labeled as *emotion* drawings. Fourth, were drawings that have their roots in the popular visual culture of childhood and adolescence, that is, cartoons and comic book-like drawings that rely on specific cultural conventions for representation.

Thus, from the 240 children and 120 adults who participated in our study, we requested four types of drawings: drawings of the *human figure, maps, emotion drawings*, and *cartoons*. In terms of the Kindler-Darras model, we consider these types of imagery to reference four different drawing repertoires.

Acquiring the drawings

The first phase of the study involved requesting four drawings each from 240 children and 120 adults in each of the three countries: Brazil, Canada, and Taiwan. Drawings were made by 5-, 8-, 11-, and 14-year-old children, adult art-novices, and adult *artists*[1]. Children made their drawings in a school setting and adult artists made their drawings in studio classes. Participants in each of the six age/expertise groups were asked to make one of the following two sets of drawings:

Set one consisted of a control drawing (a free drawing of anything they wanted and referred to here as *C*), and then three successive *emotion* drawings: *Happy, Sad* and *Angry*, (coded as HSA). Examples of drawings produced in response to these tasks are included in Figures 13.1-13.6.

For set two, we requested a control drawing from each individual and then three assigned drawings: the first showing the route of the draughtsman/woman from home to school or work (coded as *Map*, designated as M); the second showing the draughtsman/woman's favorite *cartoon* or comic book character (designated as T); and the third showing *people* engaged in some activity (designated as P). Examples of the M, P, and T drawings are presented in Figures 13.7-13.9.

By assigning the MPT task we intended to demonstrate the notion of multiple repertoires in drawing development first noted by Luquet (1927/2001) and elaborated on by Kindler and Darras (1998).

Figure 13.1 Brazilian, age 11, control drawing.

---

[1] Our *artists* were individuals with formal training in the visual arts, but they were not necessarily recognized as highly accomplished practitioners.

Discussion of Set One drawings

The *emotion* drawings (in Figures 13.2-13.6) illustrate typical developmental characteristics for this task. Younger artists and art-naïve adults tended to illustrate emotions via facial expression, gesture and/or idiosyncratic personal narratives, while the trained adult artists relied more on the formal dimensions of the drawing itself (line quality, inflection, composition, use of space) without concern for the overt content of the image. A five-year-old Canadian child, for instance, illustrated *sadness* by having the monster cry (see Figure 13.2), a five-year-old Brazilian child depicted *happiness* by facial expression and body posture (see Figure 13.3), while an eleven-year-old Taiwanese girl drew *angry* using a serial narration format to tell a story that suggests a context for anger (see Figure 13.4). The drawing shows three moments in a family conflict. The child uses a number of devices to suggest the emotional mood of the people in the story; facial emotions are clearly drawn and the use of arrows helps make the sequence of events easy to follow. Facial expressions and text establish the relationship of the siblings.

Figure 13.2 Canadian, age 5, sad.

Figure 13.3 Brazilian, age 5, happy.

Figure 13.4 Taiwanese, age 11, angry.

These children's drawings can be contrasted with those of trained adults. In Figure 13.5, an adult Brazilian artist makes metaphorical use of a ladybug and the Cross. The artist is satirical with respect to the topic of sadness and expects her audience to register the religious reference, which, ironically, contextualizes the mood of sadness.

Figure 13.6 shows an adult Taiwanese artist's response to the topic of *angry*. Unlike the Brazilian artist in Figure 13.5, he uses purely formal means – composition, and line quality – to convey the target emotion. There is no referent here and the intention is to convey feelings through *pure abstract form*. This approach demonstrates the commonly observed difference between those trained and not trained in art. Whereas the children attempt to illustrate an emotion via the concrete situation of a figure (sad is like a dragon crying), and the adolescents and non-art trained adults almost always present situations and facial expressions that carry the emotional message, it is mostly the art-trained adult participants who make drawings that have no decipherable referent (as in Figure 13.6). The art-trained participants seem to have strayed the farthest from what Willats (2005) might call *effective representation*.

Figure 13.5 Brazilian, adult artist, sad.

Figure 13.6 Taiwanese, adult artist, angry.

Discussion of Set Two drawings

Figures 13.7, 13.8 and 13.9 are drawings that were made in response to the second task and show the typical way in which writing was naturally incorporated into such images as a way to label elements. Figure 13.7, representative of *map* drawings, is by a Taiwanese 11-year-old. It incorporates a mix of overhead views (the road) and silhouette views of houses and figures. However, the image relies as much on language as imagery for conveying the bulk of its information.

Figure 13.8, by a Taiwanese 14-year-old, is based on a popular character from a Japanese cartoon series, and shows her competence in making the Kitty figure at will. Figure 13.9, drawn by a Canadian teen in response to the *draw people* task, shows the use of initial imagery (Kindler & Darras, 1997). We see a rendering of a summer scene with carefully drawn clothing and beach paraphernalia. The human body is a daunting subject for all artists, especially adolescents, so in choosing her subject and its detailed treatment, the Canadian participant demonstrated that she felt reasonably confident about producing an *acceptable* rendering of the human body.

Figure 13.7 Taiwanese, age 11, map.

Figure 13.8. Taiwanese, age 14, cartoon.

Figure 13.9 Canadian, age 14, people.

Judging the drawings

We recruited a second group of people from the Brazil, Canada and Taiwan, to judge the drawings. The judge-groups from each country consisted of 8-year-olds, 14-year-olds, adults with no art background, and adult artists. There were 192 judges in all, 64 from each country, 16 in each judge-group. Thus, we looked at judgments of children's and adults' from three geographical regions. Following the protocol developed by Pariser and van den Berg (1997, 2001), judges were shown a sub-group of 720 drawings, and were asked to sort them into three piles, according to whether or not they considered the drawings *good, fair* or *poor* (terms we deliberately did not define). The only rule was that at least one drawing had to be placed in each pile. Drawings were assigned a score of 3, 2 or 1 depending on whether they were placed in the *good, fair* or *poor* pile. Judges evaluated drawings from their own country as well as drawings from one other country.

First result: four different sorting patterns

We identified four different sorting patterns (see Table 13.1), which are presented below in the order of frequency.

Table 13.1 Showing percentages of judges' sorting patterns

	JUDGE CATEGORIES				
SORTING PATTERNS	8-year-olds	14-year-olds	Adult non-artists	Adult artists	Average %
	N=48	N=48	N=48	N=48	N=192
TRADITIONALIST (Upward-Sloping)	47.9%	68.8%	70.8%	54.2%	60.4%
ANTI-MODERNIST (Inverted U)	45.8%	29.1%	22.9%	8.3%	26.6%
MODERNIST (U-curve)	0.%	0.%	2.1%	29.2%	7.8%
NO AESTHETIC PREFERENCE (Flat Line)	6.3%	2.1%	4.2%	8.3%	5.2%
Total %	100	100	100	100	100

The upward-sloping line

The most common sorting pattern for all age groups, regardless of country, was the upward-sloping line. 60% of all judges (see Table 13.1) ranked the drawings on an upward-sloping curve. These judgments seemed to reflect a common-sense expectation about development in drawing: that as the draughtsman/woman matures, the quality of drawings improves. In the view of these judges, this kind of growth is a function of the acquisition of mastery (including technical mastery) in the use of selected pictorial repertoires. It should be noted, however, that because of the way that we collected the drawings, no images in the drawing sets that the judges reviewed reflected the very highest levels of *artistic* achievement, but some clearly exemplified greater proficiency than others in using pictorial systems for the purpose of effective representation. Furthermore, the very highest scoring drawing in the study was a control drawing (a drawing where the child was free to choose the subject). Figure 13.1 shows this drawing, a landscape by a Brazilian 11-year-old. The drawing received an average score of 2.5 (out of a possible 3). In fact, the control drawings consistently earned higher scores than all the other drawings, i.e., the drawings with assigned topics.

The *traditionalist* judges' rankings of drawings (see Table 13.1) reflected classification by age, such that the youngest children's drawings scored lower than the drawings by older children/adolescents and adults (both art-novices and artists). Almost half of the 8-year-old judges (48%), two-thirds (69%) of the 14-year-old judges, almost three-quarters (71%) of the adult art-novices, and half (54%) of the art-trained adults sorted the drawings in ways consistent with the idea that, with age and practice, drawing performance (and aesthetic merit) improves. Thus, the commonsensical notion that *practice makes perfect in drawing* is shared by at least half the judges in our sample and within our judge-groups. One must bear in mind that the judges were asked to sort the drawings according to whether they were *good*. It is likely that the judges who opted for the *traditional* sorting response were making a clear linkage between technical mastery, drawing merit and age. In fact, in earlier work (Pariser & van den Berg, 2001), we had already noticed a clear linkage among these elements for some judges.

The inverted U-curve

With this pattern, certain judges organized their drawings such that the work of the intermediate age (11- and 14-year-old) children and art-novice adults were rated more highly than the work of either the 5-year-olds or the adult artists. 26% of all judges (see Table 13.1) organized their drawings in ways that formed an inverted curve. Almost half of all the 8-year-old judges (46%) created drawing rankings that conformed to this pattern. Approximately a third (29%) of the 14-year-old judges ranked drawings in a similar way, awarding the highest scores to the work of 14-year-olds and art-novice adults. Twenty-three percent of the art-naive adult judges also created inverted curves. Only 8% of the adult artists sorted the drawings according to the inverted curve. Thus, a fair percentage of the judges who had little training in the arts organized drawings according to the inverted curve, an illustration of the judges' preference for drawings made by people who are in the middle of the age/training groups.

The inverted-U pattern could be an indication of what has been called a *plus-one* effect (Pariser, 1980). This effect is the tendency to prefer a performance that is a few steps above one's own present skill rather than preferring a skill demonstration that is far beyond one's present abilities. Golomb (1992), for example, found that a child's preferences for figure drawings tend to be "…one or two steps ahead of his own drawing achievements, suggesting an intimate link between production and aesthetic judgment" (p. 324). It could be claimed, for instance, that the 8-year-olds, 14-year-olds, and adult non-artists were all neophytes in need of skills and mastery, with the result that they gave highest assessments to the work of intermediate level draughtsmen/women, slightly ahead of themselves in terms of pictorial ability.

The prevalence of the *inverted U* pattern also demonstrates the attraction of the judges with no training in art to what has been identified as *initial imagery* (Darras, 1996; Kindler & Darras, 1997, 1998). *Initial imagery* is a system of standard graphic expression of pictorial representation that has been found cross-culturally and across time. This pictorial system "…characterizes the production of preadolescent children, *non-artistic* adolescents and adults, and art-novices, and is typified by a *simple but stable schema*" (Kindler, 2004, p. 240). These typical drawings are found throughout the world and their generic qualities corroborate Arnheim's (1974) ideas about the maker's struggle to create an image that is both effective and simple. Typically, drawings that exemplify *initial imagery* may include complementary verbal and gestural elements illustrated, for example, in Figures 13.3, 13.4 and 13.9. Even though these drawings originate in different countries (Brazil, Canada and Taiwan) and likely represent local people, the schemata used by the children (ages 5, 11, and 14 years) are hardly distinguishable. The figures are clearly identifiable as male and female, but cultural and individual differences are absent. It is also worthwhile to note that the age of the draughtsmen/women did not have a marked influence on the schemata, which is consistent with Darras and Kindler's claim that *initial imagery* is acquired early in life. It makes sense that the images favored by substantial percentages of the 8-year-old, 11-year-old, and 14-year-old judges were drawings that exemplify *initial imagery*, for these images are established early and are familiar, and are thus the easiest to understand and to assess.

In Figure 13.4, the child from Taiwan relies on written language and comic-strip panels to suggest events in a narrative. Written language is also used in the map-like drawing in Figure 13.7. Consistent with Arnheim's (1974) notions of visual simplicity, the adult non-artist who drew the map used canonical representations of objects as a way of ensuring that the information is conveyed as clearly as possible. Thus, the figures and houses are drawn full face, and pathways in their fullest extension. Again, these drawings communicate clearly to a naïve audience. These two drawings are by individuals of different ages, but, significantly, members of the groups whose drawings received the highest rankings from judges who constructed an *inverted U* with their rankings.

U-Curve

Overall, the assessments of only 8% of the 192 judges resulted in the U-curve pattern, and they were almost exclusively by adult judges with expertise in the arts. Further, the U-curve was found in the same proportion among all the artist-judges in the study. Regardless of the country of origin of the judge, one-third of the artist-judges found some aesthetic equivalencies between the work of the youngest children and that of the mature artists. As this effect was noted across all three countries, it is likely the result of contemporary instruction in fine art. This conjecture is confirmed when one listens to the judges' comments, for some would extol the authenticity and directness of the youngest children's work.

The flat line

This pattern accounted for only 5% of all the judges' sorting pattern and likely reflected the decision of some judges not to make any judgments at all. This suggests that these judges made no association between physiological development/maturation and improvement in drawing.

Second result: age affected preferences for pictorial repertoires

Apart from the control drawings, we requested four distinct *repertoires*, described earlier (HSA, M, P, T). By taking the average of the scores awarded by each of the 192 judges to each repertoire, we created a ranking for the four repertoires (see Tables 13.2 – 13.4).

Table 13.2 Brazilian judges' rankings for repertoires.

8-year-olds		14-year-olds		Adult non-artists		Adult artists**	
Map	2.09	Emotion	1.61	Cartoon	1.61	People	1.70
Cartoon	2.08	People	1.58	Emotion	1.57	Emotion	1.60
Emotion	2.04	Cartoon	1.55	People	1.53	Map	1.48
People	2.01	Map	1.53	Map	1.57	Cartoon	1.40

Average score for each repertoire is given in the second column.
** Ranking is significant at < .001 level.

Table 13.3 Canadian judges' rankings of repertoires.

8-year-olds		14-year-olds		Adult non-artists*		Adult artists**	
Cartoon	1.81	Emotion	1.71	People	1.82	People	2.04
People	1.80	People	1.70	Emotion	1.73	Emotion	1.95
Emotion	1.77	Map	1.63	Map	1.66	Map	1.92
Map	1.66	Cartoon	1.62	Cartoon	1.63	Cartoon	1.80

Average score for each repertoire is given in the second column.
* Ranking is significant at < .01 level, ** Ranking is significant at < .001 level.

Table 13.4 Taiwanese judges' rankings of repertoires

8-year-olds**		14-year-olds*		Adult non-artists**		Adult artists**	
Cartoon	1.91	People	1.68	Emotion	1.79	People	1.90
Map	1.88	Cartoon	1.62	People	1.78	Emotion	1.89
People	1.83	Emotion	1.61	Cartoon	1.70	Map	1.69
Emotion	1.66	Map	1.53	Map	1.57	Cartoon	1.68

Average score for each repertoire is given in the second column.
** Ranking is significant at < .001 level, * Ranking is significant at < .05 level.

The 8-year-old judges across all three study settings showed a consistent preference for cartoons, ranking them above most other drawing repertoires. The Taiwanese and Canadian 8-year-old judges ranked cartoons above all other imagery. No other judge groups did this. 14-year-olds and adult artists were in agreement across cultural boundaries, and none of their assessments favored cartoons.[2]

Among the assigned drawing tasks, the highest overall scores were awarded to images of people (P) and drawings expressing emotional states (HSA), followed by cartoon drawings and *maps*. The difference in rankings between the 8-year-olds and that of all other judge groups is striking and seems to confirm that there is a *narrowing* of preferences for repertoires as a function of the age of the judge. This hypothesis is based on observations made by Kindler and Darras (1997) and Kindler (2000) who argued that development in pictorial repertoires and the ability to appreciate and value them are a function of social influences that begin to show an impact well before adulthood.

Young children might be less discriminating than the other age groups in their pictorial choices and they might be open to recognizing quality within a wide range of pictorial systems. The 8-year-olds' appreciation for cartoon drawings may be rooted not only in the prevalence and accessibility of this sort of imagery in the visual culture of early childhood, but also in the fact that such young children have not yet internalized the notion that *cartoons* as a pictorial genre have a lower status in conventional *high* culture than images that conform to the standards of optical realism, or those that have been acclaimed as paradigmatic examples of great art over the centuries.[3]

On the other hand, judgments of the merit of pictorial imagery by older children, adolescents, and adults reflect socialization and the internalization of *taken for granted* cultural biases. The older judges may have ruled out *cartoons* as simply inferior to other *more serious* or more conventional sorts of drawings. They also had a more conventional set of standards for judging drawings from the different repertoires.

---

[2] Adult non-artist Brazilian judges were the only group, other than the 8-year-old judges, who gave cartoons higher scores on average than the three other sorts of drawings.
[3] The average non-art-trained adult might find it hugely amusing, not to say baffling, that a Roy Lichtenstein comic book spoof is considered a bona fide exemplar of art, just as much as a revered Rembrandt portrait. To the art sophisticates, such comparisons have merit, but to a lay person they seem like nonsense.

The average scores awarded to all drawings bear out the above observations. It should be kept in mind that the highest score possible is 3, and the lowest 1. Also, the averages listed below are based on roughly 34,500[4] drawing-judgments for each judging category. On average, all 8-year-old judges across all three countries gave the highest assessments to all drawings. The average score awarded to all drawings by all 8-year-old judges was 1.94, while the average scores by all 14-year-old judges was 1.73. For all adult non-artist judges, the overall average score was 1.76, and for all adult artist judges, it was 1.79. Clearly, the 8-year-old judges were the most *generous* in their rankings.

Third result: judgments of drawings not done by one's countrymen/women

All judges evaluated drawings from their own country and another set of drawings from one other country. It would have been easy for the judges to tell whether or not a drawing was from their own country, or from somewhere else. For example, in some map or cartoon drawings, there were tags, signs and posters, and speech balloons. Thus, it was possible to look at the degree to which judges were biased against or favorably disposed to drawings from countries other than their own, and to inquire into the possible existence of a *national aesthetics*, which would be more or less valued (see Tables 13.5, 13.6, and 13.7). Indeed, our study has shown that in the case of two countries (Brazil and Taiwan), there was a marked difference between judgments of drawings from one's own country and those from another country.

Table 13.5 Percent difference between foreign and Brazilian drawing scores awarded by Brazilian judges.

Drawings	8-year-olds	14-year-olds	Adult non-artists	Adult artists
Adult artists	- 6%**	- 8%***	-10%***	- 4%
Adult non-artists	1%	2%	5%	5%**
14 year-olds	- 2%	5%**	1%	5%**
11 year-olds	- 9 %***	- 7%***	- 6%***	- 6% **
8 year-olds	-11%***	- 6%***	- 3%	- 1%
5 year-olds	-21%***	- 3%	- 5%**	6%**

A positive percentage difference means that the judges preferred foreign drawings to those made by their countrymen. A negative percentage difference means that the judges preferred drawings by their countrymen, to those made by foreigners.* = p < .05, ** = p < .01, *** = p < .001.

---

[4] Adult artist judges made a total of 34,429 drawing judgments as did the adult non-artist judges. 14-year-old judges made a total of 34,422 drawing judgments, and 8-year-olds made a total of 33,825 drawing judgments.

Table 13.6 Percent Difference Between Foreign and Canadian Drawing Scores Awarded by Canadian Judges.

Drawings	8-year-olds	14-year-olds	Adult non-artists	Adult artists
Adult artists	15%***	7%	- 2%	- 3%
Adult non-artists	5%	2%	2%	3%*
14 year-olds	2%	- 7%***	-11%***	- 9%***
11 year-olds	4%**	- 1%	- 5%**	- 2%
8 year-olds	20%***	- 2%	- 2%	1%
5 year-olds	58%***	-11%***	3%	- 4%

A positive percentage difference means that the judges preferred foreign drawings to those made by their countrymen. A negative percentage difference means that the judges preferred drawings by their countrymen, to those made by foreigners. * = p < .05, ** = p < .01, *** = p < .001.

Table 13.7 Percent Difference Between Foreign and Taiwanese Drawing Scores Awarded by Taiwanese Judges.

Drawings	8-year-olds	14-year-olds	Adult non-artists	Adult artists
Adult artists	19%**	25%***	5%*	10%***
Adult non-artists	- 6%	17%***	0%	0%
14 year-olds	2%	26%**	10%***	15%**
11 year-olds	0%	34%***	7%***	6%**
8 year-olds	- 5%**	46%***	- 1%	2%
5 year-olds	25%***	75%***	4%*	9%***

A positive percentage difference means that the judges preferred foreign drawings to those made by their countrymen. A negative percentage difference means that the judges preferred drawings by their countrymen, to those made by foreigners. * = p < .05, ** = p < .01, *** = p < .001.

In general, Brazilians scoring non-Brazilian drawings (see Table 13.5) tended to show the greatest negative bias. The 8-year-old Brazilian judges were particularly harsh on the work of non-Brazilian 5-year-olds. As the table shows, the 8-year-old judges tended to rank drawings by non-Brazilian 8-year-olds some 20% lower than work by age-mates from Brazil. The 8-year-old judges were also hard on all other non-Brazilian drawing groups except for adult non-artists. Brazilian 14-year-olds and adult non-artists were equally critical of drawings by non-Brazilian 5-year-olds, 8-year-olds, and 11-year-olds, in all cases ranking the drawings of these groups 5 to 10% lower than the drawings of equivalent Brazilian groups. Brazilian adult-artist judges were more outward-looking, giving higher scores to drawings by non-Brazilian 8-year-olds, 14-year-olds and adult non-artists.

By contrast, the judges from Taiwan (see Table 13.7) were *outward looking* with a tendency to assess foreign drawings more highly than domestic drawings. This tendency is most clearly illustrated in the responses of the 14-year-old judges from Taiwan, who responded to foreign 5-year-olds' drawings with 75% higher rankings. Likewise, the 14-year-olds from the island awarded, on average, 25% higher rankings to non-Taiwanese drawings by all of the other drawing groups. This positive trend is visible in the responses of both groups of adult judges from Taiwan. In both cases there is a modest positive bias towards drawings by foreigners.

Canadian judges (see Table 13.6), true to form, were the most even-handed, hardly favoring or penalizing drawings by non-Canadians. The only judge-group that deviated from this restrained national pattern were the 8-year-olds who showed a marked preference for drawings by non-Canadian 5-year-olds and 8-year-olds. In the case of drawings by 5-year-olds, the response of the 8-year-old Canadian judges is dramatic, with the 8-year-old Canadian judges awarding almost 60% higher ranking to drawings by non-Canadian 5-year-olds.

Overall, it seems that there are distinctive *national patterns* of response, with the Brazilian judges being the least generous with non-Brazilian drawings and the Taiwanese judges the most generous. These variations in response to the drawings illustrate that each cultural universe (as represented by the judges from the three countries) has its own criteria for meritorious drawing, and that these criteria are not necessarily shared across the three countries in question. One has only to compare the diametrically opposed assessments of the 5-year-olds' drawings by Canadian and Brazilian 8-year-old judges. Where the Canadian 8-year-olds were apparently much more enthusiastic about non-Canadian 5-year-olds' drawings, the 8-year-old Brazilian judges tended to review Brazilian 5-year-olds' work much more favorably than they did drawings of 5-year-olds from the two other countries. The 14-year-old judges from Taiwan were also atypical in their positive response to the drawings of foreign 5-year-olds.

One further observation: the drawings of the 5-year-olds elicited the most polarized judgments from the youngest judges, suggesting that the earliest and least socialized work was the most loaded with contradictory signals for the youngest judges.

Conclusions

As a result of our studies, we now have two measures of people's informal notions about *graphic development*. Table 13.1 demonstrates that judges of different ages and backgrounds ranked drawings purely as a function of age, regardless of the visual repertoire involved. Clearly, the largest number of judges (60%) found that drawings by older subjects were better than those by the younger subjects, suggesting a connection between age and graphic mastery. However, Tables 13.2 to 13.4 present a more nuanced version of the same story. If we assume that the top-ranked repertoire for each judge group is understood as a desired developmental goal towards which the judges' graphic activity is directed, then we obtain some interesting insights into the personal graphic endpoints envisioned by the various judge-groups. In this context, it is possible to interpret their ratings as an indication of the endpoints towards which our judges believe their own drawing activity should be directed.

Table 13.2, for example, can be interpreted to show that the 8-year-old Brazilian judges see *map* drawings, which are synthetic, dynamic, and less concerned with detail, and cartoon representations as termini or worthy goals towards which achievement in drawing progresses, and thus as goals towards which their own drawing activity is oriented. The adult Brazilian artists, on the other hand, find that the pictorial genres of people and expressive drawings are the endpoints towards which pictorial efforts should aim. In fact, art-trained judges in all the three settings subscribe to this view.

This is a significant finding in the context of discussions about art education, and the goals that art teachers and their students may have in mind when they engage in pictorial activity. It is significant because apparently, the students and teachers do not share the same notions of where they are headed on the journey towards graphic mastery even though they may share a common vision of the particular graphic repertoire that is worth acquiring. Though, as we have seen with the ranking of cartoon images, this is not the case with the 8-year-olds vis-à-vis the adult judges. The discrepancy between the graphic goals of the 8-year-old judges and the adult judges, for example, may account for the fact that there is a *disconnect* between the goals of the art teacher and the younger students that they serve, particularly the 8-year-olds and quite likely the 14-year-olds. That is, teachers and students, regardless of their country, may not share the same vision of the endpoint for graphic development.

Particularly intriguing here is our finding that a third of the adult art-trained judges, who in most cases were also art teachers, do not share other judges' high regard for technical skill and mastery that result from maturation, experience, and practice. The U-shaped assessment of drawings and the comments made by these art-trained judges indicate that they value pictorial attributes that are not cherished by their students, that is, the values of authenticity and the uninhibited and perhaps even naïve uses of the graphic medium. Where most of the judges, regardless of age, saw graphic mastery as an indicator of graphic merit (e.g., drawings were better if they demonstrated more skill, hence the overwhelming dominance of the *traditionalist* sorting pattern), one third of the art-trained judges saw an aesthetic equivalence between the work of untutored children and mature artists. For these artists, graphic mastery took second place to *authentic* expression and *originality*. If what the students wish to achieve and what teachers aspire to teach do not coincide, it is necessary to be mindful of this important discord in considering curriculum and pedagogy.

We have demonstrated here that the U-curve hypothesis is of limited predictive value and, even more important, if taken too literally, it could have significant negative pedagogical implications. This study confirms that there are several ways of construing *graphic development* that are based on factors ranging from developmental issues to differences in cultural/national dispositions. By demonstrating these diverse ways of assessing drawings, our study underscores the importance of using alternative models of graphic development to understand the developmental phenomenon. In terms of its flexibility and greater reach, the Kindler and Darras model would seem a better explanatory device than either the U-curve hypothesis or the more venerable linear models that have held sway in art education since the beginning of the last century.

It is, for instance, much easier to explain the younger judges' pictorial preferences in contrast to those of the adults if we conceive of graphic development as the exploration of a set of multiple pathways rather than progress along a single well-defined path towards realism, or towards abstract expressionism. If individuals do indeed choose among different graphic pathways then clearly, different demonstrations of graphic performance will serve as desirable endpoints. This is consistent with what we have found: for the art-trained adult, the freedom and expressive directness of the child and of the trained adult will seem very much akin and emblematic of the highest achievement. For the 8-year-old and the 14-year-old, immersed in the icons of popular culture, the well-executed cartoon image and the schematic map may well seem closer to the sorts of graphic perfection that these neophytes seek. The same may be true for art-novice adults (e.g., Table 13.2 shows the Brazilian non-artist adults' preference for cartoons). We now have a way of conceptualizing the differences in rankings that we observed in relation to the concept of pictorial repertoires.

We have seen that, whereas some art-trained judges do make the U-shaped connection and equate the aesthetic qualities of young children's drawings with those of adult artists, a significant majority of our judges (60%), regardless of age and background, did not acknowledge this sort of equivalence. They made judgments of graphic excellence on the basis of the degree of skill and technical ability demonstrated and on the basis of a particular repertoire (or theme).

The educational implications of the above discussion are these: there are a number of possible definitions of *good drawing*, depending upon the sorts of functions that the drawings are to serve, and there are several pathways to achieve these desired ends. This is valuable information for the art teacher who wishes to instruct in a way that is responsive to the needs of his/her students. One thing is clear, and that is that a certain percentage of art-trained teachers do not share the prejudices and the expectations of their naïve students, children and adults alike. This is one of the clearest findings from our study. Thus, the art-trained teacher must come to terms with the fact that his/her pupils most likely value skilled demonstrations of graphic technique in the rendering of popular images taken from the media and probably do not share the *serious artists* concerns for *expression, formal explorations*, or even the *social relevance* of the image itself. If art pedagogy, especially in early childhood and adolescence, is guided by principles that do not reflect these students' pictorial needs, it is hardly a surprise that children abandon drawing as it is taught in the schools, and pursue those means of representation available in the culture at large that better respond to their ambitions and requirements.

Acknowledgement

The research presented in this chapter was supported by the Social Sciences and Humanities Research Council of Canada Grant #410-2000-0453. Support was also provided by the Concordia University Faculty Research Development Program, and by the Spencer Small Grants Program. The data presented, the statements made and the views expressed in this article are solely the responsibility of the authors.

References

Abuhamdeh, S., & Csikszentmihalyi, M. (2004). The Artistic Personality: A Systems Perspective. In R. Sternberg (Ed.), *Creativity: from potential to realization* (pp. 31-42). Washington, DC: American Psychological Association.

Arnheim, R. (1974). *Art and visual perception: A psychology of the creative eye.* Berkeley, CA: University of California Press.

Bourdieu, P. (1984). *Distinction: A social critique of the judgement of taste.* London: Routledge & Kegan Paul.

Costal, R. (1997). Innocence and corruption: Conflicting images of child art. *Human Development, 40*, 133-144.

Csikszentmihalyi, M. (1988). Society, culture and person: A systems view of creativity. In R. Sternberg (Ed.), *The nature of creativity* (pp. 325-339). New York: Cambridge University Press.

Csikszentmihalyi, M. (1999). Implications of a systems perspective for the study of creativity. In R. J. Sternberg (Ed.), *Handbook of creativity.* (pp. 314-315) New York: Cambridge University Press.

Darras, B. (1996). *Au commencement était l'image: Du dessin de l'enfant à la communication de l'adulte.* Paris: ESF.

Davis, J. (1991). *Artistry lost: U-shaped development in graphic symbolization.* Doctoral dissertation, Graduate School of Education, Harvard University.

Davis, J. (1997a). Drawing's demise: U-shaped development in graphic symbolization. *Studies in Art Education, 38*, 132-157.

Davis, J. (1997b). Does the "U" in the U-curve also stand for universal? Reflections on provisional doubts. *Studies in Art Education, 38*, 179-185.

Duncum, P. (1986). Breaking down the U-curve of artistic development. *Visual Arts Research, 12*, 43-54.

Eisner, E. (2002). *The arts and the creation of mind.* Yale, New Haven: Yale University Press.

Fransiscono, M. (1998). Paul Klee and Children's art. In J. Fineberg (Ed), *Discovering child art* (pp. 95-121). Princeton: Princeton University Press.

Fineberg, J. (1997). *The innocent eye: Children's art and the modern artists.* Princeton: Princeton University Press.

Freeland, C. (2001). *Art theory, a very short introduction.* Oxford: Oxford University Press.

Gardner, H., & Winner, E. (1982). First intimations of artistry. In S. Strauss (Ed.), *U- shaped development* (pp. 147-168). New York: Academic Press.

Golomb, C. (1992). *The child's creation of a pictorial world.* Berkeley, CA: University of California Press.

Golomb, C. (2002). *Child art in context: A cultural and comparative perspective.* Washington, DC: American Psychological Association.

Goodman, N. (1976). *The languages of art.* Indiana: Hackett Publishing Co.

Hagen, M. (1985). There is no development in art. In N. H. Freeman & M. V. Cox (Eds.), *Visual order, the nature and development of pictorial representation* (pp. 59-77). Cambridge: Cambridge University Press.

Kindler, A. M. (2000). From the U-curve to dragons: Culture and understanding of artistic development. *Visual Arts Research, 26*, 15-28.

Kindler, A. M. (2004). Researching the impossible? Models of artistic development reconsidered. In E. Eisner & M. Day (Eds.), *Handbook of research and policy in art education* (pp. 233-252). Mahwah, NJ: Erlbaum.

Kindler, A. M. (2007). Composing in visual arts. In L. Bresler (Ed.), *International Handbook of Research in Arts Education.* (pp. 543-558). Dordrecht: Springer.

Kindler, A. M, & Darras, B. (1997). Development of pictorial representation: A teleology-based model. *Journal of Art and Design Education. 16,* 217-222.

Kindler, A. M., & Darras, B. (1998). Culture and development of pictorial repertoires. *Studies in Art Education. 39,* 47-67.

Kindler, A. M., Pariser, D., & ., van den Berg, A (2000). Making drawings, judging drawings: A cross-cultural study of graphic development and aesthetic development. Proposal funded by the Social Sciences and Humanities Research Council of Canada, # 410-2000-0453.

Korzenik, D. (1995). The changing concept of artistic giftedness. In C. Golomb (Ed.), *The development of artistically gifted children* (pp. 1-30). Hillsdale, NJ: Erlbaum.

Liben, L. (2001). Thinking through maps. In Gattis (Ed.), *Spatial schemas and abstract thought* (pp. 44-77). Cambridge, MA: MIT Press.

Lowenfeld, V. (1957). *Creative and mental growth* (3rd edition). New York: MacMillan.

Luquet, G.-H. (1927/2001). *Le dessin enfantin (Children's Drawings).* Paris: Alcan Trans. Costal (2001). London: Free Association Books.

Motherwell, R. (1970). The universal language of children's art and modernism. An address opening the plenary session of the International Exchange in the Arts (April 29). *The Scholar,* 24-27.

Pariser, D. (1980). Drawing and the plus one phenomenon. How do children benefit from copying adult work? *CSEA Journal. 11,* 31-35.

Pariser, D., & van den Berg, A. (1997). The mind of the beholder: Some provisional doubts about the U-curved aesthetic development thesis. *Studies in Art Education. 38,* 158-178.

Pariser, D., & van den Berg, A. (2001). Teaching art versus teaching taste: What art teachers can learn from looking at a cross-cultural evaluation of children's art. *Poetics: Journal of Empirical Research on Literature, the Media and the Arts. 29,* 331-350.

Piaget, J., & Inhelder, B. (1956). *The child's conception of space.* London: Routledge and Kegan Paul.

Pierce, C.S. (1931-1935). *Collected papers.* Cambridge, MA: Harvard University Press.

Sze, Mai-mai (1977). Translation of the *Mustard Seed Garden Manual of Painting. A Facsimile of the 1887-1888 Shanghai Edition.* Princeton: Princeton University Press.

Willats, J. (2005). *Making sense of children's drawings.* Mahwah, NJ: Erlbaum.

Wilson, B. (2004). Child art after modernism: Visual culture and new narratives. In E. W. Eisner & M. D. Day (Eds.), *Handbook of research and policy in art education* (pp. 299-329). Mahwah, NJ: Erlbaum.

Wilson B., & Wilson M. (1981). Review. [Review of the book *Artful scribbles: The significance of children's drawings* by H Gardner]. *Studies in Visual Communication, 7,* 86-89.

Wolf, D., & Perry, M. (1988). From endpoints to repertoires: New conclusions about drawing development. *Journal of Aesthetic Education, 22,* 17-35.

Part V

Conclusion

Future Directions in Studying Children's Understanding and Production of Pictures, Drawings, and Art

Constance Milbrath
University of British Columbia

Hanns M. Trautner
University of Wuppertal

In this volume we have set out to expand the traditional cognitive approach to drawing research that puts pictures at the centre of analysis, and infers children's pictorial knowledge from their drawing production. Instead, we have taken a metacognitive perspective; one that puts children's minds at the centre of analysis and studies children's theories of pictorial representation, including their developing knowledge about artists as producers of pictures and viewers as evaluators of pictures. Our aim is not to replace the traditional cognitive approach, but to advance it by integrating it with current theory and research on children's developing understanding and production of pictures, drawings and art.

To that end, we have assembled contributions by international scholars that address what children of different ages know about the nature of pictures as representations of the world, as intentional communications conceived of by artists, and as aesthetic objects, as well as what children understand about the different ways to depict objects and scenes.

In this concluding chapter, we take stock of the diverse research and ideas presented and point to remaining questions and directions for future research. The following themes, cutting across the various contributions, organize our discussion: 1. Theories of children's understanding of pictures and the relation between picture, artist, viewer, and world; 2. Children's competence and their production of pictures; 3. Children's comprehension of pictures and its relationship to production 4. Children's evaluation of aesthetic and expressive properties of pictures; 5. Universal and cultural influences on children's drawings.

Theories of children's understanding of pictures and the relation between picture, artist, viewer, and world

The contributions to this volume begin to make a coherent statement about children's developing theory of pictures, first as an account of how infants and young children understand pictures as representations of something in the real world (the picture-referent relationship), then as to their understanding of the artist's role in making this representation (the artist-picture relationship), and finally, most delayed developmentally, children's knowledge of the contribution of the beholder in perceiving and interpreting the picture (the viewer-picture and viewer-artist relationships). Freeman (Chap. 3; Freeman & Parsons, 2001) points to these four entities, artist, picture, viewer and *state of affairs*, as the prime constituents of an ontology in the domain of pictures but demurs in crediting knowledge about these entities as the initiator of pictorial competence. Callaghan (Chap. 2) also grapples with how it is that infants and young children begin to engage with pictures. The two authors have distinctly different approaches to answering this question. Freeman takes the position that pictorial competence is a by-product of the intersection of two core domains, theory of mind and naïve physics, both of which have real evolutionary significance and which *function* by generating theory, whereas Callaghan's stance is that infants' engagement with pictures is a socially adaptive response to a symbolic heritage that values pictures. Callaghan proposes that the acquisition process is not unique to pictures but characterizes all symbolic acquisitions and that moreover symbolic acquisitions in one modality such as language can scaffold acquisitions in another such as pictures (Chap. 2). Hence while Freeman sources the human mind's propensity for theory building, Callaghan credits the social drive of humans to connect and learn from each other. Both provide fruitful theory for generating research.

We might ask as Freeman does, if it makes a difference for a research program whether or not we think children develop a theory about pictures or develop concepts relative to the domain. What issues would arise as a result of putting forward one assumption over the other? According to Freeman, making the concept assumption could lead to a more piecemeal approach in which one studies input-output relations as children learn to first allocate attention to pictures, then categorize the different types of pictorial inputs, and finally respond appropriately to these differing types. If we take the route of studying intuitive theory building in the domain, as Freeman (1995; Freeman & Sanger, 1995) has, the focus instead might be on first defining key features of the domain and then asking what children of different ages understand about the different relations among those features. This last approach liberates our research program to go beyond a narrow interest in children's understanding of pictures alone to include children's understanding of the more complex relationships between artist and picture, viewer and picture, and artist and viewer. These latter relationships invoke the intentionally communicative aspects of pictures and art as statements about *the state of affairs* in the world. Although some contributors in this volume have begun to examine these aspects of children's understanding, on the whole children's theories about these key relationships remain under researched and deserve more attention, particularly as they lead to a broader understanding of how children engage with art and how we as a society can increase this engagement.

Callaghan and Rochat (Chap. 9) address some aspects of this broader challenge in their exploration of very young children's understanding of the picture-referent relation and of the artist's intention. Liben (Chap. 8) also tackles these same issues with older children and young adults. Callaghan and Rochat present convincing evidence that children as young as five are beginning to construct a theory of the artist-picture relation that includes some reasoning about the artist's intention and mental state as an influence on the pictorial outcome. The experiments Callaghan and Rochat have undertaken are particularly potent empirical designs to address these questions with young children. The simple scaling down of tasks to incorporate the mentality of the 3-year-old as well as the 7-year-old bears considerable mention as a direction that has already and will in the future yield valuable knowledge about how young children understand the intentional relations between artist, picture and referent. In particular the pairing of pictures done by real people with those by machine and the use of film as a cue to the state of the artist were very instructive.

Liben's (Chap. 8) research suggests a more delayed development as children and even some young adults struggled with interpretations that went beyond the photograph and its referent. Liben notes that young children were very unlikely to comment on the role of the photographer but as true with other types of depictions, they judged a photograph based on its similarity to the real world referent it represented. It was not until after middle childhood on into adulthood that viewers were able to transcend the overriding picture-referent relation when looking at photographs and comprehend the photographer's use of technique and composition as an intentionally expressive tool. Indeed, surface features of the photographs, which one could equate with formal features of painted or drawn pictures (e.g., composition, style etc.), were mentioned by very few children and not all adults. Liben cautions, however, that the photographs used for those studies were created by study participants under specific instructional purposes. Therefore, one might consider the value of developing standard sets of photographs to examine different aspects (e.g., composition, emotional expressiveness, style, artist's statements about the world) of viewer's comprehension of artist's intention and its relation to the photograph. In fact, the ease of creating specific photographic effects with digital equipment, makes photographs a very appealing experimental tool. Nevertheless, it is also apparent from Liben's work that the picture-referent relation is often the predominant interpretation viewers tender when regarding a photograph. As Liben writes in her chapter: "The pervasiveness and simplicity of photography in contemporary culture undoubtedly contribute to the sense that photographs are an immediate (that is, un-mediated) representational genre" (Chap. 8, p. 155).

Freeman raises a more profound question as well; *why* do we engage with art at all; "what's in it for us?" (Chap. 3, p.39). The question might be reframed as to why it is that human's developed the habit of making pictures to begin with, a question that has been at the forefront of archeology for some time. As Freeman notes, there hardly seems a good evolutionary story to be told as to the functional significance of art "but it seems reasonable to propose that depiction exercises, stimulates, challenges and teases our computation of visual representations" (Chap. 3, p. 41). Thus while the emergence of art may not satisfy the neo-Darwinian criteria of gradual natural selection, once discovered it serves to further extend our visual capacities and becomes another communication tool, all of which may have acted to enhance survival. David Lewis-Williams (2002) puts forward a strong argument in this regard noting the particular advantages that accrued to Cro-Magnon over Neanderthals as a result of their symbolic abilities. Picture-making appeared to come on the scene quite suddenly, although one cannot discount earlier developments on ephemeral substrates. Nevertheless, picture-making of the sort found to appear abruptly during the Upper Paleolithic era coincides with other advantageous developments in tool making and signals a cultural flourishing that ends in domination by the iconic symbol users and disappearance of the Neanderthals (but see Delson & Harvati, 2006) who left no visible record of any symbolic activity. Furthermore, once this symbolic form appears it quickly evolves in complexity and sophistication successfully harnessing cognitive processes that undoubtedly do have deeper evolutionary roots (Milbrath, 2005).

Children's competence and their production of pictures

While resolving questions about *why* human's began to create and engage with pictures may remain in the realm of speculation, questions about *how* children and adults create and engage with pictures can be profitably addressed by developmental research and psychology of the arts. Morra (Chap. 4) has studied in particular, the general cognitive mechanisms that are exploited by drawing, finding that both working memory and executive control processes play a significant role in the drawing process. Morra takes considerable care to break apart the domain specific and general cognitive contributions to drawing and attempts to specify which aspects of the drawing process are guided by each. The distinction between figurative graphic schemes and operative schemes for the representation of spatial relations that Morra makes and which also appears in the work of Lange-Küttner (Lange-Küttner & Reith, 1995) and Milbrath (1998) is of significant value. Morra makes the case that although the graphic figurative scheme is not a motor program, the development of new graphic schemes requires both motor and visual experience; once formed the motor components remain flexible subcomponents in support of the visual pattern. These ideas have specific relevance to an area that remains relatively unexplored, that of the origins of formula or stereotype drawings and the development of flexibility in drawing.

Morra notes that Karmiloff-Smith's (1990) account of representational redescription of drawing procedures with development has been undermined by a host of studies that show much greater flexibility in the drawing procedures of preschoolers than would be predicted. Morra offers his own account based on working memory but notes that although working memory accounts well for increased flexibility in graphic schemes with age, it fails to explain all but a small proportion of the individual differences in flexibility at any given developmental period. Morra suggests that other important features such as reliance on visual imagery and figurative processes, differences in cognitive style, or in goal awareness and monitoring and in arts education may operate. Each of these indicates a valid area to pursue. In particular one of us (Milbrath, 1998) pursued individual differences in visual imaging and figurative processes as an explanation for the surprising flexibility of young talented drawers and autistic savants. While Milbrath studied talented children longitudinally, studies of the emergence and modification of specific drawing formulas in normative drawers as they mature might prove useful in delineating the contributions figurative and operative schemes make in normative development. Finally, if one takes Morra's analytical viewpoint, with a combination of short-term longitudinal studies one might be able to examine transition points at particular points in time, when independent schemes become unified into a single higher order scheme freeing up working memory and allowing increasing drawing complexity.

A related issue is the relationship between canonical representations of key drawing topics and the underlying mental representation of the drawing subject. In the traditional approach, the child is thought to be drawing her underlying canonical representation exemplifying a natural class. There is now general acceptance, however, that this internal model or representation is much richer than anything the normative drawer produces. But as Jolley and Rose (Chap. 10) show there is not only a discrepancy between what children are capable of producing and what they choose as a "best" drawing of a topic, younger children actually do not choose the most realistic picture when asked to choose based on drawing realism. This appears to argue against the hypothesis that young children already have a well developed internal model of objects but need to work out the myriad of practical problems that go into obtaining a more natural likeness of a drawing topic; it implies instead that a young child's internal model is more primitive than the one given directly by perception.

The alternative hypothesis, stated as a classic maxim, that children draw what they know rather than what they see, also no longer offers an acceptable hypothesis. Lange-Küttner (Chap. 5) reframes this to suggest that a child draws what she knows she can see. For Lange-Küttner this statement implies that children start with an object-centered space because their internal description of space is dominated by objects and can not yet specify how these objects are related in a spatial axis system. While much has been researched related to object-centered drawings as contrasted with view-specific drawings, the studies in this volume and published elsewhere by Lange-Küttner point to a re-conceptualization of this distinction related specifically to the type of spatial context constructed on the two-dimensional sheet of paper. What remains unclear, is whether or not any link can be made between what the child does on the paper and the visual/mental model the child has in her/his head (see also Thomas, 1995). Lange-Küttner's work might be interpreted as making a break with that tradition by tasking the child with a sort of de novo construction of a spatial context within the framework of the 2-D pictorial space. Therefore, although children may have a rich internal description of objects and a dawning awareness of real world spatial relationships, the drawing is enacted within the 2-D sheet of paper and fashioned as a new construction, not by constant referral to an internal representation of objects and their 3-D interrelations. Lange-Küttner's elegant experimental approach of giving children different drawn spatial contexts is an advancement that may allow progress in disentangling the long standing and vexing issue of the relationship between the internal model or mental representation and the drawing scheme.

Even under conditions of continuous availability of model drawings that are to be copied, the drawing level of the resulting drawings lag behind the level of the model drawings. A promising approach to analyze the mismatch between visual input and drawing production, i.e., the problems of transforming the mental representation onto the paper, is to assess the drawing process (Trautner, 1996). Careful analysis of children's procedural knowledge by studying how children adapt their drawing strategies to specific task demands, might be productive in disentangling graphic skills from object knowledge and depiction knowledge.

Children's comprehension of pictures and its relationship to production

Although much is known about both general components of cognition, (e.g., working memory, executive functions, and metacognitive abilities; see Morra, Chap. 4) and domain-specific knowledge, (e.g., figurative graphic schemes and operative schemes for the representation of spatial relations; see Lange-Küttner, Chap. 5 and Milbrath, 1998) that are involved in children's drawing, there are still gaps in our understanding of the connections between the child's knowledge about the world and its pictorial representation on the one hand, and how the child draws the world on the paper, on the other. By and large, contributors to this volume have taken the approach that children's understanding of pictures is typically at a more advanced level than their ability to produce pictures. Therefore in general, production is said to lag behind comprehension. So for example, children are able to order drawings along an assumed developmental continuum, even when the series includes drawings produced by children older or more accomplished than themselves (Trautner, Chap. 11). When children's preferences are separated from their recognition of realism, they also prefer a more advanced human figure depiction and consider it more realistic than their own level of production (Jolley & Rose, Chap. 10). It is therefore of particular interest to identify the factors that are responsible for this developmental lag between comprehension and production.

One troubling issue is the easy acknowledgment of the graphic difficulties young children encounter in producing a drawing when, as is typical, the assigned drawing task places high demands on children's graphic skills (Freeman & Cox, 1985). Might children still be able to produce competently in other selected artistic dimensions that correspond to aspects of pictorial comprehension, if graphic skill is removed as a factor?

For example, children could demonstrate similar color choices in matching emotions both in production and comprehension tasks (Burkitt, Chap. 6). Milbrath (Chap. 13) reports that visual preferences of middle and high school students for alternative types of visual balance (symmetry vs. asymmetry) showed a similar and even slightly delayed developmental course when compared with the compositions they produced; all students showed a strong preference for symmetry until 12th grade, whereas productions by 11th graders had already shifted away from symmetry toward asymmetrically balanced compositions. In keeping with her explicitly Piagetian framework, Milbrath suggests that if graphic skill is controlled, children's aesthetic productions (actions) actually may be in advance of their preferences (comprehension). Not surprisingly, when children in her study were asked about their production choices, only the oldest children were able to make comments that suggested true comprehension or awareness of why the choices they had made produced a given effect (see Milbrath 1998).

Morra's (Chap. 4) analysis of the figurative and operative scheme demands of the drawing task holds another promising direction. In comparing the delay between the onset of representational drawings and other symbolic forms in young children, Morra makes the convincing argument that drawing requires the coordination of five sensorimotor schemes, as compared to language which involves one less, since the child is already practiced in making one of the involved motor schemes (sounds) in nonsymbolic contexts. Applying this type of analysis to the production comprehension lag, by examining the information processing demands of the two kinds of tasks, might demonstrate important inequalities in the number and/or types of schemes that the child is required to coordinate and could provide one level of explanation for the observed lag. Another revealing technique might be to systematically vary the information processing demands of the drawing and comprehension tasks to see at what points equality in performance can be obtained.

An allied approach would capitalize on natural individual differences in children. Liben (Chap. 8) reports that some young children showed greater sensitivity to photographic qualities than many of the adults when asked to reproduce photographic models from different vantages with a camera. On the other hand, a number of adults showed poorer performance in comprehension tasks than the children when required to reflect on and interpret photographs. Milbrath (Chap. 12; Milbrath, 1998) presents drawings by very young highly talented children that demonstrate remarkable productive skills and also reports individual variation in children's aesthetic productions; a small group of children consistently produced sophisticated compositions from middle to high school in the free composition task. Trautner (Chap. 13) observed individual differences in children's comprehension; some of his youngest participants addressed stylistic features in their reasoning about preferred and disliked paintings, features that typically were not mentioned except by older adolescents. Assessment of consistency in performance on comprehension and production tasks in children who achieve high levels in either may be illustrative. Although Morra (Chap. 4) noted that working memory did not explain individual differences in graphic flexibility on his tasks, one cannot discount the possibility that, as is the case for the gap in onset across symbolic modalities, children who achieve high levels in production of drawings may be coordinating fewer schemes than normative drawers, because through practice they have achieved the integration of many more component schemes into unified higher order schemes. Both Liben and Morra suspect that some of such individual variation has been achieved through informal or formal tutelage by parents and teachers and both propose this as a valid inquiry into the processes that influence development in the arts. Liben describes a series of recent studies she has undertaken aimed at understanding how parents and more formal instruction influence children's and young adults' understanding of photography. More systematic study of training in the arts and its relationship to issues of production and comprehension should be pursued (see Winner, et al., 2006).

Children's evaluation of aesthetic and expressive properties of pictures

The seminal works of Parsons (1987) and of Freeman (Freeman & Parsons, 2001) have focused renewed research attention on how children, as viewers, consider the aesthetic and expressive properties of pictures and artworks and what they understand about the relationship between the artist who produces an artwork and the piece produced. Contributors to this volume have focused on children's ability to apprehend and use specific expressive and aesthetic canons of western art and their related understanding of the intention of the artist. Parsons has very much defined this area of research by showing clear developmental trends that at the highest levels appear to depend on training in the arts. The conclusions from his study and those of others have for the most part suggested that younger children respond to more concrete (i.e., subject matter and color) and/or localized (i.e., the realism of a specific figure) features of artwork and that with cognitive development, comes the ability to appreciate artwork at a deeper level, so that by pre-adolescence the emotional expressivity of a painting is discerned, and by adolescence stylistic and formal properties such as composition are appreciated. Parallel to this awakening of the self as a viewer, is the development of a sense of the artist's relationship to the work produced and of the viewer as part of a larger community that acts as a societal critic. In Freeman's (1995) terms, the child as developing theorist must coordinate an increasingly larger net of relationships that begins with her/his appraisal of the picture-referent relation, expands to include the artist-picture relation as the intentional and expressive aspects of a picture is understood, and then encompasses the viewer in relation first to the picture, and only later in relation to the artist.

Children's understanding of the artist's intentional use of technique for expressive and visual effect was taken up specifically in chapters by Burkitt (Chap. 6), Trautner, (Chap. 11) and Milbrath (Chap. 12). It is clear from Parsons and also others (see Trautner, Chap. 11) that one of the most ubiquitous findings despite the age of the viewer, is the subjective preferences for color and, the pre-eminence it is given particularly by younger children in determining pictorial preferences. But of greatest interest in relation to children's responsiveness to color, is how, they as viewers, interpret color in a picture. Burkitt (Chap. 6) reviews her own studies and those of others that examine how children understand the affective component of color. Overall this research shows that children's interpretations appear to assign negative affect to darker colors and positive affect to brighter colors. The ability to use color symbolically begins early; even very young children show flexible use of color to express affect associations. Moreover, children's color choices relate strongly to their individual color preferences and to the way they feel about the subject they are depicting. Burkitt underscores the value of taking children's color preferences into account when attempting to understand how children interpret the expressiveness of color. Of particular interest in this regard is the unresolved question of when children's color preferences leave off and the expressive power of color itself becomes central. Apropos to Freeman's model, one might ask when do children understand the artist's intentional use of color as an expressive tool and when do they begin to take the viewer into account as the interpreter of the expressive nature of color. Burkitt additionally suggests that the artist-viewer relation might be further researched by examining if and how children's understanding of color is altered depending on who the audience is. Several other issues are emphasized that bear notice in relation to undertaking research in this area. Burkitt comments that the diversity of methodologies used in studies of affective interpretations of color and the lack of a standardization of color stimuli makes it difficult to compare the results across studies. She recommends greater standardization or at least specification of color stimuli.

Most of the research cited by contributors to this volume, agrees that while younger children may be shown to be sensitive to formal properties of artwork, this awareness does not become incorporated into a theory about artists intentionality until later in adolescence (Parsons, 1987; see Trautner, Chap. 11). Nevertheless, research on children's responsiveness to the aesthetic dimension of artworks that goes beyond demonstration of preferences is scarce. The chapters by Trautner (Chap. 11) and Milbrath (Chap. 12) examine children's sensitivity to formal aesthetic dimensions. Trautner presents one of his own studies, in which he attempts to control the effects of color, subject matter, and style of stimuli, measuring both preference (and rejection) and the weight of each effect in children's reasoning about their evaluations. In the analysis of children's reasoning, Trautner replicates past findings that younger children are overtaken by bright colors and realism of subject matter whereas artistic style only becomes an important factor in considerations by older children. But Trautner also notes that style was mentioned by some young children in their judgments. From a review of the literature and his own research, Trautner concludes that sensitivity to artistic style is present well before adolescence.

Sensitivity to formal properties of art work such as style are difficult to research, especially in young children who may not have the language to talk about these more abstract elements of a picture. Nevertheless, sensitivity to style has been found in young children (see review in Trautner, Chap. 11); Callaghan and Rochat (2003) found style was discernable by six year olds using a matching task. Therefore, as Trautner cautions based on his research, there is a strong dependency between sensitivity to art work, the stimulus material used, and the methods of assessment. Considerable work in isolating what constitutes style still needs to be done. Consistent with Goodman's (1968) symptoms of the aesthetic, early work tended to concentrate on repleteness, observing children's sensitivity to variations in line quality as an indicator of style (e.g., Carothers & Gardner 1979), whereas more recent work has relied on matching the overall style of pictures sometimes attempting to control for subject matter which admittedly overpowers other aspects when young children are the beholders (see Trautner, Chap. 11 for discussion).

A return to a more nuanced attempt to define style formally for the purposes of research, could be undertaken. In a review of the art of Willem de Kooning who was diagnosed with Alzheimer's disease in the mid 1980s but who continued to paint until 1990 when he reached the age of 86, Clark, Tanner, and White (1995, p. 15) note that:

> One characteristic of 'late' styles in the age of retrospection is that they often look back to the beginnings of the artist's career and enter into dialogue with the style of the artist in his or her first maturity. I think that is true of de Kooning, and, lucky for us, the style of his first maturity is, in my opinion, his best — the style of the 1940s.

Clark, Tanner, and White (1995) refer to de Kooning's late style as a "stripped-down" style which in a comparative analysis of two paintings, one from each period, leads them to acknowledge that "de Kooning's works of the 1980s look straightforwardly like blown-up details extracted from paintings done forty years before." (p. 15). In their deliberation it is the similarity in compositional structure, the consistency of forms, and the equivalent character of the line to which they refer to as *style*. To what do we, as researchers, refer to when we use the term *style*? Can the term be defined consistently across artists, or will the style of one artist be defined by compositional elements while that of another is reliant on a correspondence of forms? Children's understanding of and response to the complex of qualities identified as stylistic features in painting and artwork should be more formally characterized and researched.

In the chapter by Milbrath (Chap. 12), an attempt is made to isolate a single formal compositional property of artwork, visual balance. Milbrath considers this fundamental to the success of an artist's communicative intention, noting that if a piece lacks visual balance the viewer will not be able to take in the whole of a piece. Little has been done in this area with children, although research on adults' perception and appreciation of visual balance has reached a very high level of sophistication (see Locher, 2006). Noting that the existing research on children has most often focused on drawing, which additionally taps graphic skill and remains confounded with drawing theme, Milbrath used 3-D abstract objects to explore children's preferences and production capabilities. The results of this work suggest that when graphic skill differences are eliminated, children throughout the school aged years are able to create 3-D pieces that are judged as visually balanced. In fact, for those students whose visual preferences as well as productions were assessed, almost all were clear in choosing visually balanced compositions over those that were unbalanced. What does develop are the strategies children evolve to produce visually balanced pieces. These reflect a slower trajectory that began in this study with the use of symmetry early in grammar school and evolved to more complex asymmetrical and dynamic compositional forms later in the high school years.

Milbrath's methodology demonstrated that most children are not only sensitive to at least one formal property of artwork, but also that they can produce visually balanced pieces. The methods introduced by Callaghan and Rochat (Chap. 9) were also successful in demonstrating younger children's sensitivity to expressive and stylistic features of pictures. Trautner (Chap. 11) was able to effectively analyze the evaluative reasoning behind choices children made but his study also pointed to methodological concerns that suggest variations in assessment and stimulus materials can lead to markedly different results. As innovations in research methods are undertaken, it becomes increasingly apparent that young children are able to discern many more dimensions of pictures than earlier research indicated. Nevertheless, the degree to which younger children are able to reflect on these aspects of artwork appears limited. If this is simply a function of the lack of language to discourse on these properties, training in the appreciation and language of the arts may provide younger children with tools to reason about that which they are able to discern. But it is also possible that early sensitivities to formal features of art remain cognitively un-integrated because young children cannot yet reflect on these abstractions. These issues have practical significance for teaching art to children and for their enculturation into an historical world view of the arts.

Universal and cultural influences on children's drawings

One of the most under researched but emerging areas of consequence is the influence diverse cultures have on children's comprehension of pictures and artistic productions. Pinto and Bombi (Chap. 7) review two major perspectives addressing the cultural influences on graphic development. The first emanates from the observation that one discerns a relatively invariant stage-like succession of basic graphic schemas in the development of children's drawings irrespective of culture. In this view cultural differences are limited to modifications of a universal or "common underlying structure" (Golomb, 1992). The alternative view resolutely maintains that culture transmits drawing conventions and standards that children emulate when learning to draw (e.g., Wilson & Wilson, 1977;1985) and therefore, that drawing is constructed and transmitted within strong cultural parameters and constraints. Unfortunately for a decisive decision on these divergent views, modern communication and schooling have resulted in a somewhat global standardization of visual images. Western culture is rich in visual imagery and increasingly this iconography has spread through technology and schooling to become universally available (Cox, 2005). The earlier dichotomy between universal and culture specific (nature vs. nurture), therefore, needs to be reframed to examine the contributions that are internal to the child, for example theory building, and those that are external and imparted by the culture in which the child is embedded, for example, geometric depictions in Muslim cultures. Both get increasingly complex for children as they mature. In point of fact, we know less about the cultural influences on children's pictorial productions and comprehension than we do about how a child's developmental level influences these competencies. A program of research that looks specifically at development within cultures that represent marked contrasts in their representational standards would add significantly to our understanding of cultural influences.

Pinto and Bombi (Chap. 7) have made a strong start in that direction by collecting drawings from cultures with marked contrasts in social structure (collective vs. individualism), environment (rural vs. urban), and societal experience (war vs. peace). They aptly trace cultural differences in the depictions of children that result from these organizational, contextual, and experiential differences. The results of their analysis suggest a more nuanced outcome, one that agrees with Cox's (2005) conclusion that children's search for graphic equivalents in human figure drawing interacts with the cultural depictions they see around them. As Pinto and Bombi (Chap. 7, p. 135) state:

> ... in all the considered cultures, children's depiction of the human figure develops in a fairly regular, even predictable way, from scribbles, to simple forms, to more complex graphic structures; at the same time iconographic conventions within each culture play a role ..., but the resulting differences are mainly stylistic and do not affect the structural characteristics of the human figure.

They acknowledge that in part this conclusion stems from the drawing topic studied, the human figure, for which "visual correspondence between referent and symbol" is fundamental. Nevertheless, they also observe that the human figure is, "extremely sensitive to the conditions under which it is produced," and as such creates an opportunity for the appearance of diverse representational goals. For these authors it is both the universal and cultural elements in a drawing that allow for its utility as a tool for studying children's social knowledge across cultures.

Characterizing the complex relationship between the universal and culture specific elements in graphic development with its explicit acknowledgement of diverse representational goals is echoed and amplified by Pariser, Kindler, and van den Berg (Chap. 13). These authors present the Kindler and Darras (1997) model as a culturally relevant proposal for how one should conceive of graphic development; "...[as] an increase in pictorial repertoires rather than as a cumulative linear growth within a system that has a single endpoint" (Kindler, 2004, p. 234). The emphasis of this model is that drawings serve diverse purposes leading to a "multiplicity of graphic repertoires" and potential developmental pathways; thus different graphic genres, for example cartoons or maps, have potentially different developmental sequences and endpoints. They extend this model to incorporate potentially diverse cultural standards as well. The research presented in their chapter, therefore, looks at both the production of and evaluations of different genres by artists and judges differing in age, nationality, and artistic expertise. Not surprisingly, there is a cultural bias in preference for drawings from one's own culture, but also a degree of genre bias depending on a judge's age, which as the authors note, has particular significance for pedagogy in the arts.

Cox (2005) illustrates a related point in noting that cultural contact with the west in the outback of Australia has meant that the Warlpiri children learn to draw both their own cultural standard for the human form that symbolizes a human in sand drawing stories and the western standard for a human figure which they learn in school. Fortes' studies (cited in Cox, 2005) of children's drawings on the Gold Coast of Africa, demonstrated as well that the establishment of schooling introduced western figure drawing standards to Tallensi children and that over successive generations, these children became much more skillful at rendering human figures (see also Martlew & Connolley, 1996). In these cultural studies, one recognizes the multiplicity of graphic repertoires that can co-exist even within the same culture but also the facility children have of developing appropriated and culturally new styles that affirms a universal capacity for producing pictures. We still know little about artistic development in cultures that do not have visual realism as the culturally transmitted standard. The arts are flourishing in some of these cultures, such as the First Nations people in Northwestern North America, and could be studied as children are apprenticed by their elders in these traditional indigenous styles.

Concluding remarks

The theories and research presented in this volume not only advance our knowledge about children's understanding and production of pictures, drawings, and art, but also point to open questions and directions for future research in the field. Several unanswered questions that could be addressed in future research were discussed in the preceding sections of this chapter. In this concluding section we highlight a final central issue that should be in the focus of future research: the understanding of the intentions and activities on which the production of pictures are based.

A basic tenet for this consideration is that, in accordance with Freeman's framework theory of pictorial representation (Freeman, 1995; Freeman, Chap. 3), research on children's understanding and production of pictures, drawings, and art has to go beyond the analysis of children's understanding of the picture-referent link to take into account their knowledge of artists as intentional producers of pictures and viewers as perceivers and evaluators of pictures. Thus, pictures are not only viewed as a medium of representation but also as a medium of communication. Moreover, when dealing with children's competence to comprehend and produce pictures, one has to consider the child artist's intention when producing a picture as well as the child's attempt to read those intentions when taking the role of viewer. The task for future research is to illuminate how it is that children acquire the ability to understand the variety of decisions and actions made by artists (themselves or others) and to understand that there are different ways to depict objects and scenes depending not only on an artist's skills but more significantly on an artist's communicative intentions. In large part, existing research imputes children's drawing intentions, as well as their attributions of others' drawing intentions, as mainly to represent the world *as it is*. This implicit assumption of a representational intention does not take into account that artists' intentions often are aesthetic and expressive or narrative (Reith, 1996) as statements about a *state of affairs* in the world.

There is relatively little in the literature on children's drawing that attempts to take account explicitly of the child's intentions when producing a drawing. One relevant issue is that when dealing with very young children, it can be difficult to ascertain intention from verbal interviews. When young children are asked, they often cannot give answers that enrich our understanding of their intentions. Although recent studies such as those presented by Callaghan (Chap. 2) and those reviewed by Freeman (Chap. 3) cleverly circumvent the verbal limitations of young children, they largely address how children understand the picture referent relationship or alternatively, another's intentions and fail to address what children themselves intend when they make certain artistic decisions. Liben (Chap. 8) has developed an interesting paradigm using photography by asking children to make photographs that are expressive of certain emotions (e.g., scary lion). It is unclear, however, how well younger children do with such a task, as Liben's youngest participants appeared unaware that the key to expressing emotion lay with the manner in which they framed or manipulated camera angles, that is in the technique they used as the photographer rather than the referent they shot.

The contributions presented in this volume, point to the conclusion that children's understanding of the role of artists' intentions and activities in producing pictures varies considerably depending on the medium and type of pictures researchers have used. While Liben (see Chap. 8) demonstrated that even young adults will focus on the picture-referent relation and the representational aspect of pictures when regarding a photograph, Callaghan and Rochat (see Chaps. 2 and 9) found evidence that young children have some understanding of the decisions and actions made by the artist when the tasks are placed in a social context. Young children were also observed to show some sensitivity to artistic style, not just the picture-referent link, when interviewed about paintings hanging in museums, (see Chap. 11). It would be of interest to analyze the factors that are responsible for these discrepant results. In the case of photographs, it might be the alleged automatic "point and shoot" of the digital camera (Liben, 2003) which minimizes taking notice of the active contribution made by the photographer and leads to a conclusion that photographs are unmediated representations of "reality" (see Liben, Chap. 8), a belief commonly shared by many adults who regard photographs not as art work in the proper sense.

Another factor influencing the delayed development of children's consideration of artists' intentions and skill beyond representing the "world", may be the quality of their experiences with photographs and pictures in their social environment. As mentioned above, western culture is rich in visual iconography, but much of this iconography is utilized simply to depict real world referents, for example as advertisements for objects or events in magazines or as depictions of objects, places, or events in school and reference books. When parents and young children begin looking at photographs in photo albums together or pictures in picture books, parents by and large refer to *who* and *what* is depicted and not to the how and why of the depictions (but see Szechter & Liben, 2004). For parents, the educational aspect of informing about what is depicted is in the foreground, not the intentions of the artist and the interpretations of the viewer, as they review people and family events with young children and teach them the names of objects and the words associated with the objects. When parents take their children for visits to art museums, there is a higher probability that they discuss the artists' specific intentions and skills. Therefore, it would be of interest to study how adults (parents, teachers) communicate with children in these different environments and the influence these communications have on how children think about the different genres of pictures they encounter (e.g., photographs, paintings). Although some contributors in this volume have begun to examine the role parents and teacher have in influencing and promoting children's understanding of pictures as intentionally expressive statements about the world, on the whole children's theories about this fundamental relationship remains under researched and deserves more attention, particularly as it could lead to a better understanding of how children engage with art and how we as a society can increase this engagement.

References

Callaghan, T. C., & Rochat, P. (2003). Traces of the artist: Sensitivity to the role of the artist in children's pictorial reasoning. *British Journal of Developmental Psychology*, 21, 415-445.

Carothers, T., & Gardner, H. (1979). When children's drawings become art: The emergence of aesthetic production and perception. *Developmental Psychology*, 15, 570-580.

Clark, T. J., Tanner, C. & White, L. P. (1995). *Painting from memory: Aging, dementia, and the art of Willem de Kooning.* Paper 7. Occasional Papers; Doreen B. Townsend Center for the Humanities. University of California, Berkeley

Cox, M. (2005). *The pictorial world of the child.* Cambridge: Cambridge University Press.

Delson, E. & Harvati, K. (2006). Palaeoanthropology: Return of the last Neanderthal. *Nature, 443*, 762-76.|

Freeman, N. H. (1995). The emergence of a framework theory of pictorial reasoning. In C. Lange-Küttner & G. V. Thomas (Eds.), *Drawing and looking* (pp. 135-146). New York: Harvester Wheatsheaf.

Freeman, N. H., & Cox, M. V. (1985). *Visual Order.* Cambridge: Cambridge University Press.

Freeman, N. H., & Parsons, M. J. (2001). Children's intuitive understanding of pictures. In B. Torff & R. J. Sternberg (Eds.), *Understanding and teaching the intuitive mind* (pp. 73-92). Hove: Erlbaum.

Freeman, N. H. & Sanger, D. (1995). The commonsense aesthetics of rural children. *Visual Arts Research, 21,* 1-10.

Golomb, C. (1992). *The creation of a pictorial world.* Berkeley: University of California Press.

Goodman, N. (1968). *Languages of art.* Indianapolis, IN: Bobbs-Merrill.

Karmiloff-Smith, A. (1990). Constraints on representational change: Evidence from children's drawings. *Cognition, 34,* 57-83.

Kindler, A. M. (2004). Researching the impossible? Models of artistic development reconsidered. In E. Eisner & M. Day (Eds.), *Handbook of research and policy in art education* (pp. 233-252). Mahwah, NJ: Erlbaum.

Kindler, A. M, & Darras, B. (1997). Development of pictorial representation: A teleology-based model. *Journal of Art and Design Education, 16*, 217-222.

Lange-Küttner, C. & Reith, E. (1995). The transformation of figurative thought: Implications of Piaget and Inhelder's developmental theory for children's drawings. In C. Lange-Küttner & G. V. Thomas (Eds.), *Drawing and looking* (pp. 75 - 92). New York: Harvester Wheatsheaf.

Lewis-Williams, D. (2002). *The mind in the cave.* London: Thames and Hudson.

Liben, L. S. (2003). Beyond point and shoot: Children's developing understanding of photographs as spatial and expressive representations. In R. Kail (Ed.), *Advances in child development and behavior* (Vol. 31, pp. 1-42). San Diego: Elsevier.

Locher, Paul (2006). Experimental scrutiny of the role of balance in the visual arts. In P. Locher, C. Martindale, & L. Dorfman (Eds.*), New directions in aesthetics, creativity, and the arts.* Amityville, NY: Baywood Publishing co.

Martlew M., & Connolley, K. J. (1996). Human figure drawing by schooled and unschooled children in Papua New Guinea. *Child Development, 67,* 2743-2762.

Milbrath, C. (1998). *Patterns of artistic development in children.* Cambridge, MA: Cambridge University Press

Milbrath, C. (2005). Epistemology and Creative Invention. *Journal of Cultural and Evolutionary Psychology, 3,* 121-142.

Parsons, M. J. (1987). *How we understand art: A cognitive developmental account of aesthetic experience.* New York: Cambridge University Press.

Reith, E. (1996). *Some useful distinctions and concepts for understanding research on the development of pictorial representation in children.* Discussion presented at the Piaget Centennial Conference "The Growing Mind", Geneva, September 14-18.

Thomas, G. V. (1995). The role of drawing strategies and skills. In C. Lange-Küttner & G. V. Thomas (Eds.), *Drawing and looking* (pp. 107-122). New York: Harvester Wheatsheaf.

Trautner, H. M. (1996). *Drawing procedures in children's free drawing, copying, and tracing of the human figure.* Paper presented at the Piaget Centennial Conference "The Growing Mind", Geneva, September 14-18.

Wilson, B., & Wilson, M. (1977). An iconoclastic view of the imagery sources in the drawings of young people. *Art Education, 30,* 5-11.

Wilson, B, & Wilson, M., (1985). The artistic tower of Babel: inextricable links between culture and graphic development. *Visual Arts research, 11,* 90-104.

Winner, E., Hetland, L., Veenema, S., Sheridan, K., & Palmer, P. (2006). Studio thinking: How visual arts teaching can promote disciplined habits of mind. In P. Locher, C. Martindale, & L. Dorfman, (Eds.), *New directions in aesthetics, creativity, and the arts* (189-205). Amytiville; NY: Baywood Publishing.

Subject Index